Computers and Programming Guide
for Scientists and Engineers

by

Donald D. Spencer

A Revision of

Computers and Programming Guide for Engineers

by Donald D. Spencer

Howard W. Sams & Co., Inc.
4300 WEST 62ND ST. INDIANAPOLIS, INDIANA 46268 USA

SECOND EDITION
FIRST PRINTING—1980

International Standard Book Number: 0-672-21693-0
Library of Congress Catalog Card Number: 80-50051

Printed in the United States of America.

Preface

Computers are being woven more and more into the lives of virtually everyone. Although much of this growth is in data processing and personal computing (microcomputers being used in the home), computers have also become essential tools for scientists and engineers. A knowledge of what computers can do and an ability to make them do it has become a necessary part of a technical education.

Computers have had a tremendous impact in science and engineering. Aeronautical engineers design supersonic aircraft with the aid of computers. Architectural firms have used computers for over a decade to help them design and plan building projects. Civil engineers use computers to aid them in designing and constructing dams, buildings, tunnels, highways, airports, transportation systems, and stadiums. Computer-aided design is an ever-increasing activity with electrical engineers. Mechanical engineers use computers to help them design automobiles, tools, and power plants. Naval architects have streamlined the art of shipbuilding by using computers. Scientists have used computers to help them make new discoveries in physics, chemistry, medicine, and other technical fields.

Nowadays, the subject of computer science, with lectures on computer principles and programming, and laboratory sessions using a computer terminal or microcomputer, is a feature of many undergraduate courses. For the many undergraduates in science and engineering who will subsequently be required to use computers effectively, a book is needed which explains the general principles on which computers operate and the means by which one communicates with them. Illustrations of the use of a computer should be within the kind of context in which students may be expected to work subsequently, so that they see it in a satisfactory relationship to the whole of their studies. Engineers and scientists should use the computer as a tool to aid them in solving problems. I attempted to keep this theme in mind while writing this book. The book is based on experience I have gained in designing scientific and real-time computer systems over the past 20 years.

The major purpose of *Computers and Programming Guide for Scientists and Engineers* is to help science and engineering students develop an understanding and appreciation of the computer, its capabilities and limitations, the concept of computer problem solving, the concepts of programming languages, and the techniques used in designing computer software systems.

A second purpose of the book is to help readers develop programming skills that will enable them to use a computer in the context of science and engineering rather than business.

The BASIC and FORTRAN programming languages are widely used in scientific and engineering applications. FORTRAN has been used by scientists and engineers for the past two decades. BASIC, a similar but easier-to-use language, is more widely used with microcomputers. Both of these languages are fully discussed in this book.

All scientists and engineers should have some knowledge of real-time systems, simulation, problem-oriented programming languages, systems design, operating systems, and teleprocessing. These subjects are all covered in this book.

Questions and exercises appear at the end of each chapter. These exercises serve to illustrate the material of the chapter, to help the reader gain computational programming skill, and to extend the material to closely related topics not covered in the chapter. A comprehensive glossary of computer-related terms is provided at the back of the book.

The future use of computers in scientific and engineering practice is limited only by the imagination of our scientists and engineers. These technical people should not lag behind in adopting the use of computers in future scientific and engineering applications.

I wish to thank the many computer manufacturers and computer users who supplied me with photographs of equipment and applications where computers are used. I also thank my wife, Rae, for typing the manuscript.

Donald D. Spencer

To my wife
Rae

Contents

CHAPTER 1

CHAPTER 2

CHAPTER 3

CHAPTER 4

CHAPTER 5

CHAPTER 6

CHAPTER 7

CHAPTER 8

CHAPTER 9

CHAPTER 10

CHAPTER 11

CHAPTER 12

Courtesy Digital Equipment Corp.

A scientist using a minicomputer system designed to collect, record, and process data from laboratory instruments.

CHAPTER **1**

USING THE COMPUTER

This is the era of automation. A variety of machines (large-scale computer systems, supercomputers, medium-scale computers, mini-computers, and low-cost microcomputers) are now available that can, by means of programmed instructions, solve difficult engineering problems, shape and machine intricate parts, control industrial systems, plot contour maps, design electronic circuits, simplify air-traffic control, land astronauts on faraway planets, and perform countless other tedious and time-consuming tasks that would have been impossible just a short time ago.

WHAT BENEFITS DO COMPUTERS OFFER SCIENTISTS AND ENGINEERS?

Most of the development concerning computers has occurred within the last two decades. The scientist and engineer, from the beginning, have been closely associated with this development. In fact, the engineer originally created much of the demand for a computing machine to aid in solving problems encountered in military applications. As soon as it became possible to solve problems previously considered impractical to solve because of time, many new computer applications became apparent in all phases of industry. The engineer and scientist now have computers available that can perform more calculations in an hour than they could do in 40 lifetimes using desk calculators.

Engineers are primarily concerned with the application of science to industrial progress. It is their objective to plan, design, develop, and construct usable devices that employ scientific principles. One of the many problems facing engineers today is the increasing complexity of their profession. Only a few years ago they were accustomed to resolving many aspects of their work with little effort; now these aspects have become complex enough to require other specialists who are as qualified in their fields as engineers are in their field.

Engineers and scientists operate at the forefront of technological development in chemistry, cryogenics, metallurgy, and the other sciences, keeping abreast of new discoveries and applying them wherever appropriate. With each passing year, successful pioneering in these areas becomes more difficult and requires increasingly improved means of communicating information and exercising control. As a result, the engineer must continue to pioneer in the field of information processing and in developing better systems for gathering, processing, storing, and disseminating information. One of the great attractions of digital computers is their ability to store vast quantities of information and to retrieve it almost instantaneously when required to do so.

By placing greater emphasis on the development and implementation of advanced information processing techniques, engineers will be better able to cope with pressing problems that are common to the entire engineering field—problems such as short time schedules, growing complexity of products, meeting stringent reporting requirements of customers, faster design and construction processes, and higher standards of product design.

The computer can relieve the engineer and scientist of many tiring and time-consuming processes, thus enabling them to spend more time on more important aspects of their profession. In addition to being able to store and retrieve vast quantities of information, the computer is also

"THE COMPUTER WILL NEVER REPLACE PEOPLE COMPLETELY — SOMEONE'S GOT TO PLUG IT IN!"

able to analyze and simulate an almost infinite number of problems. The scientist or engineer can, therefore, perform a far more rigorous analysis of design factors by using a computer than would be possible in the same period of time by using manual methods.

Unfamiliarity with computers and programming techniques in general has limited the use of this powerful tool in many technical areas. Many scientists and engineers are, in fact, openly skeptical of using a computer to carry out processes that they have done for many years by manual methods. If engineers and scientists are to obtain any benefit from using computers, they must be prepared to understand them. But before they can be persuaded to make the effort to understand and master the use of computers, they must first learn of the potential uses of computers. Let us now look at some of the tasks that computers can already undertake for the scientist and engineer, along with some possibilities for future uses.

THE APPLICATION OF COMPUTERS TO MANAGEMENT

In recent years, management has been faced with a persistent and ever-mounting pressure to keep pace with the scientific, technical, and productive capabilities of its laboratories and plants. The ability to secure new business depends to a great extent on management's proficiency. Customers weigh management performance very heavily in assessing a company's ability to meet future requirements. Even after a contract has been won, the amount of profit will frequently depend on management's ability to meet preset standards of cost, time, and reliability.

To meet this challenge, management requires an information and control system that relates each part to the other parts, with changes in one function immediately reflected in the others. It must be dynamic and capable of keeping all levels of management fully informed about activities that are of concern to them. A computerized management system can fill this role. It can produce the specific, tailor-made reports management needs. It can provide information in a form that gives management the key facts necessary for making decisions, noting especially the exceptions or critical areas requiring immediate action (Fig. 1-1). The use of such a system will assist management by contributing to:

- Improved planning of manpower, facilities, and technical abilities to meet the future market.
- Better selection of contracts that utilize existing or planned resources and capabilities.
- Better analysis of contract cost, permitting more precise bidding to meet management's profit objectives.

Courtesy Control Data Corp.

Fig. 1-1. Information being displayed on a cathode-ray tube (crt) display device that is connected to a computer located elsewhere in the building.

- Improved planning of project schedules and distribution of funds and technology.
- Faster response to deviations from the schedule or budget.

Information is the basis for management action. Only through proper use of informational resources can management establish better control and provide adequate guidance to every aspect of a company's operation.

Forecasting and Planning

Long-range planning is the process of supplying a guide for action to bring about a desired future business position. It involves setting objectives and goals, establishing guides to facilitate the accomplishment of the objectives, and following through to see that the plans are carried out to a successful conclusion.

Long-range planning involves the entire organization. The capability profile of the firm is shaped by the activities of the research and engineering organizations in developing proficiency in new areas of technology, and by the personnel and facilities groups in the development and acquisition of manpower skills, facilities, and equipment. The function of the plan is to provide for the expenditure of company resources in a manner that will provide for continuing progress of the firm. The continuing appraisal of corporate goals and strategy in the face of new market demands and opportunities is a requisite for survival. The major steps involved in long-range planning are:

- Formulation of long-term company objectives.
- Identification of alternative courses of action available to the firm.
- Statement of constraints imposed by the available and attainable company resources and capabilities.
- Balancing required capabilities with potential.
- Selection of market opportunities that promise the greatest potential return.
- Determination of the nature and timing of required decisions.
- Assignment of responsibility for the actions required to implement the plan.
- Establishment of measurement criteria to gauge the effectiveness of the plan.

The planning procedure begins with an analysis of data from a variety of sources, including information concerned with customer requirements and the action of competitors. A determination is made of the required resources in each major business area. Then, on the basis of the business dollar potential, an evaluation is made of anticipated returns versus investment requirements. This process is dynamic. Profit potential under alternative assumptions is evaluated since certain combinations of programs may reveal undesirable peaks or valleys in resource utilization. Thus, after various iterations, a plan is evolved that is satisfactory to management.

After marketing strategy has been established, a financial plan is prepared to set targets for the financial status of the company. These targets are expressed in terms of anticipated status of profit and loss, balance sheet, cash flow, and return on investment by the major business area.

Data processing offers the capability to evaluate promptly the changing internal and external conditions. It provides the facility for simulating the effect of common planning assumptions through the various operating organization levels in the company. Management will receive reports that reflect the most current information in the form of a statement of consequences based on the alternative assumptions. The ease with which data-processing equipment prepares the information needed for the planning function is an important added management capability.

Estimating and Pricing

The actual process of seeking business takes place after the business environment is determined. The estimating and pricing group has the primary responsibility for preparing sales proposals for a company. Two significant developments have occurred within engineering that increase the need and value of data-processing systems in the estimating and pricing function. First, products have become considerably more complex and diversified. Electronics, missiles, and spacecraft have increased the time and skills needed to estimate these products. Second, recent trends in proposal requirements have called for more details to be submitted to support cost estimates. This has resulted in an increased effort to control the cost elements, to prepare all proposal schedules and reports, and to make necessary revisions when the elements change. There is also an increase in the number of reestimates that require changes in rates and schedules. The result of these developments is an increase in the cost and the time pressure of preparing proposals.

Data-processing techniques for preparing proposals and cost estimates reduce the work load of the estimating and pricing department by performing much of the clerical effort and helping to control and calculate all cost elements. The necessary data is sorted, summarized, and printed into proposal reports. Adjustments and reestimates are easily prepared. As a result, the cost and time required to prepare proposals is significantly reduced.

Operational Planning

The planning, estimating, and pricing functions have one aim—to secure business that satisfies the company's profit and growth objectives. Then, having secured a contract, management is concerned with the functions of scheduling, budgeting, evaluation, and control. The following paragraphs deal with data-processing systems that supply information to assist management in improving operational effectiveness.

A schedule is a plan that specifies the objectives, the sequence of activities required to meet them, and the dates by which key events or milestones must be completed in order to ensure that the project is completed on time. A total project schedule is submitted as part of the proposal for the contract. Therefore, preliminary schedules must be determined as part of the process of preparing the proposal. A firm, final schedule is established through negotiation with the customer at the time of contract award. This must be broken down into controllable elements beginning with the management of the major segments of work, down to the various supervisory levels. Changes in project schedules may subsequently be required because of changes in customer delivery requests, product specifications changes, or schedule slippages in elements of the work.

Progress reporting starts after work begins on the contract. Actual times are compared against schedule times. Progress information is initiated on the working level and then summarized for management. This information is a basis for management evaluation of project status. The rapid rate of growth and increased size of research and development projects make it imperative that they be carefully scheduled and controlled. These same increases in growth and size, however, make scheduling and controlling by manual methods almost impossible, since it is necessary to integrate and correlate the efforts of many different departments and groups working on large, complex projects. Processing the large volumes of data for scheduling, and analyzing the completed operations against the schedules, is readily performed by data processing; thus, more time is allowed for corrective action by management. A data-processing system for scheduling may also be used to evaluate the effect of proposed changes before they are made, by executing them in the computer system for analysis only.

A budget is a financial plan of action for a specific period of time. Its purpose is to coordinate and control the activities of the various divisions of the business and to find the most profitable courses of action. To achieve this end, the budget reflects not only a plan but also a standard by which the performance and accomplishments of all levels of the organization can be measured. Since the budget is management's declaration of a plan of action, it serves as a formal means of stating corporate policy and advising all management echelons of their goals and targets. One objective of a budget system is to produce a forecasted balance sheet, profit-and-loss statement, and cash-flow statement for management. These are the summary budgets. Before they can be prepared, each element going into them must be forecast, and individual departmental or functional budgets must be prepared. Functional budgets cover sales, operations (including labor, material, and factory overhead), and the general and administrative areas.

Forecasting the future financial position of a company on the basis of estimated operations can be considered a typical simulation problem and ideally lends itself to data-processing techniques. Opening account balances are entered into the computer along with estimated operations, which are converted to appropriate journal entries. These are added to or subtracted from the affected accounts, and the projected statements are printed. The effects of changing conditions, such as the rate of progress payments on government contracts, the rate of profit, or whether a contract will be received, can be readily observed. Since many large engineering companies have a great many contracts in-house, summarizing them is a time-consuming manual task. Data-processing systems can save large amounts of time and effort in the computing and printing of the necessary reports.

In science and engineering, the trend is toward using a stand-alone microcomputer or using a remote terminal (such as the one shown in Fig. 1-2) that feeds directly to a central computer. Such a system eliminates the delays inherent in a manual entry system. After raw data is gathered for the data-processing system, it can be processed for preparation of management reports. These can be historical accounting records or evaluation reports where the data has been:

1. Summarized.
2. Compared with budget and schedule.
3. Computed for budget and schedule variance.
4. Tested against tolerance limits.
5. Printed on exception reports if called for by decision rules stored in the system.

The input data is collected from all departments via automatic data acquisition terminals and may include attendance data, requisitions, purchase orders, work orders, receiving reports, job completion notices, etc.

The success of a company is reflected in the ability of its management to plan adequately for the potential market and to control the operations. Long-range planning, estimating and pricing, and operational planning, including scheduling and budgeting, are important management functions. Effective performance of these functions results in survival and growth.

Courtesy Ferranti Ltd.

Fig. 1-2. Remote crt display and keyboard terminal is used by managers to feed data to a central computer and to display requested information.

THE APPLICATION OF COMPUTERS TO ADMINISTRATIVE TASKS

In many technical companies, computers are used for purposes of office accounting. This includes overall office accounting, individual job costing, income analyzing, expenditure analyzing, budget forecasting, payroll calculations, producing bank schedules, and many other similar tasks. Most of the administrative tasks are routine and repetitive in nature, and may easily be automated.

One of the great advantages of using computers to perform administrative tasks is the fact that it is thereby possible to standardize these particular operations. Much time can be wasted in an office instructing a constantly changing staff how to carry out their required tasks. It is a great advantage for management purposes if many of the routine administrative tasks are carried out on a data-processing system. Fig. 1-3 shows a chart describing expenditures for a small engineering company. This chart was produced by a digital plotter connected to a computer system.

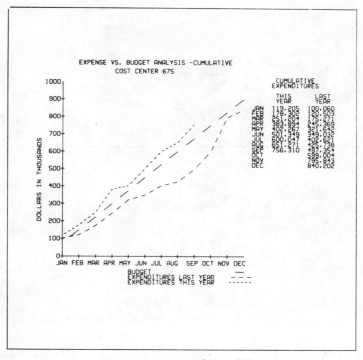

Courtesy California Computer Products, Inc.

Fig. 1-3. Graph of actual versus budgeted and last year's expenditures for a small engineering company was produced by a digital plotter connected to a digital computer.

THE APPLICATION OF COMPUTERS TO MANUFACTURING

The manufacturing process is dynamic—not static. In every phase and at every level of operations, manpower, machines, and materials are in motion and moving on a tight schedule toward completion of an end product—a product which frequently changes to accommodate revisions in design or new functional requirements. Continuous and rapid change is a dominant factor in this process. It is this rapid change that makes it so difficult for management to gather data, analyze it, make decisions, and implement them in time to be completely effective.

To cope with this problem, manufacturing management often uses a dynamic system of control—a system that facilitates continuous coordination of the planning and control functions throughout the manufacturing cycle. The engineering organization can help in

"SORRY I'M LATE. I WAS TRYING TO
BEAT THE OFFICE COMPUTER AT A
GAME OF CHECKERS."

implementing these systems. If the design data of a product is stored in a data-processing system, it can (and should) serve as the basis for all manufacturing documentation as the product is engineered. This serves to link the engineering and manufacturing groups into a more efficient team. In addition, it provides the manufacturing group with the following advantages:

- Verification that all assemblies and parts called out on a drawing eventually have a drawing themselves.
- Assurance that usage changes have been properly reflected in higher- and lower-level assemblies, and that they have been communicated to all areas requiring notice.
- Automatic preparation of parts lists from which the requirements can be planned easily.
- Acquisition of data earlier in the product cycle to allow for earlier purchasing and production planning.
- A better basis for building manufacturing cost estimates. The product support function in particular needs information early in the cycle for negotiation with the customer.

● Assurance that the engineering group has the information to take into consideration all usages of a proposed change.

The information and control systems for the manufacturing area provide management with important information of three distinct types: (1) detail data for management at the operating level, including shop orders, purchase orders, personnel, and accounting reports; (2) "exception" data for middle management, such as parts shortages, overexpenditures, and critical path changes; and (3) planning data for top management through implementation of techniques such as simulation and trend analysis. All three types of data have their source in the mainstream of manufacturing information—the flow of data that crosses all functions in the manufacturing organization.

"MISS SMITH, PLEASE HAVE THE COMPUTER CHECK THE AIR QUALITY TO SEE IF IT'S ALL RIGHT TO GO OUT FOR LUNCH."

MANUFACTURING PLANNING AND TOOLING

One of the first groups in the manufacturing organization to make use of the engineering data is the planning and tooling function. In most cases, this group has access to the information as it is being developed. It can be seen that engineering, planning, and tooling overlap considerably in the time scale. Development of the plan starts with the proposal and continues through to the completion of the contract. Because of changes in the product definition, the plan is constantly being corrected and updated. Since the changes are scheduled for a particular implementation date, the facilities requirements (tools and machines) must also be scheduled. Fast response to change is a key characteristic of a management system based on electronic data processing. The system should also have the ability to accommodate certain unexpected developments, such as the acquisition of small companies or development of new products or techniques.

The tooling operation can be aided by data processing in the following functions: tool order scheduling, tool order status, tool accountability, and tool contract estimating. The tool control portion of a management system offers many benefits. For example, it:

1. Reports precise trouble areas as they apply to tool shop load, tool design and manufacturing status, and actual tool costs versus estimated costs.
2. Supplies easily processed historical data for tool contract estimating.
3. Provides the data for preparing tool cost reports to the customer and for determining tool insurance values and tool accountability.
4. Maintains tool schedule status to provide accurate and readily available data for coordination of both tool and production manufacturing.

Materials Control

The Engineering Assembly Parts List (EAPL) provides up-to-date knowledge of the engineering status of all planned articles by serial number. It has been shown that the EAPL provides the basic information for the planning and tooling function as well as pricing and estimating for production and spares items. This information also forms the basis for materials planning and can provide all information necessary to update the manufacturing assembly bill of materials. If properly planned, one file can serve both purposes.

It is the mission of the materials control function to bring together requirements from all sources, such as the production schedule, spares requirements, engineering requirements, scrap replacement requirements, interdivisional requirements, and to provide a plan for furnishing the net requirements by time period. There not only should be a steady flow of quality materials on schedule, but there should also be a careful balancing of the cost of acquisition of material against the cost of holding and storing it.

Data processing assists materials control because it rapidly combines these varied requirements by time period and associates them with the complete manufacturing assembly parts lists to combine like requirements between separate articles, and to "net" these requirements against what is planned, committed, or already available. This is done so that manufacturing and purchasing can plan future actions on a more economical basis.

Not only does the basic parts list provide information for the materials planning aspect, but it also provides basic inventory record data so that all issues, receipts, orders, and requirements can be posted as action occurs. This is sometimes termed the *execution* phase of inventory. Data processing helps in this area mainly by providing accurate, up-to-date information through the use of data-communications terminals that transmit information on transactions as they occur. Random-access storage enables immediate inquiry into the status of materials information, as well as immediate updating of records. There are several types of actions that result from a materials requirement: a shop order is issued, purchase requisitions and purchase orders are issued, and interdivisional orders are originated.

Purchasing is a function in which data processing provides great assistance. Using the same source data, the system can provide purchase orders, requisitions, records for vendor follow-up action, and account- ing data. Interplant requirements are reflected in the input to the materials cycle in another plant. Data processing can provide great assistance in giving information on the status of all the various types of materials orders, particularly where items have become critically needed.

Shop Control

Production planning takes place after the product design has been established. After proper routing and tooling considerations have been established to plan the production process, a time estimate or standard is applied to each operation. A start or release date is set up on the basis of the required date established in the materials control section. At this point, reproduction control assumes responsibility in the manufacturing cycle.

The original assembly parts-list information in the system has provided the basis for the shop "travelers"—the bill of materials used in assembly operations and the manufacturing cost records. The requirements schedule has formed the target dates for the operational scheduling.

The many engineering changes, the short production runs, and the critical importance of the product suggest the need for tight control. Five developments in the field of data processing are of particular interest to engineering production-control managers:

1. Two-way data-communications terminals.
2. Large-capacity random-access files.
3. Data-processing systems with higher speeds and lower cost per unit of work.
4. Greater ease of computer programming through the development of better programming methods and languages.

5. Significant application and concept developments. These developments make it possible to cope with the large volume of information affecting factory operations in the small amount of time available to make decisions.

The manufacturing schedules for detail parts and assemblies are based on an operational scheduling program. Scheduled shop orders are used to establish a file, which shows the location of all open job orders. This information is also used to prepare reports showing the work load presently backed up at each work center and is also used to prepare a shop-load forecast report. A shop-order packet is prepared to accompany each order. The same information will be used to report each move of the order through the shop via data-communications terminals, so that the location and status of the order will be available on request. Data-communications terminals, located throughout the factory, also are used for recording requisitions for withdrawal of tools, materials, and parts, and to print move or split orders. Job assignment within each cost center can be handled by the computer on a real-time basis with the use of on-line communications terminals. Periodically, reports of load status and load movement and the machine utilization for each machine group and cost center can be printed. Load trends are forecasted and the total volume of shop-load input and output is measured and reported.

The shop-control systems should provide daily employee, departmental, and divisional performance information for those areas where exceptional performance is being experienced. These systems provide:

- Improved schedules for fabricated parts and assemblies.
- Improved direction to shop personnel making dispatching decisions.
- Improved information for management when contracts are cut back, stretched out, or increased. These situations require quick and accurate shop-load forecasts, machine capacity reports, and order status so that new plans can be developed.

These improvements enable management to react quickly to engineering, planning, and schedule changes; reduce investments in work-in-process inventories; increase labor efficiency; secure greater machine utilization; and improve schedule compliance. This parts discussion is related to getting the product to the customer. Support of the product after delivery also requires considerable management attention.

Product Support

The product-support organizations in engineering companies are charged with a number of responsibilities that are vital to a successful

"THAT WAS MY NEW MICROCOMPUTER!"

system installation and operation. This organization, sometimes called customer service, presents a single face to the customer representing many of the departments in the company. Product-support efforts include preparation of manuals for operating, servicing, inspecting, and maintaining the vehicle or system; test equipment; and group-support equipment. Product-support field-service engineers work with the customer to achieve the designed operation of the equipment. Service reports are prepared for use by departments charged with product design improvements. The functions directly connected with spares are an important part of product support. These functions include selection and designation of items to be listed as spares.

Consideration is made of factors such as repairable, replaceable, mean time between failure, and susceptibility to damage in view of the planned mission of the system. Results are given as a recommended quantity of spares. When a customer approves recommended spares by placing an order, a series of spares-control actions take place. Procurement, whether manufacture or purchase, and shipment in the quantity and on the schedule required is ordered by spares. A follow-up system is used to monitor status of each of the ordered items. Spares pricing and invoicing are two additional functions that are usually included as part of the spares-control system.

Many company departments provide direct service to the customer.

The primary activity of product support is to coordinate these departmental efforts into an effective supply program.

In addition to the information on the engineering configuration, the spares organization needs to know the modification status of all products and test equipment in the field so that proper support can be effected. Most of the parts-list data discussed in previous sections can be very economically shared with the product-support group through a mutual data-processing system. This information is needed to provide the customer with many different types of reports pertaining to the product.

This same information is used by the pricing and estimating department to develop spares cost. It can be seen that these two functions are closely linked through data processing, since they require the same information. An equally close relationship exists between product support (particularly the spares function) and materials control because spares requirements constitute one of the major inputs to materials planning. If spares data is controlled by data processing, the transmission of requirements to the materials-planning function becomes a much simpler task because the information is already in machine-readable form.

In addition to assuming the clerical chores of issuing production orders, shipping documents, invoicing, parts listing and pricing catalogs, data processing can help in inventory record keeping and spares inventory management, in finding optimum levels, reorder points and quantities, and in review periods. Many of the reports required by various government agencies can be prepared directly by data-processing systems (for example, provisioning parts breakdown, priced spare-parts lists, breakdown for recoverable items, and group assembly parts list). These aids to the product-support function are aimed at providing faster service to the customer, more accurate records, and a reduction of clerical effort for the manufacturer.

Product Testing

The computer can also be used in the manufacturing plant to test products. Fig. 1-4 illustrates a computer-controlled circuit-card testing machine. The operator plugs in a card which the computer will compare to a hand-tested prototype card already plugged into the left enclosure. A typewriter prints out the results of the test, including information that can be used in correcting the circuit card if there is a minor problem. The computer performs this test in seconds, as compared to about one hour to hand test a card.

Fig. 1-5 illustrates a computer-controlled quality inspection system used to check the composition of cast steel. The unit is referred to as an "ultrasonic wave cleaner" in which the computer conducts mathematical correlations. Fig. 1-6 shows quality control engineers using a minicomputer system to test the tensile strength of steel.

Courtesy Hewlett-Packard

Fig. 1-4. Operator testing a circuit card with a computer-controlled circuit-card tester.

THE APPLICATION OF COMPUTERS TO DESIGN

Since their inception, computers have been used to speed computation. Now, techniques are being implemented to employ computers as information processors. In this new role, computers are improving the analysis, communication, and control of design information. They are extending the effectiveness of the entire organization. They are solving many problems associated with the design process such as:

1. *Continuous Design Changes*—These changes occur throughout the development and service life of many products due to new functional requirements, analysis of failure data, or technological advances. Every change must be documented, communicated, and controlled.

2. *Increased Volume of Data*—The growing sophistication of modern devices is generating a flood of data. A ballistic missile system, for example, may require over 80,000 drawings and tens of thousands of data records. It is imperative that means be found to both condense and control this information as it passes through the many phases of design, production, and operation of the end product.

3. *Information Exchange*—Throughout the design process, volumes

Courtesy Digital Equipment Corp.

Fig. 1-5. Computer used as part of a quality inspection system to check the composition of cast steel.

of information must be disseminated within the engineering complex, between the engineering and manufacturing groups, and between the company and the customer.

4. *Graphic Representation*—Vehicle shape and component placement are described by tens of thousands of sketches, layouts, drawings, and schematics. These graphic representations must be generated and revised as needed, frequently on a daily basis.

5. *Rapid Changes in Product Line*—Many companies do not enjoy the stability of a long-range planned product line. Many products are designed for a special purpose, within a critically short lead

Courtesy Perkin-Elmer Corp., Computer Systems Division

Fig. 1-6. Quality control engineers using a minicomputer system to test the tensile strength of steel.

time. All components of these complex products must evolve simultaneously. At the same time, the manufacturing organization is pressing for specifications and parts requirements so they can plan for procurement, tooling, and production. Creation, dissemination, and updating of the required data—in such a limited time span—presents a monumental problem to management.

6. *Noncreative Effort*—It has been estimated that from 70% to 90% of an engineer's or scientist's time is consumed by noncreative tasks. There is an urgent need to effect a more profitable use of this important resource.

Today, computer–based information and control systems are performing a variety of important functions in the engineering area. Their more important contributions to the design process include:

1. Processing tremendous quantities of data economically, accurately, and within a limited time.
2. Recording the effect of every design revision reliably and quickly.

3. Preparing diagrams, data lists, and reports for distribution, when and where needed.
4. Relieving engineers from burdensome, noncreative activities.
5. Coordinating and integrating product data developed throughout the engineering, manufacturing, checkout, and operational cycles.
6. Responding rapidly to requests for status information.
7. Providing measures of performance, validity, and reliability of alternative product designs.

Structural and Mechanical Design

The objective of design information systems is to reduce design lead time, to improve the productivity of engineers, designers, and draftsmen, and to assure the validity of design data. The computer's high-speed record keeping and data-communications capability can be a principal factor in reducing development lead time. This is accomplished not only in engineering, but throughout the production organization because design data is communicated in computer-processed form.

Techniques to capture the physical shape of an object in computer-processed files are in an early stage of development. The present complexity of structural design has made it uneconomical to manually calculate and develop each dimension required to describe the surface contour of objects.

"Numerical design" is a computer-oriented technique for mathematically defining the geometry of an object. It is compatible with current processing capabilities, particularly numerically controlled machine tools. Numerical design is unique in that:

1. After the external shape of the object has been specified in the form of a mathematical model, it can be interrogated by various routines and programs to show several views of the object.
2. Data for use by numerically controlled machine tools can be derived from the master dimension file for use in parts manufacturing and in the production of scale models of the object for tests.
3. It provides a means of central dimensional control. This is in contrast to having the controls spread among drawings, undimensioned lines on full-size master layouts, and a full-size mockup.

Programming languages are required for encoding graphic data from sketches and layouts so that detail drawings can be generated by computers and drafting machines. After the description of a part has been recorded in a computer-processed file, changes are incorporated in computer-generated drawings by encoding the revised data and reprocessing. From a basic design of similar but not identical components encoded from a tabulated drawing, individual detail drawings are generated. Ultimately, the computer will be capable of producing perspective drawings for production illustration and maintenance manuals.

The computer generates a surface description by adding detail to the engineer's design description in accordance with programmed design rules. Thus, the quantity of informational output by the computer is many times greater than that of the source data. This output must serve the needs of a large number of widely diverse groups of people. While early system implementation may not serve all of these groups directly, their needs must be understood so that the system can be extended in the future. The system will change and grow as techniques are developed to meet new requirements, and as changes in manufacturing processes and techniques occur that affect the manner in which information is best presented to its users. Let us now briefly look at three applications where computers serve the design engineer.

Mechanical design has long depended on graphics for converting design ideas into final products. More than a decade ago, research engineers at General Motors began using digital computers in the design of automobiles. Fig. 1-7 shows a research engineer checking out a computer program that allows him to modify a design "drawing." A touch of the electric "pencil" to the crt surface signals the computer to begin an assigned task. The engineer may also instruct the computer using the keyboard at right, the card reader below the keyboard, or the program control buttons below the screen. Hundreds of special computer programs, written by research engineers, scientists, and programmers, are needed to carry out this type of work.

Several computer-generated displays are shown in Fig. 1-8. They illustrate some of the capabilities of the experimental human/computer design system used by General Motors engineers. The drawings appear on the viewing screen of the designer's console and come from a mathematical representation of the design stored in the computer's memory. In one case, the system has enabled the research engineer to make a major revision in the deck lid of a car while working at his console and to see immediately the results of his change.

Design engineers who put together aircraft cockpits and controls must know how a pilot will react physically to a particular arrangement of dials and instruments. Are emergency controls too hard to reach? Are certain instruments in the wrong place? Can movement in the cockpit be reduced by rearranging seats or controls? Manufacturing a full-scale model or mockup of every contemplated cockpit design to get these answers is expensive. Having a pilot run through simulated instrument checkouts in each mockup would be time consuming. So, before

Courtesy General Motors Corp.

Fig. 1-7. A research engineer using a computer design system for the purpose of designing automobiles.

investing time and effort in this way, designers decided to let a computer figure out whether a certain-sized pilot could operate comfortably in the cockpit of a particular design. The computer would show pilot "reach" distances and movements with mathematical precision. Fig. 1-9 shows a digital plotter under computer control drawing a human figure as specified by the designer. The plotter draws each part of the body as an individual unit. An engineer dictates where each section of the body will join the other, thus determining to a large extent the figure's action. A completed drawing of a human figure is illustrated in Fig. 1-10.

Let us now examine how a computer is used in the design of an airplane. Since this is not an easy task to describe in simple terms, we will start with the design of an airplane wing. The engineers tailor the shape of a wing to certain aerodynamic principles and requirements, and develop formulas for necessary measurements and calculations as they go along. However, an aerodynamically perfect wing is an extremely complex thing to describe mathematically and requires an

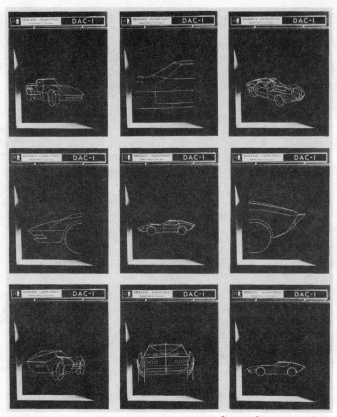

Courtesy General Motors Corp.

Fig. 1-8. Displays generated by a computer under instructions from a research engineer.

immense amount of calculation. This is where the computer comes in. Engineers no longer laboriously calculate on a slide rule the thousands of dimensions necessary to describe the contoured parts of a wing. Now they simply put the numbers into a computer and then ask the computer to make these calculations. This is the kind of work the computer does best, and it does it quickly with great accuracy.

Engineers spend long hours with the computer, changing their data, getting new calculations, and trying different design ideas in the form of mathematical models. Ultimately, though, the computer ends up with the exact dimensions of the entire wing shape, precisely as the engineers want it.

At this point, numerical control planners and programmers take over. They make a plan for a machine to cut metal in the shapes the engineers

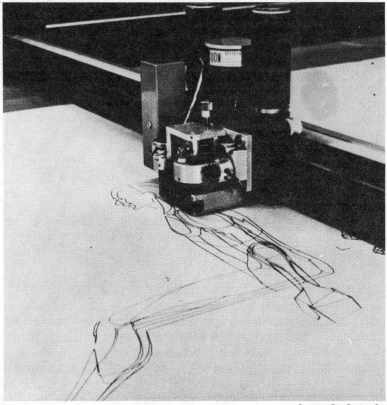

Courtesy The Boeing Co.

Fig. 1-9. Following a design engineer's instructions, a computer-controlled digital plotter draws a human figure.

have worked out on the computer. The programmers use the same numbers and calculations the engineers developed in the computer, but they translate these numbers to vertical, horizontal, and other motions of a machine cutting head. Very simply, they produce a "road map" for the cutter to follow, somewhat on the order of the numbered-dot pictures in children's activity books. In this case, metal is cut based on the engineer's mathematical points rather than pictures drawn. However, pictures can be drawn using a digital plotter (Fig. 1-11).

After the machining plan is finished, it is transferred to a punched tape which the cutting machine reads in the same way a player piano plays a punched music roll. Metal is placed on a machine, and a part is machined exactly along the pattern the programmer called for, in precisely the shape calculated by the engineer. The computer has done

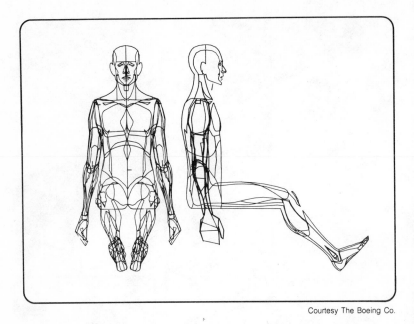

Courtesy The Boeing Co.

Fig. 1-10. A completed drawing of the human figure drawn by a computer-controlled digital plotter.

three things in this total operation: (1) It has handled the complex mathematical calculations directed by the design engineer, (2) it has stored a mathematical description of the wing, and (3) it has provided a numerical description of the cutter path which the cutting machinery follows to make the contoured parts and tools required for a wing structure.

Nowadays, much of the design information is stored in the computer, the curves and points are transferred to tapes, and the final shape is not seen until the tape-controlled drafting machine draws the picture. The heart of this operation is the computer. Everything is worked out mathematically, put on tapes, and introduced into machines. The same computer-stored information is then used to make other tapes for producing tools and parts. In short, the computer is the "junior partner" and the engineer is the "boss." The engineer determines the design control points and the computer calculates everything between these points, including the path a cutter takes to make the proper cut in metal.

Electronic Systems

Computer programs can (1) perform examinations of certain design data against prescribed rules far more exhaustively and accurately than

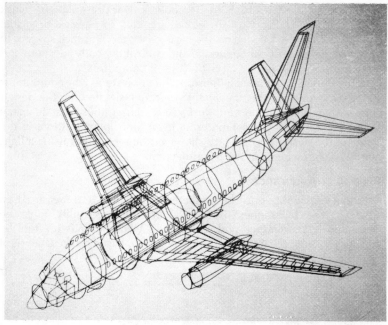

Courtesy The Boeing Co.

Fig. 1-11. Computer-generated perspective drawing of a Boeing jetliner.

can designers, and (2) control the addition of new and revised data far more reliably and quickly. Every change must be traced through the entire network to make sure it has not adversely affected the proper functioning of the system. It is this checking and backtracking, keeping track of every connection, that can consume an inordinate amount of the designer's time. The use of computers not only speeds development, but relieves engineers from burdensome, noncreative activities. In electrical design, computers were first used at the two extremes of the design spectrum:

1. Mathematical computation programs for more efficient analysis of components and circuits.
2. Maintaining, editing, and reporting production data in the interface between engineering and manufacturing.

These two aforementioned areas exhibit a critical need for computer capabilities. Exhaustive analysis of the environmental and operating characteristics of solid-state components involves so many parameter variations as to make high-speed computers essential. Translating the implemented design from its symbological representation (block diagrams, interconnection lists, equations, etc.) to physical or spatial realization (module location charts, wiring lists, etc.), in such a way as to preserve the integrity of the design and control the daily additions and modifications, also necessitates the use of computers.

In the human/machine relationship of many systems, the computer is taking over much of the noncreative routine tasks, freeing the design engineer for more important work. Research studies exist in many companies to make the computer an even more powerful tool in the hands of the designer. Fig. 1-12 shows a design engineer using a light pen to make changes in a wiring diagram.

Reliability Assurance

Product reliability must be predicted, calculated, and measured; in addition, the techniques used to assure this reliability must be continuously reexamined and reaffirmed. A computer is the tool by which a dynamic reliability assurance program, based on the analysis of

Courtesy IBM Corp.

Fig. 1-12. Engineer using crt display and light pen to update a wiring diagram.

"WHATS THIS NONSENSE ABOUT YOUR HIRING A COMPUTER ROOM MORALE BOO.... WHO?....WELL HELLO THERE!"

reliability data, may be implemented in the initial stages of a program and carried through the life of the item. Reliability is defined as the probability that a device will satisfactorily perform a specified function under specified conditions for a given period of time. Another way of expressing reliability is as a measure of effectiveness or design adequacy.

Engineering Data Control

The function of an engineering data-control system is to release new drawing and specification data and to incorporate the effect of every design revision in the engineering data records. An additional requirement imposed by design complexity is the ability to process increasing quantities of data with extreme accuracy in a limited time span.

A carefully designed engineering data system utilizing electronic data processing can minimize expediting and reduce the time span from contract award to hardware delivery. This is accomplished through elimination of duplicate files with their inherent inconsistencies, duplicate parts-listing operations, and duplicate data-handling operations. Increased accuracy can be achieved through elimination of manual transcription and through mechanization of related clerical operations. The engineering data-control system provides the capability of rapidly handling expanding volumes and increasing customer data submittal requirements. Management will achieve improved control with computer processing of engineering data. Specific advantages are that the engineering data system:

1. Establishes a single source for all users of engineering parts data, thereby assuring accuracy of parts data used in procurement, production, logistics planning, and customer data submittal because requirements information is printed from original data, rather than being copied from drawings.
2. Records parts data at the earliest possible time, assuring efficient service for all users.
3. Generates drawing usage and lower-level parts usage data on initial release, added configurations, and changes.
4. Provides machine-listed parts-list documents with integral drawing usage information meeting photo reduction requirements.
5. Reduces operating costs.

The overall effect of placing the computer in the release cycle, rather than downstream from engineering data release, can be a marked improvement in both cycle time and data accuracy. It also provides the capability for data retrieval and reporting at very low cost. Most significant is the ability to prepare customer data lists, indexes, drawing lists, and specification lists in any combination, sequence, or format. Even unanticipated requests for special reports can be met with very little effort by using a "report generator" program.

Configuration Management

Configuration management techniques have been developed in response to the requirements for successful large systems integration. The computer has made it possible to record and correlate the information necessary to control, account for, and report the planned and actual design of each article throughout its production and service life. The computer maintains a file on magnetic tape, or in random-access disk storage, of the planned constituents of each product and item of associated equipment—the "as-engineered" configuration. Another file is developed by the computer to identify the installation of components in each article—the "as-manufactured" configuration.

Subsequent revision of the configuration of each article by field modification is recorded by the computer. The engineer can determine which modifications have been incorporated in a particular product; manufacturing and operations personnel can determine which tasks remain to be accomplished at any point in time. The computer enables customer and company change-control management to determine the effect of every proposed change on the product, its associated equipment, and related documentation. The computer's ability to assimilate enormous quantities of data, maintain current records accurately, and respond to any request for configuration and implementation status information is the key to success in change control.

COMPUTER GRAPHICS

The engineer can use the computer system as a draftsman in several ways; however, the most common methods involve the use of a cathode-ray tube (crt) display device or a digital plotter. The term *computer graphics* refers to the concept of a human communicating with a computer by means of graphical symbols, such as lines, dots, curves, alphabetical or numerical symbols, etc. Computer graphics is a mode of human/machine communication that provides for a high rate of information transfer. The actual devices associated with computer graphics include cathode-ray tubes, digital plotters, keyboards, light pens, data tablets, and computers. Light pens, data tablets, and keyboards are used for entering data and modifying the information held in the computer memory. The crt's and digital plotters are used as output devices to display information.

The two major categories of crt displays are (1) *alphanumeric* and (2) *graphic*. Alphanumeric displays show only alphabetic, numeric, and special characters; graphic displays present line drawings, curves, schematics, etc., in addition to presenting alphanumeric information (Fig. 1-13). The digital plotter is used to produce conventional pen-on-paper drawings, which may consist of alphanumeric information as well as drawings (Fig. 1-14).

The use of computer graphics in design has proven very successful, since it permits efficient interaction between computers and engineers. Typical areas of application include electronic component design and network analysis and design. Electronic component design includes the entire spectrum of electrical and electromechanical hardware. In such design projects, existing components often must be modified, such as customizing a transformer design for a given application. The computer can quickly check characteristics and availability of off-the-shelf models, displaying part numbers, dimensions, electrical specifications, and available inventory either by normal printout or through alphanumeric

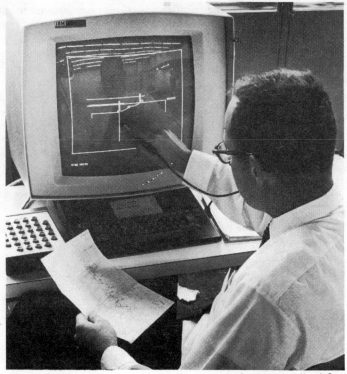

Courtesy United Aircraft Corp.

Fig. 1-13. A computer-controlled graphical crt display unit connected to a remotely located computer. The engineer is entering information with a light pen.

display terminals. Next, the engineer can use the computer to determine the minimum modification necessary to adapt an available stock item to a new set of specifications. By trial and error, the computer may explore the effects of alternate approaches and selections from inventory.

The engineer often uses special programs to help him design circuits. First, the engineer formulates a trial design. He then uses an analysis program to test his hypothetical design. If the response curve meets his original specifications, the design is complete. Otherwise, he changes certain parameters and repeats the process until the response does meet his specifications.

Network analysis relates to the computational techniques involved in the mathematical modeling and performance analysis of circuits and networks. The calculations involve complex arithmetic, matrix meth-

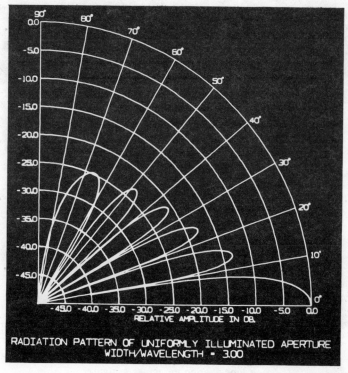

RADIATION PATTERN OF UNIFORMLY ILLUMINATED APERTURE
WIDTH/WAVELENGTH = 3.00

Courtesy Bell Telephone Laboratories

Fig. 1-14. Computer-generated polar plot of the radiation pattern of a rectangular aperture showing the relative power radiated by the antenna in different directions.

ods, and differential equations. The computer's speed makes it feasible to quickly analyze elaborate networks involving many components.

Computer graphics will permit the engineer to create the shape of a building, an automobile body, a ship hull, an electronic circuit, an airplane fuselage, or a tobacco pipe with considerable ease. The computer will behave like a skilled draftsman, working from information furnished by the engineer at the computer terminal. Fig. 1-15 shows an engineer using a digital plotter in parallel with a time-sharing terminal.

THE COMPUTER AS A CONTROL DEVICE

In a control system, the computer output is used to control, or to help control, some process or activity. In process-control applications, a computer provides signals that manipulate industrial processes.

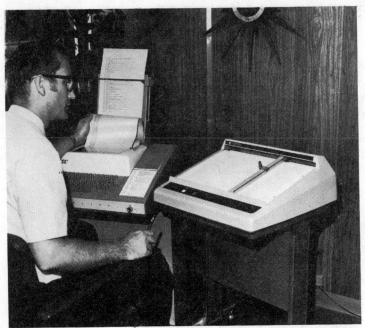

Courtesy Hewlett-Packard

Fig. 1-15. Engineer using a digital plotter in parallel with a terminal connected to a time-sharing computer system.

Automated steel mills, oil refineries, cement plants, chemical plants, utility plants, and cookie factories are examples of such applications. Process-control systems are often referred to as *closed-loop* control systems. In such systems, the computer is used to monitor control equipment (temperatures, pressures, flow rates, etc.) and when errors are detected, the computer makes the decision on what changes to make to provide optimum operation. The computer is able to perform this operation only after engineers have described the plant behavior in the form of mathematical models (mathematical equations) and represented this model in the form of computer programs. Fig. 1-16 shows systems engineers checking out the computer equipment that is used in a computer-controlled structural steel mill.

Fig. 1-17 illustrates a transit expressway system that is actually controlled by a process-control computer. The computer controls the expressway vehicles as they travel around the loop, stops them at stations, controls door openings and closings, and stops the vehicles in emergency operations. The system was developed especially for metropolitan areas with medium-density transit needs.

Another type of control system is the *open-loop* system. This system is semiautomatic, and the computer works in partnership with human operators. This is the case in an air-traffic control system in which

Courtesy Westinghouse Electric Corp.

Fig. 1-16. Systems engineers checking out the computer equipment that is used in a computer-controlled structural steel mill.

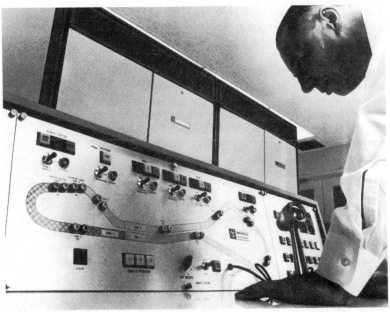

Courtesy Westinghouse Electric Corp.

Fig. 1-17. A single dispatcher, sitting in this control room, has complete control of an experimental transit expressway system.

computers, radar, and communications devices are used in conjunction with both ground-based and airborne personnel.

When the computer reacts to its input data quickly, completes its processing, and takes immediate action, the term *real-time* is sometimes used. A real-time computer system may be defined as one that controls an environment by receiving data, processing it, and taking action quickly enough to affect the functioning of the environment at that time. Systems that are usually classified as real-time systems are military command and control systems, satellite tracking systems, space communications systems, air defense systems, message switching systems, satellite information retrieval systems, simulation systems, space equipment checkout systems, traffic control systems, ship control systems, aircraft detection systems, airline reservation systems, transportation control systems, management information systems, and many others. Close human/machine cooperation and communication is characteristic of most real-time control systems.

Another control application of the computer is the numerical control of machine-tool operations. This is a system of machine-tool control in which the operation or positioning of the machine tool is determined by a sequence of coded numbers. The computer is used to develop a punched paper tape, which is then used to control the machine tool. This system results in greater accuracy and reproducibility of parts, increased productivity of the machine, as well as savings in tooling costs and in the requirements for skilled machine operators. Fig. 1-18 shows several numerically controlled sheet-metal punching machines that operate from punched paper-tape instructions produced by a computer. It is also possible for computers to directly control machines. Fig. 1-19 illustrates a Behrens punch press being controlled by a minicomputer system. Fig. 1-20 shows a technician using a minicomputer-controlled graphics system for pipeline control.

THE COMPUTER AS A LIBRARIAN

Publications, research reports, project reports, and field-trip reports are rapidly accumulating in the technical libraries of most large companies. The number of documents to be indexed, stored, and disseminated throughout each organization is increasing because

Courtesy Collins Radio Co.

Fig. 1-18. Numerically controlled sheet-metal punching machines operate from instructions produced by a computer.

Courtesy Digital Equipment Corp.

Fig. 1-19. Minicomputer interfaced to a Behrens punch press in an application where the computer controls the tool.

information is more specific and is segmented into smaller increments. Documents are produced not only by internal research laboratories and developmental projects, but also by an increasing number of outside sources, including governmental agencies, corporate and university research centers, and associate contractors.

Time is an important factor in getting this information to the user. The failure to retrieve information as soon as it becomes available can cause duplication of research and development effort. Engineers cannot wait for information to be formalized. There is a need for indexing and disseminating preliminary results—the nature of the work, the anticipated results, and knowledge of who is doing the work. This should be available to the engineer so that he can go directly to the source for discussion without the delay inherent in waiting for printed results. Finally, the engineer's time for reading is limited. Even when reports are available, he may not have the time to personally review a number of

Courtesy Digital Equipment Corp.

Fig. 1-20. Technician using a minicomputer-controlled graphics system for pipeline control.

documents in order to gather and correlate the needed information. Retrieved data must be specific. The key to effectively retrieving the specific information needed is the method of indexing. Requests for information are complex, cutting across many subject areas and technologies. Standard methods of indexing are not sufficient to meet these needs.

New techniques of indexing have been developed that enable responsive dissemination and retrieval of technical information in this interdisciplinary environment. The computer has the capacity, speed, and logical processing capability to search and correlate indexes to enormous quantities of reference data. The computer responds to search inquiries by "coordinating" index terms. That is, the document is characterized not by a single subject heading, but by 20 or 30 key words extracted from the text of the document itself. The computer brings the key words in the engineer's inquiry into correspondence with those of the document he needs. The computer combines these terms to any level of specificity desired in order to retrieve general references for one individual, or a specific document citation for another. It is not necessary to anticipate possible questions that might be asked of the system when indexing the document; the coordination of index terms takes place at the time of search.

The information system can be extended to notify engineers of the availability of new publications and reports as they are received. Selective Dissemination of Information (SDI) is accomplished by storing in the computer memory a profile of each individual's or group's interests. When a new document is indexed, a reference record is stored in a computer-processed file. At that time, the computer matches the key words of the document with the user's profiles. Wherever a sufficient correlation exists between an individual's interests and the context of the new document, he is notified of its existence.

Another aid to engineers for finding new sources of information quickly is a unique index prepared by the computer from the bibliographic references stored in its memory. This technique, known as Key-Word-In-Context (KWIC) indexing, enables preparation of literature lists at negligible additional cost. An important characteristic of the KWIC technique is that it does not depend on manual indexing. Because of the speed of electronic data-processing equipment, the elapsed time between receipt of the document and its appearance in the index can be reduced from a matter of weeks to a day or two. For this reason, the KWIC technique is frequently employed to prepare announcement lists of new documents. Its preparation requires only the entry of the document title, author, and source into the computer, which then sorts these titles into a listing in alphabetical sequence of significant words.

Another capability of the computer in a technical information system is its direct assistance to technical library personnel. Here the computer prepares catalog cards, accession lists, and query responses on its high-speed printer. The saving of time in data transcription can be an important advantage to companies using computers for information processing.

Information can be stored on magnetic tape or disk in a manner very similar to the way that music, speech, and pictures are recorded. Information contained on these tapes or disks may be used by the computer in a variety of ways. A typical computer installation used for information retrieval operations may consist of a crt display, a line printer, and a keyboard all linked to the computer. The engineer, by typing a request for certain information on the keyboard, causes the computer to display the requested information on the crt screen in the form of either written information or drawings. In some systems, when any particular item of information has been located and displayed on the crt screen, the engineer can cause a hard-copy printout to occur on a special printing or plotting device.

It is also possible to store information on microfilm and to command the computer to "read" the film and display the contents on the crt. It is then possible to carry out alterations using the light pen and then direct the computer to produce a copy of this amended information on another microfilm.

It is important that the engineer understand clearly how to use information retrieval systems and take a lead in specifying the requirements for future systems. Only the engineer knows the type of systems that are most helpful and useful to him in his job.

THE COMPUTER AS A PROBLEM SOLVER

In addition to some of the more dramatic applications of computers, such as simulation, machine control, circuit design, etc., it is possible for the engineer to use the computer as a "problem solver." Complex mathematical calculations, which might take an engineer with a desk calculator many years to complete, can be performed by the computer in a matter of hours. For example, a ten-variable multiple-correlation problem requiring hundreds of human-hours of computation with an electric desk calculator may take just two or three minutes on the computer. Many problems formerly considered impossible to solve because of prohibitive time requirements have now been placed within reach, thus allowing the engineer a greater degree of experimentation in his work. Fig. 1-21 shows an engineer using a computer system to speed the development and testing of a jet engine.

A computer program is a list of instructions which, if given to a computer, will cause it to perform a sequence of operations leading to the answer to a certain problem. The list of instructions is often prepared by a programmer; however, it may also be prepared by an engineer or scientist with some training in programming techniques. Fig. 1-22 shows an engineer writing a computer program. The engineer, then, can solve many problems by translating them into lists of instructions the computer can understand and use to produce the desired answer.

The engineer can also use computer programs that have been written by other people for use on specific computer systems. In this case, the engineer merely supplies input data to the program, which the computer then uses to produce the desired results. The following is a

Courtesy Department of the Air Force.

Fig. 1-21. Engineer using a computer system to help develop and test jet engines.

partial list of application programs that are available on many computer systems:

- Generate random numbers.
- Compute prime numbers.
- Perform algebraic operations.
- Calculate trigonometric functions.
- Calculate logarithms and exponentials.
- Generate hyperbolic functions.
- Perform numerical integrations and differentiations.
- Execute numerical solutions of differential equations.
- Perform vector operations.
- Perform matrix operations.
- Execute conversions of measurement units.
- Solve linear programming problems.
- Solve dynamic programming problems.
- Compute statistics (mean, variance, standard deviation, and correlation coefficients).

Courtesy IBM Corp.

Fig. 1-22. Engineer preparing a computer program.

- Fit data to a regression equation.
- Perform regression analysis and statistical tests, such as χ^2 test.
- Generate tables of information.
- Store and retrieve information.
- Search and sort files of information.
- Perform document information retrieval.
- Contouring program.
- Highway design.
- Traffic routing.

Fig. 1-23 shows two engineers using a computer to solve a problem. This small computer has a large library of prewritten programs that can be used for solving various engineering problems.

Many programs have been developed to aid the civil engineer. Typical of these would be programs to plot contour diagrams, plan highway routing, forecast traffic trends, produce traffic maps, design buildings, and even plot maps. An example of this latter program is SAMPS (Subdivision And Map Plotting System) which, when used with

Courtesy IBM Corp.

Fig. 1-23. Engineers using a computer to solve a problem.

a digital plotter, can do most of the drafting involved in subdivision planning and mapping (Fig. 1-24).

In addition to providing many of the previously mentioned programs with a specific computer system, the computer manufacturers usually supply several programming languages that simplify the programming task. Languages such as FORTRAN, BASIC, PL/1, APL, and Pascal are all easy to learn and are suitable for use in many engineering applications. Languages such as GPSS and SIMSCRIPT have been developed to provide the user with tools of simulation. Languages such as COGO, ICES, and STRESS have been developed to help civil and structural engineers solve many problems. For example, the STRESS system enables the engineer to write a complete input program for the solution of a structural problem even though he has had no programming experience. Such a system provides the practicing engineer with an economical way of using the computer on a day-to-day basis for the solution of routine structural problems.

Let us now consider an example where an engineer uses a computer

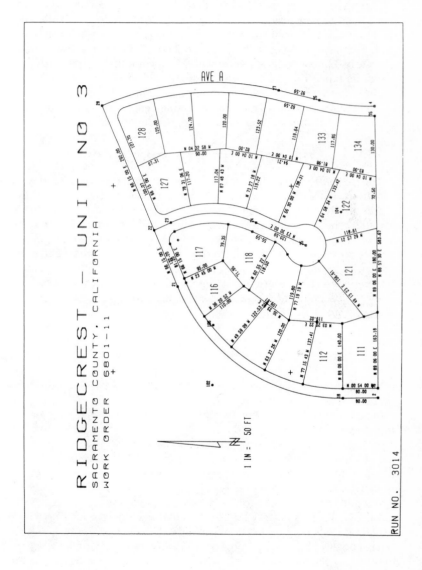

Fig. 1-24. Subdivision map drawn by a computer-controlled digital plotting system.

to help test the bullet-shaped high-speed surface vehicle shown in Fig. 1-25. This 25-ton experimental vehicle is designed to travel at 250-mi/h (402 km/h) surface speeds through densely populated corridors, such as San Diego to San Francisco and Boston to Washington. In collecting data to evaluate this linear-induction motor vehicle, a small computer (Fig. 1-26) is used to collect telemetered data from over 100 sensors at the rate of 32,000 readings per second. The incoming data is recorded on magnetic tape. Tapes filled with data are calibrated and converted to engineering terms by another program fed into the computer. The results from this test data will enable engineers to determine performance characteristics of the linear-induction motors.

THE COMPUTER AS A SIMULATOR

The computer may be used to simulate certain types of design situations. This may be accomplished by developing a model of the required situation and arranging for certain of its parameters to be varied by the engineer. In this way, it is possible to determine how the model will perform under different conditions. A computer program is written to act as a model of the system in question. It behaves like the system in some respects, but is vastly simplified. For example, a few instructions in the program may represent cars driving down a specific street, information flowing on a communications line, or even people walking into a building.

Simulation is used to study the performance of a system using a model. Models can be physical, such as a model of an airplane placed in a wind tunnel, or mathematical, where a series of equations is used to

Courtesy Varian Data Machines

Fig. 1-25. This huge linear-induction test vehicle, capable of traveling at high speeds, is being tested on a low-speed track. The trailer at the right contains instrumentation equipment, the heart of which is a minicomputer.

Courtesy Varian Data Machines

Fig. 1-26. View inside the instrumentation trailer shown in Fig. 1-25. Minicomputer and magnetic-tape recorder are in the foreground.

describe the system under study. An example of this might be a study of the trajectory of a returning satellite. There are, however, many systems that cannot be accurately modeled using either physical or mathematical techniques. These systems, such as manufacturing systems, traffic flows at major arteries, management information systems, and materials handling systems, are characterized by complex interactions between their various components.

In using a computer to study such systems, the engineer describes both the physical structure and decision logic of the system under study. He can then introduce changes into the model to see how the performance of the system will be affected. When the model is being used, input will be fed to it for a period of time, which represents the volumes and types of traffic with which the actual operational system will have to deal. The simulation program then prints out certain statistics about the behavior of the model, such as what queues develop, what response times are obtained, how heavily the various critical factors are loaded, and maximum throughput of the model. The models, once designed and programmed, can be adjusted and experimented with easily and repeatedly.

To site an example of a simulation application, let us consider the nuclear power-plant simulator. This system was designed to train power-plant utility employees in the operation of boiling-water reactor nuclear plants. The simulator system was a digital computer to control the simulation. To make the operation of the simulator as realistic as an actual plant, nuclear electric-plant equipment that is outside the control room (such as the turbine generator, auxiliary systems, circuits, pipes, pumps, and valves) is simulated by mathematical models programmed in the computer to operate continuously, realistically, and with the same timing as real equipment. The trainee must follow all the procedures for an operating plant, including paying strict attention to alarms, recorders, and indicators. A simulator of this type provides trainees with a more thorough education in plant operation.

Computer simulation of automobile crash situations has allowed safety engineers more freedom in designing, testing, and redesigning cars. This simulated "wrecking" permits the safety engineers to identify important parameters in a minimum amount of time and allows more precise and meaningful proving-ground experience. The study of apparently mundane features, such as placement of seat belt anchors, length and width of seat belts, and type of fabric to be used, requires hundreds of simulations. For example, such experiments permit the best placement of the anchor bolt in relation to the average size of the driver and passenger. In their analysis of the factors surrounding accidents, safety engineers have isolated 60 different conditions that can cause a crash. These can vary from road conditions to wind gusts to driver experience. Within each of these categories, literally hundreds of different variables can exist.

The engineer or scientist pumps these factors into the computer model, varying them frequently in an attempt to come up with the ideal design. For instance, just how forgiving should the steering system be when a driver makes a panic turn to avoid an oncoming car? Based on simulations, it can be determined what will happen if drivers whip the steering wheel over too fast or too slow, sometimes creating a skidding condition. This gives safety engineers the data needed for consideration in the design cycle.

To aid the engineer or scientist in programming a simulation model, several general-purpose simulation languages have been developed. These languages, which permit the system to be described with relative ease, are highly flexible and can simulate almost any system mechanism. A model written in such a language can be steadily increased in complexity or detail until it represents the behavior of a system very accurately.

Computers are a powerful and useful tool as simulators. The engineer or scientist can expect to see a wide variety of simulation applications where computers are used. Such applications can become complicated and require considerable imagination and skill to implement. Much time and effort are required to develop a good simulation application. Fig. 1-27 illustrates the different ways that industrial processes are affecting the climate of the earth. Scientists are simulating the process with a computer to learn more about climatic changes.

INITIATIVE REQUIRED BY SCIENTISTS AND ENGINEERS

Scientists and engineers must be capable of dealing with technological problems—not only those they learn about in college, but also new and unfamiliar ones that will arise as a result of new discoveries long after they graduate from college.

Computer scientists, researchers, and computer manufacturers have

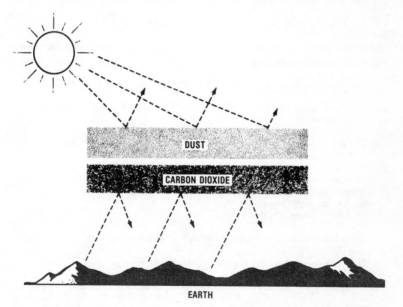

Courtesy IBM Corp.

Fig. 1-27. Two byproducts of the industrial age that may affect climate in different ways. Dust particles act as a screen that deflects the sun's rays, while the "greenhouse effect" of carbon dioxide traps heat near the earth's surface. Scientists are simulating the process with a computer to learn more about climatic changes.

done some work, such as developing programs for use by scientists and engineers and developing high-level programming languages to be used with technical applications. However, engineering, chemistry, physics, biology, and other scientific areas are professions where few people outside them have much appreciation for possible computer uses. Scientists and engineers should involve themselves in the application of computer techniques to the solution of technical problems.

It is difficult for anyone to fully appreciate the potentials of computers without having some idea of how they operate and how they may be programmed to perform various tasks. Because this fact is of such importance to the scientist and engineer, the remainder of the book is devoted to computer equipment, advanced computer concepts, and to the subject of computer programming as it relates to the technical person. Fig. 1-28 shows a laboratory technician using the computer to aid him in solving day-to-day technical problems.

EXERCISES

1. List some of the benefits computers offer to scientists and engineers.

2. What can be done to promote increased utilization of a computer facility?

3. Why is analog/digital converting equipment involved in many industrial process-control applications?

4. List some administrative applications where computers are utilized.

5. What are some advantages of numerically controlled machine tools? Why is a computer used?

6. The use of digital computers in the design and production of circuit packages and new computers is called:

   (a) Simulation.
   (b) Automation.
   (c) Design automation.
   (d) Linear programming.

7. What is meant by computer simulation? Why is it used?

8. How can computers help the manufacturing shop?

9. What are some of the major considerations in the human/machine interface?

10. One reason technical people have welcomed the use of computers is that:

   (a) The computer does all the work.
   (b) Computers have helped them solve complex problems that could not have been solved by other methods.
   (c) Computers have replaced beginning technicians.
   (d) None of the above.

Courtesy Digital Equipment Corp.

Fig. 1-28. Laboratory technician using a computer to help solve day-to-day technical problems.

11. List some of the ways computers help the design engineer.

12. Discuss some of the considerations involved in placing a computer within an existing organizational structure.

13. Simulation is a process in which (that):

   (a) The computer is used to control a process.
   (b) The computer system and program are used to produce actions similar to those in a real physical system.
   (c) Utilizes the full capacity of the computer.
   (d) Gathers data for later processing.

14. What is meant by numerical control?

15. Why are the developments in digital data transmission so significant for computer applications?

16. Real-time systems:

    (a) Process data in a manner similar to batch-processing systems.
    (b) Are effective in process control.
    (c) Process transactions by means of direct-access devices.
    (d) Were first introduced by John Faraday.

17. What aspects of computer technology are being standardized, and why is this important to a user?

18. What is meant by the term *computer graphics*?

19. List some applications where the computer is used as a control device.

20. List several applications where computers are used.

21. Name several of the ways in which computers are affecting the work life of the scientist or engineer.

CHAPTER **2**

AN INTRODUCTION TO COMPUTERS

In Chapter 1, we discussed some of the areas in which computers are used to help scientists and engineers. New applications for computers are constantly being developed. In other areas, computers are used to process payrolls, diagnose diseases, simulate physical systems, keep business records, set printing type, instruct students, perform complex experiments, make airline reservations, compose music, draw art, and perform many other interesting and unusual tasks.

Computers are just beginning to make a heavy impact in professions such as medicine and education and in other fields where human abilities are inadequate, such as air-traffic control and factory control. Space exploration would not have been possible without the help of computers.

TYPES OF COMPUTERS

There are two major classifications of computers: (1) *analog* and (2) *digital.* A third classification combines both analog and digital characteristics and is called *hybrid.* The hybrid computer combines the advantages of both the analog and the digital computer into a working system. Hybrid computers are used almost exclusively in simulation applications where it is necessary to have a close contact with the physical world. A hybrid computer system provides greater precision than can be obtained with analog computers and greater control and speed than is possible with digital computers.

The analog computer, as the name implies, processes work electronically by analogy. The most distinguishing characteristic of the analog computer is the *continuous* nature in which it solves problems. Physical phenomena are simulated by electrical or electronic analogies. These are interconnected in such a way that all phenomena affecting a physical system are simulated electronically. To illustrate, consider a gun mounted on top of a hill. At a certain time, the gun is fired. The path of the projectile is affected by several factors, including the angle of gun elevation, the force of gravity, the temperature, the shape of the projectile, the direction and velocity of the wind, the type and quantity of propellant used in the gun, the altitude of the gun, and the condition of the gun barrel.

All of these factors can be simulated electronically in the analog computer. The various electronic analogies are interconnected in such a way that virtually any desired point of information concerning the flight of the projectile can be computed. For example, it may be of interest to know how high the projectile rises before starting its descent. Or, it may be important to know how far the projectile will travel for various angles of gun elevation and propellant charge.

The analog computer does not produce numbers, as the digital computer does, but usually produces its results in the form of graphs. In the gun example, the analog computer might produce a plotter trace of a curve corresponding to the path of the projectile. The main advantage of analog computers is that they are more efficient in continuous-type calculations, such as differentiation and integration. Also, since most real-life phenomena are continuous in nature, the input and output are closer to real-life simulation.

The computer that we will be concerned with in this book is the digital computer, which solves problems by counting. The analog computer was discussed only to differentiate between the two. The digital computer is the most versatile machine in the electronic computer family. There are two main types of digital computers: (1) *special-purpose* and (2) *general-purpose*. The special-purpose computer is designed for a specific application. It may incorporate many of the features of a general-purpose computer, but its applicability to a particular problem is a function of design rather than of program. For example, a special-purpose computer could be designed to process flight information in an air-traffic control system. It would compute destination, departure time, route, payload, etc. It could not, however, be used for other applications. Special-purpose machines have been used in military weapons systems, highway toll-collection systems, airline reservation systems, and bank check-processing and self-service banking systems.

General-purpose computers are versatile in that they may be used in many different applications. The classification of general-purpose machines is determined by the power and speed of the equipment, measured in terms of the data handling and storage capacities of the machine, the variety of input/output possibilities, and the internal computer speed required to perform certain operations. The general-purpose digital computer lends itself to solving a variety of problems or applications by simply changing the instructions within the memory of the computer. This computer is capable of performing a long sequence of programmed operations without human intervention.

COMPUTER ORGANIZATION

When looking at a computer system from the outside, one is led to believe that it is just a cluster of multicolored cabinets, flashing lights, and keyboard/display devices. However, the real substance of a computer system is within the cabinets, which reveal such items as integrated circuits, mechanical gadgets, and electronic components. All computer systems are organized similarly and are composed of four basic parts: (1) a means of inputting and outputting data, (2) a means of storing data, (3) a way to perform calculations and logical operations, and (4) a means of controlling the previously described operations. To understand the purpose of these units, you must know what operations a computer must perform in order to solve a problem.

Suppose that you wish to compute the arithmetic mean of 15 numbers. To accomplish this task manually, you might perform the following steps:

1. Write the 15 numbers in a column on a sheet of paper.
2. Add the 15 numbers together to obtain their sum.
3. Divide the sum by 15 to obtain the mean of the numbers.
4. Record the result.

Now let us speculate how a computer might accomplish the task without any outside assistance or intervention during the calculations. First, there are two steps that would have to be performed by a human being:

1. A set of instructions would have to be prepared to direct the computer to perform each step in the calculation. Such a set of instructions is called a *program*. The program must be prepared in a language or form that the computer can understand.
2. The 15 numbers would have to be prepared or made available in a form suitable for entry into the computer.

To solve a problem on the computer, it is necessary to create a computer program and to prepare the input data. These two steps are described in detail in later chapters.

Now let us suppose that a program has been prepared to compute the arithmetic mean of 15 numbers, and this program has been stored in the computer. The program will direct the computer to perform the following steps:

1. Read the 15 numbers into the computer.
2. Compute the sum of the numbers.
3. Divide the sum by 15.
4. Display the result.

From this program outline, we can see that the computer must be able to read or *input* data, and it must be able to write or *output* results. It must have a *memory* to store program instructions as well as the data that are being processed.

Since the computer is directed by a program, it must have a unit that interprets the program instructions and supervises their execution. These functions are performed by a *control* unit. Finally, the computer requires a unit that can perform additions, divisions, and other arithmetic operations. This unit is call an *arithmetic/logic* unit, since it can also perform logical operations.

The relationships among the various functional units of a computer are shown in Fig. 2-1. The flow of data is shown by solid lines, while the dashed lines show the flow of control information. In most computers, two of the units previously described are integrated into a single device called the *central processing unit*, or CPU. The units are the control unit and arithmetic/logic unit. In some computers, a portion of memory is part of the CPU, while the remaining portion is external to the CPU. The CPU is discussed in Chapter 3.

MINICOMPUTERS

Until about 1965, digital computers remained large in physical size and were very expensive. However, many special applications existed that called for a computer of less power than the general-purpose scientific or business computer system. These applications existed in

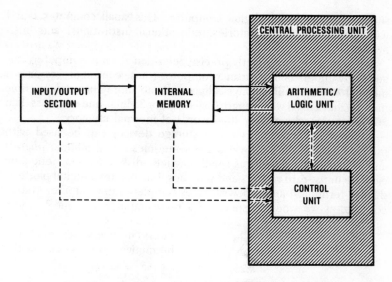

Fig. 2-1. The functional parts of a computer system.

many different areas, but they all had a common financial constraint that precluded them from using a very expensive computer system. The rapid improvement of semiconductor devices in performance, and their dramatic reduction in cost, size, and power requirements provided the answer—the *minicomputer* (see Fig. 2-2). In the mid 1960s, Digital Equipment Corporation introduced the PDP-8 minicomputer, a

Courtesy Cincinnati Milacron

Fig. 2-2. A minicomputer.

suitcase-size table-top digital computer. This small computer found widespread use in laboratories, educational institutions, and businesses.

While there is no perfectly precise definition of a minicomputer, it is generally understood to mean a computer whose central processor and internal storage unit is physically small (no more than a few cubic meters), has a fixed word length (usually 16 or 32 bits), and costs less than $6000 for a machine with 4096 words of internal memory.

A variety of input/output and storage devices can be used with minicomputers. These devices are sometimes called *miniperipherals* and include such devices as small magnetic-disk units, magnetic-tape cassette units, card readers and punches, line printers, digital plotters, display terminals, and typewriters. A complete minicomputer system consists, as we would suspect, of a minicomputer and one or more miniperipherals (see Fig. 2-3).

Minicomputers are full-scale computers in every sense of the word—except size. The small size of the minicomputer is due to the

Courtesy Data General Corp.

Fig. 2-3. A minicomputer system consisting of magnetic-disk drives, magnetic-tape units, line printer, and crt display devices.

extensive use of an electronic component, called an *integrated circuit*, in computer design. Several hundred conventional transistors, resistors, capacitors, etc., can be assembled on a silicon chip as small as 1/16 inch (1.6 millimeters) square. These chips are mounted in a plastic package with electrical contacts and then soldered on a printed-circuit board along with memory chips to form an entire minicomputer. Additional benefits gained from the use of integrated circuits include greater reliability of operation and increased speed. A minicomputer gives off virtually no heat and requires little electrical energy to operate.

A fully assembled minicomputer is small enough to be built into another machine, placed in a vehicle, or carried from one location to another.

Unlike the large computers in data centers, where the environment is sheltered, most minicomputers are designed for use in relatively uncontrolled environments. They are frequently found aboard ships, in forests, oil fields, steel mills, deserts, on farms, and in homes. Fig. 2-4 shows a minicomputer being used in an observatory high in the mountains of Chile in South America. The minicomputer is capable of withstanding more severe environments for a number of reasons, among them its physical size. Both mathematically and physically it is easy to show that the larger an object becomes, the greater its ratio of volume to surface area. Since the inverse of this holds true, it is particularly significant in cooling—it is easier to cool a minicomputer than to cool a large computer. The heat buildup is more evenly distributed in a minicomputer, and a sufficient degree of air exchange is available to keep the components of the computer within their operational tolerances.

All minicomputer manufacturers have at least one thing in common—they subject their computers to stringent tests to make their machines reliable in the field. In addition to testing the component parts and subassemblies individually, the assembled minicomputers usually undergo, to some degree, shaking, baking, and dropping tests. Almost always, these tests are dynamic; that is, the tests are performed while the minicomputer is operating.

Minicomputers are subject to a wide range of temperature testing. Many manufacturers test the assembled minicomputer in temperature cycled from as low as 0° Celsius to as high as 50° Celsius. At one manufacturer, temperature tests involve thermal shock. Each mini-computer is first tested by another computer to be sure that the new minicomputer is operating properly. Each machine is then vibrated to expose any cold solder joints, loose components, or mechanical flaws. The minicomputers are then run for 100 hours at 130° Fahrenheit, transferred to a cold chamber at 32° Fahrenheit to induce thermal shock, and after reaching cold ambient, are transferred back to the heat chamber to induce a second thermal shock.

"MS. WILSON, HAVE YOU SEEN MY MICROCOMPUTER AROUND ANYWHERE?"

Among the areas in which minicomputers have found application are numerical control automation, equipment testing, data collection, data communications, simulation, equipment control, business data processing, inventory control, and medical equipment operation. Minicomputers usually possess the hardware capability to be connected directly to a large number of measuring instruments or to analog-to-digital converters, thus simplifying their use with medical equipment, testing equipment, simulation equipment, machining equipment, etc.

MICROCOMPUTERS

A *microcomputer* is a computer manufactured on a single chip or printed-circuit board which possesses the characteristics of larger computers, including a central processing unit, a storage system, and input/output circuitry. Microcomputers are the result of modern construction technology, called *large scale integration* (LSI) circuits. Today LSI chips are available containing over 100,000 components in a space less than 1/4 inch (6.4 mm) on a side.

Some microcomputers (or microcontrollers) are manufactured on a single silicon chip (called a *computer-on-a-chip*) a fraction of a square inch in area (see Fig. 2-5). Other microcomputers are composed of a

Courtesy Digital Equipment Corp.

Fig. 2-4. Connected to analytical instruments in an astronomical observatory high in the mountains of Chile in South America, this minicomputer system withstands a wide range of daily temperature swings.

central processing unit chip (called a *microprocessor*), several memory chips, and input/output circuitry (see Fig. 2-6). A microprocessor is fabricated as a single semiconductor device; that is, the thousands of individual circuit elements necessary to perform all the logical and arithmetic functions of a computer are manufactured as a small chip (see Fig. 2-7). Microprocessor chips are also used in equipment other than microcomputers. A few devices that use microprocessors as control devices are cameras, sewing machines, video game machines, automobile electrical systems, business machines, phototypesetting

Courtesy Intel Corp.

Fig. 2-5. The Intel 8748 computer-on-a-chip microcontroller.

machines, equipment testing devices, microwave ovens, telephone dialing systems, and pinball machines.

From a functional standpoint, the microcomputer and the minicomputer are similar in nature. Both are capable of storing a program and executing instructions. The minicomputer is more powerful and can usually execute instructions at a faster rate, while the microcomputer is smaller physically and is less expensive.

The prices of microcomputers are a little short of amazing. When one considers that only about two decades ago a computer system of medium capability sold for several hundred thousand dollars, the fact that some microcomputers now sell for less than $500 is without parallel in industrial history.

"WHAT REALLY HURTS IS THAT I ONLY HAD
MY MICROCOMPUTER TWO WEEKS!"

The extremely low price of microcomputers has opened up entirely new areas of application for computers. It is now feasible to use only a minute fraction of the capability of the computer in a particular system application and still be way ahead, financially, of any other way to get the job done.

A variety of input/output and storage devices are available for use with microcomputers: floppy disks, magnetic-tape cassettes, digital plotters, visual displays, graphic pads, audio output devices, speech recognition devices, line printers, and typewriters. Fig. 2-8 shows a Radio Shack TRS-80 microcomputer system consisting of a microcomputer, a keyboard, a visual display, three floppy disk units, and a line printer. An Apple II microcomputer system is shown in Fig. 2-9 which includes a microcomputer, a keyboard, a visual display, and a floppy disk unit. Fig. 2-10 shows a Heathkit H89 desk-top microcomputer which has a built-in display and floppy disk storage.

It appears that the ultimate limits for microcomputer price and performance have by no means been reached. The speed of the central processing unit and storage speed and capacity could well increase by an additional factor of 10 or more over the next 10 years, while prices

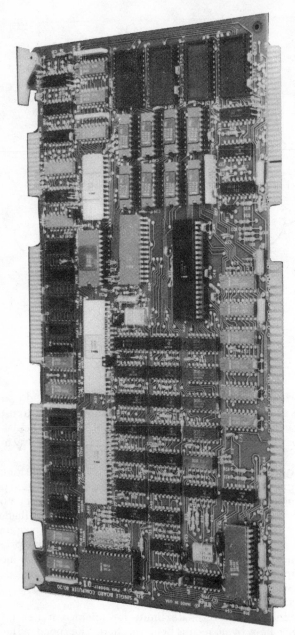

Courtesy Intel Corp.

Fig. 2-6. A single-board microcomputer.

Courtesy Intel Corp.

Fig. 2-7. Photomicrograph of a microprocessor chip.

should diminish to the point determined essentially only by the costs of marketing, distribution, and software development, with the manufacturing cost being very low in comparison.

SUPERCOMPUTERS

A few organizations require extraordinary amounts of computing power. These include the Nuclear Regulatory Commission, the military services, the National Weather Service, some airline companies, a few scientific laboratories, and NASA. In these organizations, vast amounts of information must be processed in a short time to provide fast response to users.

These relatively few organizations rely on *supercomputers*, the largest, fastest, and most expensive computers available. These computers, which cost several millions of dollars, can store several million characters of data in internal memory, and can execute instructions much faster than any other type of machine.

A few supercomputers are the Burroughs BSP (*B*urroughs *S*cientific *P*rocessor), the Cray Research CRAY-1, the Burroughs PEPE (*P*arallel

"SURPRISE, DAD! I WASHED YOUR MICROCOMPUTER BOARD FOR YA!"

Fig. 2-8. A Radio Shack TRS-80 microcomputer system.

Fig. 2-9. An Apple II microcomputer system.

Fig. 2-10. A Heathkit H89 desk-top microcomputer.

Element Processing Ensemble), the Control Data CYBER 176, the
Control Data CYBER 203, the Control Data STAR-100, the ILLIAC IV,
and the Texas Instruments ASC (Advanced Scientific Computer).

The ever-increasing computational requirements of applications such
as reservoir analysis in the petroleum industry, and computer-aided
design in the manufacturing and aerospace industries, plus the lowering
cost of semiconductor components, indicate that a broader range of
users will require supercomputers, and that supercomputer designs will
continue to emphasize new techniques for more processing power.

"MIGHTY ONE... WE'RE TRADING YOU IN FOR A LATER MODEL."

DATA REPRESENTATION

Symbols, such as those shown in Fig. 2-11, may be used to convey
information from one person to another. The most common way of
representing information to be conveyed is to use a set of symbols. In the
English language, these are the familiar letters of the alphabet,
numbers, and punctuation. The symbols are printed on paper in some
predetermined sequence and conveyed to another person who reads
and understands them.

Communicating with a computer system is similar in many ways to
communicating with another person, since the information to be
conveyed must be represented as a set of symbols that can be used by the

Fig. 2-11. Some of the symbols that are used for communication between humans.

computer equipment. This set of symbols becomes a communication language between people and machines.

Information to be used with computer systems can be recorded on a variety of media: hard magnetic disks, floppy disks, magnetic tape, tape cassettes, punched cards, magnetic-ink characters, and optically recognizable characters. Data are represented on punched cards and paper tape by the presence or absence of holes. On magnetic tapes and disks, the symbols are specific patterns of small magnetized areas. Magnetic-ink characters are printed on paper with a special ink that can be read by both humans and machines. Examples of the symbols that are used with each medium are described later in this chapter.

Information represented on recording media is read into the computer by an input device. This device converts the recorded information into electronic form, suitable for use by the computer. Output devices are used to convert information from the computer to punched cards, magnetic tape, paper tape, printed forms, visual displays, or audio devices. Information recorded on one medium can be transcribed to another medium for use with a different system; e.g., information on punched cards can be recorded on magnetic tape, or information on magnetic tape can be converted to printed reports. Communication can occur between machines in the form of electrical pulses over telephone wires, cables, or radio waves. In addition, the output of one computer system may be used as input to another computer system.

DATA REPRESENTATION IN THE COMPUTER

Data within the computer is held by electrical components: integrated circuits, magnetic cores, etc. The flow and storage of data through these components are represented as electrical pulses or indications. The presence or absence of these pulses is the method of representing data. For example, a magnetic core can be magnetized in either of two directions (see Fig. 2-12) and can be used to indicate one of two possible states (*on* or *off*, *one* or *zero*, *yes* or *no*) similar to the way the punched or unpunched hole in the punched card is used to represent the presence or absence of information. Representing data within the computer is accomplished by assigning or associating a specific value to a binary indicator or a group of binary indicators.

DATA RECORDING MEDIA

Punched Cards

Punched cards are widely used for getting information into and out of computers. Originally developed and patented by Dr. Herman Hollerith in 1889, they have since been used in many different sizes with many different coding schemes. The two most popular types of cards in present use with computers are the 80-column card (Fig.2-13) and the 96-column card (Fig. 2-14).

The 80-column card is 3¼ inches wide, 7⅜ inches long, 0.007 inch thick, and contains 12 rows and 80 columns. Information is recorded in the card by rectangular holes punched in appropriate rows and columns. The cards may be of any color and may have a corner partly cut off to

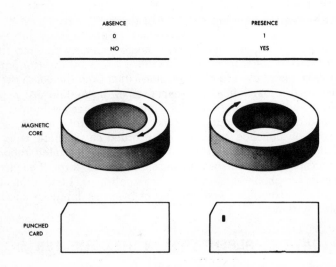

Fig. 2-12. Drawing illustrating the binary representation of the presence or absence of information.

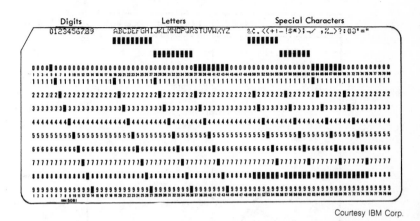

Courtesy IBM Corp.

Fig. 2-13. The 80-column IBM punched card.

facilitate manual identification. A card may be preprinted in any manner since the printing is ignored in computer reading operations.

Up to 80 columns of holes in various arrangements can be punched in the 80-column card. The 12 horizontal rows on the card consist of the positions numbered from 0 through 9, plus two unnumbered rows. The top row on the card is called the *12-row*, and the next lower one is called the *11-row*. The 80 card columns are numbered from 1 to 80 at the top and bottom of the card. The 80-column card code is shown in Fig. 2-15.

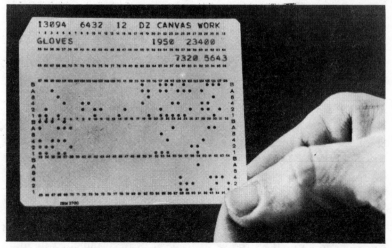

Courtesy IBM Corp.

Fig. 2-14. The 96-column IBM punched card.

CARD CODE	GRAPHIC	CARD CODE	GRAPHIC
12-2-8	¢	12-6	F
12-3-8	.	12-7	G
12-4-8	<	12-8	H
12-5-8	(	12-9	I
12-6-8	+	11-1	J
12-7-8	|	11-2	K
12	&	11-3	L
11-2-8	!	11-4	M
11-3-8	$	11-5	N
11-4-8	*	11-6	O
11-5-8	)	11-7	P
11-6-8	;	11-8	Q
11-7-8	¬	11-9	R
11	-	0-2	S
0-1	/	0-3	T
0-3-8	,	0-4	U
0-4-8	%	0-5	V
0-5-8	_	0-6	W
0-6-8	>	0-7	X
0-7-8	?	0-8	Y
2-8	:	0-9	Z
3-8	#	0	0
4-8	@	1	1
5-8	'	2	2
6-8	=	3	3
7-8	"	4	4
12-1	A	5	5
12-2	B	6	6
12-3	C	7	7
12-4	D	8	8
12-5	E	9	9

Courtesy IBM Corp.

Fig. 2-15. Card code for the 80-column punched card.

The 96-column card, introduced by IBM in 1970, is about ⅓ the size of the 80-column card, yet it can contain 20% more information than the 80-column card and allow four lines of type to be printed on the card face. The 96-column card code is shown in Fig. 2-16.

The most serious drawback to using punched cards as an input and output medium for computers is the relatively slow speed of the card reading and punching equipment compared to the internal speed of the computer itself. For example, one card reader can read at a rate of 800 cards per minute. If all the cards to be read were punched in all 80 columns, the effective reading rate would be 64,000 characters per minute. But the computer associated with this card reader can transfer

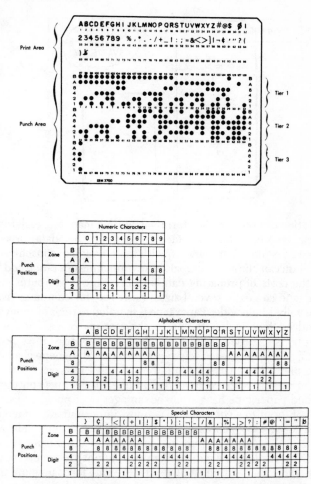

Courtesy IBM Corp.

Fig. 2-16. Card code for the 96-column punched card.

80-character records internally at a rate of 2,380,000 characters per minute, which is approximately 37 times faster than the maximum character-reading rate of the punched-card reader.

Paper Tape

Punched paper tape is a widely used medium for computer input. It has been used for many years as an input and output medium for telegraphic equipment. More recently, it has been used to record information as a by-product of document preparation or checking. Thus,

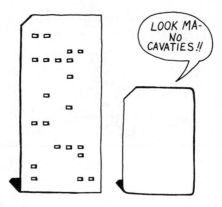

the operation of a point-of-sale terminal, adding machine, cash register, etc., can create a punched-tape record of the data processed. Combining document preparation with the creation of a machine-readable medium can eliminate a separate keypunching operation and hence reduce the costs of preparing data for entry into a computer system.

Paper tape comes in several sizes; however, for computer use, the tape is usually 1 inch wide. Paper tape is handled in reels of about 20 to a few hundred feet in length, or in short strips of only a few feet. Information is recorded as holes punched in rows across the tape width (Fig. 2-17). Generally, each row represents one alphabetic character or numeric digit. The maximum number of holes that can be punched across the tape is referred to as the number of *channels* on the tape.

Punched paper tape has certain advantages over punched cards as a medium of input to a computer. The most important advantage is that punched paper-tape records are not limited in length and can be as long or as short as desired. With punched cards, on the other hand, the entire card must be read even if only one or two columns are needed to record the data, and extra cards must be used if the data takes up more than 80 or 96 columns. Also, punched tape can sometimes be produced more quickly and less expensively than punched cards. Both the tapes and the tape-processing equipment require less space than punched cards and card-processing equipment.

Fig. 2-17. Eight-channel paper tape showing punched information.

Punched paper tape also has disadvantages as a computer input medium. Once data is punched into paper tape, it is difficult to correct errors. While certain correction procedures permit data punched into the tape to be ignored automatically, such an approach is not equivalent to the ability to delete the data completely before it enters the system. Also, after data has been recorded in punched paper tape, it cannot be manipulated; consequently, the data is often hand-sorted before being punched into the tape.

Magnetic Tape

Magnetic tape is a popular input/output recording medium for computer systems. It is also used extensively for auxiliary computer storage. Magnetic tape provides a rapid way of entering data into the computer system and an equally fast method of recording processed data from the system.

Information is recorded on magnetic tape as magnetized spots called *bits*. The recording can be retained indefinitely, or the recorded information can be automatically erased and the tape reused many times.

Magnetic tape is wound on individual reels or placed in cartridges so that it can be easily handled and processed. The most commonly used tape is ½ inch wide and is supplied in reels of 2400 feet (Fig. 2-18). A full reel weighs about four pounds and can contain information equivalent to 400,000 fully punched cards. A ⅛-inch tape is used in tape cassettes.

Data is recorded in parallel tracks (or *channels*) across the length of the tape. There are seven or nine tracks on the ½-inch tape and two tracks on the ⅛-inch tape.

Magnetic Disks

Magnetic disks are widely used for computer input/output and as auxiliary computer storage. The disks provide a relatively fast method of entering data into the internal storage of the computer and an equally fast way of recording processed data from the computer.

Magnetic disks are metal or mylar disks coated with magnetic recording material. The disks resemble phonograph records. Information is recorded on the disks in the form of magnetic spots. The information is transferred from the disk to the computer memory via a disk drive.

Floppy disks are widely used in microcomputer systems, small business computer systems, data entry systems, remote terminals, and word processing systems. A floppy disk is a compact, flexible magnetic-oxide-coated mylar disk that resembles a 45-r/min phonograph record. The disk, called a *diskette*, comes in two popular sizes—approximately 8 inches (200 mm) and 5 inches (125 mm) in diameter. The 5-inch diameter disk is called a *minifloppy* disk. The

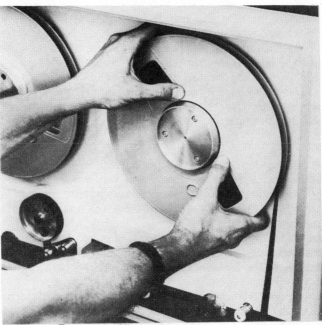

Courtesy Xerox Corp.

Fig. 2-18. A reel of magnetic tape being loaded onto a tape-transport mechanism.

diskette is enclosed in a jacket for protection, with a slot for access by the disk reading and writing mechanism. Information is recorded in a digital fashion on the magnetic surface of the disk while the disk is rotating.

Magnetic-Ink Characters

The set of magnetic-ink characters is shown in Fig. 2-19. The type font which MICR (*M*agnetic-*I*nk *C*haracter *R*ecognition) devices can read,

Numeric Symbols

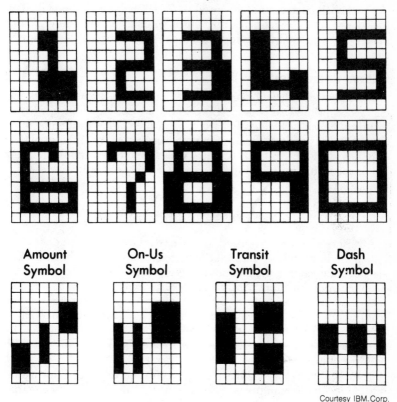

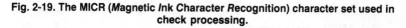

Courtesy IBM.Corp.

Fig. 2-19. The MICR (*Magnetic Ink Character Recognition*) character set used in check processing.

was developed by the American Bankers Association in cooperation with the MICR equipment manufacturers. The character set comprises the 10 numeric symbols and four special symbols used in check processing. The special symbols are the *dash*, used in account numbers; the *amount* symbol, which sets off the amount field; the ABA *transit* routing symbol, which sets off the numerical code of the drawee bank; and the *on-us* symbol, which is put on a check only by the drawee bank and marks off a field used for internal accounting codes.

Fig. 2-20 shows a check using the MICR characters. The first group of digits to the left constitutes the check routing number and the ABA transit number. The second collection of digits constitutes the account number in the drawee's bank. The group of digits to the right indicates the amount for which the check was drawn and is printed on the check at the time of payment by the paying bank.

The MICR characters are printed on paper with a magnetic ink. The ink looks like a normal black ink, but it contains a very finely ground magnetic material and a binder to make the magnetic particles adhere to the paper.

Optical Characters

Several devices have been built that can read a variety of marks and characters printed on paper. At present, the size, type font, quality of printing, and positioning of characters on the source document must meet several standards before the data can be read reliably by optical scanning devices. An OCR (*Optical Character Recognition*) character font is shown in Fig. 2-21. Fig. 2-22 shows a utility bill printed with OCR characters.

DATA PREPARATION

A variety of devices are used to record data from a source document onto a medium suitable for input to a computer system. These devices are not connected to the computer but are used merely to produce the machine-readable input data. The routine of translating raw source data into machine-readable form often involves keypunching information from forms, orders, records, etc., into punched cards, punched paper tape, or onto magnetic tape or disks. It may also be transcribed by typewriter for processing by an OCR reader or printed for use with MICR equipment.

The *keypunch* (Fig. 2-23) is a unit that is used to punch information into cards. An operator presses a key on the keypunch and it punches the

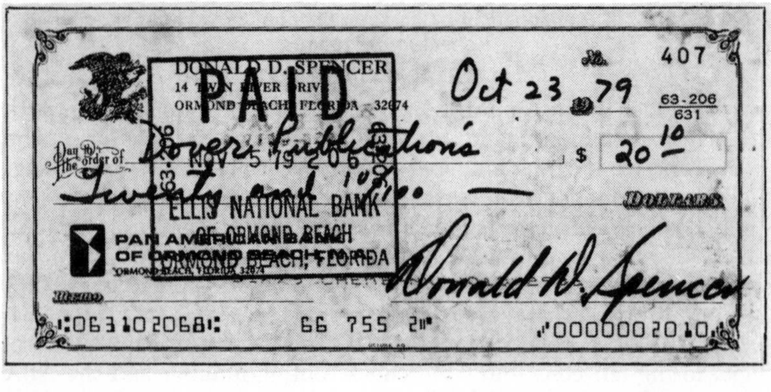

Fig. 2-20. A cancelled check illustrating the use of the MICR character set.

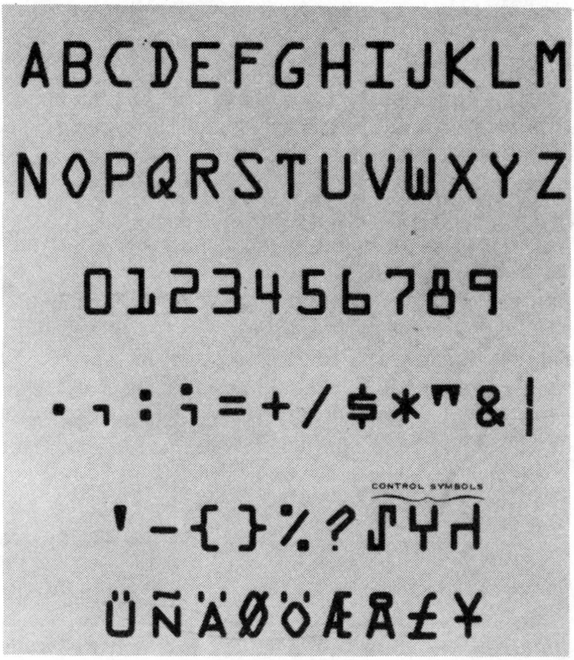

ABCDEFGHIJKLM
NOPQRSTUVWXYZ
0123456789
• ⌐ : ⌐ = + / $ * " & |
' - { } % ? ♪ЧП

ÜÑÄØÖÆ£¥

Fig. 2-21. An OCR (Optical Character Recognition) character set.

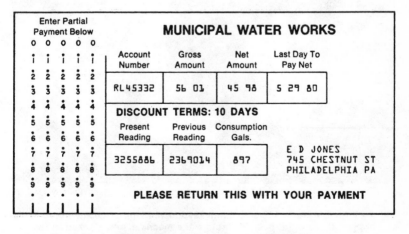

Fig. 2-22. A utility bill illustrating the use of OCR characters.

appropriate hole or holes in a card column. A printing/punch would also print the character, in the same column, on top of the card.

Some examples of devices that are used to punch information into paper tape are point-of-sale terminals, bookkeeping machines, and cash registers. Some punching units simply punch the tape while other units punch the tape and also produce a readable copy of the information being punched. A unit of this type is the teletypewriter with attached paper-tape reader and punch. This machine, which is shown in Fig. 2-24, will produce a punched paper tape containing all keyboard operations in coded form.

The reading of punched cards and paper tape is a slow process. The conversion of data from a slow input medium to a faster medium can be accomplished by feeding the cards or tape into a converter that reads these media and records their data in an input form, such as magnetic tape or disk. The magnetically recorded data is then available for high-speed input into the computer system. Several manufacturers

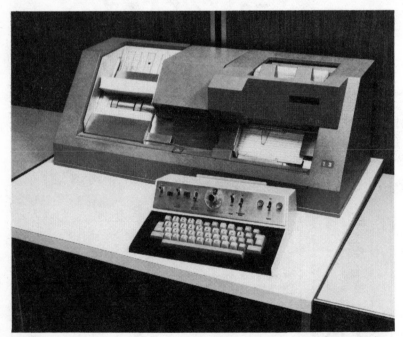

Courtesy IBM Corp.

Fig. 2-23. An IBM Model 129 80-column keypunch. Blank cards are stored in the hopper at the right, passed through the machine, and stacked in the hopper at the left.

make equipment for converting practically any type of machine-readable record to practically any other type of machine-readable record. This includes the conversion of punched cards to magnetic tape or disks, paper tape to magnetic tape, and magnetic tape to punched cards.

There are also devices that will record keyed data directly onto standard 2400-foot reels of magnetic tape, on magnetic-tape cassettes, and on disk packs. Fig. 2-25 shows a key-to-disk system that will allow several keyboard operators to record data onto a disk pack—all at the same time. The system uses a small computer to accumulate operator inputs and to control the data being recorded on the disk.

Fig. 2-26 shows an operator feeding printed information into an optical reading-to-tape system. The system, which uses a minicomputer, reads either typed or printed information, edits and formats it, and then produces a magnetic tape output of digital data. This output can then be fed to a computer. The system replaces keypunching or key-to-tape operations.

Courtesy General Electric Co.

Fig. 2-24. Teletypewriters may be used to produce a punched paper tape and a readable copy of the information that was punched.

Courtesy Varian Data Machines

Fig. 2-25. A key-to-disk data preparation system accepts information from several keyboard operators and stores it on a disk pack.

EXERCISES

1. What are the two major classifications of electronic computers?

2. What is an important difference between an analog computer and a digital computer?

3. What is a hybrid computer?

4. A digital computer performs its computations by:

    (a) Mechanical means.
    (b) Analogy.
    (c) Guessing.
    (d) Counting.

Courtesy Varian Data Machines

Fig. 2-26. Operator feeding printed information into an optical reading-to-tape system.

5. Microcomputers are _____ than the early computers.

   (a) faster and larger
   (b) less reliable
   (c) larger and stronger
   (d) faster and smaller

6. What disadvantages did vacuum-tube computers have compared with computers using transistors or integrated circuits?

7. What are the four basic parts of a computer system?

8. What is a minicomputer? A microcomputer? A microprocessor?

9. In what ways do minicomputers differ from microcomputers?

10. What is a microcomputer system?

11. Which was developed first, the minicomputer or the microcomputer?

12. What is a miniperipheral?

13. List several areas where minicomputers are used.

14. List several areas where microprocessors are used.

15. List five peripheral devices that may be used with microcomputers.

16. What is a supercomputer?

17. List common data-recording media used with computers.

18. List some disadvantages to using punched cards as an input to computers.

19. What are some of the main advantages of magnetic tape over punched cards?

20. What is the primary advantage of reading data in the form of magnetic-ink characters or optically readable characters?

21. What is meant by the two acronyms OCR and MICR?

22. Describe some common business situations in which OCR capabilities might be used.

23. What is a keypunch?

CHAPTER **3**
THE COMPUTER SYSTEM

A computer system may be classified into four basic functions: (1) *input*, (2) *processing*, (3) *output*, and (4) *storage*. The input function consists of getting information into the computer and is accomplished by various input devices. The output function consists of producing results in a desired form and is accomplished by various output devices. The central processing unit performs the processing function. The storage of information within the computer itself is accomplished by memory devices. The remainder of this chapter is devoted to discussing these four basic functions.

THE CENTRAL PROCESSING UNIT

The *central processing unit* (CPU) controls and supervises all operations of the computer. For all practical purposes, it *is* the computer. The central processing unit, which is sometimes called the *main frame*, consists of the *control* section and the *arithmetic/logic* section.

The control section directs and coordinates the entire computer system. It performs the following control functions: (1) fetching information from storage and placing information into storage, (2) executing instructions in the sequence prescribed by a computer program, (3) transferring information between computer storage and input/output devices, (4) transferring information between the arithmetic/logic section and storage, and (5) controlling the arithmetic/logic section.

The arithmetic/logic section performs all mathematical operations, such as adding, subtracting, multiplying, and dividing. It also performs such operations as comparing, sorting, selecting, editing, shifting, or converting information.

The overall control of the CPU is guided by two governing and regulating units: (1) a computer *program* and (2) an internal *clock*, which measures off time into working segments.

Registers and Consoles

The CPU contains several *registers*, which are devices that are capable of receiving information, holding it, and then transferring it as directed to some controlling circuitry. Some types of registers and their functions are:

1. *Accumulator*—Holds the results of a calculation.
2. *Address Register*—Holds the address or designation of a storage location or device.
3. *Instruction Register*—Holds the instruction currently being interpreted or executed.
4. *Storage Register*—Holds data taken from storage or being sent to storage.
5. *Index Register*—A counter whose contents may be increased or decreased.
6. *General Register*—Holds several types of data.

Information placed in registers may be shifted to the right or left within the register, or in some cases between two registers. A register may temporarily hold information while other parts of the CPU analyze the data. Logical operations (such as AND or OR) and arithmetic operations (such as multiply or divide) can be performed on information in registers. The value of single characters, bits (binary digits), or combinations of bits may be checked or set in registers.

The more important registers of the CPU, particularly those used in normal processing and data flow, are represented on an *operating console*. The contents of registers may be displayed as binary values, or as octal representations of binary values. Fig. 3-1 shows binary information being displayed on the operator's console of an IBM System/370 computer.

By means of displayed information, the computer operator or maintenance technician can inspect the contents of certain registers and determine what instructions are being executed. In addition to register displays, the console panel contains control switches, buttons, keys, and dials which enable the operator to start or stop the execution of a computer program, or to modify or send new instructions or data to the computer.

Machine Cycles

All computer operations are performed in fixed intervals of time, measured by regular pulses emitted from the CPU's electronic clock at extremely high frequencies (several million per second). A machine cycle is measured as a fixed number of pulses. In most second-generation computers, the memory cycle time was measured in microseconds; however, it is not unusual to find third-generation machines with a

Courtesy IBM Corp.

Fig. 3-1. Computer operators using information displayed on the control panel of an IBM System/370 computer.

memory cycle time in the nanosecond range. It is often difficult to conceive of such extremely short units of time without comparison with some known reference. The information in Table 3-1 should be helpful in this respect.

Within a machine cycle, the CPU can perform a specific machine operation. Several machine operations are combined to execute an instruction. In many CPUs, most of the instructions can be executed in two or three machine cycles. Instructions such as multiply, divide, and

Table 3-1. Time Units and Their Fractional Equivalents

Time Unit	Fractional Equivalent
1 second	1 second
1 millisecond	1/1000 second
1 microsecond	1/1,000,000 second
1 nanosecond	1/1,000,000,000 second
1 picosecond	1/1,000,000,000,000 second

shift often take several machine cycles. A CPU performs an addition operation by executing two successive machine cycles: (1) an *instruction* cycle and (2) an *execution* cycle. During the instruction cycle, the CPU takes the instruction from the program in internal storage, places the instruction in the instruction register, and decodes the instruction. The instruction then informs the CPU of what it must do, places the data address in the address register, and brings the data to be processed into the data register. At this point, the CPU knows what it is to do and has the data to be processed in the registers. During the execution cycle, the CPU adds the data to the contents of the accumulator, thus completing the addition operation. The sum is found in the accumulator at the termination of instruction execution.

Word Length

Fixed and variable *word* length describes the units of data that can be addressed and processed by the CPU. In a fixed-word computer, information is addressed and processed in words containing a fixed number of positions. The word size varies with the computer; however, word sizes consisting of 12, 16, 24, 32, and 36 bits are common. A few machines have word sizes of 18 and 48 bits. In most modern computers, the word size is a multiple of eight; 8, 16, and 32 bits being the most used sizes. In many computers, the word size represents the smallest unit of information that can be addressed for processing in the CPU. However, in some computers, it is possible to work with bytes (8 bits), half-words (½ standard word) and double-words (two standard words). Registers, accumulators, storage, and input/output data channels are primarily designed to accommodate the fixed word.

In a variable-word computer, information is processed serially as single characters. Information may be of any practical length within the capacity of the available storage. For example, in a variable-word computer, the addition of 4326814903 and 763214264312 is performed character by character starting at the right: $2 + 3$, then $1 + 0$, then $3 + 9$ carry 1, then $4 + 4 + 1$, then $6 + 1$, etc., until the sum is computed. This is exactly how one would perform this operation with pencil and paper.

Some computers have the facility for working with fixed-word as well as variable-word data. Computers such as the IBM System/370 provide both the efficiency of fixed-word operation and the flexibility of variable data-length handling.

In applications where computational speed is important (real-time systems, scientific processing, simulation, etc.), the fixed-word computer is usually preferred. The process of performing operations on all digits of information simultaneously is called *parallel-mode* operation and is usually associated with computers that utilize a fixed-word format. *Serial-mode* operation is the process of performing operations on individual characters in a sequential manner. This mode of operation is much slower than parallel operation and is usually restricted to some business applications where computational speed is of secondary importance.

Input/Output Channels

The process of transferring information into and out of the internal-storage unit is called an *input/output* operation. Input/output operations are performed by input/output channels which connect the input and output devices with the CPU. The input/output channel acts like a small subsystem of the CPU that allows input/output communications to occur independently of computing. The input/output channel relieves the CPU of the task of communicating directly with input/output devices. On most computers, there are two types of input/output channels: (1) *selector* channel and (2) *multiplexer* channel (see Fig.3-2).

A selector channel is used to transmit information to or from one input or output device at a time. This channel is often used when high-speed input/output devices are connected to a computer.

A multiplexer channel permits the simultaneous operation of several input and output devices. This channel allows both low-speed and high-speed input/output devices to be operating simultaneously. Reading, writing, and computing can take place simultaneously when

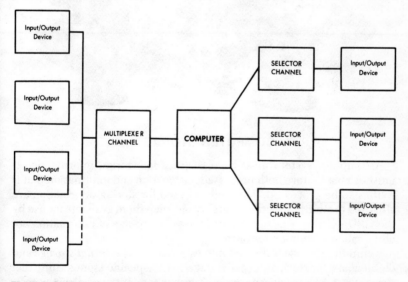

Fig. 3-2. Selector input/output channels provide for data communications with one device. Many devices can be connected to a multiplexer input/output channel.

the multiplexer channel is used. In selector channels, this can only occur when two or more channels are used.

In some computer systems, the input/output data channels are called *input/output systems* or *input/output processors*. A data channel is more than wires connecting input/output devices to the computer. It is constructed with electronic circuitry and is capable of responding to its own commands. It may be built physically into the CPU, or it may be a separate unit.

COMPUTER STORAGE

A computer system must have facilities for storing information. It must be able to store both processed information and information that is waiting to be processed. The facilities used for storing information are also used to store computer programs and keep them available for use by the CPU whenever needed. The devices for storage of information are often called *computer memory*.

Computer storage is divided into two classes: (1) *internal storage* and (2) *auxiliary storage*. Internal storage is the specific storage unit that serves the CPU. Auxiliary storage is either sequential or direct access. *Sequential access*, such as that used with magnetic tape, involves examining sequentially all recorded information. This form of storage necessitates tape searching by starting at the beginning of the tape and continuing to search through all records until the desired information area is found. In contrast, *direct-access* (or *random-access*) devices provide immediate access to individual records and do not require reading from the beginning of a file to find a particular record.

Two terms used in the preceding paragraph demand further definition. A *record* refers to a group of logically related items read as a single unit into internal storage or written from storage in the same manner. The term *file* refers to a group of logically related records. For example, the name of an employee might be one item. All data about the employee (age, sex, marital status, work experience, number of children, etc.) might be contained in one record. The data for all employees in a company might be contained in a file.

Sequential-access storage is *nonaddressable*; that is, an operator cannot directly refer to the contents of a particular storage location. Direct-access storage is addressable; a given item can be selected from anywhere in storage by simply specifying the address where it is located.

The *capacity* of a storage device is expressed as the number of words, bytes, characters, or bits it can store at one time. The cost of storage is directly determined by the capacity of the device and its type.

The time the computer takes to locate and transfer information to or from storage is called *access time*. Access to some storage units is so rapid it is measured in nanoseconds (billionths of a second).

For years, magnetic-core storage was the primary type of internal storage for computers. Today, however, computer manufacturers are using semiconductor memories in most computers. All minicomputers and microcomputers, and many larger machines as well, use semiconductor memory for their internal storage.

Auxiliary storage devices include magnetic tapes, magnetic disks, and magnetic drums. Magnetic tape is the only sequential storage device discussed in this book; all the other auxiliary storage devices are of the direct-access type. These various forms of storage will be discussed in this chapter.

Internal Storage

As mentioned earlier, modern computers employ two memory technologies for internal storage: (1) semiconductor (integrated circuit) memory and (2) magnetic-core memory. The trend is toward semiconductor memory, although core memory manufacturers are working to reduce the cost of their product, and so remain competitive. A typical magnetic-core storage unit is made up of thousands of tiny doughnut-shaped rings of a ferromagnetic material assembled on a crosshatch of fine wires (Fig. 3-3).

A semiconductor memory uses silicon chips with interconnecting on/off switches (called *flip-flops*). The direction of the electric current

Courtesy Honeywell, Inc.

Fig. 3-3. A magnetic-core memory plane.

passing through each cell determines whether the position of the switch is *on* or *off*; that is, whether the bit is 1 or 0. Each silicon chip is about ⅛ inch (3.2 mm) square (see Fig. 3-4). Semiconductor memories provide increased storage capacity and low access time. It is also possible to design logic into these memories.

Semiconductor memories can be found in many large computers as well as in small computers. Semiconductor memories are used as the internal storage in all minicomputers and microcomputers.

The most common (and least expensive) kind of microcomputer memory is called RAM (*R*andom-*A*ccess *M*emory). It is used primarily to store user programs and data; however, the contents are lost when the power to the microcomputer is shut off. So a small amount of another kind of memory is needed in the microcomputer: ROM, PROM, or EPROM.

*R*ead-*O*nly *M*emory (ROM) is used to store monitors, interpreters, input/output drivers, or special application programs. It is not possible to write into ROM memory as it is into RAM memory. ROM memory, however, is not user programmable; the contents of the ROM were put there by the manufacturer.

Another memory, called PROM (*P*rogrammable *R*ead-*O*nly *M*emory), does not forget what it knows when the power to the microcomputer is turned off, and is used in many microcomputers to contain monitors, input/output drivers, and special application programs. The PROM

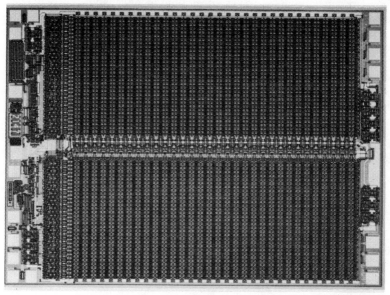

Courtesy Intel Corp.

Fig. 3-4. Photomicrograph of a semiconductor memory chip.

chips can be purchased blank and then programmed by using a special machine called a *PROM programmer* or *PROM burner*. Once programmed, the PROM memory behaves the same as the ROM.

Erasable *PROM* (EPROM) is one of the latest types of semiconductor memory. It can be programmed by the user, and it can also be erased and reprogrammed with different information. Once it has been programmed, EPROM memory acts just the same as ROM. The EPROM is the program memory most frequently used by users who must make frequent changes in their programs. They can do it themselves if they have a PROM programmer.

Semiconductor and magnetic-core memories are direct-access memories. That is, the computer can access (transfer information to or from) any memory location chosen at random, instead of having to access the locations in some particular sequence. For this to be possible, every storage location must be provided with an address. When the CPU needs the information in a certain storage location, it transmits the address of that location to the storage section. The storage hardware decodes the address and sends back the contents of the specified location. Storing information is accomplished in a similar way. We can thus visualize the internal storage of a computer as a set of postoffice boxes. Each box will hold a certain amount of information, and each has a unique address by which it can be identified.

In some computer systems, the working capacity of internal storage can be increased by programming a portion of auxiliary storage to augment internal storage. Called *virtual storage,* this procedure has the effect of increasing the working capacity of internal storage. Virtual storage is discussed later in this chapter.

Other types of internal storage that are less well known are magnetic-bubble storage, laser-holographic storage, and thin-film storage. These memory types are discussed later in this chapter.

Auxiliary Storage

A computer system may have a number of different storage devices other than internal storage. These devices, called *auxiliary storage* devices, are used to store programs and data. They can be used to receive input information that is to be processed in the CPU, or to store the output of the CPU and hold it for reference, for printout, or for further processing. There are three commonly used auxiliary memory devices: magnetic tapes, magnetic disks, and magnetic drums. These devices are discussed in the following three sections.

Magnetic Tape—Magnetic tape is one of the more popular media for representing information. It is used not only as a fast way of getting information into and out of the computer, but also as auxiliary storage.

A tape unit reads from and writes on tape. Before the tape unit can perform read or write operations, it must be prepared for operation. This preparation involves loading two reels on the tape unit and threading the tape through the tape transport mechanism. Fig. 3-5 shows an operator loading a magnetic-tape reel on a tape unit.

During tape read or write operations, the tape moves from one reel across a read/write head to the other reel. Writing on tape is *destructive*; that is, as new information is written, old information is erased. Reading is *nondestructive*; the same information can be read again and again. Information is written on tape by magnetizing areas in parallel tracks along the length of the tape. In the tape unit, there is one read/write coil in the head for each recording track, where electrical current flowing through the coils magnetizes the iron-oxide coating of the moving tape and erases previously written information. The execution of a "program write" command results in one or more records of data being written. A 0.6-in (15.24-mm) *interrecord gap* (IRG) is left after each "write" has been completed. The gap serves to separate one record from another and allows distance for both stopping the tape after an operation is completed and accelerating the tape to the proper speed when starting a new operation.

File protection rings are often used with magnetic tape to prevent the accidental writing of information on a tape. This ring, which is made of

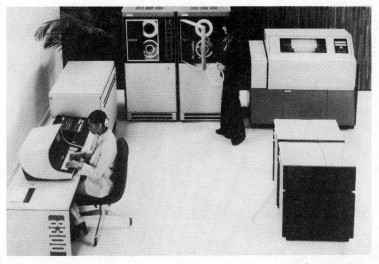

Courtesy NCR Corp.

Fig. 3-5. Operator loading a magnetic-tape reel on a tape unit.

plastic, fits into a circular groove on the tape reel. Writing is prohibited whenever the ring is absent.

Magnetic-tape units read tapes at speeds up to 112.5 inches per second (285.75 centimeters per second). Information can be recorded on a tape up to 1600 characters per inch. This is referred to as the *tape density*. Data recorded at 1600 c/in and reading at 112.5 in/s (285.75 cm/s) allows 180,000 characters to be transmitted each second. This high-speed operation is the primary reason that magnetic tape is used as a primary input/output method for many medium and large-scale computer systems.

Many businesses store all their information on magnetic tape, building up large tape *libraries*. Data is often recorded on magnetic tape by using a *card-to-tape conversion* procedure or a *key-to-tape recorder*. In card-to-tape conversion, the source data is initially recorded on punched cards. Then, using the card reader, the computer, and a magnetic-tape unit, the data is recorded on magnetic tape. The key-to-tape recorder is a device that can be used to record data directly onto magnetic tape.

Computer systems often require large quantity storage of data that is used only occasionally. In large systems, this requirement is often met by using a magnetic tape. Minicomputers and microcomputers often have these same requirements, although usually on a smaller scale. The magnetic-tape units available for large systems, although a possible solution, are not often used because their cost is generally higher than that of a minicomputer or microcomputer. Recently, several container-loaded magnetic-tape units, designed as low-cost storage devices for minicomputers and microcomputers, have been made available.

A *cassette* unit is a digital tape recorder that operates with tape 3.785 mm ± 0.025 mm wide (commonly referred to as ⅛-in tape) that has been previously loaded in some form of container. The container is open at one end to permit insertion of magnetic heads and the drive mechanism. The remainder is completely enclosed. Cassette units are basically simple, modest-performance devices. They are relatively easy to operate and their cost is fairly low. Hence, these devices provide a low-cost solution to the problem of large-capacity storage for small digital computer systems. A cassette is shown in Fig. 3-6. Fig 3.7 shows a cassette tape recorder.

Magnetic Disks—Magnetic disks are a very popular type of auxiliary storage. The physical characteristics of all magnetic disks are similar. Each one is a thin metal disk coated on both sides with magnetic recording material (Fig. 3-8). The disks are mounted on a vertical shaft and are slightly separated from each other to provide space for the movement of read/write assemblies. The shaft revolves, spinning the disks. Data is stored as magnetized spots in concentric tracks on each surface of the disk. Disk units have several hundred tracks on each surface for storing data. The tracks are made accessible for reading and writing by positioning the read/write heads between the spinning disks. The read/write head mechanism is hydraulically driven to move all heads simultaneously to any track position. After horizontal movement is completed to a specified track, the read/write heads can be directed to perform the reading and writing on the track.

Fig. 3-6. A magnetic-tape cassette.

Courtesy Ohio Scientific

**Fig. 3-7. A microcomputer system using an unmodified audio tape cassette
recorder for data storage.**

Fig. 3-9 illustrates a disk assembly. This assembly is composed of six
disks mounted on a vertical shaft. The disk assembly provides 10
surfaces on which information can be recorded. The top and bottom
surfaces are used as protective plates and are not used for recording
purposes. Information is read from or written on the disks by read/write
heads mounted on a comb-like access mechanism which has 10
read/write heads mounted on five access arms. Each read/write head can
either read or write information on the corresponding upper or lower
disk surface. The entire access mechanism moves horizontally so that
information on all tracks can be either read or written.

A magnetic-disk assembly can have several disks. A disk unit with 25

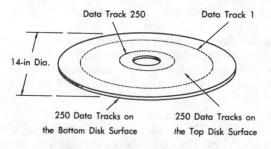

Fig. 3-8. Diagram of a magnetic disk.

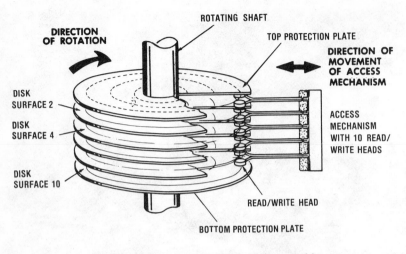

Fig. 3-9. Diagram of a magnetic-disk assembly.

disks can have a storage capacity of over 100 million characters of information. This information can be transmitted to and from a computer at rates of over 150,000 characters per second.

The magnetic-disk data surface can be used repetitively. Each time new information is stored on a track, the old information is erased as the new information is recorded. The recorded data may be read as often as desired; data remains recorded on the tracks of a disk until it is written over.

The simplified disk assembly shown in Fig. 3-9 illustrates the read/write head mechanism moving in a horizontal direction. In this manner, the disk mechanism is able to position itself at any specified track. The time required to locate a specific track is called the *disk access time*. This time is related to the lateral distance that the read/write head mechanism moves.

In addition to access time, there is another timing factor associated with disk read/write operations. The *rotational delay time* is the time required for the disk to attain the desired position at the selected read/write head. The maximum revolution time for a disk is the time required for one full revolution. The average rotational delay time is one-half the disk revolution rate. For example, if the disk revolves at 2400 revolutions per minute, then the average rotational delay time would be slightly over 11 milliseconds.

Some disk units have removable and replaceable disk packs or cartridges. (Fig. 3-10). These disk units are used as input/output units as well as storage devices. The disk pack or cartridge is popular because it allows a user to move the data stored in one disk unit conveniently to

Courtesy Data General Corp.

Fig. 3-10. Dustproof cover being removed from a disk pack mounted on a disk drive unit.

another place so that it can be processed on various computer systems. Replacement of one disk pack by another takes less than a minute.

There is one other type of disk unit. This unit, called a *fixed-head disk*, has a stationary read/write head for each track. These head-per-track devices are much faster than other disk units since there are no moving parts; only the rotational delay time determines the access time. In fact, access times of the fixed-head disks are similar to magnetic drums. Fixed-head disk units are, however, more expensive than other types of disks. Fixed-head disks will probably be replaced by magnetic-bubble memory chips in future computer systems.

A newer type of disk has proved to be a strong competitor with the previously mentioned disk units. These disks, called *floppy disks*, are flexible, made of oxide-coated mylar, and are stored in paper or plastic envelopes. The entire envelope is inserted in the disk unit, effectively protecting the contents of the disk surfaces. The disk surfaces are rotated inside the protective covering. The disk head contacts the track positions through a slot in the covering.

The person in Fig. 3-11 is placing a floppy disk (or diskette) into the

Courtesy Digital Equipment Corp.

Fig. 3-11. Floppy disk (or diskette) being inserted into the disk unit of a minicomputer system.

disk unit. Disk units such as these are relatively inexpensive, and the disks themselves are cheap. It is estimated that eventually a diskette will cost around 50 cents. Because of their low cost and high speed, the floppy-disk units are being widely used, especially in minicomputer and microcomputer systems.

Magnetic Drum—A magnetic drum is a metal cylinder coated with magnetically sensitive material on its outer surface. The drum rotates at a constant speed. The drum surface is divided into several *tracks* or *channels*. Each track has an associated read/write head mechanism that is used to read and write data on the drum surface. A read/write head is suspended a very slight distance from the drum surface. Whenever new data is recorded, the old data is automatically erased.

As the drum rotates, reading and writing occurs when the specified area of the track (on some drums, a track is subdivided into several *sectors*) passes under the read/write mechanism for that track. Writing results in magnetized spots on the drum surface. Reading involves only sensing the magnetized areas.

"MR. SMITH, THE STAFF REFERS TO YOU AS 'BUBBLEHEAD'!"

MAGNETIC-BUBBLE STORAGE

Magnetic-bubble memory has advanced considerably since the concept was introduced by Bell Laboratories in 1967. Several companies, including Texas Instruments, Inc., Intel Corp., IBM Corp., Rockwell International, and Bell Laboratories, have been actively experimenting with magnetic-bubble technology.

What is a magnetic-bubble memory? The bubble is so called because to the Bell Laboratories people, who developed it, it seemed to behave "like a bubble floating in a magnetic sea." Actually, bubbles are cylinders of magnetic material that are "floating" in a film of magnetic material. Magnetic bubbles are tiny cylindrical magnetized areas—less than 1/16 the diameter of a human hair—contained in a thin film of magnetic material such as a garnet layer. These areas can be moved about electronically so they can be used for computing and storing data. The bubbles are polarized in the opposite direction from the rest of the material. With the proper magnetic bias, which is provided by external permanent magnets, the bubbles are astonishingly stable; they do not disappear or appear unless they are supposed to. Methods have been developed for creating and destroying bubbles and for moving them around.

It is important to emphasize that although the bubbles move, the magnetic material does not. There are no moving parts, and no wear and tear. In terms of what they accomplish, bubble memories are closer to disks than to the semiconductors which they resemble. A number of metal paths are laid on top of the bubble chip in loops. Bubbles are switched about the chips like trains on tracks. Each loop can be thought of as corresponding to a track on a disk. With faster access than a disk drive, the bubble memory is not nearly as fast as a semiconductor RAM. Bubble memory is nonvolatile; therefore, the data is retained even when power is no longer applied to the chip.

Since the diameter of a bubble is so small, many thousands of data bits can be stored in a single bubble memory chip. Texas Instruments and Rockwell International have developed chips that store over a quarter of a million bits of data. Intel Magnetics, a subsidiary of Intel Corp., has announced a million-bit memory device—the 7110 bubble-memory chip. IBM has developed a bubble-memory chip with a 10-million-bit storage capability. Using such a compact memory, one could store the whole Library of Congress in the cubic space taken up by the average size console tv set. Within the next five to 10 years, the capability to store all the knowledge of mankind in the corner of a room should exist. Texas Instruments is currently developing a 16-million-bit chip.

Perhaps one of the most important features of the manufacture of bubble memories is the compatibility of the new developments with semiconductor processing technology. Many of the same manufacturing techniques developed for semiconductors can be applied directly to magnetic bubbles. The years of semiconductor experience can be readily transferred to the emerging magnetic-bubble field.

The compatibility of these two important technologies should have a profound impact on the microelectronics industry. The future of magnetic-bubble memory is certainly debatable; however, it seems clear that these memory chips will be used in future microcomputers. The advantages of magnetic-bubble memories over random-access memories (RAMs) are nonvolatility, potentially lower price per bit, and more bits per chip. The RAM, however, has the advantage of much better access time, higher transfer rate, and simpler interfacing. Bubble memories will also replace fixed-head disks in many future computer systems, and they may even displace moving-head disks.

"IT'S OUR NEW BUBBLE MEMORY!"

LASER-HOLOGRAPHIC STORAGE

As computers continue to grow in size and complexity, storage will have to be increased significantly at no sacrifice in speed. This means the information will have to be packed much more densely in whatever storage device is used. Holography is a technique that can further the development of large storage devices. With recent advances in holography and laser-beam technology, computer developers are studying optical memories whose ultimate storage capacity may well be in excess of 100 million bits of data, and whose random-access time may be as short as one microsecond.

Holograms make use of a high-energy laser beam to store or display three-dimensional images. The image produced by a hologram can easily be read by a photodetector, and information can be stored redundantly.

A *holographic memory* is made on a special recording medium somewhat similar to conventional photographic film. The recording process starts with the construction of a data mask that represents the contents of a page. Each mask is basically an array of pinholes, blocked where 0s are to be recorded and transparent where 1s are needed. Each data mask is recorded holographically, one at a time, on the recording medium. Information is retrieved from the memory by projecting the data recorded on the hologram onto a light-sensitive detector. The detector converts the optical information into electronic signals that the computer can process.

Several experimental laser-holographic memory systems have been developed. IBM has developed a system that stores more than 100 million bits of information on a 9-in^2 (58-cm^2) holographic plate. A system developed by a Japanese firm is capable of accommodating a telephone directory of 3800 pages on 16 pieces of film, each measuring 5 in^2 (32.26 cm^2). It has a capacity much greater than present storage units and is considerably faster than conventional magnetic tapes or disks in information readout.

Another system has been developed that can record over 70,866 bits of information onto a 1.0-centimeter length of 8-mm photographic film at a rate of over 10 million bits per second.

VIRTUAL STORAGE

System designers and programmers have typically had to be concerned with internal memory capacity to make sure that they could fit their computer programs and working data into the available space. If the programs were too large for memory, the programmer would segment the program, putting the first part in internal storage and the other segments in auxiliary or secondary storage. When the first section was complete, the second section would be brought into internal storage (overlaid in the same memory area that contained the first section). The use of overlays can be limited to smaller sections, so that a main segment is kept intact and smaller portions are overlaid.

The concept of *virtual memory* is to have the hardware and software *automatically* segment the program and to move segments into storage when needed. The auxiliary storage, usually disk units, is, in effect, utilized as an "extension" of the internal memory of the computer. Virtual memory is the memory space defined by a range of addresses specified by the programmer and different from the addresses utilized by the memory system. A device is required for translating the addresses used by the program into the correct memory location addresses. The size of virtual memory is consequently limited only by the addressing capability of the computer and not by the number of locations in its internal memory. With virtual memory, the programmer has the illusion that the memory of the computer is larger than it really is.

The basic element of a virtual memory is a program segment or *page*—a fixed-size unit of storage, usually 2048 or 4096 bytes. The pages of memory are swapped back and forth in such a way that the internal memory (real memory) of the computer is expanded to many times its actual capacity. The process of swapping programs of data back and forth is referred to as *page-in*, since the page goes from disk to internal memory, and *page-out* as a page leaves the internal memory and is stored on the disk unit.

The difficult part of any memory organization is keeping track of what part of the program is in internal storage and what part is stored on the disk. A technique called *dynamic memory allocation* is used in the management of memory resources. This technique divides a selected area of internal memory into pages. Any available page may be assigned for different purposes, depending on the requirements of the moment. A control routine keeps account of which pages are free so that the available memory space can be immediately assigned as needed. This is accomplished by a technique wherein available pages are linked together in the form of a chain. When a memory page becomes available, it is appropriately added to the chain. The control routine shuffles programs or data from auxiliary storage into available memory pages as required.

Virtual memory allows a programmer to write a program as if internal memory were limitless. With virtual memory, the computer takes care of the difficulty of scheduling the swapping of data and programs.

THIN-FILM STORAGE

Thin-film storage, which utilizes concepts similar to those that magnetic-core storage is based on, has been used as internal storage for some recent computers. It is, however, more compact, more expensive, and faster in access time than is magnetic-core storage.

One form of thin-film memory consists of a series of metallic-alloy dots, a few millionths of an inch thick, deposited on a glass, ceramic, or plastic plate. The dots are connected by very fine wires and perform the same as magnetic cores. The dots can be magnetized in either of two stable preferred directions. Several thousand dots may be deposited on a 1.0-in (2.54-cm) square plane. Because the thin films consist of so many small dots, the arrangement of circuits to perform reading and writing operations is difficult. A common method is to etch copper wires onto an insulating material. Then, by closely positioning these circuits, the dots can be magnetized and their direction of magnetization sensed.

INPUT AND OUTPUT DEVICES

For a computer to be useful there must be convenient ways of putting the information to be processed into it and getting the results out. This is the mission of the input/output devices. Input and output devices are the means by which the computer communicates with the outside world. Input units transfer data to the computer and output units receive data from it. When input or output units are connected directly to the computer, they are considered to be *on-line*. When they operate independently of the computer, they are called *off-line*.

The off-line concept involves separating the slow input/output equipment from the central processing unit by intermediate storage: magnetic tape or disk pack. This separation maximizes the usage of the central processing unit, since it allows input/output operations to occur at a higher rate.

A large computer system may involve many different types of off-line equipment: punched cards to magnetic tape, paper tape to magnetic tape, keyboard to magnetic tape, keyboard to disk pack, magnetic tape to printed form, magnetic tape to digital-plotted form, magnetic tape to microfilm, and printed document to paper tape.

From the early stages of computer development, input and output equipment have acted as restraining factors on the high speed of the computer. Since most of the data that a computer uses or produces must go through input/output equipment, it is understandable that there is much concern over the speed of these devices. The relatively slow speed of devices such as card readers and paper-tape readers is the reason many computer systems use magnetic tape and removable magnetic disks as the primary method of communicating with the computer. Data is recorded on magnetic tape or magnetic disk prior to its use on the computer. This can be accomplished by using off-line data preparation equipment or even a small off-line computer system dedicated to this purpose. Likewise, computer output can be recorded on magnetic tape or disk packs and later transcribed to printed or other forms by off-line equipment.

Input/output devices operate under the control of the computer as directed by a stored computer program. For example, an instruction to read a card would cause the card reader to read a card and transmit the information to computer storage. An instruction to print a message would cause one or more lines of copy to be printed on a printing device such as a typewriter or line printer. Thus, instructions in the program select the required device, direct it to read or write, and indicate the location in computer storage where data will be inserted or retrieved.

In this section, we will look at some of the most common input/output devices. Fig.3-12 shows some devices and identifies them as input, output, or both.

Visual Display Terminals

The *cathode-ray-tube* (crt) terminal is used widely as a computer input/output device. A crt terminal looks like a cross between a

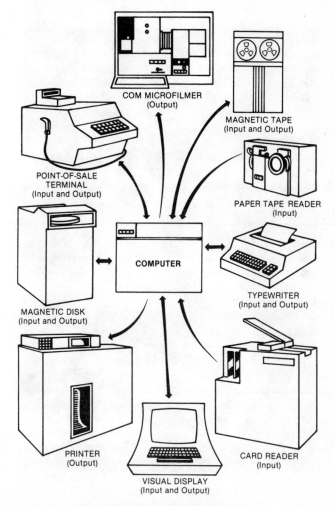

Fig. 3-12. Input and output devices.

typewriter and a tv set (Fig. 3-13). Information sent from the computer to the terminal is displayed on the screen. In most instances—though not always—the crt terminal is equipped with a keyboard to give it two-way communications capability.

In a typical computer system, the terminal would be connected by wire with the computer. This may be a hard-wired connection directly with the computer, or the terminal may be one of many in a system network, operating under the control of multiplexers or a communications control computer. If the crt terminal is at a remote location, its connection with the computer usually would be through telephone lines.

Fig. 3-13. A crt terminal.

Some crt terminals can only display text; others can also display drawings. Some terminals are equipped with a *light pen* (Fig. 3-14), which can be used to make drawings on the screen that are subsequently transmitted to the computer.

The visual display terminal is the most useful microcomputer output device. This is primarily because it is fast, quiet, and costs less than a printing device. The two most common types of terminals used in microcomputer systems are the video monitor and the tv receiver.

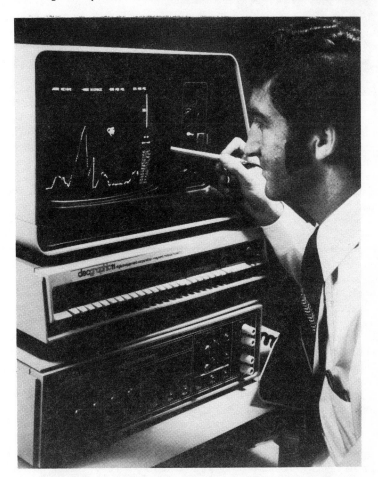

Courtesy Digital Equipment Corp.

Fig. 3-14. Spacecraft (light-colored shape on crt) is guided across jagged mountain peaks in a moon flight simulated by a minicomputer system. The operator is using a light pen.

A *video monitor* is made specifically for information display and is very similar to a home tv set, except that it does not include the electronics for receiving signals from a distant tv station. A *tv receiver* used with computers is simply a modified home tv set. Fig. 3-15 illustrates a video monitor that is used with the Radio Shack TRS-80 microcomputer.

Fig. 3-15. Video monitor used with the Radio Shack TRS-80 microcomputer.

Another type of visual display is called a *plasma panel*. Unlike other display systems, plasma panels do not use crt or tv tubes. They substitute etched glass plates separated by a gas which glows when excited by an electrical pulse. Plasma panels do not require constant reexcitation; once a particular point on the display is turned on, it continues to glow a bright orange until it is turned off. The display consists of a series of bright dots that can be formatted into alphanumeric characters and diagrams.

Several kinds of *keyboards* are often used with display devices (Fig. 3-16). An *alphanumeric* keyboard allows the operator to compose messages or make inquiries. A *function* keyboard permits the operator to make coded inquiries or to establish operating modes. Some function keyboards use coded, changeable overlays so that the meaning of the function keys can be changed by the operator.

A *graphic tablet* is an electronic unit that converts pen position into digital form while the pen is normally writing, drawing, or pointing on the tablet surface. A spot or line corresponding to the stylus position can be made to appear on the screen. The tablet may be used as a scratch pad, a graphic pointer, a means for entering written characters, and a means for tracing drawings.

The *joy stick* and *track ball* are devices that allow the operator to mechanically control two orthogonal analog-to-digital converters. The outputs of the two converters are sensed, and a spot appears on the display screen at the location determined by these positions. It is a computer program function to compare the dot position generated by the device with computer-generated data.

Printing Devices

Printing devices provide permanent and readable records of information from the computer. The printing device receives informa-

tion in electronic form which activates printing elements in the printer, thus causing information to be printed. There are three main printing devices used with computers: the typewriter, the line printer, and the teletypewriter.

The *typewriter,* which may be used as a keyboard input device as well as an output printing device, provides a method for printing limited amounts of information. This device can print up to 200 characters per second. Typewriters, such as the one shown in Fig. 3-17, are commonly used as control devices in medium- and large-scale computer systems, and as primary input/output devices in many small-scale computer systems.

The *line printer,* which is the most important hard-copy output device to be used with computers, prints a line at a time at a very fast rate. This device is used to produce reports, summaries, and similar output on continuous paper forms (Fig.3-18). The paper may be blank, lined, or printed in any form. Fig. 3-19 shows the line printer that is used with the Radio Shack TRS-80 microcomputer.

There are two major categories of printing techniques. In *impact printing,* a type carrier contacts an inked ribbon and paper. In *electrostatic printing,* the paper is charged with line images and is passed through an ink fog. Ink adheres to the charged portions of the

Courtesy Perkin-Elmer Corp., Computer Systems Division

Fig. 3-16. Chemists, mathematicians, physicists, astronomers, and other scientists use computers to help them conduct research studies. A crt display and keyboard are shown in the foreground.

paper. Heat is then used to fix the line images. Electrostatic printing is faster than impact printing because of simpler mechanical construction, but impact printing is the more common method.

Many computer systems use a typewriter-like device, called a *teletypewriter*, as a method of getting information into or out of the computer.

Courtesy Perkin-Elmer Corp., Computer Systems Division

Fig. 3-17. A typewriter designed for use with a computer as both a keyboard input device and an output printing device.

Card Reader and Punch

A *card reader* is a device that accepts punched cards and senses what is on each card (reads it). The information punched on the cards is then transmitted to the memory of the computer. Fig.3-20 shows two types of punched cards. The 80-column card at the top is the standard-size card used with most data-processing equipment. The 96-column card at the bottom is used with some newer computer systems.

Card readers are of two basic types: (1) mechanical and (2) optical. Mechanical card readers use metal brushes, which feel for holes in the cards. Once the holes have been found, electrical circuits are established which enable the card reader to transmit data, in the form of characters, to computer memory. Optical card readers operate similarly to mechanical ones except that light beams detect the holes, electrical circuits are established, and information is transmitted. Mechanical card readers read cards at the rate of about 250 cards per minute. Optical card readers read cards at rates of up to 2000 cards per minute. At the fastest speeds, card readers supply information to computer memory at a rate of over 2500 characters per second. Fig. 3-21 shows a punched-card reader.

Courtesy Teletype Corp.

Fig. 3-18. A Teletype Model 40 terminal (left) with line printer (right.)

The *card punch* punches information from computer storage into blank cards. The card punch has a hopper that holds many blank cards. The blank cards are moved under the punch knives, one at a time, where holes are punched in the card after the proper knives have been activated.

Paper-Tape Reader and Punch

Perforated paper tape with its *holes* and *no-holes* coding is used to input information into the computer and to record information from the computer in much the same manner as punched cards. Reading speeds vary from a few hundred characters per second up to a thousand characters per second. Punching speeds are somewhat slower, being in the range of several hundred characters per second.

There are numerous makes and models of *paper-tape readers* and *punches*. Fig. 3-22 shows a reader. Many paper-tape punches are attachments for adding machines, cash registers, typewriters, point-of-sale terminals, and bookkeeping machines. When punched with information, the tape may be used in a paper-tape reader for direct transmission to computer memory or for recording on magnetic disk or tape for faster computer input.

Magnetic-Ink Character Reader

The *magnetic-ink character reader* is a special-purpose input device that was designed as an aid to the automation of the banking industry. This device can read card and paper documents inscribed with a special magnetic-ink character font. The printed check is the most common form of document that uses these printed characters.

"MY MOTHER WORKS IN A BANK..."

Optical Character Reader

Another character-reading device that can be used as input to computers is the *optical character reader*. This device reads letters, numbers, and special characters that are printed on paper documents. Documents to be read are placed in a hopper and then transported in the reader past an optical scanning position where a powerful light and lens enable the machine to distinguish the letters, numbers, and special characters as patterns of light. These light patterns are converted into electrical pulses for use by the computer.

The action of optical scanning is similar to the action of the human eye. Fig. 3-23 illustrates that the eye, in order to see an object, must have some illumination. Reflected light then passes through the lens of the eye and is focused on the retina. The retina converts this image to nerve impulses that are sent to the brain, and some action is then instituted. In

Fig. 3-19. Line printer used with the Radio Shack TRS-80 microcomputer.

the optical scanner, illustrated in Fig. 3-24, the character to be read is illuminated; then reflected light passes through a lens and is directed to a photomultiplier, which converts the light to electrical impulses. The electrical impulses are then sent to the computer to be recognized, and some action is taken.

While the OCR reader is similar to the human eye, it is not as versatile as the human eye. It cannot make allowances for poor printing, sloppy writing, writing on brown paper, and many other such limitations that the human eye can overcome. But what the OCR reader can and does read, it reads very fast.

There are four general types of optical character readers: (1) page readers, which read 8½ × 11-in (21.59 × 27.94-cm) documents; (2) document readers, which read a line or two from small documents about 4 × 8 in (10.16 × 20.32 cm) or 2 × 4 in (5.08 × 10.16 cm); (3) reader/punches, which read data printed on a card and punch the data into the same card; and (4) journal-tape readers, which read printed cash-register or adding-machine listing tapes.

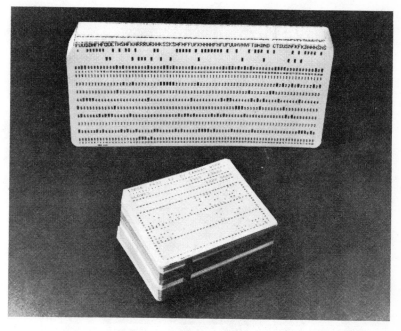

Courtesy IBM Corp.

Fig. 3-20. Two types of punched cards.

Page readers tend to be large, expensive multifont machines because of the flexibility required to scan the loose formats of varying pages. Document readers, journal-tape readers, and reader/punches are somewhat smaller and less expensive because of a simpler transport mechanism and the smaller scanning areas required for their types of input.

Optical character readers are widely used by utility companies, oil companies, department stores, mail-order houses, and credit-card companies. The use of these readers simplifies the computer input process.

Optical Mark and Mark-Sense Readers

In the last section, we discussed the optical character reader. Some optical character readers have the ability to read both alphabetic characters and marks. Optical mark and mark sensing is performed by detecting the presence or absence of pencil marks in specified positions on a form. Many areas of data collection are simplified by using preprinted forms that require only that the user fill in appropriate boxes

Courtesy Hewlett-Packard

Fig. 3-21. Card readers, such as the one shown here, can read punched cards at rates between 200 and 600 cards per minute.

with pencil marks. Such forms are commonly used for collecting inventory information, taking school attendance, conducting a census, recording a public opinion poll, or taking a test. Forms of this type may be read by *optical mark* and *mark-sense readers*.

The mark-detection system of an optical mark reader generally consists of a light source, mirrors, and light-sensitive photocells. A mark is detected when a drop occurs in the amount of light arriving at the photocells after being reflected by the document being scanned. In contrast, the mark-detection system of a mark-sense reader generally consists of sets of three brushes each of which make contact with marks. A voltage is applied to the outer two brushes of the sets, and a mark is

Courtesy Digital Equipment Corp.

Fig. 3-22. Peripherals are often small and can be rack mounted with the computer. Shown here from the top down are a peripheral controller, a crt display, a paper-tape reader, and a minicomputer.

detected when a current passes through the graphite mark to the center brush.

Documents that are to be read by an optical mark reader can be marked with standard lead pencils. Documents that are to be read by mark-sense readers must be marked with special pencils containing soft and highly conductive leads. Fig. 3-25 shows an optical mark reader that reads both punched and pencil-marked cards.

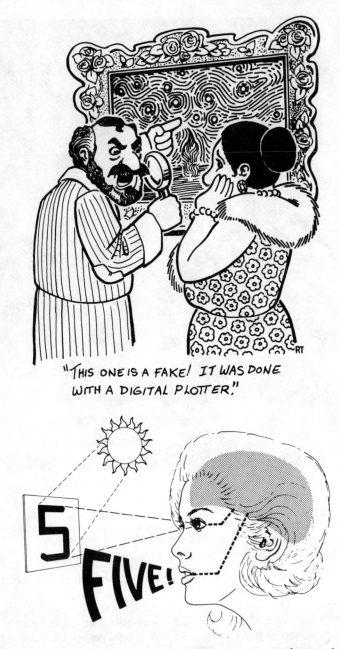

Fig. 3-23. Sketch illustrating how the human eye scans a document using illumination, lens, retina, nerve impulses, and brain.

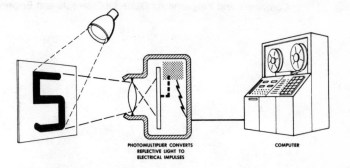

Fig. 3-24. Sketch illustrating how the OCR reader scans a document using illumination, lens, photomultiplier, electrical impulses, and electronic computer.

Digital Plotters

Automatic plotting devices are used with computers to produce pictorial or graphic representations of information. The *digital plotter* is a device that can draw under control of the computer. Typical applications might be the drawing of graphs (Fig. 3-26), land contour maps (Fig. 3-27), weather maps, mathematical functions (Fig. 3-28), subdivision maps, electrical network drawings, machine part drawings, or highway maps.

Courtesy Hewlett-Packard

Fig. 3-25. Desktop optical mark reader that reads both punched and pencil-marked cards.

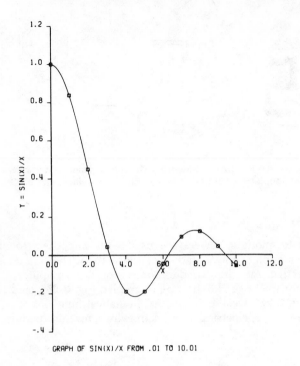

GRAPH OF SIN(X)/X FROM .01 TO 10.01

Fig. 3-26. Graph produced by a digital plotter.

The two most common forms of plotters are the *drum* and *flatbed* types. The pen of a drum plotter is driven in one axis while the paper moves positively or negatively in the other axis. The flatbed plotter moves the pen in both the X and Y axes, and the table is usually fixed. The computer provides pen movement and functional commands to the plotter in digital form, and these commands are then converted into pen motions. Fig. 3-29 illustrates a digital plotter being used to produce a diagram.

Intelligent Terminals

The term *intelligent terminal* designates a terminal in which a number of computer processing characteristics are physically built into, or attached to, the terminal unit. This enables the terminal to perform some functions normally handled by the computer, thus relieving the load on the computer system or data transmission lines. Specifically, the intelligent terminal detects and corrects certain operator errors, relieves the computer of some routine tasks, speeds up processing, and makes information available more easily and more quickly.

Intelligent terminals are usually cathode-ray-tube (crt) units

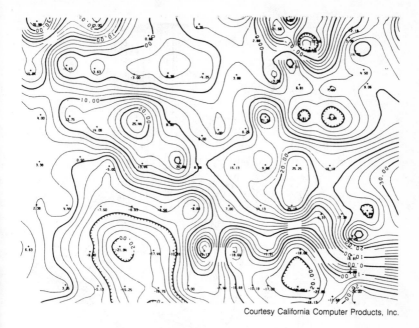

Courtesy California Computer Products, Inc.

Fig. 3-27. Contour map produced by a digital plotter.

equipped with a keyboard. They may be connected (interfaced) with a number of other input/output devices, such as card readers, printers, and cassette recorders. The intelligent terminal, coupled with other input/output devices, greatly increases the capability of a computer.

An important function of the intelligent terminal is to capture and enter raw source data at the remote location of its origin, such as a sales office, branch office, or mobile office. Since the terminal can be programmed for specific applications, this assures that entries are made in the proper places in fill-in blanks. Operators always know exactly what is being entered and where entries are to be made through visual verification with the crt display. Each entry is checked as it is made, and the operator can make corrections before committing data to the computer by simply rekeying the data.

Many of the intelligent terminals use microcomputers or microprocessors to control various functions. These micro's can be programmed to perform many unique and special functions that may be required for a special application.

Audio Response Terminals

Computers can now talk! A program looks up words to be spoken in a dictionary stored in a computer memory, and determines how they are

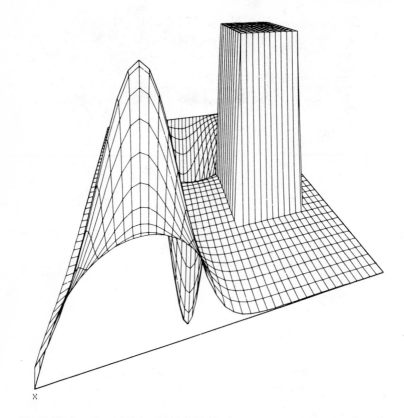

X

Fig. 3-28. Drawing of a mathematical function produced by a digital plotter.

to be pronounced and stressed. It then calculates how the human vocal system would move in speaking the words, in order to determine what sounds would be produced. This information is then passed on to an electronic device that actually produces the sound.

Audio response, or *voice synthesizing*, systems are used in a wide variety of businesses. The uses to which banks can apply voice response techniques are extensive. A teller's inquiry can get a response regarding the existence or nonexistence of an account, or whether the balance is sufficient to cover a check. A bank officer can be informed of the status of a loan, a trust account, or the details of a mortgage. In a retail store, audio response provides instant and private advice at the point of sale regarding a customer's credit, and also provides credit-card verification. A long list of audio response uses could be made for such diverse businesses and industrial activities as real estate, transportation, manufacturing, insurance, wholesale, and many others.

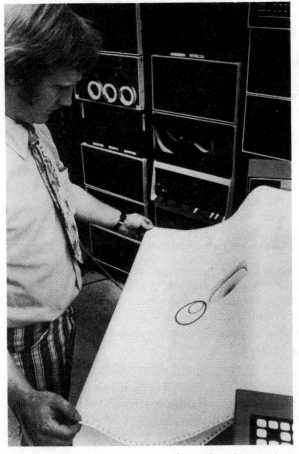

Courtesy Digital Equipment Corp.

Fig. 3-29. Computers and digital plotters are used to produce many types of drawings.

Fig. 3-30 shows the voice synthesizer for the TRS-80 microcomputer. This device translates the output of the computer into recognizable, intelligible speech.

Voice Recognition Units

Voice recognition devices are used to convert audio signals into digital impulses. Input is rather slow if vocal input occurs at the normal speaking rate; however, a much faster method of input could result if the spoken words were recorded on magnetic tape or disk. This input could then be transmitted to the computer at a faster rate.

Courtesy Radio Shack, a Division of Tandy Corp.

Fig. 3-30. Voice synthesizer for the Radio Shack TRS-80 microcomputer.

At the present time, voice input of data to computers is only in the early stages of development, but it holds much promise for the future as a method of human/machine communications. Several units are currently available for use with TRS-80 and Apple II microcomputer systems.

Point-of-Sale Terminals

Computer users are starting to realize the potential advantages of capturing data at the source. Some of the benefits of a good data collection system are: reduction of clerical costs; increased accuracy of information because of the elimination of the manual handling and transcribing of data; more effective cost control; and sounder operating decisions by management, because they are getting timely management information, not history.

Useful data must have at least two characteristics: (1) it must be accurate and (2) it must be timely. Neither of these characteristics can be overlooked. The person who is capturing the data should do the fewest number possible of the simplest things possible.

Characteristics of point-of-sale systems are: the input device should be installed as close as possible to the point where the data is generated, the device should be easy to operate by the person at that location who is familiar with the characteristics of the data and with the important effect of errors in the data, precoded information should be used when possible, and a method of visual verification and correction is desirable.

For a number of years, some cash registers have been equipped with a paper-tape punching mechanism to record the facts of each sale when these facts are entered on the keyboard of the machine. For example, the sales clerk enters the amount of sale, tax, and other charges and credits, if any. The clerk may also enter the stock number and unit quantity of merchandise sold as well as any other data desired. While this is being done, the machine punches a paper tape with the amount and identification of each item. At the end of the day or period, the punched tape is removed from the cash register and placed in a device that records the data from the paper tape to magnetic tape to feed the sales for the day to the computer, which updates the accounts receivable, cash on hand and stock records, and produces sales analysis reports for the store management.

This semiautomatic method of capturing data is certainly better than complete manual systems; however, there is still much more room for improvement. Today, several companies are producing systems that eliminate the manual keying of data (an excellent place for error to creep into a point-of-sale system).

Today, computerized supermarkets throughout the country are becoming commonplace. The key to these checkout systems is an optical scanning device which "reads" an identification code placed on each item of merchandise, and transmits this information to a computer. The

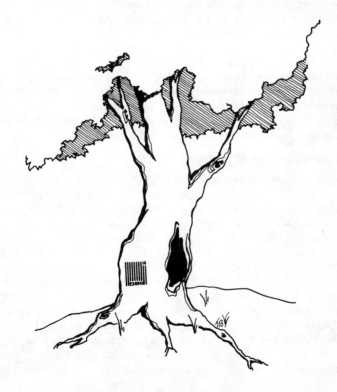

computer uses this information to create a perpetual inventory control system.

The code used to identify products is the Universal Product Code (UPC), a 10-digit numbering system for identifying items sold by stores. The first five digits in the code identify the manufacturer; the second five digits identify that manufacturer's product. This 10-digit code is expressed in a symbol as a series of vertical bars that can be understood by computer equipment. This symbol is printed on most of the 10,000 items sold in a typical supermarket. Upon receiving the code, the computer immediately matches it with product information such as price. It then relays this data to a cash register where it is visually displayed to both the customer and the checker. Simultaneously, the price is printed on the customer's receipt along with the product name.

Placing the price in computer memory eliminates the tedious job of price-marking items and also eliminates checkout errors that occur because of illegible price marks and ring-up mistakes. The store manager can also use the system to check the inventory of any product, to determine sales up to the moment at any checkstand or in any department, to know total sales, and to change prices of products.

We briefly discussed two areas (retail stores and supermarkets) where point-of-sale terminals are used. The capturing of data at its source is commonly referred to as *source data automation*. No additional steps are needed to transcribe the data to computerized form. Point-of-sale terminals, magnetic-ink character reading devices (such as those used by banks), optical character reading devices (such as those used by utility companies), and other recognition devices offer the possibility of preparing data only once at the original source and sending this data directly to the computer. There are many application areas that could be drastically improved by using source data automation systems.

Computer Output Microfilm

With the increasing calculating speeds of computers, a growing problem is how to obtain output from the computer. Printers have become faster, but are slow in comparison with the speeds at which computers can generate output.

Computer Output Microfilm (COM) has recently come of age. Although COM does not solve all problems associated with computer output, it does provide an additional option that system designers may consider. Fig. 3-31 shows how the COM microfilmer interfaces with a computer. Instead of printing pages on the printer, the computer generates an output magnetic tape. This magnetic tape is used as input to a COM unit. (An example of a COM unit is Kodak's KOM-90, shown in Fig. 3-32). The COM unit reads data from the magnetic tape, displays it on the face of a cathode-ray tube, and photographs it onto 16-mm roll microfilm. Data recording is accomplished at a rate up to 120,000

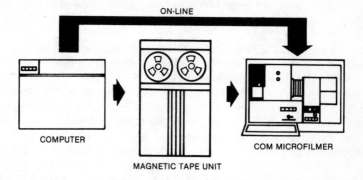

Fig. 3-31. Illustration of how a COM microfilmer interfaces with a computer.

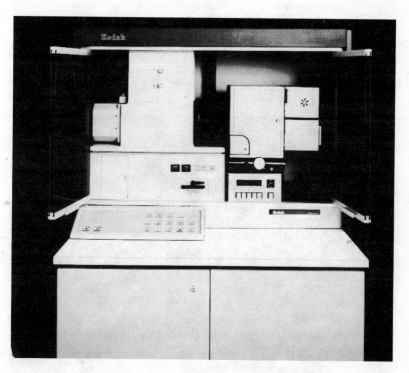

Courtesy Eastman Kodak Co.

Fig. 3-32. The Kodak KOM-90 microfilmer.

characters per second or 26,000 lines per minute, approximately equal to 300 printout pages per minute. The Bell & Howell 3800 COM system is shown in Fig. 3-33.

As shown in Fig. 3-31, the COM microfilmer can be directly connected to the computer (on-line), thus eliminating the necessity of recording the data on magnetic tape.

Alternative to the reel of microfilm is *microfiche*, a 4 × 6-in (10.16 × 15.24-cm) sheet of microfilm that contains 208 or more full pages of information. Microfiche films are simple to file and quick to retrieve. When placed in a microfiche viewer, the single page needed is shown in full size on the screen for easy reading and, if desired, a full-size photocopy of the single page may be printed out in seconds. Typical output speeds of computer-stored data to microfiche is one microfiche per minute, or approximately 12,000 pages per hour.

The uses for computer output microfilm are probably limitless. Microfilm reduces a high volume of documentary data to manageable proportions and frees the user from time-consuming searches. It also frees the computer from high-volume printing tasks. Some fundamental applications of COM are the following:

- Business-oriented listings with a low or high frequency of reference, but with an infrequent need for updating.

Courtesy Bell & Howell

Fig. 3-33. The Bell & Howell 3800 COM system.

- Computer-generated data bases, such as catalogs, indexes, directories, bibliographies, abstracts, and financial data.
- Libraries.
- Engineering drawings, including plots, graphs, maps, charts, circuit designs, etc.
- Management information reports requiring both alphanumeric and graphic output for proper display of data.
- Insurance; examples are agents' commission statements, agents' digest system, positions' records, vendors' records, etc.
- Animated movies.
- Educational and training films for industry, hospitals, business, government, and schools.

Computer Networks

Data communications involves the transmission of information from one point to another. A system for data communications consists of some type of terminal that is used to generate and receive electronic signals transmitted over communication lines. In addition, a *data set* is often required. This device converts digital signals for transmission over communications lines. Information to be transmitted is first converted by the terminal into an intermediate form acceptable to a data set. The data set converts the signals to a form that can be transmitted over a common communications line (see Fig. 3-34). At the other end of the communications line is another data set and another terminal to perform the conversions in reverse order.

A variety of devices may be used as remote terminals for data communications systems: point-of-sale terminals, digital plotters, minicomputer systems, microcomputer systems, card readers, line printers, teletypewriters, data collection equipment, pushbutton telephones, visual display systems, and others.

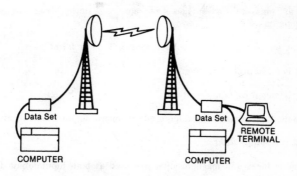

Fig. 3-34. Illustration of data transmission between two computers or between a computer and a remote terminal.

EXERCISES

1. What are the logical components of the central processing unit?

2. What are the major arithmetic operations that a computer can perform?

3. What are registers?

4. Describe the difference between a selector channel and a multiplexer channel.

5. Name the two major classifications of storage used with computer systems.

6. Define access time.

7. Name three types of internal storage.

8. What is a semiconductor memory?

9. Identify the following acronyms:

   (a) ROM
   (b) PROM
   (c) RAM
   (d) EPROM

10. What is meant by a direct-access memory?

11. What is the difference between direct access and sequential access?

12. Can a magnetic-tape device be called a direct-access device? If not, why?

13. Internal storage usually has a faster access time than most auxiliary storage devices. True or false?

14. List three examples of auxiliary storage.

15. Explain the difference between magnetic drums and disks.

16. What are some of the advantages of random-access storage devices as compared to magnetic tapes?

17. Writing on magnetic tape is nondestructive. True or false?

18. What is a file protection ring?

19. What is meant by tape density?

20. Magnetic-tape cassettes are widely used with microcomputer systems. Explain why.

21. What is a floppy disk?

22. Magnetic tapes and magnetic disks are used as both input/output devices and auxiliary storage units. True or false?

23. What is meant by magnetic-bubble memory?

24. Give several reasons why magnetic-bubble memory may be used in future microcomputer systems.

25. It is not practical to use holograms as a method to store information. True or false?

26. Why does the virtual-memory concept permit the user to run larger programs than could be run without virtual memory?

27. What is a "page"?

28. What is dynamic memory allocation?

29. List six devices that may be used to get information in and out of computer storage.

30. Compare punched cards, punched paper tape, and magnetic tape with respect to:

    (a) Ability to reuse.
    (b) Speed of reading information into the computer.

31. Why is printing a practical form of output?

32. How fast can line printers print output data?

33. What output device would be best to use if one wanted to draw a plot plan for a housing subdivision? A circuit diagram? A graph?

34. Identify the following acronyms:

    (a) OCR.
    (b) MICR.
    (c) CRT.

35. What is a light pen? How is it used?

36. Describe how you might use a graphic tablet in some engineering application.

37. What is a point-of-sale terminal?

38. What is an intelligent terminal?

39. What is meant by source data automation?

40. Briefly describe how a point-of-sale terminal might be used.

41. A code used to identify products:

    (a) Price-Tag Code (PTC)
    (b) Supermarket Price Code (SPC)
    (c) Universal Product Code (UPC)

42. Explain the difference between a COM unit and an OCR unit.

43. Explain how a data set is used in a data communications system.

CHAPTER **4**

STEPS IN PROBLEM SOLVING

A digital computer does not do any thinking and cannot make unplanned decisions. Every step of a problem must be accounted for by a computer *program*. A problem that can be solved by a digital computer need not be described by an exact mathematical equation, but it does need a certain set of rules that the computer can follow. If a problem needs intuition or guessing, or is so badly defined that it is hard to put into words, the computer cannot solve it. Considerable thought must be put into defining the problem and setting it up for the computer in such a way that every possible alternative is taken care of by the computer program.

When the engineer begins to develop a program, he must be familiar with several aspects of the situation:

1. He must thoroughly understand the problem and be able to determine if it is feasible to solve it on a computer.
2. He must know the different operations that can be performed by the computer system available to him.
3. He must understand what the program output is to be.

The engineer should remember that computers are used to implement the solutions to problems. Computers do not solve problems—*people* solve problems. The computer carries out the solution as specified by people.

There are six steps that the engineer must use when he solves a problem with a computer:

1. Problem analysis.
2. Flowcharting.
3. Coding.
4. Translation.
5. Testing.
6. Documentation.

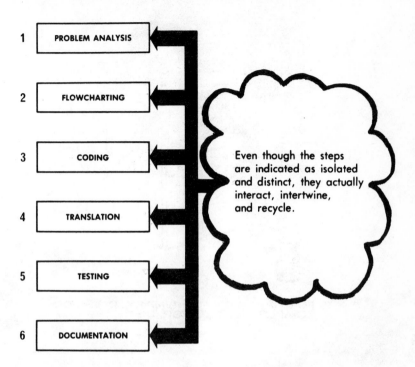

Fig. 4-1. Steps used in solving a problem with a computer.

Fig. 4-1 indicates these steps and calls attention to the recycling among them. This chapter will consider each of the six steps.

PROBLEM ANALYSIS

Before a problem can be solved on a computer, the following questions must be answered:

1. Is the problem worth doing?
2. Can the problem be solved with a computer?
3. Do we know how to solve the problem on a computer?
4. Can the computer in question solve the problem?
5. What are the inputs and outputs?
6. What language will be used?
7. Have parts of the problem already been programmed?

After the engineer answers these questions, he can better determine whether or not a problem should be solved by a computer.

"A IS FOR APL, B IS FOR BINARY, C IS FOR
COMPUTER, D IS FOR DISK..."

The problem-analysis step includes the proper definition of the problem. Although it sounds strange, we must know *exactly* what the problem is before attempting to solve it. People often ask such questions as: "Can you play chess with a computer?" "Can you simulate the operations of a jet aircraft with a computer?" "Can you automate a business accounting system on a computer?" "Can you monitor the operation of our plant with a computer?" Of course, all of these things can be accomplished with a computer; however, it may take several human-months or even human-years to define the problem adequately.

Generally, a problem is defined when you have identified all the inputs and outputs and are in a position to flowchart a solution to the problem. Prior to flowcharting, however, a method of solution must be selected. In engineering work, we often use an *algorithm*, which is an efficient step-by-step procedure for solving a complex problem. It is a defined process that guarantees an answer. If an efficient procedure is not available, it is perfectly proper to use a less sophisticated method; i.e., a crude, brute-force, inefficient method of solution. After this unsophisticated method is working on the computer, the engineer can usually find better and more clever ways of rewriting part of the program. The important thing to remember is that some method of solution must be available before a computer can be used.

FLOWCHARTING

As shown in Fig. 4-1, after we analyze a problem, we should make a *flowchart* of the solution. A flowchart is a drawing that helps organize a problem. It is a pictorial view of the logic used to solve the problem. A flowchart is composed of special symbols connected by straight lines. Perhaps the best way to explain a flowchart is to show one and describe how it works. Fig. 4-2 is a flowchart of a program to perform a simple read-compute-print operation. Let us trace the flow of the program by using this flowchart.

The program starts with the oval box (box 1) at the top and proceeds in the direction of the arrows. In box 2, the program reads a card. The next box (box 3) indicates that some computation is to be performed. Box 4 specifies that the computed answer is to be printed. The next step (box 5) is to determine if the program is to read more cards. If it is, the program then goes back to the top and reads another card. The program repeats itself as long as there are more cards to read. This repeating process is called *looping*. When there are no more cards to read, the program stops (box 6).

The flowchart in Fig. 4-2 uses five different symbols to indicate different operations. Using different shapes for different functions helps to organize the flowchart and makes it easier to read. To increase the probability that one engineer will be able to understand another's flowchart, certain conventional symbols have been standardized and widely adopted for flowcharting procedures. The symbols shown in

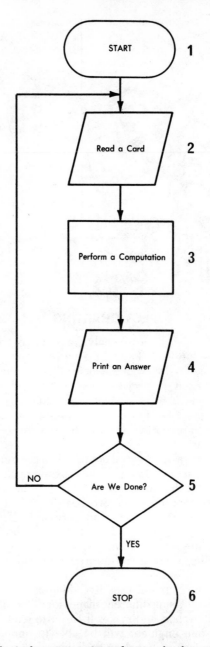

Fig. 4-2. Flowchart of a program to perform a simple read-compute-print operation.

Table 4-1 are sufficient to flowchart most engineering problems. These are the only symbols used in flowcharts in this book.

To aid in the preparation of flowcharts, special plastic templates (Fig. 4-3) containing cutouts of the flowchart symbols are obtainable from a number of sources, such as the various computer manufacturers, college bookstores, etc.

Table 4-1. Standard Flowcharting Symbols

Symbol	Symbol Name	Symbol Use
	Process Symbol	Used to define a process, an operation or set of operations, memory assignments, arithmetic calculations, and other instructions or operations not assigned to any other symbol.
	Decision Symbol	Used to indicate points in a program where a change in program control is to be made based on some type of decision or logical choice.
	Terminal Symbol	Used to indicate the beginning or end of a program.
	Predefined Process Symbol	Used to indicate a subroutine; i. e., prewritten program steps that are specified elsewhere.
	Preparation Symbol	Used to initialize or set up a storage location.
	Input/Output Symbol	Used to indicate any input/output operation not covered by a specific symbol.
	Connector Symbol	Used to indicate a junction in the logic flow. Represents an entry from, or an exit to, another part of the flowchart.
	Flowline Symbol	Used to indicate the sequence or continuity of operations in a flowchart. Direction is indicated by arrows.
	Annotation Symbol	Used to add descriptive comments or clarifying notes about the program.

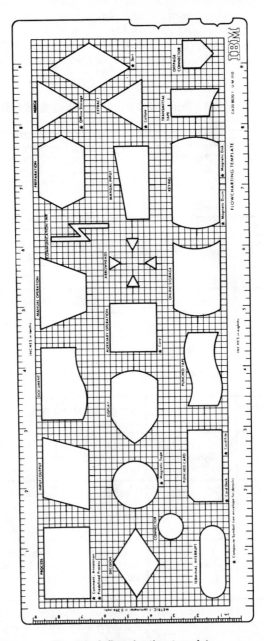

Fig. 4-3. A flowcharting template.

As indicated in Table 4-1, oval boxes are used to show a *start* or *stop* point. The diamond-shaped box is used for making a *decision*. Calculations such as

$$A = \pi r \left(r^2 + h^2\right)^{1/2}$$

are placed in rectangular *process* boxes. Prewritten programs, such as subroutines, are identified by using the *predefined process* symbol. A small circle identifies a junction point of the program. Input/output operations are placed in the *input/output* symbol. Comments are added to flowcharts by using the *annotation* symbol. All of these symbols are connected by directional *flowlines*; i.e., straight lines with arrows.

There are several reasons why we draw flowcharts:

1. To present the logic used in solving a problem in pictorial form.
2. To provide a means of communicating the program logic to other people.
3. To divide a large problem into several smaller, more manageable segments. The smaller segments can be coded by one or several people without regard to the complete problem.
4. To provide a visual description of the data process, which allows better control over computer operations.
5. To provide engineers and programmers with a detailed blueprint to be used in writing a computer program.
6. Flowcharts are relatively simple, easy to prepare, easy to read and use, and are free of ambiguities.

Flowcharting is, perhaps, the best method available for expressing what computers can do—or what you want them to do. The flowchart shown in Fig. 4-2 is a simple one. Most programs and flowcharts are not that simple. Let us now look at several other problems and flowcharts.

The angular *mil* is a very useful unit for some special aspects of angle and arc measurement. Some conversion factors for the angular mil are:

$$1° = 17.777778 \text{ mils}$$
$$90° = 1600 \text{ mils}$$
$$1 \text{ mil} = 0.05625°$$
$$1 \text{ mil} = 0.00098175 \text{ radians}$$

The length of arc on the circumference of a circle of radius, r, is approximately

$$\frac{r\alpha}{1000}$$

where α is the subtended angle in mils.

The flowchart in Fig. 4-4 shows a program that will print a table for

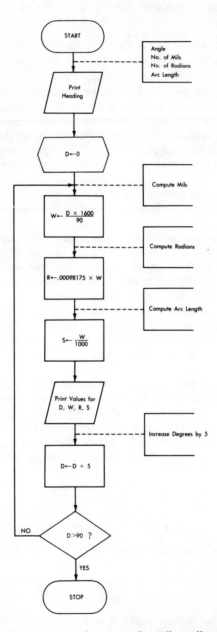

Fig. 4-4. Flowchart of a program for computing mils, radians, and arc lengths.

angles 0°, 5°, 10°, . . ., 90° showing mils, arc lengths, and radians. Let us trace the flowchart step by step.

The program begins at the START symbol at the top and goes in the direction of the arrows at all times. The first step is to print a heading with listings for ANGLE, NO. OF MILS, NO. OF RADIANS, and ARC LENGTH. The program then sets D to be equal to 0. This will be the value of degrees at this point.

The program then enters a loop—a series of steps repeated over and over a number of times. The loop starts with a calculation for mils (W). The next block in the flowchart shows the calculation of radians (R). An arc-length (S) computation is specified by the next box. Then the program prints values for D (degrees), W (mils), R (radians), and S (arc length).

Next, the program adds 5 to the number of degrees (D) and repeats the calculations for mils, radians, and arc length, this time with D equal to 5. Then it prints the number of degrees (D), calculates new values for mils, radians, and arc length, and prints them. Again 5 is added to the number of degrees, and the computations are repeated with D equal to 10. The loop has an end, however, when the number of degrees exceeds 90 (D > 90). Thus, as long as D is less than or equal to 90, the program runs as before. But when D exceeds 90, the decision box takes the program out of the loop and into the STOP symbol.

The previous example for calculating mils, radians, and arc lengths had only one loop. Let us now draw a flowchart with two loops, one inside the other. This flowchart also includes a subroutine with a single loop.

Fig. 4-5 shows the flowchart of a program that computes the base 3, 6, 8, and 2 equivalents of the base 10 numbers 5, 10, 15, 20, 25, . . . , 150, and prints a table similar to the following:

NUMBER	BASE 3	BASE 6	OCTAL	BINARY
5	12	5	5	101
10	101	14	12	1010
•	•	•	•	•
•	•	•	•	•
•	•	•	•	•

(Note: OCTAL is base 8 and BINARY is base 2.)

The program uses the following procedure in converting a number from base 10 to another base: Assume that you wanted to find the base 8 equivalent of decimal (or base 10) number 100. One proceeds as follows:

$$
\begin{array}{r}
8\ \underline{|\ 100} \\
8\ \underline{|\ 12}\quad \text{remainder} = 4 \\
8\ \underline{|\ 1}\quad \text{remainder} = 4 \\
0\quad \text{remainder} = 1
\end{array}
\left.\vphantom{\begin{array}{c}1\\2\\3\\4\end{array}}\right\}
\begin{array}{l}
\text{Read the} \\
\text{remainder} \\
\text{values in} \\
\text{reverse order.}
\end{array}
$$

152   Computers and Programming Guide for Scientists and Engineers

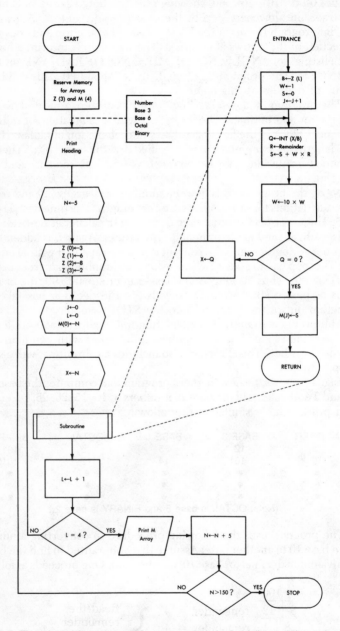

Fig. 4-5. Flowchart of a program for converting decimal (base 10) numbers to four other bases.

Thus, 100 (base 10) = 144 (base 8).

For another example, find the base 3 equivalent of 85 (base 10):

$$
\begin{array}{r l}
3 \;\rule{0.5pt}{0pt}\; 85 & \\
3 \;\rule{0.5pt}{0pt}\; 28 & \text{remainder} = 1 \\
3 \;\rule{0.5pt}{0pt}\; 9 & \text{remainder} = 1 \\
3 \;\rule{0.5pt}{0pt}\; 3 & \text{remainder} = 0 \\
3 \;\rule{0.5pt}{0pt}\; 1 & \text{remainder} = 0 \\
0 & \text{remainder} = 1
\end{array}
$$

Thus, 85 (base 10) = 10011 (base 3)

We start at the top of the flowchart. The first box after the START symbol specifies that computer storage is to be reserved for arrays Z and M. The next box causes a heading to be printed. The next step is to set N to 5. This will be the first value to be converted to bases 3, 6, 8, and 2. The next box sets the values 3, 6, 8, and 2 in $Z(0)$, $Z(1)$, $Z(2)$, and $Z(3)$. The program next enters a loop that starts with J and L being set to 0, and $M(0)$ being set to N. The next box starts another loop with X being set to N. The box labeled *Subroutine* is not just one operation, but actually an entire series of steps. This shows that a flowchart can be as simple or as complicated as we wish. The subroutine includes the operations required to compute an equivalent number in a specified number base; $Z(L)$ contains the specified number base and X is the number. After performing this computation, the subroutine returns control to the main program.

After referencing the subroutine to compute a number base conversion, the program increases the counter L by 1 until L reaches 4. The decision box containing L = 4? will either direct the program to loop back and perform another number conversion (by referencing the subroutine again) or to perform the next in-line step, printing the contents of array M. At this point, array M contains the converted values: $M(0)$ = decimal number N, $M(1)$ = base 3 equivalent of N, $M(2)$ = base 6 equivalent of N, $M(3)$ = octal equivalent of N, and $M(4)$ = binary equivalent of N. The next box specifies that N is to be increased by 5. If N does not exceed 150, then the next decision box loops the program back to perform the same computations with a new value for N. If N exceeds 150, then the decision box takes the program out of the loop and into the STOP symbol.

CODING

Coding means writing instructions for a sequence of computer operations. Normally, one codes from flowcharts. One flowchart symbol may become several instructions or statements. These are recorded on

preprinted coding sheets such as the one shown in Fig. 4-6. These statements are then usually keypunched into punched cards.

Few engineers (or programmers) can write a program involving a hundred or more statements without error. Some of the more common types of errors are:

- Keypunching errors.
- Confusion of characters; e.g., S for 5, 1 for I, Z for 2, etc.
- Unreferenced symbols.
- Ambiguous decisions.
- Unprogrammed branches.

An engineer can find many program mistakes by reviewing the flowcharts of processing operations and associated coding sheets very carefully. Some have other engineers check their work. This checking process is often called *desk checking*. Desk checking usually does not detect all errors but does detect enough to make the process worthwhile.

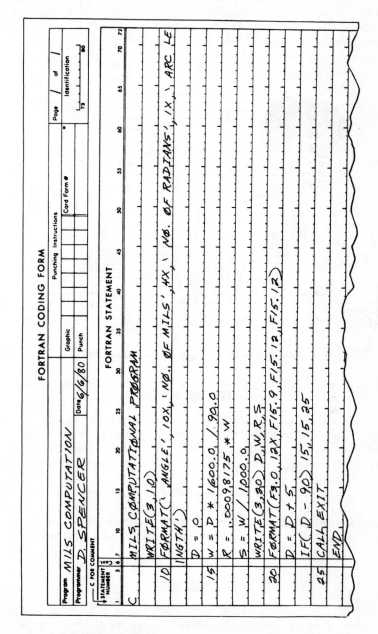

FORTRAN CODING FORM

Program MILS COMPUTATION

Programmer D. SPENCER   Date 6/6/80

Punching Instructions

Graphic   Punch

Card Form #

Page 1 of 1

Identification

FORTRAN STATEMENT

```
C      MILS COMPUTATIONAL PROGRAM
       WRITE(3,10)
10     FORMAT(' ANGLE', 10X, 'NO. OF MILS', 4X, ' NO. OF RADIANS', 1X, ' ARC LE
      1NGTH')
       D = 0
15     W = D * 1600.0 / 90.0
       R = 1.0009875 * W
       S = W / 1000.0
       WRITE(3,80) D,W,R,S
20     FORMAT(F3.0, 12X,F15.9,F15.12,F15.12)
       D = D + 5
       IF( D - 90) 15,15,25
25     CALL EXIT
       END
```

Fig. 4-6. FORTRAN program of the flowchart shown in Fig. 4-4.

Fig. 4-6 illustrates the coded program of the flowchart shown in Fig. 4-4. This program was coded in a language, used by many engineers, called FORTRAN. Another programming language that engineers use considerably is called BASIC. Fig. 4-7 illustrates a BASIC program of the flowchart shown in Fig. 4-5.

TRANSLATION

After all mistakes detected in the desk check have been diagnosed and corrected, the program (called a *source-language* program) is ready to be translated into instructions that the computer understands. This translated program is an end product of the translation process and is called an *object* program.

The translation process is discussed in detail in Chapter 5. This process also produces messages (called *diagnostics*) indicating the type and location of additional mistakes in the program. It is the engineer's job to respond to these diagnostic messages by making the indicated or necessary modifications to the program.

TESTING

After the program has been translated into a language that the computer understands, it is necessary to execute the program on the computer. It is in this step that the engineer determines if his program

```
10    REM   NUMBER CONVERSION PROGRAM
20    DIM Z[3]
30    DIM M[4]
40    REM   PRINT HEADING
50    PRINT "NUMBER","BASE 3","BASE 6","OCTAL","BINARY"
60    PRINT
70    LET N=5
80    LET Z[0]=3
90    LET Z[1]=6
100   LET Z[2]=8
110   LET Z[3]=2
120   LET J=0
130   LET L=0
140   LET M[0]=N
150   LET X=N
160   REM   REFERENCE SUBROUTINE
170   GOSUB   280
180   REM   RETURN FROM SUBROUTINE
190   LET L=L+1
200   IF L<4 THEN   150
210   PRINT M[0],M[1],M[2],M[3],M[4]
220   REM   INCREASE N BY 5
230   LET N=N+5
240   REM   LOOP IF N DOES NOT EXCEED 150
250   IF N<=150 THEN 120
260   STOP
270   REM   START SUBROUTINE
280   LET B=Z[L]
290   LET W=1
300   LET S=0
310   LET J=J+1
320   LET Q=INT(X/B)
330   LET R=X-B*Q
340   LET S=S+W*R
350   LET W=10*W
360   IF Q=0 THEN   390
370   LET X=Q
380   GOTO 320
390   LET M[J]=S
400   REM   END OF SUBROUTINE
410   REM   RETURN TO MAIN PROGRAM
420   RETURN
430   END
```

Fig. 4-7. BASIC program of the flowchart shown in Fig. 4-5.

works properly (it usually does not on the first try) and, if not, he makes the necessary program revisions to make it work properly. This step is called program *testing* or *debugging*.

Programming is an exercise in logical thinking. There is no place for loose ends or fuzzy thinking; otherwise, program mistakes are bound to occur and will show up during the testing process. Computer manufacturers often offer software routines to help the engineer test his programs. Debugging aids such as trace routines, memory-dump routines, and register-dump routines are often helpful in testing programs. Debugging systems are available on many computers that provide the engineer with routines designed specifically to help him detect program errors. These systems allow the engineer to enter breakpoints (where the computer will stop) and to use the typewriter to enter data into the computer and to receive printouts. Debugging aids help the engineer obtain clues to his program errors. Perhaps the engineer should remember some of the so-called "axioms" of programming:

- Every computer program contains at least one "bug." (A bug is a program mistake.)
- If there is a bug, the computer will find it.
- If anything *can* go wrong, it *will*.

DOCUMENTATION

After the program is working, the engineer should put together a documentation package for others to use. This package should include at least:

1. An English language description of the problem.
2. A flowchart.
3. A symbolic listing of the program.
4. A list of instructions needed to operate the program, including console switch settings.
5. Description of files and record layouts.
6. Test cases and sample results.
7. A list of error conditions.
8. A source-language deck of punched cards or roll of punched paper tape.

The documentation of programs contributes to their usefulness. Well-documented programs are extremely valuable whenever the program is to be rewritten on another computer or whenever someone other than the originator is to modify the program. There is no excuse for poorly documented programs.

" BILL ... THERE'S GOT TO BE MORE TO A VACATION THAN TENNIS AND TOURING COMPUTER STORES ! "

EXERCISES

1. Discuss the main aspects of the problem situation with which the engineer must be concerned before solving a problem on a computer.

2. List and briefly discuss the six steps the engineer uses when solving a problem on a computer.

3. Identify the following flowcharting symbols.

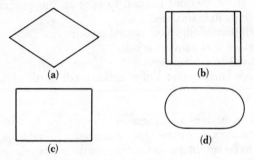

(a)   (b)

(c)   (d)

4. What is a template?

5. Draw a flowchart of a procedure that will loop and compute the value of c, represented by the following:

$$c = \sum_{i\,=\,1}^{4} a_1b_1 + a_2b_2 + a_3b_3 + a_4b_4$$

6. A manufacturer of commercial hardware makes many different parts. He keeps his inventory by punching a card for each part made. These cards contain such information as the part number, color, cost, and selling price. The plant manager has asked for a program to count the number of red, right- and left-handed "woozles" now in stock. Draw a flowchart for a program that can accomplish this.

7. Draw a flowchart to read 100 numbers, to count the number of positive numbers in the list, and to calculate their sum. Print the number of positive numbers and the sum.

8. Draw a flowchart of a program used to calculate the volume of the solid shown in the accompanying sketch. Assume that only the dimensions shown are stored in the computer's memory.

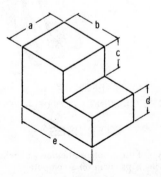

9. Draw a flowchart that will read the value of x and calculate the value of sine x correct to ±0.0005. Use the series approximation:

$$\sin x = x - \frac{x^3}{3!} + \frac{x^5}{5!} - \frac{x^7}{7!} \dots$$

You will have to determine how many terms are required for the given accuracy. Assume x will be:

$$0 < x < \frac{\pi}{2}$$

10. Draw a flowchart of a program that can be used to compute the focal length of a convex lens (see the accompanying sketch):

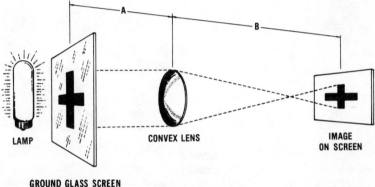

LAMP   CONVEX LENS   IMAGE
                                                                   ON SCREEN

GROUND GLASS SCREEN
WITH CROSS AS OBJECT

By varying the distance A, and the resultant distance B, a series of values of A and B can be obtained. Assume that ten pairs of values for A and B are used and determine an average value of F using the formula:

$$F = \frac{AB}{A + B}$$

The program should read in one pair of A and B values at a time, calculate the equivalent F value, and then accumulate the F values until the end of the program. The total F values should then be divided by 10 to give an average F value.

11. The "Southern Aircraft Company" has been taking hundreds of exhaust temperature readings of their newest engine. The engineers require a program that will give them the average temperature, the number of readings processed, the number of readings below 1000°C, and the number above 2000°C. Draw a flowchart of this program.

12. Draw a flowchart of a procedure to read a value for N, and calculate and print N! (read N-factorial); that is,

$$N! = N (N - 1) (N - 2) \dots (1)$$

For example:

$$7! = 7 \times 6 \times 5 \times 4 \times 3 \times 2 \times 1$$

13. Define coding.

14. What is meant by a program "bug"?

15. Why is it necessary to debug a computer program?

CHAPTER **5**

THE LANGUAGE OF COMPUTERS

The key to the successful use of a computer is *programming*. The computer cannot add two numbers unless it has been so directed. In fact, the simplest task can be a major problem for the computer if poorly programmed; paradoxically, however, the most complex problem can be a simple task when properly programmed.

Programming involves writing a set of instructions in a sequence that will produce a desired result when the sequence is executed on the computer. These instructions are stored in the internal memory of the computer. The data, or information upon which these operations are performed, is also stored in the internal memory of the computer.

As stated in Chapter 4, writing sequences of instructions is called *coding*. Coding can take place at various levels, ranging from machine language (basic language of the computer) to problem-oriented language (programming language in problem terminology). These different levels are:

- Machine language.
- Assembly language.
- Procedure-oriented language.
- Problem-oriented language.

All coding levels except machine language are symbolic in nature and must be translated into machine-language instructions. The computer operates at the level of machine coding; therefore, all other codes must eventually be translated into that form.

THE STORED-PROGRAM CONCEPT

The first electronic digital computer, ENIAC (*E*lectronic *N*umerical *I*ntegrator *A*nd *C*alculator), was directed to perform its functions by means of wired control panels and switches. ENIAC had more than a hundred control lines along which instructions could be sent. Basically,

ENIAC could be instructed to solve a problem in two ways: (1) the plugging of the control lines into sockets or hubs and (2) the setting of switches. The difficulty with ENIAC was that with each new problem a new set of control lines had to be plugged into different sockets to enter the new set of instructions. Sometimes it took several days to perform this operation.

Even before ENIAC was completed, the group at the Moore School of Electrical Engineering of the University of Pennsylvania—John W. Mauchly, J. P. Eckert, A. W. Burks, H. H. Goldstine, and others—together with consultant Dr. John von Neumann, talked over ideas for a new machine called the EDVAC (Electronic Discrete Variable Automatic Computer), which was to have an internally stored program.

In 1945, Dr. von Neumann wrote a document entitled *First Draft of a Report on the EDVAC*. Imbedded in this document was the remarkable idea of a *stored program*, now universal to computers. He suggested that the instructions for the computer—always before entered on punched paper tape, or by wired plugboards—could be stored in the computer's electronic memory as numbers, and treated in exactly the same manner as numerical data. For the first time, then, logical choices of program sequences could be made *inside* the machine, and the instructions could be modified by the computer as it went along.

Another stored-program computer, called the EDSAC (Electronic Delay Storage Automatic Computer), was being developed at Cambridge University in England at about the same time. This computer used the same concepts that Dr. von Neumann had proposed for the EDVAC.

MACHINE-LANGUAGE PROGRAMMING

Basic instructions to a computer consist of operations such as *add, subtract, multiply, divide, store, load, read, write, shift*, etc. A machine-language instruction consists of an *operation code* and one or more *operands*. Fig. 5-1 illustrates a machine-language instruction with two operands. The operation code refers to the part of the instruction that specifies the operation to be performed, such as *add* or *read*. The operands refer to the part of the instruction that references a location within the computer where the data to be processed is stored. In the example, the operation code (34) indicates that the computer is to perform an addition operation. The operands (20100 and 26430) specify the computer memory locations of the data to be added.

A *program* is a meaningful sequence of instructions or statements possessing an implicit or explicit order of execution. A program written in machine language is a sequence of numbers, such as that shown in Fig. 5-2.

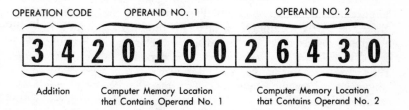

Although machine language provides for economy of construction, it is usually inconvenient for direct human use. Machine language also requires that the user have a thorough knowledge of the computer, its peculiarities, and its intricate details. It was inevitable that languages

Fig. 5-1. A machine-language instruction.

MACHINE-LANGUAGE CODING FORM			
OPER	OP1	OP2	COMMENTS
42	00003	26400	LOAD REGISTER WITH C
14	00003	32000	MULTIPLY BY B
34	00003	25300	ADD A
27	00003	41000	STORE AS D

Fig. 5-2. Machine-language program to compute $d = a + b \times c$.

had to be developed that were easier to learn, easier to write, and easier to remember. It was also inevitable that numbers be replaced by symbols and words that could be better understood by the human user.

SYMBOLIC LANGUAGES

Symbolic languages were developed to overcome the many inconveniences of machine language. Symbolic coding involves programming a computer to recognize instructions in a language more easily understood by the user, and then translating these expressions into machine language. This concept has led to the development of a large number of different symbolic programming languages that are easy to use and understand.

Before looking at the various types of symbolic languages, let us define several terms. As stated earlier, a *program* is a meaningful sequence of *statements*. Statements, in turn, are strings of symbols from a given alphabet composed of letters, digits, and special characters. The form of each statement obeys a set of rules *(syntax)* and possesses an operational meaning *(semantics)*. Collectively, the alphabet, syntax, and semantics are termed a *language*.

A *source program* is a computer program written in a symbolic language. The instructions or statements of a source program are processed in the computer in order to produce a program that can eventually be executed on the machine. This processing function is called *translating*, and the processor program is called a *translator*. Thus, the translator converts a program written in a symbolic source language into machine language. This machine-language program is called an *object program*. A translator, then, converts a source program into an object program. The object program is the program that is run on the computer to produce the desired results.

Symbolic languages are more suitable for human use than is machine language. They are designed to facilitate computer programming, and they tend to be associated in some sense with the problems under consideration. One of the features that hastened the widespread acceptance of programming languages is the fact that computer programs written in this more convenient form could be translated into machine language by another computer program running on the same or possibly a different computer. One of the significant aspects of the philosophy behind the use of symbolic languages and translator programs is the fact that the same computer may process programs written in many different languages, provided that a translator program has been written for each language.

"RALPH, OUR COMPUTER HAD A MALFUNCTION...
CAN YOU THINK IN MICROSECONDS ?"

ASSEMBLY LANGUAGE CODING

The most primitive type of symbolic language is known as *assembly language,* which provides operations that are very similar to the machine language of the computer being used. In this language, all operation codes of the computer are given a *mnemonic* designation. All machine addresses in the commands are written using symbolic designators. This type of language relieves the programmer of many intricate coding details; however, it takes as many symbolic instructions to solve a problem as it does machine instructions. As in machine-language coding, the user must have a thorough knowledge of the computer and its operation.

There are three advantages to using assembly-language coding rather than machine-language coding:

1. It is easier to write.
2. It is easier to read.
3. It is easier to modify.

Many assembly-language assemblers contain facilities for establishing constants and storage areas, for communicating with the assembler program itself, and for incorporating sets of standard instruction sequences into the machine-language program.

A statement in assembly language consists of one to four entries: (1) *location*, (2) *operation*, (3) *operand*, and (4) *comment*. An *add* operation in assembly language would look like the following:

ADD REG3, TEMP

The ADD in the instruction is the symbolic code for the addition function, and REG3 and TEMP in the operand portion of the instruction provide for a symbolic representation of the storage locations.

If we wanted to compute $d = a + b \times c$ in assembly language, we might write the sequence of symbolic instructions shown in Fig. 5-3. Before the computer could use this program, it would be necessary to translate these symbolic instructions into machine-language form.

Assembly language was certainly a significant improvement over machine language. However, even with the use of assembly language, it has been reported that over 90% of the time required to solve problems utilizing a computer was devoted to defining the problem, writing the program, and correcting mistakes that had occurred during the

ASSEMBLY-LANGUAGE CODING FORM				
LOCATION	OPERATION	OPERAND 1	OPERAND 2	COMMENTS
BEGIN	LD	REG 3	C	LOAD C INTO REGISTER 3
	MUL	REG 3	B	MULTIPLY REGISTER 3 BY B
	ADD	REG 3	A	ADD A TO REGISTER 3
	STR	REG 3	D	STORE REGISTER 3 AT D

Fig. 5-3. Assembly-language program to compute $d = a + b \times c$.

programming process. It has been found in many installations that approximately 80% of the cost of solving an engineering-type problem is caused by the extensive time required to program the computer. Only 20% of the cost is for the actual utilization of the computer.

In the mid 1950s, several projects were started to develop programming languages that were easier to use and that would not require the user to have a detailed knowledge of the internal characteristics of the computer system. These programming languages were called *procedure-oriented* and *problem-oriented* languages.

PROCEDURE-ORIENTED LANGUAGES

In contrast to assembly language and machine language, in which the source language is still highly dependent upon a particular hardware system, *procedure-oriented* languages relate to the procedures being coded and are, thus, relatively machine-independent. Therefore, a program coded in a procedure-oriented language can be executed on any computer system that has a translator available for that programming language.

Many procedure-oriented programming languages have been developed. This is primarily because this type of language simplifies the programming task. The use of a procedure-oriented language reduces the requirement that the user have a detailed knowledge of digital computers. This, in turn, allows the user to concentrate more deeply on steps that are more closely related to the problem. Procedure-oriented programming languages are widely accepted and used by persons not having a strong background in machine-language programming or computer equipment.

A program can be written in a much shorter time period when a procedure-oriented language is used, primarily because the language includes a set of very powerful instructions. A procedure-oriented language instruction may accomplish the same operation as several lower-level machine instructions. Both the coding and debugging tasks are simplified when one uses a procedure-oriented language. Many of these languages are self-documenting; i.e., a listing of the program will suffice for documentation purposes. However, this usually applies only to very small programs. A brief description of several procedure-oriented languages follows.

The major procedure-oriented programming languages are BASIC, FORTRAN, COBOL, and, to a lesser extent, PL/1, Pascal, APL, and RPG. These languages were developed by computer manufacturers and by committees consisting of representatives from manufacturers and users to make the computer available directly without having to work through an intermediary symbolic or machine-language programmer. The ease of learning and the ease of coding make it possible for a computer user to learn programming in a short time. Through the use of a terminal, or by coding the program on the proper coding form, the user can run the programs and produce the answer with little effort.

The FORTRAN language is discussed in Chapter 6, and BASIC is covered in Chapter 7. In the following sections, PL/1, APL, COBOL, Pascal, and RPG are briefly described.

"OF COURSE NOBODY UNDERSTANDS YOU; YOU ONLY SPEAK PL/1!"

PL/1 (Programming Language/1)

PL/1 is a general-purpose programming language that can be used for both commercial and scientific applications. PL/1 aims at combining the problem-solving facilities of scientific languages with the data-handling capabilities of commercial business languages in order to produce a language that may be used equally well in either application.

While PL/1 can be a very simple language to use, it can also be employed to handle extremely complex computing problems. One of its most important characteristics is its modularity; that is, the presence of different subsets of the language for different applications at different levels of complexity. The language has a block structure that allows program segmentation into blocks of language statements or subroutines of a total program.

PL/1 is versatile enough to process a wide variety of data types, such as fixed and floating-point numbers, and character and bit strings. The language structure is *free form*. No special forms are needed for coding, since the significance of each statement depends on its own format and not on its position within a fixed framework. Each PL/1 statement terminates with a semicolon (;). Because the PL/1 compiler recognizes the semicolon as a terminator, part of a statement, or many statements, can be written on one coding line.

PL/1 has the best debugging capability of all existing programming languages. A *default* feature, by which every error or unspecified option is given a valid interpretation, minimizes the effect of programming errors. For example, a PL/1 compiler, when confronted with an unmatched left parenthesis, will automatically insert a right parenthesis in the proper place.

Fig. 5-4 shows a PL/1 program that will read the maximum and minimum temperatures for every day of the week, and calculate and print the average daily temperature.

" I THINK IT'S A SUBSET OF THE APL LANGUAGE! "

```
WEATHER: PROCEDURE;
      DECLARE MAXDAY(7), MINDAY(7), AVERAGE(7);
      READ LIST ((MAXDAY(I), MINDAY(I)) I = 1 TO 7);
      AVERAGE = (MAXDAY + MINDAY) / 2;
      WRITE ((MAXDAY(I), MINDAY(I), AVERAGE(I))
      I = 1 TO 7) (2F(5), F(8, 1), SPACE);
END WEATHER;
```

Fig. 5-4. A PL/1 program to compute average daily temperature.

APL (*A Programming Language*)

APL is a language for describing procedures in the processing of information. It can be used to describe mathematical procedures having nothing to do with computers, or to describe (to a human being) how a computer works. Most commonly, however, it is used for programming in the ordinary sense of directing computers how to process numeric or alphabetic data.

APL is one of the most concise, consistent, and powerful programming languages ever devised. Operations on single items extend simply and naturally to arrays of any size and shape. Thus, for instance, a matrix addition that in other higher-level languages might require two loops and a half-dozen statements, becomes simply A + B in APL.

The language is very mathematically oriented. It is, however, finding widespread acceptance among a variety of users, many of them in business and education. Fig. 5-5 shows an APL program that computes the total sales of five salesmen, each of whom sells the same three products.

COBOL (*COmmon Business-Oriented Language*)

COBOL is an internationally accepted programming language developed for general commercial and business use. It is a high-level compiler language in which the source program is written using statements in restricted English, but in readable form. A program coded in COBOL bears little resemblance to a computer machine code. For example, in an accounting program where new stock received is added to inventory, the COBOL statement might appear as "ADD RECEIPTS TO STOCK ON HAND."

The COBOL compiler would examine each word of this statement separately. "ADD" becomes an operating instruction. "RECEIPTS" is a location where data are located. "TO" directs attention to what follows, "STOCK ON HAND." "STOCK ON HAND" represents data stored

```
        ∇SALES1
 [1]    'ENTER P'
 [2]    P←□
 [3]    'ENTER S'
 [4]    S←3 5ρ□
 [5]    J←1
 [6]    TOTAL←+/P×S[;J]
 [7]    'TOTAL SALES FOR SALESMAN ';J;' IS ';TOTAL
 [8]    →6×ι5≥J←J+1
        ∇

        SALES1
ENTER P
□:
        1.25 4.30 2.50
ENTER S
□:
        40 20 37 29 42 10 16 3 21 8 35 47 29 16 33
TOTAL SALES FOR SALESMAN 1 IS 180.5
TOTAL SALES FOR SALESMAN 2 IS 211.3
TOTAL SALES FOR SALESMAN 3 IS 131.65
TOTAL SALES FOR SALESMAN 4 IS 166.55
TOTAL SALES FOR SALESMAN 5 IS 169.4
```

Fig. 5-5. An APL program.

somewhere in computer storage. After thus analyzing this statement, the COBOL compiler would generate several machine-code instructions that could be used to carry out this specific calculation.

COBOL provides facilities for describing the program, specifying the computer it is to be run on, indicating the data formats and files it will use, and stating the operations to be performed on the data. Each COBOL program is broken down into four major divisions:

1. THE IDENTIFICATION DIVISION is used to identify the programmer's name, the name of the program, the outputs of the compilation, along with the date, location, and security classification of compilation.

2. THE ENVIRONMENT DIVISION is used to identify the equipment needed for compiling the source program and for executing the object program.

3. THE DATA DIVISION is used to describe the files and records that the object program is to manipulate or create.

4. THE PROCEDURE DIVISION is used to tell the computer the steps to be performed using data described in the DATA DIVISION in order to solve the problem.

COBOL uses a large number of reserved words that have special meanings. For example, reserved words such as "MULTIPLY," "INSPECT," "SORT," and "ASSIGN" have special meaning to the COBOL compiler and must be used according to COBOL language rules. These words, which number about 300, are an inherent part of the COBOL language and are not available for use as data or procedure names. In the statement, "ADD OVERTIME TO NORMAL HOURS," the reserved words are "ADD" and "TO," which instruct the COBOL compiler to generate the machine code necessary to perform addition. "OVERTIME" and "NORMAL HOURS" (defined in the DATA DIVISION) will be names or labels referring to units of data.

Fig. 5-6 is a sample COBOL program. It is easily read, even by a nonprogrammer, because of its similarity to English. Since COBOL programs are relatively machine-independent, they can be compiled and run on a variety of different machines. Many users develop all their programs in this language, mainly to bridge the gap between the computer they are using today and computer systems that will eventually replace them.

IBM

COBOL Coding Form

GX28-1464-5 U/M 050*
Printed in U.S.A.

SYSTEM					
PROGRAM	SAMPLE PROGRAM		PUNCHING INSTRUCTIONS		PAGE / OF /
PROGRAMMER	D. D. SPENCER	DATE 10/16/78	GRAPHIC		CARD FORM #	*
			PUNCH		

SEQUENCE		CONT	A	B	COBOL STATEMENT	IDENTIFICATION
(PAGE)	(SERIAL)					
3 4	6	7 8	12 16	20 24 28 32 36 40 44 48 52 56 60 64 68 72 76 80	
0 0 1	0 1 0		IDENTIFICATION DIVISION.		
0 0 1	0 2 0		PROGRAM-ID. SAMPLE.		
0 0 1	0 5 0		AUTHOR. D. D. SPENCER.		
0 0 1	0 4 0		DATE-WRITTEN. OCTOBER 16, 1978.		
0 0 1	0 5 0		DATE-COMPILED. OCTOBER 18, 1978.		
0 0 1	0 6 0	*	THE SAMPLE PROGRAM COMPUTES AND PRINTS THE PRODUCT OF		
0 0 1	0 7 0		THE VALUES 643 AND 761.		
0 0 1	0 8 0		ENVIRONMENT DIVISION.		
0 0 1	0 9 0		CONFIGURATION SECTION.		
0 0 1	1 0 0		SOURCE-COMPUTER. IBM-370.		
0 0 1	1 1 0		OBJECT-COMPUTER. IBM-370.		
0 0 1	1 2 0		DATA DIVISION.		
0 0 1	1 3 0		WORKING-STORAGE SECTION.		
0 0 1	1 4 0		77 TOTAL PICTURE 9(6).		
0 0 1	1 5 0		77 NUMBER-ONE PICTURE 999 VALUE IS 643.		
0 0 1	1 6 0		77 NUMBER-TWO PICTURE 999 VALUE IS 761.		
0 0 1	1 7 0		PROCEDURE DIVISION.		
0 0 1	1 8 0		CALCULATION. COMPUTE TOTAL = NUMBER-ONE * NUMBER-TWO.		
0 0 1	1 9 0		DISPLAY TOTAL. STOP RUN.		
0 0 1	2 0 0		END PROGRAM.		

*A standard card form, IBM Electro C61897, is available for punching source statements from this form. Instructions for using this form are given in any IBM COBOL reference manual. Address comments concerning this form to IBM Corporation, LDS Publishing, Dept. J04, 1501 California Ave., Palo Alto, Ca. 94304

*No. of forms per pad may vary slightly

Fig. 5-6. A sample COBOL program.

Pascal

Pascal is a programming language developed during the early 1970s by Professor Niklaus Wirth in Zurich, Switzerland. Pascal is not an acronym, but was named in honor of the French mathematician and philosopher, Blaise Pascal (1623–1662).

Pascal is one of the newest languages to be used on microcomputers. Although relatively easy to use, it is more powerful than BASIC, FORTRAN, or assembly language. The language has been accepted at many universities for several years and is now becoming more commonplace in industry and business.

Pascal is a highly structured programming language that is extremely popular in the computer science field. It has a number of inherent features that make it highly suitable for the development of sophisticated software using the technique of structured programming. One of the outstanding features of Pascal is that well-written Pascal code is very readable; more so than most other programming languages.

Pascal is a relative newcomer to the world of programming languages. The following table shows just how new Pascal really is. Remember that most compilers are not introduced until three to five years after the initial language specification. For example, Pascal was initially specified in 1968 and the first compiler was available in 1971.

Programming Language	Introduction Date
FORTRAN	1957
ALGOL	1960
LISP	1961
SNOBOL	1962
BASIC	1965
PL/1	1965
APL	1967
Pascal	1971

Pascal was the first major new language to be developed after the concept of structured programming was introduced. The future should see a continued growth in the acceptance of the language in both the academic and commercial environments.

RPG (Report Program Generator)

RPG is a language that has received wide acceptance since the introduction of small third-generation computer systems. The language was designed for business applications in which there is a need for the generation of routine business reports. RPG is easy to use and clerical in nature. Programs are recorded on a series of specification forms. To instruct the computer, the user merely records a series of entries on the specification forms that describe the files, the input, the calculations to be performed, and the output to be produced.

PROBLEM-ORIENTED LANGUAGES

There is really no doubt that procedure-oriented languages have proven their usefulness; there are several hundred different languages of this type currently being used. The main emphasis of this type language development was on the simplification of problem solving. However, certain types of problem calculations recur so frequently in both scientific and business areas that it is worthwhile to have a language for the specific application of these calculations. This led to the development of *problem-oriented* languages. A problem-oriented language is one that is restricted to the description of specialized problems.

A problem-oriented language is designed so that a user can express a problem in a language with which he is familiar. In this way, a problem can be expressed more easily than in a general language such as PL/1 or COBOL. A problem-oriented language is designed for one specific type of problem. A brief description of several problem-oriented languages follows.

COGO (COordinate GeOmetry)

This language provides the capabilities of solving civil engineering, coordinate geometry problems. Civil engineers working on surveying, layout, and highway design problems use certain common terms and operations; e.g., *point, line, area, station, coordinate, azimuth,* and *intersect.* With COGO, the engineer writes a simple listing to locate points, find areas, and do those calculations that occur frequently in his work. Words such as *angle, distance,* and *area* permit him to find the angle formed by three points, the distance between two points, and the area of a polygon—all without writing a single equation.

GPSS (General-Purpose Systems Simulator)

Another example of a problem-oriented language is GPSS, a language that permits a system with queues to be described with relative ease and from which a model may be generated. This language is highly flexible and can simulate many different systems. A model written in GPSS can be steadily increased in complexity or detail until it represents very accurately the behavior of a specific system.

APT (Automatically Programmed Tools)

APT is a language used in numerical control applications for programmed control of machine functions. The APT language allows a user to define points, lines, circles, planes, conical surfaces, and geometric surfaces.

STRESS (STRuctural Engineering Systems Solver)

STRESS is a language designed for use by engineers in analyzing framed structures.

The user of a problem-oriented language need not be a trained programmer; however, the user should be familiar with the problem area in question. If the problems to be solved have complicated descriptions, the user of the problem-oriented language may be required to devote time and effort to learning the details of the language; however, for a given problem area, the learning effort will always be far less for a problem-oriented language than for another type of symbolic language. Problem-oriented languages are discussed in more detail in Chapter 8.

SIMULATION LANGUAGES

In recent years, computer modeling and simulation techniques have been developed and have received widespread attention and application. Simulation languages, such as GPSS and SIMSCRIPT, have been developed to provide the user with tools of simulation. These languages are designed to eliminate much of the tedium involved and to simplify the procedures in preparing simulations for computer implementation. The simulation languages are subdivided into two language types: (1) flowchart-oriented languages and (2) statement-oriented languages.

In the flowchart-oriented languages, the user defines and assembles blocks into a program structure that represents the system to be simulated. The most notable example of this language type is GPSS.

The statement-oriented languages use programming statements to define conditions that must apply before certain actions can take place and to describe the results of the actions. SIMSCRIPT is an example of this type of language.

Chapter 9 discusses simulation languages in more detail.

LANGUAGE TRANSLATION

As previously noted, the computer can execute instructions only in machine-language form. Therefore, a program written in symbolic form must first be translated into machine-language instructions prior to execution on the computer. When assembly language is used, the translator is called an *assembler*. When procedure-oriented or problem-oriented languages are used, the translator is called a *compiler*.*

---

*Both procedure-oriented languages and problem-oriented languages are sometimes called *compiler* languages.

"THIS LETTER FROM HIS TEACHER SAYS HE PRO-
GRAMMED THE COMPUTER TO CHEAT AT CHECKERS!"

Fig. 5-7 illustrates the steps in assembling a program. When the source-language program, written in assembly language, is presented to the computer with the assembler already loaded, the computer translates these symbolic statements into a machine-usable form. The computer does not execute the statements but writes out the object program on punched cards, punched paper tape, magnetic tape, magnetic disk, etc. Then the object program is fed into the computer, and this time the computer executes the machine-language statements, runs the problem, and produces the calculated results. Note that the program must be presented to the computer twice, the first time in source language (the engineer's language) and the second time in object language (the machine's language).

The previous process is used on many smaller computers with limited storage facilities; however, there is another approach called *assembling and running* that combines the two operations.

Fig. 5-8 illustrates a process with the intermediate output process eliminated. The computer assembles the source-language program but instead of outputting the object program, the computer stores it in its own memory. After the object program has been assembled, the

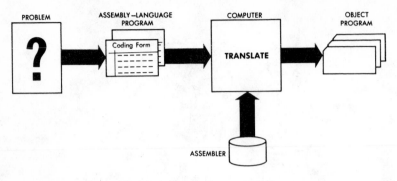

(A) Assemble program process.

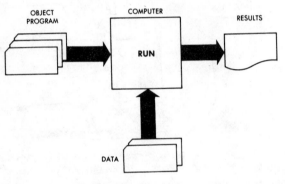

(B) Execute program process.

Fig. 5-7. Assemble and execute programs separately.

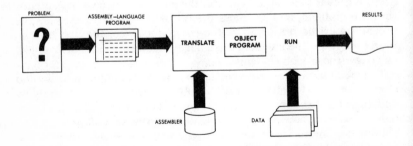

Fig. 5-8. Assemble and immediately execute program (load-and-go.)

computer immediately starts executing it. This mode of operation is called *load-and-go*.

The computer is extremely good at the translation process, which allows the engineer to write his program in a language that is convenient to him and places on the computer the whole burden of translating the program into a set of instructions that the computer can then execute. There is no need to address the computer in *its* language; we can teach it to understand *our* language.

Let us now consider writing programs in a programming language that is more acceptable to engineers, such as FORTRAN, BASIC, PL/1, or APL. How do we teach the computer to accept these languages? Since the computer can only do what we order it to do, it must be provided with a translating program that must be placed in the computer memory before the FORTRAN (or BASIC, PL/1, APL) program is read in. The preparation of the translating program is the difficult part. Compilers to translate FORTRAN programs include several thousand instructions.

For input, the compiler uses the source-language program (FORTRAN, BASIC, PL/1, or APL). The object program is the compiler output. The compiler program is analogous to a bilingual person serving as translator and interpreter for those who must communicate in different languages. The compiler is prepared only once and must be stored in the computer before any source program is read in.

As in the assembling process, the process of carrying out a particular computation consists of two stages. First, the source-language program is translated, or compiled, into the equivalent object program; second, the object program is executed. The two stages are kept separate. Compilation is completed before any actual computation begins, and, in fact, the entire object program is stored away before any part of it is executed.

At the completion of the compilation, one of two things may happen. The object program may be immediately executed (as illustrated in Fig. 5-9), or it may be recorded on some suitable medium, such as punched cards, punched paper tape, magnetic tape, or magnetic disk for use later (as illustrated in Fig. 5-10). In the latter case, the object program must be read back into the main computer memory before the program can be executed by the computer. The two-stage process provides for the source-language program to be compiled on one computer and later executed on the same or a different computer. The compile and immediately execute process is often called the *compile-and-go* process.

Both assemblers and compilers provide auxiliary functions that assist the engineer in documenting and correcting the instructions written. These functions include program listings and error indications that are detected during the translating process. Fig. 5-11 illustrates a segment of an assembly-language program listing generated by the assembler

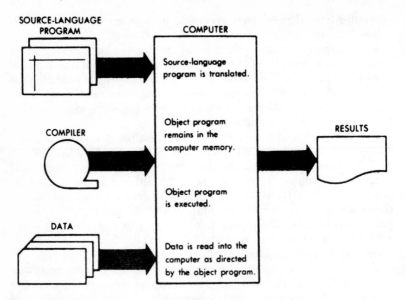

Fig. 5-9. Compile and immediately execute program (compile-and-go.)

with the detected errors. The errors detected by the assembler or compiler are called *diagnostics*. The process of correcting errors is commonly referred to as *program debugging*.

INTERPRETIVE LANGUAGES

Interpretive coding permits programming in a language that is easier to learn than machine language. Many interpretive languages are similar to machine language; however, they provide features and operations that are not inherent in the computer used for executing the program. Interpretive systems are used primarily on computers that are too slow to permit efficient use of algorithmic languages, and on microcomputers that have implemented high-level programming systems such as BASIC or FORTRAN. They are also commonly used on small computers to provide a language that resembles machine language but is actually much easier to learn and use. A program written in such a language is ordinarily executed one instruction at a time by a translator called an *interpreter*.

The interpreter is a computer program that must be entered into the memory of the computer and remain there during the execution of a program written in interpretive language. For example, when an ADDF instruction is encountered, the interpreter interprets it as a *floating-point add* instruction to be simulated within the interpreter,

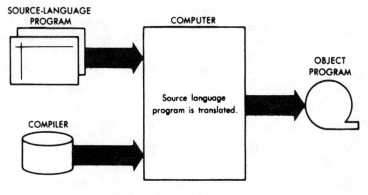

(A) Compile program process.

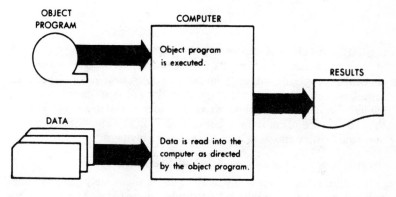

(B) Execute program process.

Fig. 5-10. Compile and execute programs separately.

rather than as a machine-language *add* instruction. Interpreters are usually lengthy programs that can occupy several hundred or even several thousand locations of computer memory. Hence, an interpreter may occupy a major portion of the memory of a small computer.

COMPARING PROGRAMMING LANGUAGES

The successful application of computing equipment to a problem solution may be critically affected by the software skills of the programming staff. Return on the investment of computing equipment

Error Flag	Machine Code	Assembler Instruction	Error Type
A	00012 020766	LDA 0,400	Address Error.
UB	00014 024023	LASL: LDA 1,23	Bad character in label.
UUE		REG= 3+B	Equivalence error.
F	00015 143000	ADD 2	Format error.
N	00020 000007	C77: 7A	Number error.
O	00021 020016	LDA 4,.−3	Field overflow.
R		.RDX 20	Radix error.
U	00022 030015	LDA 2,B	B is undefined.
Q		+.END	Questionable.

Fig. 5-11. Partial program listing showing errors detected during the assembly process.

is partly a function of expressing instructions in a language powerful enough to obtain useful results at a reasonable cost. This means that choosing a programming language has thus become a major task in many installations and among many communities of computer users. The choice of language can often have more effect on the success of a project than the choice of computer. Let us now look at some of the problems one faces when choosing a programming language.

Programming Languages Are Not Standard

It is difficult to compare any two languages adequately since neither is defined precisely enough so that direct comparisons can be made.

Compilers Are Not Standard

There is usually more than one compiler for each language, which implies that more than one version of the language is actually implemented. This is more often true when the compilers are on different computers; however, it is also true when two different compilers for the same language are for the same computer.

Users Are Not Standard

One must consider the language preferences of the different users. One group of users may prefer using a language that is disliked or ignored by another set of users. This is often due to different educational backgrounds, professional backgrounds, stubbornness, or company preference.

Operating Systems Are Not Standard

One must consider the operating system under which the processor and translated program operate. Many systems allow on-line usage of languages, while other systems allow programs to run off-line.

Benchmarks

The following benchmarks must be considered when comparing programming languages:

1. *Fast Object Code and Efficient Storage Utilization*—Assembly-language coding (on any computer) written by an experienced programmer produces the "best" code. "Best" here implies faster operating time and less storage space. A good compiler cannot produce as good coding as a good machine-language programmer can; however, a good compiler can produce more efficient coding than an inexperienced programmer can. A rule-of-thumb estimate is that good assembly-language programs often run three or four times faster than compiler-produced codes and take about half as much storage.

   Most compiler languages manipulate words (groups of bits) rather than single bits or characters, thus making a very poor memory-utilization comparison with assembly language where data is always packed in the minimum amount of storage.

2. *Ease of Learning*—Problem-oriented and procedure-oriented languages are generally best for most users. These languages are easier to learn than is assembly language of the same complexity.

3. *Self-Documenting*—Documentation is a discipline in which all those who write programs must become adept, regardless of the programming language used. Higher-level programming languages can be written so that the programs are often self-documenting. To do this, however, the engineer must use comment statements describing operations, variables, and the functions of different program paths.

4. *Ease of Coding and Understanding*—It is easier to code programs in problem-oriented or procedure-oriented languages since the notation is considerably more problem-oriented. It is also much easier to understand the programs after they have been written.

5. *Ease of Debugging*—Freedom for the engineer is the salient feature of assembly language. This means freedom to improve efficiency and sophistication, and to make sophisticated errors. Higher-level languages provide safeguards that protect the engineer from his own failings.

   A problem written in a higher-level programming language is generally easier to debug than one written in assembly language. One reason for this is that the notation is more natural, and more attention can be paid to the logic of the problem being solved, with less worry about the details of assembler coding. Another reason is that the source program will generally be shorter, thereby reducing the chance for additional errors.

6. *Ease of Maintaining*—Because of the notation, higher-level language programs are easier to modify. One of the great difficulties in modifying assembly-language programs is to make sure that a change in one instruction does not create major problems elsewhere in the program.

7. *Ease of Conversion*—The costs associated with converting a library of existing programs from one computer to another are very high. Higher-level programming languages are relatively machine-independent, thereby relaxing the conversion task between different hardware systems.

8. *Program Development Time*—The use of higher-level programming languages will reduce the total amount of elapsed time from the inception of a problem to its solution. This is the greatest single overall advantage of higher-level languages. On large problems, the elapsed time may be reduced from months to weeks, while on smaller problems, the elapsed time may be reduced from days to hours.

9. *Translating Time*—The computer time required for translating source-language assembler programs is much less than that required to compile higher-level source-language programs into machine code. The compilation time varies with each processor; however, it is a significant factor that must be considered when developing programs with a higher-level programming language.

10. *Inability of the Language To Express All Needed Operations*— Some higher-level programming languages do not allow one to do all the operations that are required for the proper solution to a given problem. Many of the higher-level languages have weak or inadequate input/output facilities, no bit-handling capabilities, inabilities to manipulate characters of information, etc. This problem usually occurs when a user has chosen the language unwisely for his particular application.

11. *Control Over Program and Data Location*—Many small computers depend on the location of programs and data for efficiency in both execution time and memory utilization. Higher-level languages offer less flexibility than assembly language in specifying program layout and data storage.

CHOOSING A PROGRAMMING LANGUAGE

In the early days of electronic computing there was no choice of programming languages. By choosing a computer, one automatically

"DO YOU HEAR ME WORLD? MY PROGRAM WORKS!"

chose the assembly language and machine language that went with it. Today, however, a variety of programming languages are available for most of the existing computers. The following is a list of the various types of languages that are presently available:

1. *Machine Language*—All computers can be programmed in the basic language of the computer.
2. *Assembly Language*—All computer manufacturers offer a symbolic assembly language for each computer. Many computers have assembly languages of different levels.
3. *Business-Oriented Compiler Language*—COBOL and RPG are the most popular business programming languages.
4. *Scientific-Oriented Compiler Language*—FORTRAN is available on all large- and medium-scale machines, many small-scale machines, most minicomputers, and some microcomputers. BASIC is available on all microcomputers and most other computers. APL is available on a few large-scale machines and microcomputers.
5. *General Compiler Languages*—PL/1 is available on several

large-scale computer systems. Pascal is available on several large-scale machines as well as several microcomputers.

6. *Application Languages*—Problem-oriented languages, such as COGO, STRESS, GPSS, APT, etc., have been made available on a few machines.

The choice of language narrows somewhat when the user selects a specific computer. Some machines have two or more assembly languages. Some machines have more than one scientific-oriented language; e.g., FORTRAN, PL/1, APL, and BASIC may be available. In short, the choice appears narrow, but the user does have a wide choice as to what type of language to use—assembly language or higher-level language, business-oriented language or scientific-oriented language, procedure-oriented language or problem-oriented language, on-line conversational language or batch-processing language, or general programming language or COBOL/FORTRAN combination.

Some criteria that should be considered in the selection of a programming language are:

1. *Ease of Use*—Problem-oriented languages, such as COGO, GPSS, or APT, are the easiest to use. Languages such as BASIC, FORTRAN, Pascal, COBOL, and PL/1 are the next easiest to use. Less convenient are the symbolic assembly languages, and one should never even consider using machine language. For convenience in learning, the higher-level languages are favored because the user need not have a detailed working knowledge of the computer.

2. *Personnel Competence*—The chosen language is often the language best known at a particular facility. If most of the engineers know FORTRAN, then it is a simple task to produce a working program. If the staff is more familiar with assembly language, or BASIC, or PL/1, etc., then it is the logical choice.

3. *Language Suitability for Problem*—The language chosen should contain all the elements needed to solve the particular class of problems for which it is being considered. For example, a language that provides good computational facilities (APL, FORTRAN) may not provide the alphanumeric character-manipulating ability required for a specific inventory control problem. Conversely, a language that contains too many facilities is not desirable, since the user pays a heavy price for the facilities not needed for his specific problem.

4. *Availability*—Before the user selects a programming language, he should make sure that the language has been implemented on the machine configuration being considered. It is useless to select a language and then find out that the compiler will not run on a

specific hardware system because it lacked a tape transport, card reader, disk file, etc.

5. *Speed of Operation*—Some high-level language compilers produce object programs that are as efficient as those obtained from an intermediate-level programmer using an assembly language.

6. *Speed of Compilation and Programming*—Compiling time is worth money, and this time varies between different languages and different implementations of the same language. Although generally slower in compilation speed than assembly language, the higher-level languages allow programming work to be done more rapidly than is possible with assembly language.

7. *History of Previous Use*—When a user has tentatively selected a language and has determined that a compiler is available for his specific hardware configuration, he should then investigate the history of usage of this language. Were previous users satisfied with the language? How difficult is it to train people to use the language? What conversion problems will there be if this language choice is finalized, etc.?

8. *Nature of the Job*—Certain languages are better suited for certain specific applications, as outlined in the following:

- Business problems, which usually require a small amount of computation and a large amount of input/output data handling, can best be programmed in either PL/1, COBOL, RPG, or assembly language.
- In engineering programming, where the problem can conveniently be expressed in mathematical notation, languages such as FORTRAN, PL/1, BASIC, Pascal, or APL are usually chosen.
- Manipulation languages, such as SNOBOL, are best suited to applications where the main requirement is the manipulation of strings of symbols.
- Heuristic processes, which are by nature continually changing and expanding so that the relationship between the data are "tree-like," are best programmed in languages like LISP.
- Control programs and input/output routines such as executive routines, monitors, disk-handling routines, card-reader routines, etc., which usually have a time and space requirement, are most often programmed in assembly language. However, where time and space requirements are not a problem, higher-level languages could be used.
- Simulation languages, such as GPSS and SIMSCRIPT, have been designed to simplify the programming of simulation applications.

- Problem-oriented languages, such as COGO and STRESS, have been developed to aid civil engineers in the solving of some of their problems.
- Conversational languages, such as BASIC, are ideally suited for educational programming. The languages can be learned in a matter of hours and are well suited for solving typical classroom problems in chemistry, engineering, mathematics, biology, psychology, etc.

OPERATING SYSTEMS

When computers were first developed, they were usually put to work solving jobs that had previously required a great deal of routine human activity. For example, basic accounting, record keeping, and problem solving were a few of these early applications. By and large, the automatic processing of such jobs proved the speed, economy, and reliability of electronic data processing.

A few years later, computer users began to use computers for applications that went far beyond the mere mechanization of manual operations. Process control systems, medical diagnosis systems, management information systems, computer-assisted instruction (CAI) systems, and storage and retrieval systems are a few recent examples of such applications.

Today, as a result of this rapid progress, most data-processing installations are facing an increase in the number of conventional applications as well as in the scope and complexity of new system applications. To cope with these problems, a data-processing system must efficiently apply all of its resources—hardware, information, and human. These resources represent a considerable investment and must be used efficiently. Hardware and information resources must be readily available so that the CPU can be kept busy processing data. Human resources must be relieved of tasks that the computing system can perform.

An *operating system* is an organized collection of programs and data that are specifically designed to manage the resources of a computer system, and to facilitate the creation of computer programs and control their execution in that system. The primary purpose of operating systems is to reduce the cost of running problems (production programs) by increasing the use of the various computer system components and by avoiding lost time. Through the use of operating systems, the computer user delegates part of the burden of improved information processing efficiency to the computer itself.

For an operating system to achieve the high efficiencies of which present information processing systems are capable, it should be able to handle the following functions:

- Scheduling and performing input/output and related functions for programs.
- Interpreting human operator commands and/or control cards which describe to it the work to be done.
- Handling requests for all allocation of system resources.
- Controlling the stacking of jobs for continuous processing.
- Allocating space for external storage devices.
- Governing the operation of compilers, assemblers, and other manufacturer-provided software.
- Readying programs for execution.
- Monitoring the execution of processing programs.
- Protecting the various programs from one another.
- Providing a variety of user services.

Operating systems range in complexity from simple systems, which manage only simple functions, to very complex ones. In general, the more sophisticated the computer system is, the more complex is the operating system required to manage its use. The philosophy underlying the operating system is that the computer should perform those operator tasks that it can do faster and more accurately, and that the computer should be kept operating as continuously and as effectively as possible.

A small-scale computer system may have a very minimal operating system that deals primarily with input/output activities. Minicomputers and microcomputers may not have operating systems, since they may be dedicated to particular tasks. In most medium- and large-scale systems, however, the operating system controls the total computer environment.

One of the major features of an operating system is that the computer operator can stack the jobs for continuous processing (batch processing), which, of course, greatly reduces the setup time between jobs. The system will then take advantage of all the facilities offered in the system by calling special programs, routines, and data as needed. The operator uses a *job-control language* to give instructions to the computer. The job-control language statements permit the computer operator to communicate wishes to the computer in a language that both parties can understand. The user may, for instance, use job-control language to request that a PL/1 program be compiled or that a program that has been stored in the auxiliary memory of the computer be executed. No matter what the request is, the operating system software processes job-control language statements. After checking the job-control statements to be sure that valid requests have been made, the operating system software locates, in auxiliary storage, needed programs and brings (loads) them into the internal memory of the computer.

Other operating system software is responsible for initiating input/output operations, checking and creating file labels, processing interrupt signals, responding to end-of-file conditions, error recovery, printing control messages for the computer operating, and a variety of other tasks.

The utility system component of an operating system assists the computer user by performing library maintenance, diagnostics, sorting and merging, and job reporting. Library maintenance routines consist of software that can add, delete, or copy programs into or from the various program libraries located in auxiliary storage. Diagnostic software provides the computer user with error messages when conditions exist that make it difficult or impossible for the computer to continue processing a job.

The sort and merge programs are designed to reorder data files. Job-reporting software records information that will be used to evaluate the efficiency with which the computer system is run, and to bill computer users. This software stores the name of every program run on the computer, when the program was run and how much time it took, and the name of the person or department responsible for having the program run.

The operating system functions mentioned in this section are merely an indication of the type of programs that are included in operating systems. Additional operating system software is required for computer systems that support such features as time sharing, multiprogramming, virtual memory, or remote processing. In all cases, operating system software exists to provide the computer user with a workable system.

EXERCISES

1. What is meant by the *stored-program* concept?

2. What is an instruction?

3. What is the purpose of using a programming language?

4. Name four kinds of programming languages. How are they classified in the hierarchy of programming languages?

5. Distinguish between:

   (a) Computer-oriented and problem-oriented programming languages.
   (b) Scientific- and business-oriented programming languages.

6. Define the following terms:

   (a) Source program.
   (b) Object program.
   (c) Assembler.
   (d) Syntax.

(e) Program.
(f) Translator.

7. What is machine language?

8. What is assembly language?

9. What is a procedure-oriented programming language?

10. List four procedure-oriented programming languages.

11. Name two problem-oriented languages discussed in this chapter.

12. What is the function of a *compiler*?

13. Name two simulation programming languages.

14. Name one language that is widely used on microcomputers.

15. What kinds of applications are most suitable for FORTRAN? For COBOL? For PL/1?

16. Describe how a civil engineer would solve a problem using COGO.

17. Design a flowchart that will show all the steps involved in solving a problem on a computer.

18. Discuss the similarities and differences of assembly language and procedure-oriented languages.

19. What is meant by a *compiler* language?

20. What is meant by the *compile-and-go* process?

21. What benefits might be realized by users if a common programming language were developed that could be utilized for all applications?

22. What is an *interpreter*?

23. List some of the problems one encounters when comparing programming languages.

24. List some factors that one may use in the selection of a programming language.

25. What is the function of an operating system?

CHAPTER 6

FORTRAN PROGRAMMING

FORTRAN is an acronym for *FOR*mula *TRAN*slation. It identifies a closely related family of procedure-oriented programming languages and compilers for solving problems on a digital computer. These languages are especially useful for solving engineering and mathematical problems.

FORTRAN CHARACTERS

Fig. 6-1 illustrates a typical FORTRAN program to calculate the frequency of a pendulum. When a pendulum is set in motion, its period (the time it takes to complete one oscillation) is related to the length of the pendulum. The relationship is shown in the formula:

$$T = 2\pi \sqrt{\frac{l}{g}}$$

where,
    T is the time in seconds for one complete oscillation,
    $\pi = 3.14159$,
    l is the length of the pendulum in feet,
    g is the acceleration due to gravity (32 ft/s²).

The frequency is the reciprocal of the period:

$$f = \frac{1}{T}$$

The reader should not at this time try to determine how the FORTRAN program works. This example is presented here only to illustrate what a program looks like. In the following paragraphs, several references will be made to the program.

FORTRAN has an alphabet consisting of:

- The upper case letters of the alphabet (A, B, C, . . . , Z).
- The numerical digits (0, 1, 2, . . . , 9).
- The special characters $+ - * / ( ) = .$, blank.

```
C      FREQUENCY OF A PENDULUM
       K = 0
       READ(5,10) ALENG
   10  FORMAT(F10.5)
       K = K + 1
       PI = 3.14159
       G = 32.0
       T = 2.0 * PI * (ALENG / G) **.5
       FREQ = 1.0/T
       WRITE(6,20) ALENG, T, FREQ, K
   20  FORMAT('L=',ALENG,'T=',T,'FREQUENCY=',FREQ,'K=',K)
       STOP
       END
```

Fig. 6-1. FORTRAN program to compute the frequency of a pendulum.

It can be seen from Fig. 6-1 that a FORTRAN program consists of a series of statements using the preceding alphabet. This alphabet is used with punctuation or is joined together to form *words*, which, in turn, make up the statements. Since FORTRAN is an engineering-type language, its words consist essentially of constants, variables, and special symbols. All of these must be presented to the computer in certain specific ways. The basic unit of the FORTRAN language is the *statement*, of which there are four types, as follows:

1. *Arithmetic* statements, which specify the mathematical operations to be performed.
2. *Input/output* statements, which control the transfer of data into and out of the computer.
3. *Program-control* statements, which direct the sequence of operations to be performed by the computer.
4. *Specification* statements, which allocate computer storage and specify the types and formats of data and variables.

Let us now study some of the basic elements that are used to construct these statements.

NUMBERS

In FORTRAN, a *constant* is a fixed number that never varies. For example, in Fig. 6-1 the numbers 3.14159, 32.0, 2.0, and 1.0 are fixed constants that never vary throughout the running of the program. The two most used types of FORTRAN constants are *integer* constants and *real* constants.

Integer constants (sometimes called *fixed-point* constants) are whole numbers written without a decimal point. For example, the number 468 is an integer constant, whereas 24.9 is not. The integer constant may be either negative or positive. It may not, however, contain any commas.

Real constants (sometimes called *floating-point* constants) always include a decimal point and may or may not have a fractional part. Typical examples are 8.0 and 83.2. Real constants may also contain an *exponent*. For example, the value 24.8×10^3, where 24.8 is the mantissa, 10 is the base, and 3 is the exponent, would be represented in FORTRAN by the real constant 24.8E3, where 24.8 is the mantissa, 3 is the exponent, and E means *with exponent*. The number is always to the base 10. In a real constant, both the mantissa and the exponent may be either positive or negative.

This form of constant allows us to express very large or very small numbers. For example, an ounce of gold contains approximately 8,650,000,000,000,000,000,000 atoms. In this form, the number would be difficult, if not impossible, to represent in most computers. This number can be written as 8650 times 1,000,000,000,000,000,000. In FORTRAN the number is written as 8650.E18.

Some typical examples of integer and real constants are shown in Table 6-1.

Table 6-1. Examples of Integer and Real Constants

Integer Constants	Real Constants
23	0.0006
0	−8.7
+69	21.0
−43	5.2E2
123456	0.0
21	69.0

FORTRAN VARIABLE IDENTIFIERS

Whereas constants are fixed and never vary, *variables* are quantities that may be changed many times during the same program. For this reason they are identified by letters, not numbers. For example, in the mathematical expression

$$26a + 14b - 3c$$

the constants are 26, 14, and 3, and they never vary. The variables are a, b, and c, and they can take on different values at different times.

A FORTRAN variable may be either a single symbol, such as X or S, or it may be a name consisting of up to six* letters and numbers, the first of which must be a letter. Several examples are HOUR, D123, COST, FORCE, and SUM. Special characters or spaces may not be used in variable names. In Fig. 6-1, the following are variables: ALENG, K, PI, G, T, and FREQ.

There are several types of variables. However, the two most used types are *integer* (fixed-point) variables and *real* (floating-point) variables (see Table 6-2). An integer variable is one that may be assigned any of the values permitted for an integer constant and is represented by a name starting with one of the letters I, J, K, L, M, or N.† The name of a real variable must begin with a letter other than I, J, K, L, M, or N.†

Table 6-2. Examples of Integer and Real Variables

Integer Variables	Real Variables
JOHN	SPEED
M26	ALPHA
KOUNT	TAX
NUMBER	A14
N	Z

ARITHMETIC OPERATIONS AND EXPRESSIONS

An *arithmetic expression* is a properly arranged set of variables, constants, functions,‡ and *arithmetic operators*. The five arithmetic operators are:

+   addition
−   subtraction
*   multiplication
/   division
**   exponentiation

The order in which expressions are evaluated is governed by the rules of precedence, with all operations of a higher precedence being performed prior to those of a lower precedence. When parentheses are used, the operations contained within the parentheses are performed first. Operations of equal precedence are performed from left to right. The following hierarchy of operations may be used to determine priority order:

---

*Depending on the computer, the maximum might be more or less than six.
†By using a special statement, this can be changed. INTEGER and REAL *type* statements are discussed later.
‡Functions are discussed in a later section.

1. Operation within parentheses.
2. Exponentiation.
3. Multiplication and division.
4. Addition and subtraction.

The simplest expression is a single constant or variable. If the quantity is an integer quantity, the expression is said to be in the *integer mode*. If the quantity is a real quantity, the expression is said to be in the *real mode*. The modes of constants and variables should be the same; that is, integer and real quantities should not be mixed in the same expression. Many FORTRAN systems, however, will allow *mixed-mode arithmetic*. An exception to mixed-mode arithmetic is a real quantity raised to an integer power, such as X**2. Some examples of mixed-mode arithmetic and their correct form are shown in Table 6-3. The arithmetic expressions in Fig. 6-1 are:

```
K + 1
3.14159
32.0
2.0 * PI * (ALENG/G) **.5
1.0/T
```

Table 6-3. Examples of Mixed-Mode Arithmetic and Their Correct Form

Mixed Mode	Correct Form (Same Mode)
X = 13	X = 13.0
M8 + 26.0	M8 + 26
FORCE + 88 − W	FORCE + 88.0 − W
K + 14*R	K + 14*IR

Several other FORTRAN arithmetic expressions and their mathematical equivalents are shown in Table 6-4.

Table 6-4. Some FORTRAN Expressions and Their Mathematical Equivalents

FORTRAN Expression	Mathematical Expression
I + J − 3*K	$i + j - 3K$
(A + B)/2.0	$\dfrac{a+b}{2}$
B**2 − 4.0*A*C	$b^2 - 4ac$
(A**2 + B**2)**.5	$\sqrt{a^2 + b^2}$

FORTRAN ARITHMETIC STATEMENTS

In FORTRAN, an *arithmetic statement* is quite similar to the conventional algebraic equation. It consists of the variable to be computed on the left side of the statement, followed by a *replaced by* symbol (=), and an arithmetic expression on the right side of the statement. The general form of the arithmetic statement is

$$variable = expression$$

The arithmetic statement

$$K = K + 1$$

is interpreted as follows: (1) K + 1 is evaluated by adding 1 to the current value of K, and (2) K is then set equal to the value of the expression. This has the effect of replacing K with K + 1. In Fig. 6-1 the following are arithmetic statements:

```
K = K + 1
PI = 3.14159
G = 32.0
T = 2.0*PI*(ALENG/G)**.5
FREQ = 1.0/T
```

If the mode of the expression is different from that of the variable on the left of the *replaced by* symbol, then the expression is converted to the mode of the variable. One must not confuse mixed-mode arithmetic with different modes on opposite sides of the *replaced by* symbol. Mixed-mode applies *only* to the mixing of variable and constant modes within an expression. It is often desirable to perform some computation in one mode—real mode, for example—and store the result as an integer value. In the statement

$$J = 18.6 + 32.8 + 26.0$$

the value of the expression is first determined as 77.4, then *truncated* to 77, and then assigned to the integer variable J.

FORTRAN LIBRARY FUNCTIONS

Some mathematical functions are in such frequent demand by engineers that to save each person from having to write a program to calculate the functions, they are incorporated in the FORTRAN system. Thus, to calculate the square root, sine, cosine, and absolute value of a variable (A), one need only write down the expressions SQRT (A), SIN (A), COS(A), or ABS(A) at the appropriate point in the program, and the FORTRAN system will return the required value. The value contained within parentheses is called the *argument* and can be any expression, not just a variable as used in the previous example. A few commonly used library functions that are available in all FORTRAN systems are listed in Table 6-5.

Table 6-5. Commonly Used FORTRAN Library Functions and Their Mathematical Equivalents

FORTRAN Library Function	Mathematical Equivalent
SQRT(X)	$\sqrt{x}$
SIN(X)	sin x
COS(X)	cos x
TAN(X)	tan x
EXP(X)	e^x
ARCOS(X)	arcos x
ARSIN(X)	arcsin x
ATAN(X)	arctan x
ABS(X)	$|x|$
FLOAT(K)	Convert k to Real
FIX(X)	Convert x to Integer

Library functions are used in arithmetic expressions in the same way that variables and constants are used. For example, the statement in Fig. 6-1

$$T = 2.0 * PI * (ALENG/G) **.5$$

could also have been written using a library function as

T = 2.0 * PI * SQRT (ALENG/G)

TERMINATING A FORTRAN PROGRAM

Every FORTRAN program must end with an END statement. It is a signal to the FORTRAN compiler that the end of the source program has been reached and that compilation of the program is to terminate.

The STOP statement is written to stop the computation. In many computer systems this statement returns control back to the *operating system* rather than stopping the computation. A CALL EXIT statement is also used to terminate a program and return computer control to the operating system. The program in Fig. 6-1 contains both a STOP statement and an END statement.

PREPARING FORTRAN PROGRAMS FOR THE COMPUTER

As stated previously, FORTRAN programs are composed of many FORTRAN statements. The statements are written on coding forms, such as that shown in Fig. 6-2. The FORTRAN coding form has 72

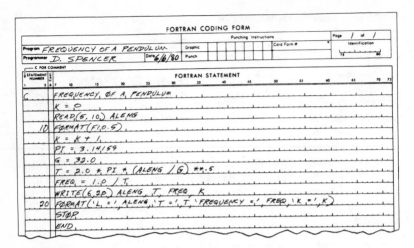

Fig. 6-2. Program of Fig. 6-1 written on a FORTRAN coding form.

columns on it. A comment is made by placing a C in column 1, and the comment (any English language remark) in columns 2 through 72. Comments do not become part of the machine-language program and they will not be executed when the program is executed on the computer. It is advisable to use comments freely throughout your programs.

The *statement number* belongs in columns 1 through 5. This number is often called a *label* and is used for reference by other statements in the program. It is not necessary to number all statements—only those being referenced by other statements.

Column 6 is the *continuation* column and is used only when a statement exceeds one line of the coding form. For example, a three-line FORTRAN statement would have a blank in column 6 on the first line and nonzero characters (1, 2, 3, . . ., 9) in column 6 on the next two lines. The body of the statement is written in columns 7 through 72.

After the FORTRAN program is written on coding forms, it is then usually punched on cards. One line of the coding form is keypunched into one punched card. A FORTRAN statement card is shown in Fig. 6-3. A FORTRAN data card is usually a blank card. A complete FORTRAN program keypunched on cards is called a *source deck*. Fig. 6-4 illustrates the source deck for the program shown in Figs. 6-1 and 6-2.

READING AND PRINTING

Input/output statements make it possible for the computer to communicate with peripheral devices external to the computer, such as

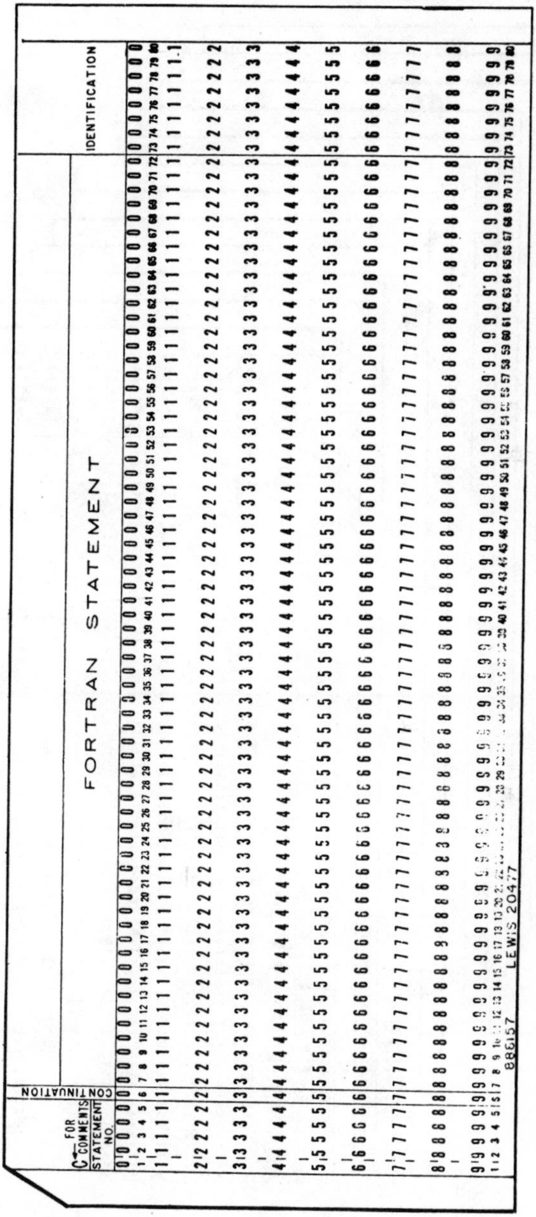

Fig. 6-3. Punched card for FORTRAN statements.

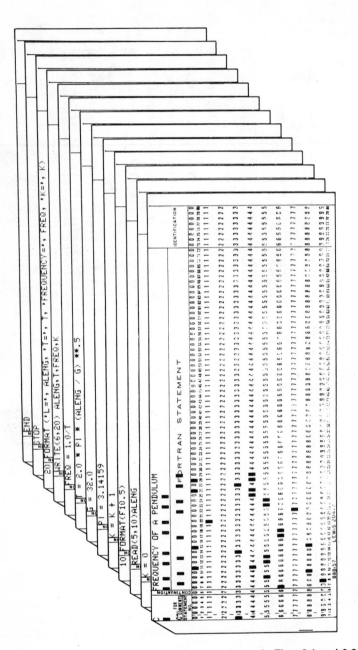

Fig. 6-4. Source card deck for the program shown in Figs. 6-1 and 6-2.

card readers, line printers, typewriters, magnetic-tape units, magnetic-disk units, card punches, etc. Input statements enable a program to receive data from input devices, while output statements transmit data from computer storage to an output device. In this section we will discuss three input/output statements: (1) the READ statement, (2) the WRITE statement, and (3) the FORMAT statement. The program in Fig. 6-1 contained the following input/output statements:

```
    READ (5,10) ALENG
10  FORMAT(F10.5)
    WRITE(6,20) ALENG, T, FREQ, K
20  FORMAT('L = ',ALENG,'T = ',T,'FREQUENCY = ',FREQ,'K = ',K)
```

The READ and WRITE statements include a *list* which defines what data are to be processed by the statement. In the preceding READ statement, ALENG is the list. Input lists specify variables to which incoming data are assigned. Output lists specify variables whose values are to be transmitted to an output device. The elements of a list are specified in the order of their appearance in the list (from left to right). An example of an output list is shown in the preceding WRITE statement: WRITE (6,20) ALENG,T,FREQ,K. As shown in this example, if the list contains more than one variable name, the names are separated by commas. A list must not contain constants.

The READ statement is of the form

$$READ(u,f)list$$

The u stands for the input device we want to use, f is the statement number of the FORMAT statement associated with this READ statement, and *list* is an input list. The input device number will change, depending on the computer system being used. Most computer systems use the number 5 to represent a card reader. A magnetic tape unit could be 2 and a disk drive could be 3.

When you write

```
    READ (5,40) VOLT, MASS, BRIDGE

40  FORMAT(_____)
```

the program will read from a punched card (data card) the values for the variables VOLT, MASS, and BRIDGE. The data on the card must be in the same order as the variables in the input list. Every READ statement has an associated FORMAT statement, identified by a statement number. Later we will see how the FORMAT statement is written, but for now we will just use a long dash.

Consider another example of a READ statement:

READ(5,60) X1,X2,Y1,Y2,Z1,Z2

60   FORMAT(_____)

This READ statement would be used to read six numbers. The number farthest to the left on a data card would be assigned as X1, the second X2, the third Y1, the fourth Y2, the fifth Z1, and the sixth Z2.

Whereas the READ statement is used to specify that data be transmitted from punched cards to the computer, the WRITE statement is used to specify that data be transmitted from the computer to some output device. It is in this manner that calculated results are made available for human use. The WRITE statement is of the form

$$\text{WRITE } (u,f) \text{ } list$$

where u is a number that identifies the output device that we want to use, f is the statement number of an associated FORMAT statement, and $list$ is an output list. In this case, the output device could be a line printer, a card punch, a magnetic-tape unit, or a disk drive. Usually, the number 6 is assigned to the line printer.

The elements of the output list are converted and positioned as specified by the associated FORMAT statement. The output list actually specifies what quantities are to be transmitted from the computer. The WRITE statement

WRITE(6,100) TEMP,PRES,VOL
100   FORMAT (_____)

would direct the computer to output to the line printer the current numerical values of TEMP, PRES, and VOL according to the specifications of FORMAT statement 100.

It is possible to use the WRITE statement without an output list. A statement such as

WRITE(6,300)
300   FORMAT(_____)

would inform the computer to produce output on the line printer using FORMAT statement 300. This FORMAT statement would contain the actual information to be printed.

Let us now examine the FORMAT statement. Remember *every* READ and WRITE statement has an associated FORMAT statement. The general form of the FORMAT statement is as follows:

$$f \text{ FORMAT } (specification \text{ } codes)$$

where f stands for the statement number of the FORMAT statement. This statement number is the same as the number used in the associated

READ or WRITE statement. The *specification codes* are always enclosed in parentheses. There are many different codes, and each one is used for a specific thing. For example, the slash (/) code will cause the line printer to skip a line, the X code is used to skip columns on a punched card, and the I code is used when reading or writing integer values.

The FORMAT statement is not executable; therefore, it may be placed *anywhere* in the program.* Many people place all FORMAT statements together at the end of the program, while others prefer to place each statement right after the associated READ or WRITE statement that uses it. Let us now examine the different specification codes that may be used with the FORMAT statement.

I Specification Code

The I specification code is used when reading and writing *integer* data. This code has the form Iw. This specifies that the number to be read from a punched card, or to be printed, is an integer constant covering w columns of the card or paper. For example, the code I6 means an integer having up to six decimal digits. The code I12 means that the number may be up to 12 digits long.

F Specification Code

The F specification code is used for *real* numbers. The general form is F$w.d$. As before, the number w tells the computer the width of each number (how many places to set aside for each), and the number d tells the computer how many places to put to the right of the decimal point. The decimal point between the w and d numbers must always be included. For example, the code F10.4 means that a real number may have a total width of up to 10 places, with four decimal places to the right of the decimal point. The total width, w, includes the whole number part, the fractional part, the decimal point, and a possible sign.

E Specification Code

The E specification code is used for printing real numbers that would be too long if printed with an F specification code. For example, assume we wanted to print the number of miles in a light year (5,880,000,000,000). If we were to print it with an F code, we would need the code F13, which would be too long for some computers. Instead, if we represent the number in exponential form as

$$0.588 \times 10^{13}$$

---

*Some compilers do not permit FORMAT statements to appear as the first statement in a program.

it would be acceptable to even the smallest computer. The E code is used to print a number in this form. If the specification code E8.3 were used with the previous number, then the following value would be printed:

$$0.588E13$$

The general form of the E specification code is $Ew.d.$, where w and d are the same as described for the F specification code.

X Specification Code

The X specification code is a method that FORTRAN provides for skipping spaces on a line, card, record, etc. The general form is wX, where the number, w, could be the number of card columns to be skipped on input or the number of blank spaces to insert when printing. For example, the code 14X would skip 14 spaces.

Slash Specification Code

Whenever a slash (/) appears in a FORMAT statement, it means either a new card or a new line of print. When used with a READ statement, the slash means to read a new card. When used with the WRITE statement, the slash means to start a new line of print. Thus, the statements

```
          WRITE(6,300)A,B,C
     300  FORMAT(F10.0,/,F10.0,/,F10.0)
```

would result in A being printed on one line, B on the next line, and C on the third line.

H Specification Code

The H specification code provides a method for transmitting nonnumeric data in or out of the computer. It is most often used to print messages or headings. The general form is wH, where w specifies the number of characters immediately following the H to be transmitted. Any FORTRAN character, *including blanks*, may be used with this specification. When using the H specification code, it is not required to put anything in the list of the associated READ or WRITE statement. If we wanted to print the message

TENSION IN THE CABLE IS

the statements

```
          WRITE (6,200)
     200  FORMAT(23HTENSION IN THE CABLE IS)
```

would accomplish this task. The 23 was obtained by adding the 19 characters of the message and the four blank spaces between words.

The first column of a printed page is reserved for controlling the carriage on the printer. The control characters are:

> 1 —Skip to start of new page.
> 0 —Double spacing.
> + —Suppress spacing.
> blank—Single spacing.

In the previous example, if we had wanted to print the message at the top of a new page, the following FORMAT statement should be used:

        20   FORMAT(24H1TENSION IN THE CABLE IS)

Let us now print another message, this time letting the FORMAT statement contain a value to be printed:

        WEIGHT OF TANK IS *n*

where "WEIGHT OF TANK IS" is printed using the H specification code, and *n* is the value of the variable "TANK" and is printed using the specification F10.3. Assume that "TANK" has a value of 86.400 in the computer memory, then the statements

        WRITE(6,480) TANK
    480 FORMAT(18H1WEIGHT OF TANK IS, F10.3)

would cause the following message to be printed at the top of a new page:

        WEIGHT OF TANK IS 86.400

Quotes as a Specification Code

Quotes are used in a FORMAT statement for the same purpose as the H specification code. They are, however, much easier to use since one does not have to count the number of characters to be read or printed.

As an example, suppose the program computed a result of 432., and we wish to print this value out along with the phrase "AIR RESISTANCE EQUALS." A way of doing this is

        WRITE(6,100)AIRRES
    100 FORMAT('AIR RESISTANCE EQUALS', I4)

The computer then causes the phrase inside the quotes to be printed, followed by the numerical value of AIRRES:

        AIR RESISTANCE EQUALS 432.

Repeat Specification Codes

The specification codes I, F, and E may be repeated by placing a repeat factor in front of the specification designator. For example, the specification nIw means that there are n integers, $nFw.d$ means that there are n real values, and $nEw.d$ means that there are n real values with exponents. In other words, 4I5 is the same as I5,I5,I5,I5 and 3F10.5 is the same as F10.5,F10.5,F10.5.

GO TO STATEMENT

The GO TO statement permits one to transfer program control to another statement in the program—*unconditionally*. For example, if we wanted to transfer program control to statement number 100, we use the instruction

GO TO 100

After the statement identified by 100 is executed, control continues with the statements following statement number 100.

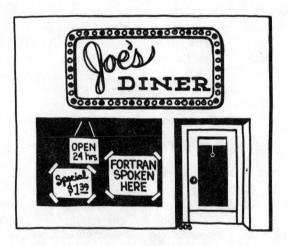

COMPUTED GO TO STATEMENT

The *computed* GO TO statement can cause program control to be transferred to one of several places in the program, depending on the value of some number. The statement is of the form

GO TO (a,b,c, . . .,n), i

where a, b, c, . . ., n are statement labels, and i is an integer. Execution of this statement causes the statement identified by one of the statement labels $a, b, c, \ldots, n$ to be executed next, where the specific $a, b, c, \ldots,$ n is determined by the value of i at the time of execution. For example, if one wrote

GO TO (20,30,40,50,60), K

the computer transfers control to statement number 20 if K equals 1 at execution time, to 30 if K equals 2, to 40 if K equals 3, and to 60 if K equals 5 at execution time.

DO STATEMENT

A program loop consists of one or more statements to be executed a number of times, each time altering one or more variables in the statements so that each pass through the loop is different from the preceding one. An *index* must be initialized before the loop, incremented once each time around the loop, and tested to see whether it is time to leave the loop. The DO statement does all this in one statement. A loop controlled with a DO statement is usually called a DO loop.

In Fig. 6-5, the DO statement instructs the computer to do 200 times all the instructions from the DO statement up to and including statement number 40. On the first pass through the loop, N equals 1; on the second pass, N equals 2; on the third pass, N equals 3; and so on until N equals 200 on the last pass.

The general form of the DO statement is illustrated in Fig. 6-6. At the beginning of the loop, the variable i will be set equal to the value of a. When the value of i exceeds the value of b, the computer will stop going through the loop and will continue with the next statement in the program. The c stands for the number that should be added to i each time the computer goes through the loop. As an example, the DO statement

DO 400 K = 1,22,3

will cause K to be initially set to 1. All statements following the DO statement will be executed until statement 400 is reached. After executing statement 400, 3 will be added to the current value of K and a check made to see if this value is greater than 22. If it is not, the computer will loop back and execute the statements again. This will continue until the value of K, which has had 3 added to it each time through the loop, goes over 22. Then the computer will stop the loop and continue with the statement following statement 400.

A few rules which apply to the DO statement are:

Rule 1.   The variables a, b, and c must be only integer or real variables.

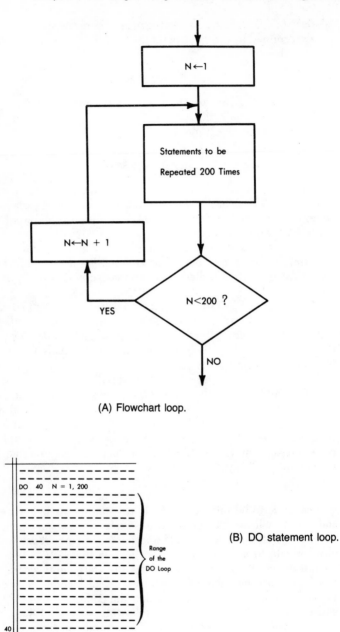

(A) Flowchart loop.

(B) DO statement loop.

Fig. 6-5. Looping with the DO statement.

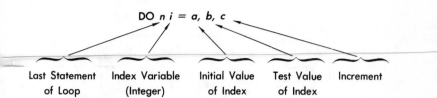

DO *n i = a, b, c*

| Last Statement of Loop | Index Variable (Integer) | Initial Value of Index | Test Value of Index | Increment |

Fig. 6-6. The general form of the DO statement.

Rule 2.   Once the loop has been executed the appropriate number of times, the index is not available for use.

Rule 3.   If *c* is absent, it is understood to be 1.

Rule 4.   The values of *a, b,* and *c* must not be changed in the middle of a DO loop. At the time of execution they must be greater than zero.

Rule 5.   If the value of *b* is smaller than the value of *a*, the DO loop will not be executed.* The value for *a* must be less than or equal to the value for *b*.

Rule 6.   The last statement in the loop cannot be a GO TO, IF, DO, STOP, or END statement.

Rule 7.   DO loops may be *nested*† if all statements in the inner loop are contained in the outer loop. Both the inner and outer loops may end on the same statement.

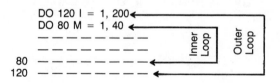

Rule 8.   Control may be transferred from a DO loop but not into it.

Rule 9.   Control can be transferred to and from an inner DO loop; however, none of the DO loop parameters (index, increment, etc.) can be modified.

Rule 10. The DO loop index may be used by any statement in the loop.

Rule 11. Statements within a DO loop will always be executed at least once.

---

*Some FORTRAN systems will execute the loop once.

†A *nesting loop* is a programming technique in which a loop of instructions contains another loop, which may in turn contain another loop, and so on. Loops contained within other loops are called *inner loops*. The highest-level loop is called an *outer loop*.

" FRED, WOULD YOU LIKE A SUGGESTION ?"

CONTINUE STATEMENT

The CONTINUE statement is a *do-nothing* statement and is often used as the last statement in a DO loop. The statement is useful in cases where the last statement in a DO loop would normally be a transfer-of-control statement. For example, we could not use the program segment

```
      DO 200 K = 1, 60
200   IF(R − 27.0) 100, 150, 180
```

However, the segment

```
      DO 200 K = 1, 60
      IF(R − 27.0) 100, 150, 180
200   CONTINUE
```

is perfectly legal.

ARRAYS

An *array* is a group of variables called by the same name. Suppose, for example, that we wanted to store in computer storage the final examination grades of 180 engineering students. It would require considerable time to write a program if we had to give each grade a separate name and handle the grades one by one. Instead, we can group the entire set of 180 grades together into an array and give it one name.

A value in an array is located by using a *subscript*. For example, if the previous array of 180 grades was named GRADE, then GRADE (1) could be used to specify the first grade, GRADE (2) the second grade, GRADE (3) the third, and so on. The value contained within parentheses is called the subscript. This means that every variable in an array must have a subscript and is called a *subscripted variable*. Thus, GRADE (84), PRICE (60), SCORE (N), and A(4*N) are all subscripted variables. The last two examples illustrate that subscripts can be variables and limited expressions as well as constants. Arrays can hold either integers or real numbers, depending on whether the array name is an integer or a real variable name.

In FORTRAN there are three distinct types of arrays: (1) *one-dimensional*, (2) *two-dimensional*, and (3) *three-dimensional*. If the listing is simply sequential, then the array is called a *one-dimensional* array* and only one subscript is needed to locate any element within the array. For example, any item in the following array can be located with a subscript ranging between 1 and 8:

```
VOLT(1)
VOLT(2)
VOLT(3)
VOLT(4)
VOLT(5)
VOLT(6)
VOLT(7)
VOLT(8)
```

A *two-dimensional* array † uses two subscripts separated by a comma. This type of array is used when both *rows* and *columns* of values are present. For example, the "tic-tac-toe" board shown in Fig. 6-7 is used to illustrate the use of subscripts in a two-dimensional array.‡ The name of this array is TIC and it contains 3 rows and 3 columns (called a 3 by 3 array). The first subscript denotes the row, and the second subscript denotes the column. Thus, TIC(2,2) specifies the board position in the second row and second column, TIC(1,2) the first row and second column, and TIC(3,3) the third row, third column, etc.

A *three-dimensional* array needs three subscripts to identify its items. We can think of this type of an array as a three-dimensional box having length, width, and height. The first subscript identifies the *row*, the second subscript the *column*, and the third subscript the *layer*. Given the three subscripts, we can locate any value in the array.

The DIMENSION statement is used for informing the computer of

---

*Sometimes called a *list* (in BASIC) or a *vector*.

†Sometimes called a *table* (in BASIC) or *matrix*.

‡Numbers in a two-dimensional array are not stored inside the computer in boxes. This drawing is used only for the purpose of illustrating a two-dimensional array.

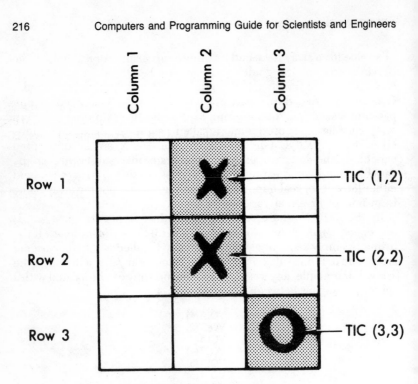

Fig. 6-7. A two-dimensional array.

the names of all the different arrays in a program and how many locations in computer storage to reserve for each array. The DIMENSION statement has the form

$$\text{DIMENSION } a, b, c, \ldots$$

where the letters $a, b, c, \ldots$ represent the list of the array names used in a program. Each one of these names must be followed by a set of numbers which show the greatest value that the subscripts of that array can have.

A DIMENSION statement to allocate storage for a list of 300 items (named PRICE) would appear as

DIMENSION PRICE(300)

The statement

DIMENSION TEST(10,14)

reserves storage for a two-dimensional array of 140 items.

Several arrays may be dimensioned in one DIMENSION statement.

For example, the statement

DIMENSION TITLE(80), TEMP(18,40), CROSS(20,20,8)

causes the computer to reserve storage for an 80-item one-dimensional array called TITLE, an 18 by 40 two-dimensional array called TEMP, and a three-dimensional array called CROSS that contains 20 rows, 20 columns, and 8 layers.

Previously, we discussed READ and WRITE statements with lists containing only variable names. Now that we have learned how to reserve blocks of computer storage for an array, let us examine how numbers are read into and printed from an array.

Subscripted-variable names and subscripted-variable names with indexing can also be used in the list of READ and WRITE statements. For example, the statements

```
        READ(5,240) A(5), B(8), C(2)
    240 FORMAT(3F10.2)
```

would cause three values to be read from a data card and assigned to the fifth position of array A, the eighth position of array B, and the second position of array C. The statements

```
        DO 100 K = 1, 60
        READ(5,50) X(K)
     50 FORMAT (F10.5)
    100 CONTINUE
```

would cause 60 different numbers (each on a separate punched card) to be read into array X. This is just a shorter way of writing the statements

```
        READ (5,50) X(1)
        READ (5,50) X(2)
        READ (5,50) X(3)
                  .
                  .
                  .
        READ (5,50) X(59)
        READ (5,50) X(60)
     50 FORMAT (F10.5)
```

The DO loop method of reading data into arrays is satisfactory, but there is an even easier method. It involves something similar to a DO loop except that it is part of the input/output list and is called an *implied* DO loop. The best way to describe this method is to illustrate how it works.

The statements

```
        READ (5,700) (X(K),K = 1,30)
    700 FORMAT (F8.2)
```

will set up a loop that will read 30 values into array elements X(1), X(2), X(3), . . ., X(30). A statement that would read the data associated with a two-dimensional array would have the form

READ(5,20) ((SUM(J,K),J = 1,2),K = 1,3)

This statement would read data into the computer in the following order:

SUM (1,1)
SUM (2,1)
SUM (1,2)
SUM (2,2)
SUM (1,3)
SUM (2,3)

If the previous statement had been written

READ(5,20) ((SUM(J,K),K = 1,3),J = 1,2)

the data would have been read in the sequence

SUM (1,1)
SUM (2,1)
SUM (3,1)
SUM (1,2)
SUM (2,2)
SUM (3,2)

An example of a WRITE statement is

WRITE(6,40) ((NUM(I,J), I = 1,3), J = 1,3)
40   FORMAT(3I6/3I6/3I6)

These statements would cause the elements of array NUM to be printed in the following manner:

26	32	12
14	81	23
11	16	19

assuming that the values in computer storage were

NUM(1,1) = 26
NUM(2,1) = 14
NUM(3,1) = 11
NUM(1,2) = 32
NUM(2,2) = 81
NUM(3,2) = 16
NUM(1,3) = 12
NUM(2,3) = 23
NUM(3,3) = 19

DATA STATEMENT

Two common ways to make numeric assignments in a program are to use an arithmetic statement or to read the data value into computer storage. Both of these assignments are made while the program is being executed. Another way is to assign data values to a variable at *compilation* time. In this way, the data values become part of the source program. This method uses the DATA statement, which has the general form

$$\text{DATA } a/d_1, d_2, d_3/, b/d_1, d_2/, c/d_1/, \ldots$$

where $a, b, c, \ldots$ represent variables to receive data values, and the d's are the actual data values to be assigned to variables in the list. For example, the statement

DATA A/3.7/, B/423.9/, N(3)/80/

would assign 3.7 to A, 423.9 to B, and 80 to N(3). This statement is accomplishing the same assignments as the arithmetic statements

$$A = 3.7$$
$$B = 423.9$$
$$N(3) = 80$$

FORTRAN SUBROUTINES

Occasionally when writing computer programs one finds a certain set of calculations that are to be repeated many times with different data. Instead of writing the same set of statements many times, FORTRAN allows the statements to be put into a program of their own. This program is called a *subroutine*. Once written, a subroutine can be referenced by a FORTRAN program whenever desired.

The subroutine starts with a statement that has the word SUBROUTINE, the name, and the arguments. For example, the following statement could be the first statement in a subroutine:

SUBROUTINE ERROR(X,Y,Z)

The name of the subroutine is ERROR and the arguments are X, Y, and Z. It is not required that a subroutine have arguments. Arguments are merely used to pass data to the subroutine for subsequent calculations, or to pass subroutine calculated results back to the referencing program. A subroutine must contain a RETURN statement, which transfers program control back to the referencing program. A subroutine to compute the factorial of a positive integer follows:

```
      SUBROUTINE FACT(N,IFACT)
      IFACT = 1
      DO 10 K = 2,N
   10 IFACT = IFACT * K
      RETURN
      END
```

The input is the argument N. This is to be supplied by the main program when it calls for this subroutine. The output is the value of IFACT.

Subroutines are referenced in a program by the CALL statement, which has the general form

CALL *name (arguments)*

The *name* stands for the name of the subroutine and the *arguments* stands for the list of values to be passed to and from the subroutine.

When a CALL statement is used in a program, the computer will transfer control to the subroutine, execute it, and come back to the main program when it reaches a RETURN statement in the subroutine. It will enter the main program at the statement that immediately follows the CALL statement.

The following CALL statement could be used to reference the subroutine FACT:

CALL FACT(N, IFACT)

LOGICAL COMPUTATIONS

Logical computations may also be performed in FORTRAN. A *logical expression* is an expression consisting of a sequence of *logical variables*, *logical constants*, or certain arithmetic expressions separated by either logical or relational *operators*. A logical constant can represent either *true* or *false*. A logical variable is a variable that has been declared so in a LOGICAL *type* statement.* A logical constant must be either .TRUE. or .FALSE.; a logical variable can take on only the values .TRUE. or .FALSE.. Likewise, the solution to a logical expression is a value that is either *true* or *false*.

The simplest form of logical expression is a single logical variable which can be assigned either a true or false value. Another common form of logical expression is the *relational expression*. This has the general form

$$e \ r \ e$$

where *e* is an arithmetic expression and *r* is one of the following *relational operators:*

.GT.	Greater than (>)
.LT.	Less than (<)
.GE.	Greater than or equal to (≥)
.LE.	Less than or equal to (≤)
.EQ.	Equal to (=)
.NE.	Not equal to (≠)

The relational operators are always preceded and followed by a period. This is to distinguish them from other FORTRAN variables, such as GT, LT, or EQ.

The .EQ. operator has the same meaning as the "equal to" sign (=) in an algebraic equation.

Examples of logical IF statements using relational expressions are

```
IF (X .LE. Y) GO TO 300
IF (SPEED .EQ. 431.7) S = R + 837.82
IF (A .GT. 400) GO TO 80
```

More complicated logical expressions can be expressed using the *logical operators*

$$.AND. \quad\quad .OR. \quad\quad .NOT.$$

to combine other logical or relational expressions.

Expressions using the logical operators have the following form:

$$a \ .AND. \ b \quad\quad a \ .OR. \ b \quad\quad .NOT. \ a$$

Type statements will be discussed in the next section.

where a and b are logical or relational expressions. In the expression a .AND. b, the effect of the operator is to make the total expression *true* only if a and b are both true, but *false* if both a and b are false, or if either a or b is false. In the expression a .OR. b, the effect of the .OR. operator is to make the total expression *true* if either a or b is true, or both a and b are true, but *false* only if a and b are both false. The expression .NOT. a makes the total expression *true* only if a is false, but *false* only if a is true. The logical operators are also preceded and followed by a period.

Logical and relational expressions will be processed by the FORTRAN compiler from left to right, using the hierarchy of operations to determine the priority. If parentheses are absent and the operators are of equal priority, then the operations will be performed from left to right. If the operators are of different priority, the one with the highest priority will be processed first. Quantities within parentheses will always be processed first. The hierarchy of operations is as follows:

1. Quantities within parentheses.
2. Evaluation of functions.
3. Exponentiation.
4. Multiplication and division.
5. Addition and subtraction.
6. Relational operators.
7. .NOT.
8. .AND.
9. .OR.

A *logical statement* has the general form

$$a = le$$

where a is a logical variable and le is a logical expression. In the statement

A = X .GT. Y

the variable A will be set to *true* if the value of X is greater than the value of Y, and to *false* if X is equal to or less than the value of Y. Both X and Y, and A must have previously appeared in a LOGICAL *type* statement. Some other examples of logical statements and their mathematical equivalents are shown in Table 6-6.

The logical IF statement has the form

$$IF(e) \ le$$

where e is a logical expression and le is any executable statement except another logical IF statement, a DO statement, or a nonexecutable

Table 6-6. Examples of Logical Statements and Their Mathematical Equivalents

Logical Statement	Mathematical Statement
Y = (A .AND. B) .OR. C W = .NOT. X A = B .LT. R	$y = (a \wedge b) \vee c$ w is not x $a = b < r$

statement such as FORMAT or END. The operation of the logical IF statement is illustrated by the following examples:

$$\text{IF (X .GT. Y) GO TO 400}$$

This statement causes a transfer of control to statement 400 if X is greater than Y.

$$\text{IF (A .GT. B .AND. C .EQ. D) GO TO 80}$$

This statement causes a transfer of control to statement 80 if *both* the conditions "A greater than B" *and* "C equal to D" are true. If one (or both) is false, then the GO TO statement will not be executed and control will pass to the next statement in the program.

$$\text{IF(A .EQ. B .OR. R .LE. 40) VOLT} = 1.0$$

In this case, the statement VOLT = 1.0 will be executed if *one* or *both* of the conditions "A equal to B" and "R less than or equal to 40" is true. Only when they are both false will the statement VOLT = 1.0 be ignored.

$$\text{IF(.NOT. X .GT. Y) GO TO 60}$$

This statement has the same effect as the statement

$$\text{IF (X .LE. Y) GO TO 60}$$

The .NOT. operator reverses the truth value of whatever follows. Therefore, the GO TO statement will be executed if "X greater than Y" is *not* true.

The IF statement is often used to write a *loop*. For example, if one wanted to perform the same set of statements 100 times, you could set up a single loop as shown in Fig. 6-8.

REAL, INTEGER, AND LOGICAL DECLARATIONS

In general, we know that *integer variable* names begin with I, J, K, L, M, or N, and *real variable* names start with other letters. There are times, however, when we would like to change that rule. *Type*

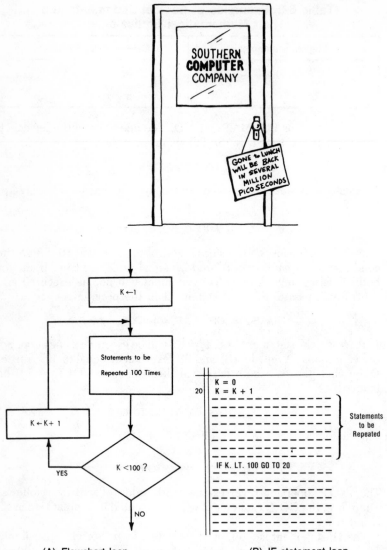

(A) Flowchart loop.   (B) IF statement loop.

Fig. 6-8. Looping with the IF statement.

statements are used to override variables named *implicitly;* that is, by
the conventional "IJKLMN" naming rule.

The INTEGER *type* statement has the general form

$$\text{INTEGER } a, b, c, \ldots$$

where a, b, c, . . . can represent real variable or subscripted variable names. A statement such as

INTEGER AREA, SUM, R

will cause the variables AREA, SUM, and R to be treated as integer variables in a program.

The following REAL *type* statement:

REAL NAME, MATH, J

will cause the variables NAME, MATH, and J to be treated as real variables in the program.

Before an *explicitly* defined variable name can be used in an executable FORTRAN statement, it must previously have been defined in a *type* statement. All variables and arrays that are to be of the *logical* mode must be defined in the list of a LOGICAL *type* statement. This statement has the form

$$\text{LOGICAL } a,b,c,...$$

where a, b, c, . . . are variable or array names. As discussed in the last section, a logical variable can take on only the values *true* and *false*.

EXERCISES

1. Circle the illegal FORTRAN variables:

    (a) GO   (d) K + 27
    (b) R23   (e(A63
    (c) HOTLIP   (f) JACK

2. Which of the variable names in Exercise 1 are integer?

3. Write FORTRAN expressions for each of the following mathematical expressions:

    (a) $a + b^4 - 6$
    (b) $b + 6^{x-y}$
    (c) $ax^3 + bx^2 + cx - d$
    (d) $d^2 + 4.6c - 77$

4. Write FORTRAN statements for the following mathematical statements:

    (a) $y = ax^3 + bx^2 - cx + 36$

    (b) $a = b + c^2 - 63$

    (c) $m = \sqrt{a + b^2 - 6}$

    (d) $z = \sqrt{\dfrac{a + b}{3}} + \dfrac{x + y}{6}$

(e) $s = \dfrac{V_2^2 - V_1^2}{2g}$

(f) $r = \dfrac{WV_1^2}{2g} - \dfrac{WV_2^2}{2g}$

5. If Y = 2.0, Z = 3.0, N = 2, and K = 3, what will be the result of the following FORTRAN statements?

    (a) X = Y * Z / 3.0
    (b) X = Z**4
    (c) J = K/N
    (d) J = (N*K)**2/2.0

6. Express the following mathematical statements in FORTRAN:

    (a) $V = \pi r \sqrt{r^2 + h^2}$

    (b) $A = \dfrac{rl - c(r - h)}{2}$

    (c) $s = vt - \dfrac{at^2}{2}$

    (d) $y = |v + a| - 36$

7. What would be the value of W after executing the following sequence of FORTRAN statements?

$$
\begin{aligned}
X &= 3.0 \\
Y &= 2.0 \\
Z &= 5.0 \\
R &= X + Y \\
S &= R + Z - X \\
W &= S * Y/4.0
\end{aligned}
$$

8. The following card contains values for X and Y:

888.0   632.4

Write READ and FORMAT statements that will read these values into computer storage.

9. Which one of the following FORTRAN statements will transfer control to statement 22 when X is negative, and to statement 44 when X is zero or positive?

    (a) IF(X) 44,22,44
    (b) IF(X) 22,44,44
    (c) IF(X) 22,22,44
    (d) IF(X) 44,44,22

10. Write a program to read A; compute $X = A^2$, $Y = \sqrt{A}$, and $Z = A^2 + 73$; and print X,Y, and Z.

11. Write READ and FORMAT statements that would cause the values shown on the cards to be assigned in computer storage as follows:

$$IA = \qquad IB = \qquad IC =$$

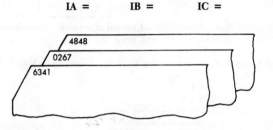

12. Write a program to read A, B, and C; compute $S = \frac{1}{2}(A+B+C)$, $AREA = \sqrt{S(S-A)(S-B)(S-C)}$; and print AREA. Assume that the following values are punched on one data card: $A = 12$, $B = 8$, $C = 14$.

13. Write a program to calculate 10!.

$$10! = 1 \times 2 \times 3 \times 4 \times \ldots \times 10$$

14. Draw a flowchart and write a program to compute the sum of the first 300 integers squared:

$$\sum_{n=1}^{300} n^2$$

15. Write a program that will compute the period of a pendulum. Use the following equation:

$$T = 2\pi \sqrt{\frac{l}{g}}$$

where,
  T is the period in seconds
  l is the length of the pendulum in feet,
  $g = 32.2$ ft/s^2.

Compute the period for a pendulum having a length of 20 feet.

16. Write a DO statement that causes a DO loop to perform as follows:

(a) Iterate a loop 40 times with the loop index K successively assuming the values 2,4,6, . . .
(b) Iterate a loop 200 times with the loop index assuming the values 15, 16, 17, . . .
(c) Iterate a loop with the loop index assuming all the values between 2 and 150.

17. Find the intermediate and final values of X in the following program segment:

```
        X = 3.0
        DO 100 K = 1,4
100     X = X*2 + S(K)
```

Array S
S(1) = 2.0
S(2) = 0.0
S(3) = 3.0
S(4) = 4.0

18. Write a program that will read the 10 values of array B into computer storage, calculate the sum of these values, and print the sum.

19. Write a DO loop that will accomplish what the following IF loop is doing:

```
        I = 0
100     I = I + 1
        _ _ _ _ _ _ _
        _ _ _ _ _ _ _
        IF (I .LT. 20) GO TO 100
```

20. Find the final value of N in the following program:

```
        N = 1
        DO 200 I = 1,2
        DO 200 K = 1,2
200     N = N + X(I,K)
```

Array X

2	2
3	4

21. Write a FORTRAN program to calculate the time it takes to fill a water tank, which

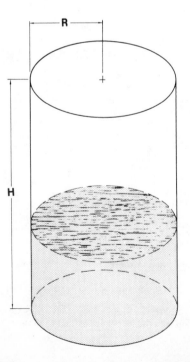

is determined by dividing the volume of the tank by the rate of filling. The volume is given by

$$V = \pi R^2 H$$

where R is the radius and H is the height of the tank. The time to fill the tank is given by

$$Hours = \frac{\pi R^2 H}{Q}$$

where Q is the filling rate in ft³/h. Use the following data values: R = 6.0 ft, H = 18.0 ft, and Q = 40.0 gal/min. There are 7.481 gallons per cubic foot.

22. The heights of the 10 members of the "Space University" basketball team, in inches, are

63   65   66   68   71   71   72   72   74   78

Write a program that will compute the mean average height of the team.

23. The wavelength of a sound is a function of its frequency. A high-fidelity system can reproduce sounds as low as 15 vibrations per second (with waves more than 70 feet long) and as high as 30,000 vibrations per second (with waves less than half an inch long). The formula for this function is

$$W = \frac{1100}{F}$$

where W is the wavelength in feet, and F is the frequency in vibrations per second. Draw a flowchart and write a program to compute a table of values of W and F for all values of F in the range $10 \le F \le 100$.

24. Two square matrices can be added by adding their corresponding elements:

$$A = \begin{bmatrix} a_1 & b_1 \\ a_2 & b_2 \end{bmatrix} \qquad B = \begin{bmatrix} c_1 & d_1 \\ c_2 & d_2 \end{bmatrix}$$

then A + B = C:

$$C = \begin{bmatrix} a_1 + c_1 & b_1 + d_1 \\ a_2 + c_2 & b_2 + d_2 \end{bmatrix}$$

Write a program to add two matrices, A and B, each of which can contain up to 20 by 20 elements. The program should read the input data into computer storage, calculate C, and output the C matrix.

25. The "Colorado Research Company" is running a contest in which they will send the winner some money every day for one month. The amounts are $100 the first day, $200 the second day, $300 the third day, $400 the fourth day, and so on. Assuming that you won the contest, draw a flowchart and write a program that will compute how much money the "Colorado Research Company" will send you for 30 days.

26. An electric circuit contains three pure resistances in parallel: R_1, R_2, and R_3. Write a FORTRAN program to compute a table of values for R_T using the following data values: $R_1 = 5$ ohms, $R_2 = 8$ ohms, and $R_3 = 2, 3, 4, 5, 6, \ldots, 15$ ohms. Use the following equation:

$$\frac{1}{R_T} = \frac{1}{R_1} + \frac{1}{R_2} + \frac{1}{R_3}$$

27. Write a program to calculate sine x by the infinite series expansion:

$$\sin x = x - \frac{x^3}{3!} + \frac{x^5}{5!} - \frac{x^7}{7!} + \frac{x^9}{9!} \ldots$$

Use sufficient terms so that the error in the nth term is less than 0.00001. Compute sine x values for $x = 0.0, 0.1, 0.2, 0.3, \ldots, 1.0$. Compare results produced by the program with standard table values.

28. The number of chirps that a cricket makes in a minute is a function of the temperature. As a result, it is possible to tell how warm it is by using a cricket as a thermometer! A formula for the function is

$$T = \frac{N}{4} + 40$$

where T represents the temperature in degrees Fahrenheit, and N represents the number of cricket chirps in one minute. Write a program that will compute and print the approximate temperatures for 100, 105, 110, 115, 120, . . ., 230 chirps per minute.

29. Write a program that will compute the volume of a hollow torus. Use the formula

$$V = \frac{\pi^2 D \left[d_1^2 - d_2^2 \right]}{4}$$

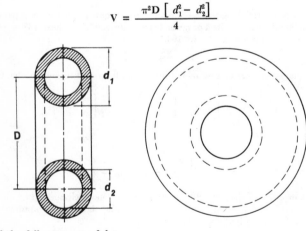

and the following sets of data:

D	d_1	d_2
6.0	3.0	2.0
10.2	4.8	2.6

18.0	5.6	4.1
20.0	5.6	4.4
20.0	5.8	4.4
32.2	6.8	3.2

30. The equation which expresses the variations of electric current with time in an inductive circuit is

$$i = I_0 \, \varepsilon^{-Rt/L}$$

where,

   i is the current in amperes,
   I_0 is the original steady-state value of current (a constant),
   ε is the base of the natural system of logarithms and is approximately 2.7183,
   R is the resistance in ohms in the circuit (a constant),
   t is the time in seconds measured as the current i varies,
   L is the inductance in henrys (a constant).

Write a FORTRAN program to calculate and print values of i as t varies from 0 to 0.5 second. Use the following data values: $I_0 = 0.16$ ampere, R = 1.2 ohms, and L = 0.5 henry.

31. A series of weighings of a sample of metal powder are made with the following results:

Weight in Grams of a Sample

2.020	2.021	2.019	2.019	2.021
2.018	2.021	2.021	2.017	2.018
2.017	2.020	2.019	2.020	2.016

Write a program to compute the mean and standard deviation for the weighings. Use the following equations:

$$X = \sum_{i=1}^{n} \frac{X_i}{n} = \frac{X_1 + X_2 + X_3 + \ldots X_n}{n}$$

$$\sigma = \sqrt{\frac{\Sigma \, (X_i - \bar{X})^2}{n-1}}$$

where,

   $\bar{X}$ is the arithmetic mean,
   σ is the standard deviation,
   Σ is the symbol for "summation of,"
   X_i are the individual measurements,
   n is the total number of measurements.

32. If two sides and the included angle are known, the third side of a triangle can be found by the *Law of Cosines:*

$$c^2 = a^2 + b^2 - 2ab \cos C$$

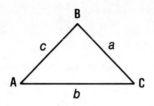

Draw a flowchart and write a program that will compute 50 values of side c according to 50 given values of side a, side b, and angle C. Array A contains 50 values of side a, array B contains 50 values of side b, and array ANGLE contains 50 values of angle C. Output the values for sides a, b, and c in the following format:

SIDE A	SIDE B	SIDE C
a_1	b_1	c_1
a_2	b_2	c_2
a_3	b_3	c_3
.	.	.
.	.	.
.	.	.
a_{50}	b_{50}	c_{50}

33. Write a program to show the relationship between horsepower transmitted by various diameters of cold-drawn steel shafting for a speed of 72 r/min based on the formula

$$hp = \frac{D^3R}{50}$$

where,
    hp is the horsepower,
    D is the diameter of the shaft in inches,
    R is the revolutions per minute of the shaft
      = 72.
The program should produce a printout showing values for every inch diameter up to and including 22 inches.

34. A switching path between parallel railroad tracks, A and B, is to provide a reasonably smooth crossing. It must leave track A tangentially, to avoid a sharp corner there, and join track B at a point 4 units of distance to the east and 2 units to the north, again tangentially. One relatively simple curve that meets these requirements and also has the desirable feature of being symmetrical about the central point, labeled (2,1) is the "cubic polynomial":

$$Y = \frac{(6 - X)X^2}{16}$$

As shown in the drawing, X and Y represent distance eastward and northward from (0,0). For laying the track, the values of Y at positions X = .01, .02, . . ., 2.00 are needed; the other half will be determined by the symmetry. Write a program to output these values.

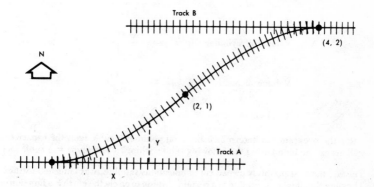

35. Write a program that will compute the total capacity of the water tank shown in the accompanying sketch. For convenience, you may consider the tank to be in three

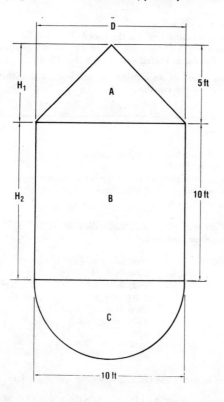

parts: a cone (A), a cylinder (B), and a hemisphere (C). Use the following formulas:

$$\text{Volume of cone (A)} = \frac{\pi\, D^2 H_1}{12}$$

$$\text{Volume of cylinder (B)} = \frac{\pi\, D^2 H_2}{4}$$

$$\text{Volume of hemisphere (C)} = \frac{\pi\, D^3}{12}$$

$$\text{Total volume} = A + B + C$$

After the program has determined the total volume in cubic feet, the capacity in gallons can be found using the following relationship: 7.481 gallons = 1 cubic foot.

36. Telstar, the first privately owned communications satellite, was launched in 1962. The time that it takes a satellite at a certain altitude to circle the earth is a function of the speed of the satellite. The formula for an altitude of 100 miles is

$$T = \frac{1540}{S}$$

Where T is the time in minutes, and S is the speed of the satellite in thousands of miles per hour. Draw a flowchart and write a program that will compute and print a table of values of T for the following values of S: 16, 17, 18, . . ., 24.

37. The minimum flying speed of an airplane at sea level and with standard air conditions is expressed in the equation

$$V^2 = \frac{W}{(P/2)\, C_L S}$$

where,
    W is the weight of the airplane and its cargo,
    S is the wing area = 330 ft^2,
    C_L is the maximum coefficient of lift of the wing section = 2.0,
    P is the mass density of air = 0.07651 lb/ft^3,
    V is the landing speed in ft/s.

Write a FORTRAN program to compute the landing speeds (in ft/s) for the following airplane weights (airplane and cargo):

                    3000 lb
                    3400 lb
                    3800 lb
                    4200 lb
                    4600 lb
                    5000 lb
                    5400 lb
                    5800 lb
                    6200 lb

38. Write a program to compute the landing speeds in miles per hour (Exercise 37).

39. Write a *type* statement to make the variables S, AREA, and VOL of *integer* mode.

40. **Write a DATA statement that could replace the following arithmetic statements:**

$$
\begin{aligned}
J &= 672 \\
R &= 36.0 \\
T &= 41.66
\end{aligned}
$$

41. **Write a subroutine that will compute the smallest number of X, Y, and Z. Inputs to the subroutine are X, Y, and Z. The output from the subroutine is the smallest number SMALL. The referencing statement for this subroutine is**

CALL SMNUM(X,Y,Z,SMALL)

CHAPTER 7
BASIC
PROGRAMMING

BASIC is an acronym for *Beginner's All-purpose Symbolic Instruction Code*. The language was developed in 1963–1964 by a small group of undergraduate students under the direction of Professors John G. Kemeny and Thomas E. Kurtz at Dartmouth College. It was developed at a time when the interest in time sharing was focused on large research-oriented, experimental systems. Today BASIC is the most widely used programming language. It is available on almost all computers, including minicomputers and microcomputers.

In Chapter 6, we discussed the FORTRAN programming language. Since BASIC is similar to FORTRAN and shares many points in common with it, knowledge of either language helps with the learning of the other. BASIC, however, represents a considerable simplification of FORTRAN. BASIC is a programming language for the engineer who:

1. Has a problem.
2. Wants to solve it easily, quickly, and conveniently.
3. Prefers to describe his own problems to a computer rather than describe them to a programmer.
4. Will have modest amounts of input data to be used by the program.

BASIC permits the engineer to communicate a problem to the computer in a language that uses statements and equations. It permits the engineer to define and rapidly solve programming problems. Although a simple language, BASIC can be used for the solution of complex mathematical and engineering problems. Using BASIC, an engineer can easily solve problems using a desk-top microcomputer or a terminal connected to a remotely located computer.

FUNDAMENTALS OF BASIC

A BASIC program is made up of meaningful symbols, including numbers, letters, and special characters. The symbols are used in

punctuation or are joined together to form words, which, in turn, are grouped into statements. The vocabulary of words and grammatical rules for making statements and punctuating are the basic tools of any language; however, in BASIC, as in any other programming language, the tools are necessarily stylized and rigid to permit the computer to interpret its instructions without ambiguity.

Since BASIC is an engineering language, its words consist essentially of variables, numbers, and operators. All of these must be represented to the computer in certain specific ways, which we shall explore in some detail. The basic unit of the BASIC programming language is the *statement*, of which there are four types, each having different functions:

1. *Arithmetic Statements*—These statements specify the mathematical operations that the computer must execute.
2. *Program Control Statements*—These statements direct the sequence of operations in the program.
3. *Input/Output Statements*—These statements describe the input/output operations needed to enter data and print results.
4. *Specification Statements*—These statements allocate storage space.

As we proceed through the chapter, we shall discuss and illustrate each of these types of statements. Examples of *programs* (and *subprograms*) composed of various statements will also be presented.

Before we actually start to write programs, let us consider some fundamental rules of BASIC programming:

- A line can contain only one statement.
- Every BASIC program *must* terminate with an END statement.
- Each statement must have a *line number,* an integer between 1 and 99999.
- Statements are executed in the order of their line numbers, not in the order of entry at the terminal.
- Spacing between words, variables, numbers, and symbols is usually not important. Within limits, you may put spaces in or leave them out as you see fit.

Fig. 7-1 shows an example of a complete BASIC program that will compute and print the value of the following mathematical expression:

$$\sqrt{a_1^2 + a_2^2 + a_3^2 + a_4^2}$$

where $a_1 = 2$, $a_2 = 8$, $a_3 = 21$, and $a_4 = 17$.

As can be seen from this example, a program consists of a simple sequence of statements. Each statement has a *line number* and begins on a new line. A program may contain *comments,* which are to be printed with the program but otherwise ignored. Each comment statement must start with the word REM.

```
10    REM   SAMPLE PROGRAM
20    DIM A[4]
30    LET X=0
40    FOR I=1 TO 4
50      READ A[I]
60      LET X=X+A[I]↑2
70    NEXT I
80    LET S=SQR(X)
90    PRINT S
100   DATA  2, 8, 21, 17
110   END

RUN
  28.2489
```

Fig. 7-1. Example of a complete BASIC program.

THE CHARACTER SET

BASIC makes use of all letters of the alphabet (A, B, C, . . . Z), the digits (0, 1, 2, . . . 9), and the special characters shown in Table 7-1. Some of the special characters are not available on all keyboard devices. For example, Fig. 7-2 illustrates the keyboard of the Radio Shack TRS-80 microcomputer. Notice that this keyboard does not have the symbols ≤, ≥, and ≠. Thus, some BASIC implementations have improvised and created their own characters: > = is the same as ≥; < = is the same as ≤; and < > is the same as ≠. The keyboard of an IBM communications terminal is shown in Fig. 7-3. This keyboard contains all of the previous symbols.

Table 7-1. Special Characters Used in BASIC

+	Plus Sign	'	Single Quote
−	Minus Sign	"	Double Quote
↑	Up Arrow	<	Less-Than Sign
/	Slash	≤	Less Than or Equal To
*	Asterisk	=	Equal Sign
(	Left Parenthesis	>	Greater-Than Sign
)	Right Parenthesis	≥	Greater Than or Equal To
,	Comma	≠	Not Equal To
.	Period, Decimal Point	!	Exclamation Point
&	Ampersand	$	Dollar Sign
;	Semicolon	@	At Sign
:	Colon	#	Number Sign
	Blank		

Fig. 7-2. Keyboard of the Radio Shack TRS-80 microcomputer.

Fig. 7-3. Keyboard of an IBM communications terminal.

VARIABLES, NAMES, VALUES, AND CONSTANTS

The fundamental quantities in BASIC are called *variables*, which are identified by their *names*. Each variable can take any *value* within a certain *domain*, and the value may be changed during the computation. A statement involving variables is to be treated in the same way, regardless of the actual values that the variables have. Some statements allow the current values of variables to be tested and, thus, determine subsequent action.

Names, which identify variables in BASIC, consist of a letter, or a letter with a digit. Thus, in the program of Fig. 7-1, the variables are called I, X, S, and A (I). The variable A (I) is called a *subscripted variable* and is discussed in a later section. There is one additional type of variable in BASIC called a *string variable*, which is denoted by a letter followed by a $; for example, D$, or R$. Variables such as A, X7, or S2 are called *simple variables*. The following are *not* variables in BASIC:

2S	(first character must be a letter)
AB6	(contains more than one letter)
AR	(second character must be a digit)
26	(first character must be a letter)
A163	(contains more than one digit)

A string variable can take on the value of a *string*, which is simply an alphanumeric name of up to 15 valid characters, such as ENGINEERING or THE END.

When we speak of "the value is N2" or "there are K equations" we are really referring to the current value of the variable whose name in this context is given.

Numerical *constants* are written using the ordinary decimal notation. A scale factor (integral power of 10) may be included after the letter E. Constants may be either *integer* or *real*, with or without a scale factor. An integer constant (also called a *fixed-point* constant) is a value that does not contain a fractional part or a decimal point. Real constants (also called *floating-point* constants) always include a decimal point and may or may not have a fractional part. Thus,

- 16428 and 1043 are integers.
- 5.6, 15.16, and 0.281 are real (without exponent).
- 1.432E2 and 61.40E−3 are real (with exponent).

The notations 4.16, 0.416E1, 416.E−2, and 0.00416E3 are different ways of writing the same constant. In the example 0.416E1, the *mantissa* is 0.416, 1 is the *exponent*, and E simply means *with exponent*.

"IT GIVES THE ANSWER AS 36,427,942,018. BUT IT SAYS IT'S JUST A WILD GUESS!"

Commas must not appear in constants. For example, the number 74,162 would not be allowed. A negative constant *must* start with a minus (−) sign. A plus (+) sign for a positive number is optional. If a number is unsigned, it is assumed to be positive. Fractions cannot be used directly, but must be written in decimal form. For example, the fraction 1¾ would be represented as 1.75.

EXPRESSIONS

Several kinds of statements may contain *expressions*, which are written similar to algebraic notation, and cause the current values of the

specified elements to be combined in the specified ways. An element in
an expression may be one of the following:

- Simple variable (A6).
- Constant (2317.0).
- Subscripted variable (R (6)).
- String variable (B$).
- Library function* (SQR (X)).
- String (ENGINEER).

The elements may be combined using the following arithmetic
operators:

+	addition
−	subtraction
*	multiplication
/	division
↑	exponentiation

Thus, the following combinations are valid expressions:

```
A + B − C
R + 36.4
S/A − 6 + 32.4
```

Expressions are evaluated according to the rules of precedence; all
operations of a higher precedence are performed before those of a lower
precedence. When parentheses are used, the operations contained
within parentheses are performed first. Operations of equal precedence
are performed from left to right.

In an expression with no parentheses, operations are evaluated in the
following order:

1. Exponentiation.
2. Multiplication and/or division.
3. Addition and/or subtraction.

The order of precedence for evaluating the subexpressions is
illustrated in Fig. 7-4.

Two operation symbols must not be used in succession, unless
separated by parentheses. Thus, the incorrect expression

$$X = Y * − Z$$

---

*Library functions are discussed later in the chapter.

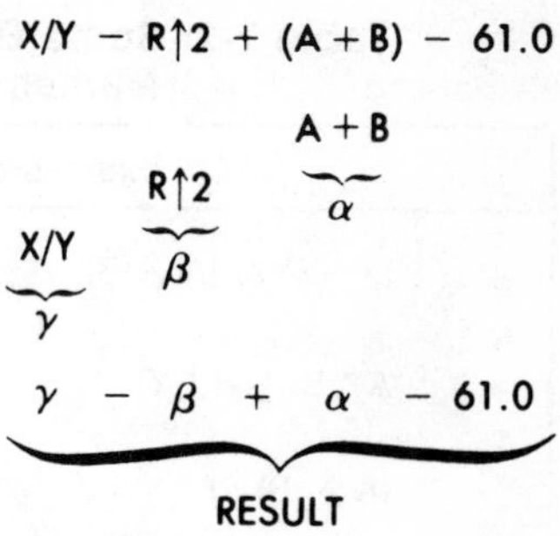

$$X/Y - R\uparrow2 + (A+B) - 61.0$$

$$\underbrace{X/Y}_{\gamma} \quad \underbrace{R\uparrow2}_{\beta} \quad \underbrace{A+B}_{\alpha}$$

Fig. 7-4. Illustration of the order of precedence for evaluating expressions in BASIC.

$$\underbrace{\gamma \quad - \quad \beta \quad + \quad \alpha \quad - 61.0}_{\text{RESULT}}$$

should be writen

$$X = Y * (- Z)$$

or

$$X = - Z * Y$$

An expression may also be a string or a string variable. Thus, the string variable

$$P\$$$

and the string

POWER

are valid expressions. The string

"POWER IS ON"

is also an expression. Whenever a string contains characters such as the comma, semicolon, space, and other special characters, the entire string must be enclosed in quotation marks. Unquoted strings always begin with alphabetic characters.

Some examples of BASIC expressions and their mathematical equivalents are listed in Table 7-2. Had the last example in the list

$$X/ (Y + Z)$$

been written without using parentheses,

$$X/Y + Z$$

the computed result in algebraic notation would have been

$$\frac{x}{y} + z$$

Table 7-2. Some BASIC Expressions and Their Mathematical Equivalents

BASIC Expression	Mathematical Expression
(X + Y) / (A + B)	$\dfrac{x + y}{a + b}$
A * B − H * Y	$ab - hy$
(A + B) / 6	$\dfrac{a + b}{6}$
3 * X ↑ 2 + 2 * X − 3	$3x^2 + 2x - 3$
A ↑ (2 ↑ 2)	A^{2^2}
(A + B) / (X * Y)	$\dfrac{a + b}{xy}$
(1 −X) * (V + 2) / ((1 + X) * (V − 2))	$\dfrac{(1 - x)(v + 2)}{(1 + x)(v - 2)}$
X/(Y +Z)	$\dfrac{x}{y + z}$

instead of

$$\frac{x}{y + z}$$

Let us now examine some BASIC statements and explore their applications.

LET STATEMENT

The principal computational statement in BASIC is the LET statement, which has the form

$$\text{LET } v = x$$

where v is a variable and x is an expression. The = symbol in BASIC is not a mathematical equal sign; it means *is replaced by*. Thus, this statement is interpreted to mean "The value of the expression on the right of the *is replaced by* sign replaces the value of the variable on the left."

The LET statement in BASIC is very similar to the familiar arithmetic statement used in everyday mathematics and performs a function similar to the arithmetic assignment statement in the FORTRAN language. Some typical examples of the LET statement are as follows:

```
40   LET X = X + 1
70   LET R = 14
20   LET X = Y + 10
65   LET B$ = Z$
43   LET S2 = 0
50   LET R = A + B + C + D + E + F + G + 34109
10   LET A$ = RESISTANCE
```

The example

```
40   LET X = X + 1
```

results in the value 1 being added to the value X in storage. The new sum replaces the original value of X. The statement

```
70   LET R = 14
```

causes the number 14 to be assigned to R.

The LET statement may be used to initialize a variable (set the variable to some starting value) or to modify the value of the variable during a computation.

Let us now examine some additional examples. The polynomial

$$y = x^4 - 4x^3 + 8x^2 - 12x + 18$$

can be written

```
10 LET Y = X ↑ 4 − 4 * X ↑ 3 + 8 * X ↑ 2 − 12 * X + 18
```

The equation

$$y = \sqrt{abc}$$

can be written

```
40   LET Y = (A * B * C) ↑ .5
```

The equation

$$\frac{1}{x} = \frac{1}{y} - \frac{1}{z}$$

must first be rearranged in mathematical notation as a function of x:

$$x = \frac{1}{\dfrac{1}{y} - \dfrac{1}{z}}$$

and then the equivalent LET statement is

```
40   LET X = 1 / ((1/Y) − (1/Z))
```

There is one other form of the LET statement, which permits *multiple variable replacement*. Thus, the statement

```
40   LET A = B = C = X + 326
```

is a simplified way of writing

```
40   LET A = X + 326
41   LET B = X + 326
42   LET C = X + 326
```

The statement

```
70   LET X1 = Y2 = Z3 = A/3 − D
```

would have the effect of dividing the value of A by 3, subtracting D from the result, and assigning the resulting numerical value to the variables X1, Y2, and Z3.

"*I KNEW IT WAS A MISTAKE BUYING THIS IMPORTED MODEL!*"

READING AND WRITING

To do even a simple arithmetic problem in BASIC, we need a way of putting numbers into the computer and a method of printing our computed answer. One way to read data is to use the READ and DATA statements. Results may be printed by using the PRINT statement. For example, the program segment shown in Fig. 7-5 will compute and print the sum of the numbers 10, 14, and 26. The READ statement directs the

Fig. 7-5. Segment of BASIC program
illustrating the use of the READ, DATA,
and PRINT statements.

```
10  READ  A,B,C
20  LET  X=A+B+C
30  PRINT  X
40  DATA    10, 14, 26
```

computer to go to the DATA list and read numbers from it. In this particular program, this involves reading the number 10 and assigning it to A, then reading the number 14 and assigning it to B, and then reading the number 26 and assigning it to C. The LET statement computes the sum of 10, 14, and 26 and assigns the sum to X. Then the PRINT statement directs the computer to output (print) the value of X.

The general form of these three input/output statements is as follows:

$$READ \ a, \ b, \ c, \ . \ . \ .$$

where a, b, and c are variables (simple, subscripted, or string) separated by commas.

$$DATA \ x, \ y, \ z, \ . \ . \ .$$

where x, y, and z are digits separated by commas.

$$PRINT \ x, \ y, \ z, \ . \ . \ .$$

where x, y, and z are expressions separated by commas.

One may think of all the DATA statements in a program as being assigned to a first-in/first-out *data bank*, such as that illustrated in Fig. 7-6. In this example, the data values are placed in the data bank in the order 16, 23, 14, 163. When the program is executed, the statement

```
10   READ A, B
```

```
10  READ  A,B
20  LET  C=A+B
30  READ  D,E
40  LET  F=C+D+E
50  PRINT  F
60  DATA    16
70  DATA    23, 14
80  DATA    163
90  END
```

Data Bank

| 16 |
| 23 |
| 14 |
| 163 |

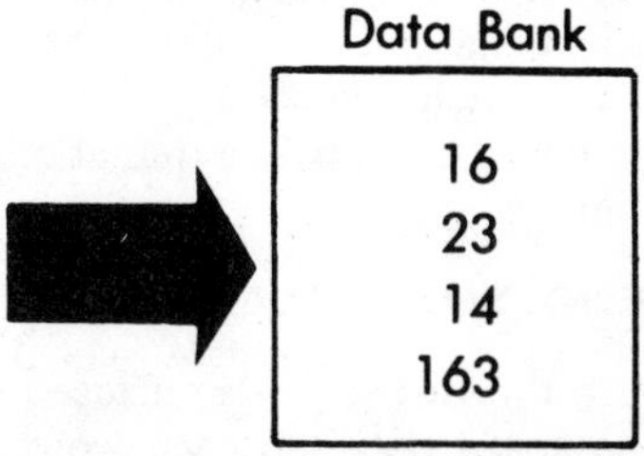

Fig. 7-6. DATA statements assign values to the data bank.

uses the first two numbers, 16 and 23. The statement

    30   READ D, E

reads the remaining numbers, 14, and 163. The same would have been accomplished if the program in Fig. 7-6 had been written as shown in Fig. 7-7A.

```
10 READ A,B,D,E              10 DATA  16, 23, 14, 163
20 LET C=A+B                 20 READ A,B,D,E
30 LET F=C+D+E               30 LET C=A+B
40 PRINT F                   40 LET F=C+D+E
50 DATA  16, 23, 14, 163     50 PRINT F
60 END                       60 END

RUN                          RUN
 216                          216
         (A)                          (B)
```

Fig. 7-7. DATA statements can be located anywhere in the program.

The placement of data actually occurs when the program is read into computer storage rather than at the time of execution. Therefore, even though a DATA statement follows a corresponding READ statement in a program, the data to be read is already accessible when the READ statement is executed. Thus, DATA statements can be located anywhere in the program. The program of Fig. 7-6 could also have been written as shown in Fig. 7-7B. It is good practice, however, to collect all of the DATA statements and place them together just before the END statement as shown in Fig. 7-7A.

There are several other forms of the PRINT statement.

    20   PRINT

causes a line to be skipped on the printing device.

    30   PRINT "THIS IS A MESSAGE"

causes the message contained between quotation marks to be printed.

A PRINT statement containing quotation marks is the only one in BASIC in which *blanks* are counted. The computer will print the message enclosed between quotation marks exactly. For example, the statement

    40   PRINT "SNOOPY FOR PRESIDENT"

will cause the three words enclosed in quotation marks to be printed with one space between each word. The statement

    60   PRINT "SNOOPY   FOR   PRESIDENT"

will cause four spaces to appear between the words SNOOPY and FOR, and seven spaces to appear between FOR and PRESIDENT. In each case, the skipped spaces precisely match the skipped spaces in the statement.

Let us now examine how columns of data can be printed. Suppose that we have written a program to compute electric power for several sets of values of resistance and current (power = $I^2 R$, in which I is current and R is resistance). Let us assume that our column headings are to be

```
        POWER      RESISTANCE         CURRENT
```

To obtain this heading, we write

```
20  PRINT "POWER", "RESISTANCE", "CURRENT"
```

To obtain the values, we write

```
80  PRINT P, R, C
```

Thus, the program segment

```
20  PRINT "POWER", "RESISTANCE", "CURRENT"
 •
 •
 •
80  PRINT P, R, C
90  END
```

would cause printed output similar to the following:

POWER	RESISTANCE	CURRENT
56.423	54.232	1.020
136.041	55.121	1.571
229.109	57.220	2.001
268.872	57.789	2.157
381.210	58.032	2.563

The *commas* contained in the PRINT statement caused the headings and values to be displayed or printed in specific column areas. The display or print area is divided horizontally into five 15-column zones, as shown in Fig. 7-8. When only one value is printed, as in a PRINT R statement, it is placed in zone 1, beginning in column 1. When more than one value is printed, as in a PRINT X, Y, Z statement, the second value is placed in zone 2, the third in zone 3, etc. When more than five values are printed, the first five are placed in the five zones in order. The sixth value is printed on the next line in zone 1, the seventh in zone 2, etc. Whenever the value to be printed exceeds 15 characters, any intervening zone boundary is ignored.

BASIC also has a variable-zone format. Values will be printed in the zones indicated in Table 7-3. A *semicolon* is used in the PRINT

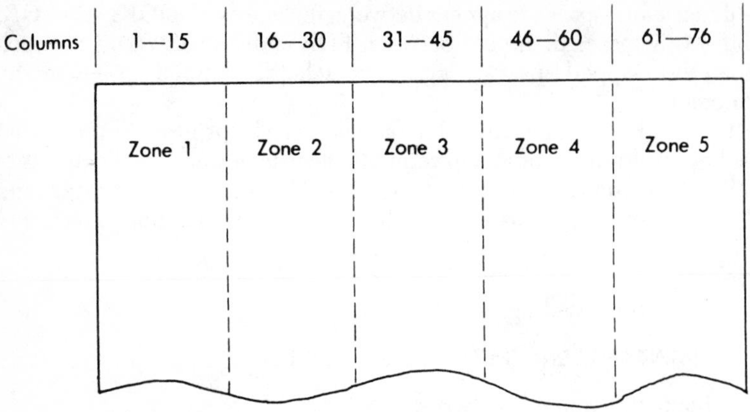

Columns	1—15	16—30	31—45	46—60	61—76
	Zone 1	Zone 2	Zone 3	Zone 4	Zone 5

Fig. 7-8. Display or print area divided into five, 15-column zones.

Table 7-3. Sizes of Values and Zones in Variable-Zone Format

Size of Value (Digits)	Number of Zones	Size of Zone
1	24	3
2, 3, or 4	12	6
5, 6, or 7	8	9
8, 9, or 10	6	12
11	5	15

statement to specify the shorter zone formats. For example, the statement

70   PRINT A; B; C; D; E; F; G

will cause all seven values (provided the values of the variables do not exceed six digits) to be printed on one line. Had the statement

70   PRINT A, B, C, D, E, F, G

been used, then two lines would have been used. To summarize:

PRINT K   Will print the value of K in zone 1, and the next value to be printed will be on the next line.

PRINT K,   Will print the value of K in zone 1 of a five-zone format, and the next value to be printed will be in zone 2.

PRINT K;   Will print the value of K in zone 1 of a
                      variable-zone format, and the next value to be
                      printed will be in zone 2.

PRINT   Will print a "blank line"; i.e., will advance the
                      teletypewriter paper one line, leaving a blank
                      line if the type head is already at the start of a
                      line.

PRINT "MESSAGE"   Will print whatever is contained between the
                      quotation marks.

Messages and variables can also be mixed in the same PRINT statement. For example, the statement

80   PRINT "POWER = ", P

will cause the *message* "POWER =" to be printed in zone 1, and the *value* of P to be printed in zone 2. Thus, if the current value of P was 56.32, then the following would be printed:

POWER = 56.32

Let us now examine several sample BASIC programs using the statements that we have discussed so far. Suppose we wanted to compute the area of a flat ring that had an ouside radius of 8 inches and an inside radius of 6 inches, as shown in Fig. 7-9. The area is obtained by

$$AREA = \pi (R^2 - r^2)$$

The program shown in Fig. 7-9 would accomplish this and, when executed, would print the result: 87.9645.

The last statement in the program of Fig. 7-9 should be explained. Every BASIC program *must* be terminated with an END statement. The END statement, therefore, must have the highest-numbered line number in the program. This statement identifies the end of the program.

Suppose an engineering student wanted to use BASIC to compute the diameter and area of a circle having a radius of 2163 inches. The program shown in Fig. 7-10, when executed, would compute and print the following line of data:

RADIUS = 2163   DIA = 4326   AREA = 1.46981E + 7

This example illustrates that integers containing more than nine digits will be printed as follows: the first digit, followed by a decimal point; the next five digits; the letter E; and the appropriate exponent value.

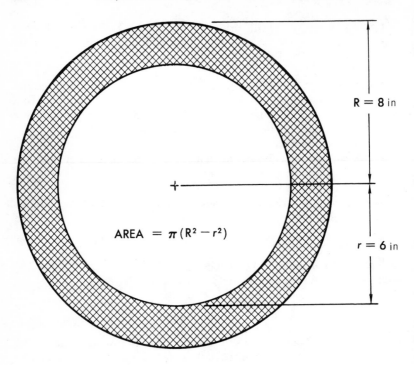

$$AREA = \pi(R^2 - r^2)$$

R = 8 in

r = 6 in

```
200 READ R1,R2
300 LET A=3.14159*(R1↑2-R2↑2)
400 PRINT A
500 DATA  8, 6
600 END

RUN
 87.9645
```

Fig. 7-9. BASIC program to compute the area of a flat ring.

Let us now write a program to compute the voltage across terminals A and B of the circuit shown in Fig. 7-11. This voltage is equal to the source voltage (E) multiplied by $R_1/(R_1 + R_2)$. The program shown in Fig. 7-11 determines that the voltage is 83.3887 volts. This program uses the REM statement to give the program a title.

The *arithmetic mean* of a set of numbers, X_1, X_2, X_3, . . . , X_n is denoted by $\overline{X}$ (read "X bar") and is defined as

$$\overline{X} = \frac{\Sigma X}{n} = \frac{X_1 + X_2 + X_3 + \ldots X_n}{n}$$

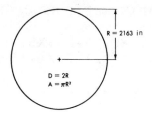

```
10  READ R
20  LET D=R*2
30  LET A=R↑2*3.14159
40  PRINT "RADIUS = ";R,"DIA = ";D;"AREA = ";A
50  DATA   2163
60  END
```

RADIUS =   2163 DIA =   4326 AREA =   1.46981E+7

Fig. 7-10. BASIC program to compute the diameter and area of a circle.

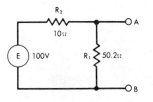

```
10  REM   CIRCUIT PROBLEM
20  READ E,R1,R2
30  LET A=E*R1/(R1+R2)
40  PRINT A
50  DATA  100, 50.2, 10
60  END

RUN
   83.3887
```

Fig. 7-11. BASIC program to compute the voltage across terminals A and B.

The program in Fig. 7-12 computes the arithmetic mean of the grades Steven Spencer made on his last six engineering examinations: 84, 91, 87, 72, 78, and 68. The program computed and printed the value 80.

PROGRAM CONTROL STATEMENTS

The sequence in which the computer executes statements is normally determined by the order in which the statements are physically arranged. Thus far, we have only discussed BASIC programs that are composed of statements to be executed in an unchanging sequence. However, few problems suitable for computer processing can be solved by a simple sequence of arithmetic statements. In many cases, the program will arrive at certain points when it must decide where to go next on the basis of some condition it finds; for example, a number that may be positive, zero, or negative. Depending on the outcome, the

```
100 REM   ARITHMETIC MEAN CALCULATION
200 LET N=6
300 READ X1,X2,X3,X4,X5,X6
400 LET X=(X1+X2+X3+X4+X5+X6)/N
500 PRINT X
600 DATA  84, 91, 87, 72, 78, 68
700 END

RUN
  80
```

Fig. 7-12. BASIC program to compute the arithmetic mean of a set of numbers.

program either continues processing in a straight-line order, jumps back to an earlier step in the program, jumps forward to a later step in the program, or branches to an entirely different program sequence, as shown in Fig. 7-13.

There are several statements in BASIC that allow the engineer to specify the sequence of program execution; thus, altering program paths may depend on a specific condition at the time of execution. Line numbers serve as markers by which program control statements can direct the sequence of a program. Program control cannot be transferred to *nonexecutable* statements such as DIM, REM, DATA, or DEF.

The simplest statement for altering the sequence of execution is the GOTO statement. Suppose, for example, that we wanted to compute values for y in the equation

$$y = x^3 + 7x - 3$$

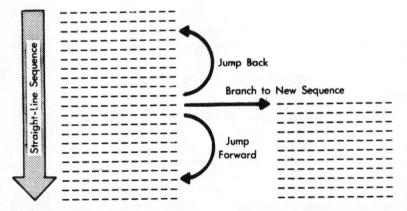

Fig. 7-13. Processing sequences that are possible in a BASIC program.

when x has the values 6, 12, 14, 9, 26, and 41. We could, of course, write the program as shown in Fig. 7-14A. This program requires 19 statements and will perform the required calculations. However, if we make use of the GOTO statement, we can write a program that will produce the same result in six instead of 19 statements as shown in Fig. 7-14B. This program computes and prints values for y and keeps returning control to line number 10 until all data have been used. Program execution then terminates and some special message is printed; for example,

OUT OF DATA IN 10

would have been displayed or printed.

To summarize, the GOTO statement consists of the word GOTO followed by a line number. When the computer encounters the GOTO statement, it causes program control to be transferred to the line number specified in the GOTO statement. Thus, if we said

40 GOTO 107

the computer would transfer control to the statement at line number 107, regardless of where it might be in the program.

It may be desirable to transfer control to a particular statement in a program under certain circumstances but not in others, depending on the results of intermediate calculations. This is accomplished in BASIC by using the IF-THEN statement. Such a statement, called a *conditional transfer* statement,* transfers control only if a certain condition is met.

The general form of the IF-THEN statement is

IF $e\ r\ e$ THEN ln

where e is an expression, ln is a line number in the program, and r is one of the following relational operators:

Relational Operator	Meaning
<	less than
<=	less than or equal to
>	greater than
>=	greater than or equal to
=	equal to
<>	not equal to

*The GOTO statement is called an *unconditional transfer* statement, since it always transfers program control.

```
10 LET X=6
15 LET Y=X↑3+7*X-3
20 PRINT Y
25 LET X=12
30 LET Y=X↑3+7*X-3
35 PRINT Y
40 LET X=14
45 LET Y=X↑3+7*X-3
50 PRINT Y
55 LET X=9
60 LET Y=X↑3+7*X-3
65 PRINT Y
70 LET X=26
75 LET Y=X↑3+7*X-3
80 PRINT Y
85 LET X=41
90 LET Y=X↑3+7*X-3
95 PRINT Y
99 END
```

(A) Program written without using the GOTO statement requires 19 statements.

```
RUN
 255
 1809
 2839
 789
 17755
 69205
```

```
10 READ X
15 LET Y=X↑3+7*X-3
20 PRINT Y
25 GOTO 10
30 DATA  6, 12, 14, 9, 26, 41
35 END
```

```
RUN
 255
 1809
 2839
 789
 17755
 69205
```

(B) Program written using the GOTO statement requires only six statements.

Fig. 7-14. Two methods of writing a BASIC program to solve the same mathematical equation.

In some BASIC systems, the symbols $\leq$, $\geq$, and $\neq$ are used instead of $<=$, $>=$, and $<>$. This depends on the terminal keyboard that is used.

Suppose we wanted to compute $y = 13x^2$ if the value of $a^2 - 2b^2$ is negative, otherwise compute $y = 217x^3$. A flowchart of the program is shown in Fig. 7-15, and the program itself is shown in Fig. 7-16. The program uses the following data values: $a = 28$, $b = 14$, and $x = 12$.

The program tests the value computed for $a^2 - 2b^2$ at statement 400. If the value is less than zero, then the next statement to be executed by the computer will be statement number 700, which computes $y = 13x^2$. If

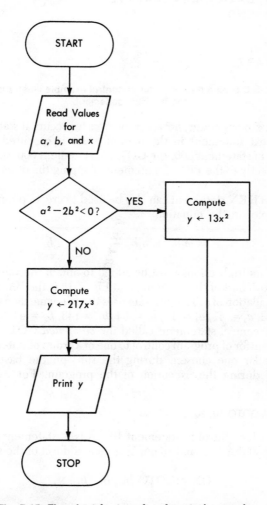

Fig. 7-15. Flowchart for transfer-of-control example.

```
100 REM TRANSFER OF CONTROL EXAMPLE
200 READ A,B,X
300 REM GO TO 700 IF A ↑2-2*B↑2<0
400 IF A↑2-2*B↑2<0 THEN  700
500 LET Y=217*X↑3
600 GOTO 800
700 LET Y=13*X↑2
800 PRINT Y
900 DATA   28,  14,  12
999 END

RUN
  374976
```

Fig. 7-16. BASIC program for transfer-of-control example illustrating the use of the IF-THEN statement.

$a^2 - 2b^2$ is zero or greater, however, no transfer occurs at statement 400, and the next statement in the natural order is executed. After y is computed in statement 500, the GOTO in statement 600 causes control to pass directly to the PRINT statement, skipping the other calculation for y.

The IF-THEN statement can also be used to create program *loops*.* For example, in the equation

$$c = a_1 b_1 + a_2 b_2 + a_3 b_3 + a_4 b_4$$

a series of multiplications must be added to obtain the value of c. Fig. 7-17 is a flowchart of the program, and Fig. 7-18 is the BASIC program for the calculation of c. The program uses the following data values: $a_1 = 13$, $a_2 = 63$, $a_3 = 47$, $a_4 = 12$, $b_1 = 64$, $b_2 = 143$, $b_3 = 41$, and $b_4 = 16$.

Another control statement, called the *computed* GOTO statement, permits transfer of program control to one of a group of statements, with the particular one chosen, during the run, on the basis of results computed during the execution of the program. For example, the statement

300 ON A GOTO 10, 20, 30, 40, 50

would transfer control to statement 10 if A is 1, statement 20 if A is 2, statement 30 if A is 3, and so on. The general form of the statement is

$$\text{ON } e \text{ GOTO } ln_1, \ ln_2, \ ln_3, \ \ldots$$

---

*Looping is discussed in greater detail in the next section.

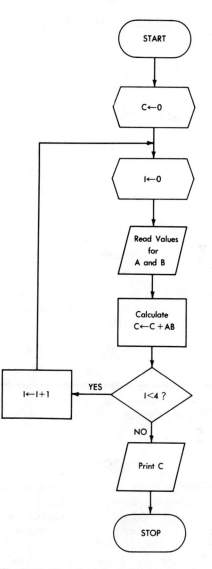

Fig. 7-17. Flowchart for looping example.

where e is a valid BASIC expression other than a string or string variable, and ln_1, ln_2, . . . , are line numbers in the program. Execution of this statement causes ln_i to be executed next, where i is the integer value of the expression. If computation of the expression produces a result other than an integer, the result is *truncated* to its integer value,

```
100 REM CALCULATION OF C
150 LET C=0
200 LET I=0
250 LET I=I+1
300 READ A,B
350 LET C=C+A*B
400 IF I<4 THEN  250
450 PRINT C
500 DATA  13, 64, 63, 143, 47, 41, 12, 16
550 END
```

```
RUN
 11960
```

Fig. 7-18. BASIC program illustrating the use of the IF-THEN statement to create program loops.

regardless of the value of the fractional part. For example, if the expression is $X - Y$ and $X = 4.6$ and $Y = 1.2$, the difference, 3.4, will be truncated to 3, and when the statement

```
100 ON X - Y GOTO 10, 30, 44, 63
```

is executed, control is transferred to statement 44, the third line number in the control statement. The engineer must be sure that the expression in the computed GOTO statement produces a result of at least one, but no more than the number of line-number labels contained in the statement.

LOOPING

One of the most important techniques in programming is the ability to create *loops*. A loop consists of the repetition of a group of statements a number of times, usually with different values of one or more variables at each execution. As illustrated in the previous section, loops can be written using the GOTO and IF-THEN statements. But in BASIC (as in most high-level programming languages), a special statement is available for this purpose. The combination of the FOR and NEXT statements is used to create loops in a BASIC program. A BASIC loop using these statements is illustrated in Fig. 7-19.

The loop starts with the FOR statement and ends with the NEXT statement. The FOR statement instructs the computer to execute 200 times all the instructions between the FOR statement and the NEXT statement. On the first pass through the loop, the variable K is 1, on the

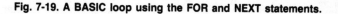

Statements that are
to be repeated in
the loop.

```
10    FOR K = 1 TO 200
 -    - - - - - - - - - -
 -    - - - - - - - - - -
 -    - - - - - - - - - -
 -    - - - - - - - - - -
70    NEXT K
```

Fig. 7-19. A BASIC loop using the FOR and NEXT statements.

second loop K = 2, on the third loop K = 3, and so on until K = 200 on the last loop. The general form of the FOR statement is

$$\text{FOR } v = a \text{ TO } b \text{ STEP } c$$

where v is the index, a is the initial value of the index, b is the terminal value of the index, and c is the value by which the index is modified for each pass through the loop. When c is equal to 1, the general form may be simplified to

$$\text{FOR } v = a \text{ TO } b$$

The general form of the NEXT statement is

$$\text{NEXT } v$$

where v is the same variable (used as an index) that is used in the corresponding FOR statement. Fig. 7-20 is a sample BASIC program illustrating the use of the FOR and NEXT statements. Note that all loop control information is contained in the one FOR statement: The index is X; the starting value is 1; the terminating value is 40; and since no STEP value is specified, the index increment is understood to be 1. A few rules that apply to the FOR statement are:

- Every FOR statement must have an associated NEXT statement.
- The number of statements that may appear between the FOR and NEXT statements is unlimited.
- The FOR loop index may be used by any statement in the loop.
- For a *positive* STEP value, looping will be terminated when the value of the index is greater than b; for a *negative* STEP value, looping will be terminated when the value of the index is less than b.
- The index may not be changed during the course of the FOR-NEXT loop.

```
100 REM TABULAR VALUES OF X
105 PRINT "X","X2","X3","1/X","SQUARE ROOT"
110 FOR X=1 TO 40
115   LET X2=X*X
120   LET X3=X*X*X
125   LET R=1/X
130   LET S=X↑.5
135   PRINT X,X2,X3,R,S
140 NEXT X
150 END
```

RUN

X	X2	X3	1/X	SQUARE ROOT
1	1	1	1	1
2	4	8	.5	1.41421
3	9	27	.333333	1.73205
4	16	64	.25	2
5	25	125	.2	2.23607
6	36	216	.166667	2.44949
7	49	343	.142857	2.64575
8	64	512	.125	2.82843
9	81	729	.111111	3
10	100	1000	.1	3.16228
11	121	1331	9.09091E-2	3.31662
12	144	1728	8.33333E-2	3.4641
13	169	2197	7.69231E-2	3.60555
14	196	2744	7.14286E-2	3.74166
15	225	3375	6.66667E-2	3.87298
16	256	4096	.0625	4
17	289	4913	5.88235E-2	4.12311
18	324	5832	5.55556E-2	4.24264
19	361	6859	5.26316E-2	4.3589
20	400	8000	.05	4.47214
21	441	9261	.047619	4.58258
22	484	10648	4.54545E-2	4.69042
23	529	12167	4.34783E-2	4.79583
24	576	13824	4.16667E-2	4.89898
25	625	15625	.04	5
26	676	17576	3.84615E-2	5.09902
27	729	19683	.037037	5.19615
28	784	21952	3.57143E-2	5.2915
29	841	24389	3.44828E-2	5.38516
30	900	27000	3.33333E-2	5.47723
31	961	29791	3.22581E-2	5.56776
32	1024	32768	.03125	5.65685
33	1089	35937	.030303	5.74456
34	1156	39304	2.94118E-2	5.83095
35	1225	42875	2.85714E-2	5.91608
36	1296	46656	2.77778E-2	6
37	1369	50653	.027027	6.08276
38	1444	54872	2.63158E-2	6.16441
39	1521	59319	.025641	6.245
40	1600	64000	.025	6.32456

Fig. 7-20. BASIC program illustrating the use of the FOR and NEXT statements.

Often it is useful to have loops within loops; that is, a loop completely contained within another loop. This is called *nesting*, and loops may be legally nested as shown in Fig. 7-21A. Fig 7-21B, however, illustrates the illegal nesting of loops—each loop must be completely contained

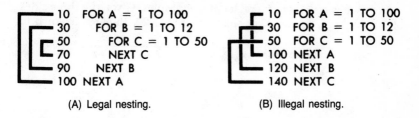

(A) Legal nesting.   (B) Illegal nesting.

Fig. 7-21. Legal and illegal nesting of program loops.

within another loop. (NOTE: As shown in Fig. 7-21A, it is conventional in writing BASIC programs to indent all statements contained within each FOR-NEXT loop. This practice clearly outlines the scope of the loop, particularly nested loops.)

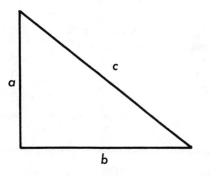

$$s = \frac{a + b + c}{2}$$

$$AREA = \sqrt{s(s-a)(s-b)(s-c)}$$

```
10 REM   COMPUTE AREA OF TRIANGLE
15 PRINT " A"," B"," C"," AREA"
20 FOR R=1 TO 2
25    READ A,B,C
30    LET S=(A+B+C)/2
35    LET A7=(S*(S-A)*(S-B)*(S-C))↑.5
40    PRINT A,B,C,A7
45 NEXT R
50 DATA   3, 4, 5
55 DATA   30, 20, 40
60 END
```

```
RUN
A                  B                  C                  AREA
3                  4                  5                  6
30                 20                 40                 290.474
```

Fig. 7-22. BASIC program to compute the area of a triangle for two sets of data values.

Let us now consider several looping examples. Given the three sides of a triangle, a, b, and c, as shown in Fig. 7-22, the area is equal to

$$AREA = \sqrt{s\,(s\,-\,a)\,(s\,-\,b)\,(s\,-\,c)}$$

where

$$s = \frac{a\,+\,b\,+\,c}{2}$$

The program shown in Fig. 7-22 computes the area of the triangle for two sets of data: $a = 3$, $b = 4$, $c = 5$; and $a = 30$, $b = 20$, $c = 40$. A flowchart of the program is shown in Fig. 7-23. By changing the FOR statement and adding additional DATA statements, this program would compute the area for an unlimited number of triangles.

There are four scales to measure temperature: (1) Fahrenheit (F), (2) Celsius (C), (3) Kelvin (K), and (4) Rankine (R). Fahrenheit temperatures may be converted to Celsius by subtracting 32° from the Fahrenheit readings and multiplying the difference by 5/9:

$$C = 5/9\,(F\,-\,32°)$$

Kelvin temperatures may be obtained by adding 273° to the Celsius readings:

$$K = C\,+\,273°$$

Rankine temperatures are obtained by adding 460° to the Fahrenheit readings:

$$R = F\,+\,460°$$

The program shown in Fig. 7-24 computes a table of values for the following 12 Fahrenheit temperature values: 14, 63, 22, 68, 26, 78, 54, 102, 72, 107, 99, and 47. A flowchart of this program is shown in Fig. 7-25.

Any traveler who has flown in a jet aircraft is used to such statements as "The aircraft is now cruising at 31,000 feet," or "The ceiling is 60,000 feet." Although this information is informative, one may still wish to know what the altitude is in miles. The program shown in Fig. 7-26 performs this computation for values of 0 to 200,000 feet in steps of 10,000 feet. The conversion is accomplished by dividing the altitude in feet by 5280, the number of feet in a mile. This program illustrates the use of the STEP in the FOR statement. After each pass through the loop, the value of 10,000 is added to the index A. A flowchart of this program is shown in Fig. 7-27.

" First we were captured, then they started
punching our keys, yelling stuff like,
'Do you understand basic?' 'What is your
memory capacity?.... "

ARRAYS

An *array* is an ordered arrangement of items all identified by a name.
There are two types of arrays in BASIC: (1) a *one-dimensional* array,
often called a *list* or a *vector;* and (2) a *two-dimensional* array, often
called a *table* or a *matrix*. In this section we will use the names *list* and
table.

An array name in BASIC must be a single alphabetic character; for
example, B, R, and Z are valid array names, whereas A6, AB, or 2H are
not. Consequently, there are precisely 26 valid names for lists or tables.

Individual members of the array are specified by the array name
followed by either one or two *subscripts*, separated by a comma and
enclosed in parentheses. This is called a *subscripted variable* and is used
to designate an individual item in an array. Examples of subscripted
variables are:

```
A (4)                    H (I - 3)
D (2, 8)                 K (A, R * 3)
X (A + B - C/D)          W (A + B, I * K + 3)
```

A subscript can be any form of expression except a string or a string
variable.

The number of subscripts, and the range of values they may take

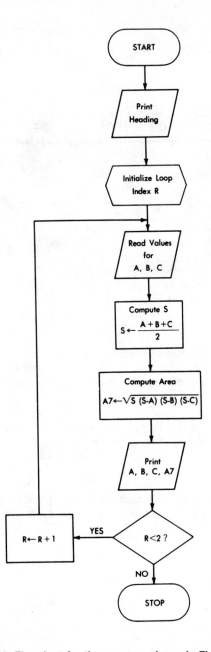

Fig. 7-23. Flowchart for the program shown in Fig. 7-22.

```
100 REM TEMPERATURE CONVERSION PROGRAM
101 PRINT "FAHRENHEIT","CELSIUS","KELVIN","RANKINE"
102 FOR S=1 TO 5
103    PRINT
104 NEXT S
105 FOR I=1 TO 12
106    READ F
107    LET C=5/9*(F-32)
108    LET K=C+273
109    LET R=F+460
110    PRINT F,C,K,R
111 NEXT I
112 DATA  14, 63, 22, 68, 26, 78, 54, 102, 72, 107, 99, 47
113 END
```

| RUN
FAHRENHEIT	CELSIUS	KELVIN	RANKINE
14	-10	263	474
63	17.2222	290.222	523
22	-5.55555	267.444	482
68	20	293	528
26	-3.33333	269.667	486
78	25.5555	298.556	538
54	12.2222	285.222	514
102	38.8889	311.889	562
72	22.2222	295.222	532
107	41.6667	314.667	567
99	37.2222	310.222	559
47	8.33333	281.333	507

Fig. 7-24. BASIC program for converting Fahrenheit temperature values to Celsius, Kelvin, and Rankine values.

(lower and upper bounds), are fixed properties of the array. These properties are associated with the array name by specifying its *dimensions*. In BASIC, the DIM statement assigns names to lists and tables, and specifies the size of them. BASIC automatically saves computer storage for any list of no more than 11 elements, whose subscripts fall in the range 0 to 10. For example, BASIC would automatically save enough storage for a list of seven elements or a table with four *rows* and six *columns*. However, it would *not* automatically reserve storage for a list of 15 items, or a table consisting of 16 rows and 20 columns. To reserve storage for such lists and tables, the statement

20 DIM A (15), B (16, 20)

could be used. In this example, the 15-item list is named A and the 16 by 20 table is named B.

A single DIM statement can reserve storage for a combination of lists and tables. For example, the statement

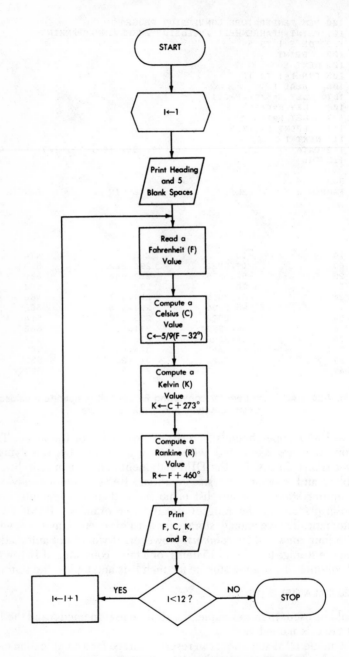

Fig. 7-25. Flowchart for the program shown in Fig. 7-24.

```
10 REM FEET-TO-MILES CONVERSION PROGRAM
20 PRINT "ALT IN FEET","ALT IN MILES"
30 FOR A=0 TO 200000 STEP 10000
40    LET M=A/5280
50    PRINT A,M
60 NEXT A
70 END
```

```
RUN
ALT IN FEET        ALT IN MILES
 0                  0
 10000              1.89394
 20000              3.78788
 30000              5.68182
 40000              7.57576
 50000              9.4697
 60000              11.3636
 70000              13.2576
 80000              15.1515
 90000              17.0455
 100000             18.9394
 110000             20.8333
 120000             22.7273
 130000             24.6212
 140000             26.5151
 150000             28.4091
 160000             30.303
 170000             32.197
 180000             34.0909
 190000             35.9848
 200000             37.8788
```

Fig. 7-26. BASIC program for converting altitude in feet to altitude in miles.

100 DIM X (27), E (10, 16), R (22, 33), C (104)

reserves computer storage for two lists named X and C, and for two tables named E and R. The DIM statements are not executed by the computer and may be placed anywhere in the program. It is good practice, however, to place them at the beginning of the program.

Let us now study an example that uses a list. Suppose we wanted to find the sum of 10 integers $(y_1, y_2, y_3, \ldots, y_{10})$, the values of which are

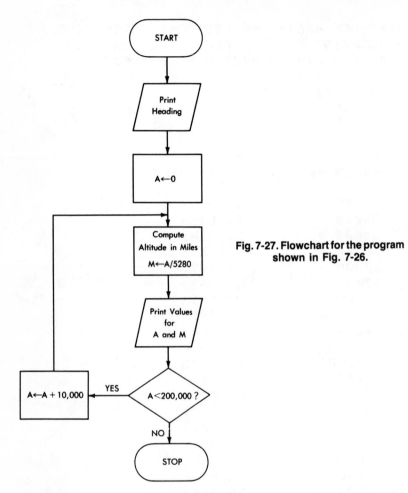

Fig. 7-27. Flowchart for the program shown in Fig. 7-26.

as follows: $y_1 = 14$, $y_2 = 63$, $y_3 = 28$, $y_4 = 47$, $y_5 = 81$, $y_6 = 7$, $y_7 = 12$, $y_8 = 34$, $y_9 = 54$, and $y_{10} = 78$. We could, of course, give these 10 variables 10 different and distinct variable names and obtain the sum by using the program shown in Fig. 7-28. However, note the length of the READ, LET, and DATA statements, and then visualize what would happen if we were to compute the sum of 100 or 1000 integers by this method. It is much easier to establish a list name and use subscripted notation. The program shown in Fig. 7-29 uses a list named Y to contain the 10 integers. Statement 65 causes the 10 values of Y to be placed in the data bank prior to program execution. When the program is executed, statements 20 to 30 cause the values to be read from the data bank into array Y. Statement 40 is an initializing statement; it sets the

```
100 REM SUM OF 10 NUMBERS
110 READ Y1,Y2,Y3,Y4,Y5,Y6,Y7,Y8,Y9,W1
120 LET S=Y1+Y2+Y3+Y4+Y5+Y6+Y7+Y8+Y9+W1
130 PRINT S
140 DATA  14, 63, 28, 47, 81, 7, 12, 34, 54, 78
150 END

RUN
 418
```

Fig. 7-28. BASIC program to compute the sum of 10 integers without using subscripted notation.

value of the partial sum at zero to start. The FOR statement (45) causes statement 50 to be executed 10 times. Each time the statement is executed, the index J is incremented by one, and another value of Y is added to the partial sum. Exit from the iteration loop takes place when all 10 numbers have been added. Statement 60 causes the sum to be printed.

A table is composed of horizontal *rows* and vertical *columns*. Therefore, each item in a table has two subscripts. The first subscript refers to the row number, the second to the column number. For example, a table of three rows and four columns might be shown in mathematical notation as follows:

$$x_{1,1} \quad x_{1,2} \quad x_{1,3} \quad x_{1,4}$$
$$x_{2,1} \quad x_{2,2} \quad x_{2,3} \quad x_{2,4}$$
$$x_{3,1} \quad x_{3,2} \quad x_{3,3} \quad x_{3,4}$$

In BASIC, the elements of a table named X would be written as X (1,1), X (1,2), X (1,3), X (1,4), X (2,1), X (2,2), X (2,3), X (2,4), X (3,1), X (3,2), X (3,3), X (3,4).

The reader trained in engineering will find tables of this type familiar, since they are similar to determinants:

$$\begin{vmatrix} a_{11} & a_{12} & a_{13} \\ a_{21} & a_{22} & a_{23} \\ a_{31} & a_{32} & a_{33} \end{vmatrix}$$

or to matrices:

$$\begin{bmatrix} P_{11} & P_{12} & P_{13} & P_{14} & P_{15} \\ P_{21} & P_{22} & P_{23} & P_{24} & P_{25} \end{bmatrix}$$

```
10  REM SUM OF 10 NUMBERS
15  REM READ VALUES INTO ARRAY K
20  FOR K=1 TO 10
25    READ Y[K]
30  NEXT K
35  REM DETERMINE SUM
40  LET S=0
45  FOR J=1 TO 10
50    LET S=S+Y[J]
55  NEXT J
60  PRINT S
65  DATA  14, 63, 28, 47, 81, 7, 12, 34, 54, 78
70  END

RUN
 418
```

Fig. 7-29. BASIC program to compute the sum of 10 integers using subscripted notation.

As a simple analogy, let us consider the familiar chessboard as a table containing 64 squares in eight rows and eight columns (Fig. 7-30). Applying BASIC terminology, we will give the chessboard a name (A) and specify a few locations on it. Any location in table A can be specified by A (I, J), where I represents the row and J the column. Thus, location A (4,3) is the square in the fourth row, third column. To specify the square in the first row, fifth column, we use the subscripted variable A (1,5).

Let us now consider a BASIC program that uses a table. The program (Fig. 7-31) is named MOVE, and it transfers nine numbers from a table named M to a table named B. A flowchart for the MOVE program is shown in Fig. 7-32.

The MOVE program is straightforward enough to cause no difficulty, but two statements in it,

160 PRINT B (I,K),

and

180 PRINT

should be explained. The comma at the end of statement 160, called a *dangling* comma, will cause the next PRINT command that is to be executed to start printing in the next available zone rather than in the first zone of a new line. Statement 180, called a *vacuous* (or *blank*) PRINT statement, will advance the paper in the teletypewriter one line. It will also return the type head to the beginning of the new line. Thus, the following group of statements:

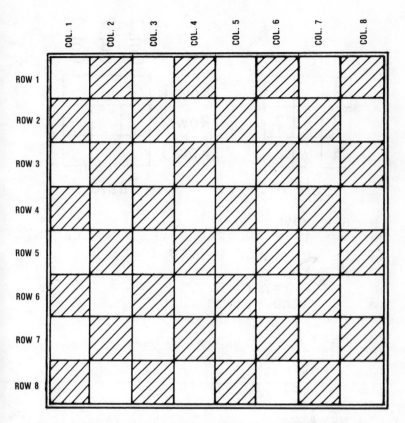

Fig. 7-30. Chessboard consisting of eight rows and eight columns.

```
140   FOR I = 1 TO 3
150      FOR K = 1 TO 3
160         PRINT B (I, K),
170      NEXT K
180      PRINT
190   NEXT I
```

will cause the contents of B (1,1), B (1,2), and B (1,3) to be printed on line 1; the contents of B (2,1), B (2,2), and B (2,3) to be printed on line 2; and the contents of B (3,1), B (3,2), and B (3,3) to be printed on line 3, as seen in Fig. 7-31. Without statement 180, the following printout would have occurred:

```
RUN
8       1       6       3       5
7       4       9       2
```

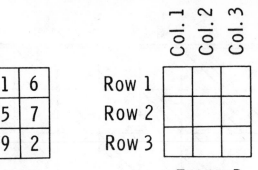

Table M   Table B

```
10    REM MOVE
20    REM THIS PROGRAM MOVES ALL ELEMENTS
30    REM OF TABLE M INTO TABLE B
40    FOR X=1 TO 3
50       FOR Y=1 TO 3
60          READ M[X,Y]
70       NEXT Y
80    NEXT X
90    FOR G=1 TO 3
100      FOR H=1 TO 3
110         LET B[G,H]=M[G,H]
120      NEXT H
130   NEXT G
140   FOR I=1 TO 3
150      FOR K=1 TO 3
160         PRINT B[I,K],
170      NEXT K
180      PRINT
190   NEXT I
200   DATA   8, 1, 6, 3, 5, 7, 4, 9, 2
210   END

RUN
 8              1              6
 3              5              7
 4              9              2
```

Fig. 7-31. BASIC program for transferring the numbers from table M to table B.

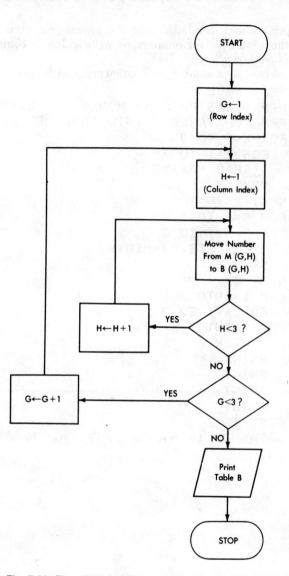

Fig. 7-32. Flowchart for the program shown in Fig. 7-31.

If statement 160 had been written without the dangling comma

160 PRINT B (I,K)

each value would have been printed on a separate line. Thus, the
dangling comma, in conjunction with the blank PRINT statement, is

used to print values in tabular form. To provide more blank space between the printed lines of numbers, we write additional blank PRINT statements as shown in Fig. 7-33.

Before we examine a number-summation program, let us consider the

```
10    REM    MOVE
20    REM    THIS PROGRAM MOVES ALL ELEMENTS
30    REM    OF TABLE M INTO TABLE B
40    FOR X=1 TO 3
50      FOR Y=1 TO 3
60        READ M[X,Y]
70      NEXT Y
80    NEXT X
90    FOR G=1 TO 3
100     FOR H=1 TO 3
110       LET B[G,H]=M[G,H]
120     NEXT H
130   NEXT G
140   FOR I=1 TO 3
150     FOR K=1 TO 3
160       PRINT B[I,K],
170     NEXT K
180     PRINT
182     PRINT
184     PRINT
186     PRINT
190   NEXT I
200   DATA    8, 1, 6, 3, 5, 7, 4, 9, 2
210   END

RUN
 8                      1                      6



 3                      5                      7



 4                      9                      2
```

Fig. 7-33. BASIC program of Fig. 7-31 illustrating the use of additional blank PRINT statements to provide more blank space between the printed lines of numbers.

procedure for setting all elements of a table to zero by means of a three-statement loop. The following group of statements sets to zero all elements of a 10 by 15 table named S:

```
1000  DIM S (10,15)
1001  FOR I = 1 TO 10
1002      FOR J = 1 TO 15
1003          LET S (I,J) = 0
1004      NEXT J
1005  NEXT I
```

Given the following table of numbers in six rows and five columns:

40	32	16	19	24
17	6	31	92	91
16	22	11	47	55
83	64	87	71	3
14	33	16	92	18
36	14	9	76	84

find the sum of all the numbers in the table except those that do not lie on the border; i.e., the sum of the numbers enclosed in the rectangle. The program shown in Fig. 7-34 computes and prints the entire table (named H), the numbers that do not lie on the border, and the computed sum of the nonborder numbers. This program first initializes a variable (S), which will ultimately be the sum of the nonborder numbers. Statements 30 through 70 cause 30 numbers from the data bank to be read into table H. The sum of the nonborder numbers is computed by statements 80 through 120. Statements 140 through 200 cause all the numbers in table H to be printed. Three blank lines are printed by statements 220, 230, and 240. Statements 260 through 320 cause the nonborder numbers to be printed, and statement 340 causes a message and the sum to be printed. Statements 350 through 390 are the DATA statements specifying the 30 numbers that were read into the data bank. A flowchart of this program is shown in Fig. 7-35.

PRINTING COLUMNS OF DATA

One way to specify a columnar format in output is to use the TAB function, the general form of which is

$$\text{PRINT TAB } (c_1); \; v_1; \; \text{TAB } (c_2); \; v_2$$

where c is a constant that specifies the position in the line where the immediately following variable v is to be printed. Fig. 7-36 is an illustration of the TAB function and its effect on the printed output. This program caused the 10 values of K to be printed starting in column 4, the 10 values of K + 1 in column 23, and the 10 values of K + 2 in column 34. Note that each argument in statement 200 is one less than the column it specifies because the print positions on the terminal being used are numbered 0-74.

A more complicated but also more flexible way of controlling output involves writing an "image" of the desired format into the program and referring to it by means of the PRINT USING statement. The image consists of symbols, which represent types of data written in the order and quantity in which the data are to be printed. The image statement is characterized by a colon immediately following its line number. Its

```
 10   REM SUM OF CENTER ELEMENTS
 20   LET S=0
 30   FOR W=1 TO 6
 40      FOR X=1 TO 5
 50         READ H[W,X]
 60      NEXT X
 70   NEXT W
 80   FOR A=2 TO 5
 90      FOR B=2 TO 4
100         LET S=S+H[A,B]
110      NEXT B
120   NEXT A
130   REM PRINT ENTIRE TABLE
140   FOR I=1 TO 6
150      FOR K=1 TO 5
160         PRINT H[I,K],
170      NEXT K
180      PRINT
190      PRINT
200   NEXT I
210   REM PRINT THREE BLANK LINES
220   PRINT
230   PRINT
240   PRINT
250   REM PRINT NUMBERS THAT DO NOT LIE ON THE BORDER
260   FOR I=2 TO 5
270      FOR J=2 TO 4
280         PRINT H[I,J],
290      NEXT J
300      PRINT
310      PRINT
320   NEXT I
330   REM PRINT SUM OF NUMBERS
340   PRINT "SUM OF NUMBERS THAT DO NOT LIE ON THE BORDER = ",S
350   DATA   40, 32, 16, 19, 24
360   DATA   17, 6, 31, 92, 91
370   DATA   16, 22, 11, 47, 55
380   DATA   83, 64, 87, 71, 3
390   DATA   14, 33, 16, 92, 18
400   DATA   36, 14, 9, 76, 84
410   END
```

Fig. 7-34. A BASIC

general form is

$$ln : line\ image$$

Before we examine the contents of the image statement, let us look at the general form of the PRINT USING statement,

$$\text{PRINT USING } ln \text{ of image statement, } v_1, v_2, \ldots$$

in which v_1 and v_2 are variables to be printed as indicated in the image statement.

Five symbols are used in the image statement. One, the quotation mark ("), has been used in a related way before, but there are two important differences. Whereas in a regular PRINT statement quotation marks enclose an actual message, in an image statement they establish a *field*. That is, they specify the amount of space that will be occupied by the related variable in the PRINT USING statement. The second difference is that the field specified equals the space occupied by the quotation marks themselves, in addition to what is enclosed within

```
RUN
40        32        16        19        24

17        6         31        92        91

16        22        11        47        55

83        64        87        71        3

14        33        16        92        18

36        14        9         76        84


6         31        92
22        11        47
64        87        71
33        16        92
SUM OF NUMBERS THAT DO NOT LIE ON THE BORDER =          572
```

number-summation program.

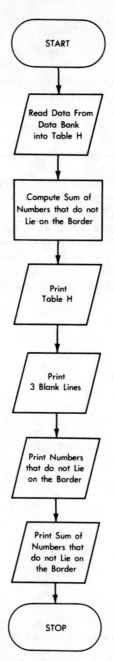

Fig. 7-35. Flowchart for the program shown in Fig. 7-34.

```
100 FOR K=1 TO 10
200     PRINT  TAB (3);K; TAB (22);K+1; TAB (33);K+2
300 NEXT K
400 END

RUN
      1                    2                3
      2                    3                4
      3                    4                5
      4                    5                6
      5                    6                7
      6                    7                8
      7                    8                9
      8                    9               10
      9                   10               11
     10                   11               12
```

Fig. 7-36. BASIC program illustrating the use of the TAB function.

them. These details will become clear in the examples presented later, but first we must identify the four other symbols used in the image statement.

1. The *apostrophe* (') specifies a one-character field, which may contain either an alphabetic or a numeric character.
2. The *pound sign* (#) specifies numeric data, and the number of pound signs must be equal to or greater than the magnitude of the largest value to be printed.
3. The *period* (.) represents a decimal point within numeric data.
4. The set of four *up-arrows* (↑ ↑ ↑ ↑) specifies numeric data in scientific notation (exponential).

These symbols in the image statement, singly or in combination, can specify five types of fields: (1) *integer*, (2) *decimal*, (3) *exponential*, (4) *alphanumeric*, and (5) *literal*.

An *integer* field is specified by pound signs (see Fig. 7-37).

Numbers within an integer field are right-justified (to adjust to the rightmost part of the specified field area) and truncated if they are not integral. The user must allow space within the field for the algebraic sign of a value.

A *decimal* field is specified by using a period in conjunction with pound signs (see Fig. 7-38). Numbers printed under the direction of a decimal field will be rounded off to the number of places specified by the pound signs to the right of the decimal point.

An *exponential* field consists of a decimal field followed by four up-arrows (see Fig. 7-39). The four-character field specified by the

```
10 REM EXAMPLE USING INTEGER FIELDS
20:    ####     ###    ####    ####
30 READ A,B,C,D
40 PRINT USING 20,A,B,C,D
50 DATA 635.7, -23.407, 68.2, -3.0007
60 END


RUN


     635     -23     68     -3
```

Fig. 7-37. BASIC program illustrating the image and PRINT USING statements using integer fields.

```
10 REM EXAMPLE USING DECIMAL FIELDS
20:    ##.##     ##.####     ####.
30 READ X,Y,Z
40 PRINT USING 20, X,Y,Z
50 DATA 674.326, -6.143769, -68.3
60 END


RUN
     674.33          -6.1438          -68.
```

Fig. 7-38. BASIC program illustrating the image and PRINT USING statements using decimal fields.

```
10 REM EXAMPLE USING EXPONENTIAL FIELDS
20:    #.####↑↑↑↑     ##.##↑↑↑↑     ##.↑↑↑↑
30 READ A,B,C
40 PRINT USING 20,A,B,C
50 DATA 627.423, -374.689, 26.8
60 END

RUN
     .6274E+03          -3.75E+02          3.E+01
```

Fig. 7-39. BASIC program illustrating the image and PRINT USING statements using exponential fields.

up-arrows will contain the letter E, the sign of the exponent, and the two-digit exponent itself, in that order. The number of pound signs preceding and following the decimal point in the first part of the exponential field specifies the magnitude of the mantissa. In other words, the pound signs determine the format of the factor by which the power of 10 specified by the exponent is to be multiplied.

An *alphanumeric* field can be specified by either the apostrophe or a pair of quotation marks (see Fig. 7-40). Since the apostrophe specifies a one-character field, its practical value is primarily limited to data in that form. However, it can also be used for printing only the first character of a string. For example, the apostrophe can be used to print initials of first names, even though full names have been placed in the data bank. Quotation marks are used to specify a field of two or more characters. However, the "message" enclosed in the quotation marks is not itself printed. The enclosed material here, together with the quotation marks, simply specifies the size of the field. In an alphanumeric field of two or more characters, the string is left-justified (to adjust data to the leftmost part of the specified field area). When the string is shorter than the specified field, the remaining space is left blank. When longer, it is truncated on the right.

```
10 REM EXAMPLE USING ALPHANUMERIC FIELDS
20:   "1234"        "PUT TITLE HERE"      '        '
30 READ RS, SS, TS, US
40 PRINT USING 20, RS, SS, TS, US
50 DATA ABCDEFGH
60 DATA SPEED
70 DATA CDEF
80 DATA AB
90 END

RUN
    ABCDEF        SPEED                    C        A
```

Fig. 7-40. BASIC program illustrating the image and PRINT USING statements using alphanumeric fields.

A *literal* field is made up of printable constants and will appear in printed form exactly as it appears in the image (see Fig. 7-41). In an image statement, the literal field is *not* enclosed in quotation marks.

The attention of the reader is called to the fact that spacing is significant in all image statements. In other words, the "image" includes whatever spacing is written into it. The only BASIC statement so far encountered in which spacing was important was the PRINT statement

```
10 REM EXAMPLE USING LITERAL FIELDS
20:    THE SQUARE ROOT OF 81 IS        ##
30 LET A = SQR(81)
40 PRINT USING 20, A
50 END

RUN
    THE SQUARE ROOT OF 81 IS          9
```

Fig. 7-41. BASIC program illustrating the image and PRINT USING statements using literal fields.

for messages enclosed in quotation marks. In a sense, the combination of the PRINT USING and image statements can be thought of as a variation of that technique, with an added flexibility. The image statement provides an exact format in which data of varying magnitude can be printed. Therefore, the user need not specify spacing in his PRINT USING statement; he is similarly free of the automatic spacing dictated by the comma or the semicolon.

The program shown in Fig. 7-42 illustrates the use of four of the five types of fields that can be specified in image statements. The program computes and prints the sales records for the month of July of five salesmen working for a manufacturer of computers and related equipment. The PRINT USING statement at line number 220 references image statement 230, which specifies a literal field and an alphanumeric field. The first output line shows the effect of these two statements. The PRINT USING statement at line number 300 references statement 310, which first specifies a long literal field, then a one-character integer field, then a short literal field (IS $), and finally a decimal field. The remaining five lines of output resulted from this combination of image and PRINT USING statements. A flowchart for this program is shown in Fig. 7-43.

By now the reader should be familiar enough with BASIC techniques to find the answers to the following questions in the previous program: How many individual products were involved? What is the price of each? How many of each did each man sell?

KEYBOARD INPUT DURING COMPUTATION

The engineer might prefer to supply the numbers to be used in the program from the terminal keyboard during the running of the program, instead of specifying these values in a DATA statement. If so, a program similar to the one shown in Fig. 7-44 might be used. The first thing this program would do is print the message,

```
100 REM COMPUTER SALESMAN PROGRAM
110 REM READ PRICE INFORMATION INTO LIST Y
120 FOR K = 1 TO 4
130     READ Y(K)
140 NEXT K
150 REM READ PRODUCTS SOLD INTO TABLE Z
160 FOR I = 1 TO 4
170     FOR J = 1 TO 5
180         READ Z(I,J)
190     NEXT J
200 NEXT I
210 LET E$ = "JULY"
220 PRINT USING 230, E$
230:    COMPUTER EQUIPMENT SALES FOR THE MONTH OF "123"
240 REM COMPUTE TOTAL SALES FOR EACH SALESMAN
250 FOR B = 1 TO 5
260     LET Z = 0
270     FOR A = 1 TO 4
280         LET Z = Z + Y(I) * Z(A,B)
290     NEXT A
300     PRINT USING 310, B,Z
310:    TOTAL SALES FOR SALESMAN # IS $######.##
320 NEXT B
330 DATA 10260, 3000, 12000, 26000
340 DATA 1,3,4,1,4
350 DATA 2,3,6,2,4
360 DATA 1,0,1,1,0
370 DATA 2,0,1,1,0
380 END

RUN
   COMPUTER EQUIPMENT SALES FOR THE MONTH OF JULY
   TOTAL SALES FOR SALESMAN 1 IS $156000.00
   TOTAL SALES FOR SALESMAN 2 IS $156000.00
   TOTAL SALES FOR SALESMAN 3 IS $312000.00
   TOTAL SALES FOR SALESMAN 4 IS $130000.00
   TOTAL SALES FOR SALESMAN 5 IS $208000.00
```

Fig. 7-42. BASIC program illustrating the use of four of the five types of fields that can be specified in image statements.

WHAT ARE THE VALUES FOR A, B, AND C?

The INPUT statement causes a question mark to be printed immediately following the C in the previous message. Had the semicolon at the end of statement 20 not been present, the question mark would have appeared as the first character on the next line. Whenever an INPUT statement is reached, the computer will pause and wait until the values for A, B, and C are typed on the keyboard. When this is done, the program will resume computation and give the following output as specified by statement 80:

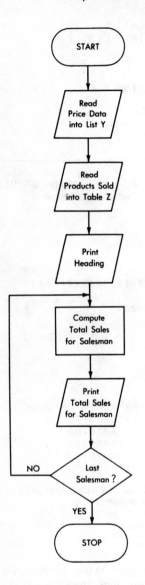

Fig. 7-43. Flowchart for the program shown in Fig. 7-42.

THE SUM OF 144, 167 and 83 IS 394

The INPUT statement is ideally suited for use in programs that have two-way communications with the terminal user.

"WHAT DO YOU MEAN, YOU FORGOT !"

```
20 PRINT "WHAT ARE THE VALUES FOR A, B, AND C";
40 INPUT A,B,C
60 LET S=A+B+C
70 PRINT
75 PRINT
80 PRINT "THE SUM OF ";A;",";B;"AND";C;"IS";S
90 END

RUN
WHAT ARE THE VALUES FOR A, B, AND C? 144? 167? 83

THE SUM OF  144 , 167 AND 83 IS 394
```

Fig. 7-44. BASIC program illustrating the use of the INPUT statement.

RESTORE STATEMENT

In the program shown in Fig. 7-45, the DATA statement (statement 70) causes three numbers to be placed in the data bank. The first time statement 20 is executed, values for A, B, and C are taken from the data bank. The program computes and prints a value for D by adding to the last D the sum of A $\uparrow$ 2, B $\uparrow$ 2, and C $\uparrow$ 2. If the computed value for D is less than 20,000, program control is transferred back to statement 20, in order that new values for A, B, and C may be read. However, since the DATA statement originally placed only three numbers in the data bank, and we used them when we executed statement 20 the first time,

```
10 LET D=0
20 READ A,B,C
30 LET D=D+A↑2+B↑2+C↑2
40 PRINT D
50 REM  --- PLACE TO ADD RESTORE STATEMENT
60 IF D<20000 THEN  20
70 DATA  2, 6, 8
80 END

RUN
 104
```

Fig. 7-45. BASIC program illustrating the use of the RESTORE statement.

the data bank is now empty. Whenever the data bank is empty and a READ operation is attempted, the computer prints

OUT OF DATA IN *ln*

where the referenced line number is that of the READ statement.* However, if we replace statement 50 of the program with a RESTORE statement, the computer will return to the DATA statement, which again places the same three numbers in the data bank. The program then reads the same values for A, B, and C and computes a new value for D on subsequent passes through the program until the computed value of D exceeds 20,000.

The RESTORE statement, frequently used for accessing data that will be used several times in the program, eliminates the need for writing duplicate DATA statements for the same data. Whenever the RESTORE statement is encountered in a program, the computer reestablishes data in the data bank for use by subsequent READ statements.

FUNCTIONS

Very often when a program is being written, a situation arises that can easily be handled by a *function,* which is a device by which a specific task can be performed on more than one occasion. The BASIC language includes two types of funtions: (1) *library* functions and (2) *user-defined* functions. The BASIC language has 11 library functions as shown in Table 7-4.

---

*This message will vary with the specific BASIC system that you are using.

Table 7-4. Library Functions Used in BASIC

Function	Description of Function
SIN (X)	Sine of *x*.
COS (X)	Cosine of *x*.
TAN (X)	Tangent of *x*.
ATN (X)	Arctangent of *x*.
	x is expressed in radians
ABS (X)	Absolute value of *x*.
SQR (X)	Square root of the absolute value of *x*.
EXP (X)	Exponent, *e*, to the *x* power.
LOG (X)	Natural logarithm of the absolute value of $x(\log_e x)$.
INT (X)	Integer part of *x*.
SGN (X)	Sign of *x* (0 if *x* is 0; 1 if *x* is positive; −1 if *x* is negative).
RND (X)	Pseudorandom-number generator.

To *call* (i.e, to make use of) a library function, we need only to write the name of the function, followed by parentheses enclosing the expression for which the function is to be computed. For example, the following LET statement containing the sine function:

```
100   LET A = SIN(X)
```

will cause the sine of angle *x* to be computed and the result to be assigned to the variable A. (As indicated in Table 7-4, *x* must be expressed in radians.)

The 11 listed mathematical functions are normally sufficient for most users of the BASIC language, but even these functions can be combined to produce additional capabilities. For example, if we wanted to compute the cotangent of *x*, we could use the SIN(X) and COS(X) functions, as in the statement

```
LET T = COS(X) / SIN(X)
```

where T represents the computed value, the cotangent of *x*.

The X in the listed functions is a general letter representing an expression, and it is called the *argument* of the function. The argument is always enclosed in parentheses. Any valid expression (other than strings or string variables) may be substituted for X in any of the functions. For example, the root mean square, or quadratic mean, of a set of numbers $x_1, x_2, x_3, \ldots, x_n$ is defined by the formula

$$\text{RMS} = \sqrt{\frac{\Sigma x^2}{n}}$$

A program to compute the root mean square of the set of numbers 1, 3, 4, 5, and 7 is shown in Fig. 7-46. In this example, the argument of the function in statement 120 is (X1 ↑ 2 + X2 ↑ 2 + X3 ↑ 2 + X4 ↑ 2

```
100 REM ROOT MEAN SQUARE
110 READ N,X1,X2,X3,X4,X5
120 LET Y=SQR((X1↑2+X2↑2+X3↑2+X4↑2+X5↑2)/N)
130 PRINT "ROOT MEAN SQUARE = ",Y
140 DATA  5, 1, 3, 4, 5, 7
150 END

RUN
ROOT MEAN SQUARE =                        4.47214
```

Fig. 7-46. BASIC program to compute the root mean square of a set of numbers. This program illustrates the use of the SQR library function.

$+X5 \uparrow 2)$ /N. Some mathematical expressions and their BASIC equivalents using library functions are given in Table 7-5.

The argument of one library function can itself contain functions. Thus, the mathematical expression sine e^z would be represented in BASIC as

$$\text{SIN (EXP (Z))}$$

and would be perfectly acceptable.

Consider the program shown in Fig. 7-47, which employs the Newton-Raphson method for finding the cube root of a number. Given an approximate value, y_0, an improved value, y_1, can be obtained from the relation

$$y_1 = \frac{1}{3} \left(\frac{x}{y_0^2} + 2y_0 \right)$$

Table 7-5. Some Mathematical Expressions and Their BASIC Equivalents Using Library Functions

Mathematical Expression	BASIC Expression
$\sin (x + y)$	SIN (X + Y)
$\lvert x - 2 \rvert$	ABS (X − 2)
$a \cos \theta$	A * COS(T)
$\dfrac{c^2 \sin 2a}{4}$	C ↑ 2 * SIN (2 * A)/4
$\sqrt{a^2 + b^2 - 3}$	SQR (A ↑ 2 + B ↑ 2 − 3)
$\dfrac{\lvert a - b \rvert}{\sin \theta}$	ABS (A − B) / SIN(T)

21

$$y_{i+1} = \frac{1}{3} \left(\frac{x}{y_i^2} + 2y_i \right)$$

This process is repeated until two successive iterations agree to some specified degree of accuracy, E:

$$|y_{i+1} - y_i| < E$$

The program in Fig. 7-47 calculates the cube root of 106 and stores the calculated answer in the variable Y1. The DATA statement contains the number 106, the approximate value 14, and the accuracy constant 0.0001. The program will, of course, calculate the cube root of any value. Only the DATA statement needs to be changed. A flowchart of this program is shown in Fig. 7-48.

A pseudorandom number* can be generated very easily in BASIC by using the RND function; however, this function has been implemented differently on different computer systems. For example, the expression RND (20) on the TRS-80 microcomputer will cause a number between 1 and 20 to be produced, the expression RND (8) on the Apple II microcomputer will cause a number between 0 and 7 to be produced, while on other computers, the expression RND (-1) will produce

---

*The term used for numbers generated by computers in a deterministic manner. However, pseudorandom numbers have been subjected to many statistical tests of randomness and for practical purposes may be considered random numbers.

```
10  READ X,Y,E
20  LET Y1=.333333*(X/Y↑2+2*Y)
30  IF ABS(Y1-Y)<E THEN 60
40  LET Y=Y1
50  GOTO 20
60  PRINT "CUBE ROOT OF",X,"EQUALS",Y1
70  DATA   106,  14,  .0001
80  END

RUN
CUBE ROOT OF      106          EQUALS        4.73262
```

Fig. 7-47. BASIC program for finding the cube root of a number. This program illustrates the use of the ABS library function.

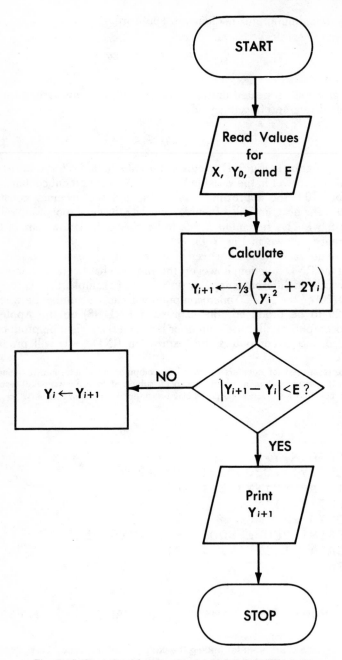

Fig. 7-48. Flowchart for the program shown in Fig. 7-47.

six-digit numbers that lie between zero and one. Before using this function, be sure and check to see how the RND function works on the computer that you are using. The program shown in Fig. 7-49 will generate 110 pseudorandom numbers in the range from 0 to 37.

Let us now examine the SGN function, which will generate the values +1, 0, or -1, depending on the value of the argument. Consider the following examples:

Value of x:	0	-0	634	.140	-36	-.004
Yield of SGN (X):	0	0	+1	+1	-1	-1

```
10 FOR A=1 TO 110
20    PRINT INT(37*RND(-1)),
30 NEXT A
40 END
```

RUN

7	5	31	34	6
16	20	7	26	1
21	0	10	14	9
26	7	29	0	24
31	24	6	10	22
13	4	33	32	9
10	34	36	27	35
27	13	7	21	24
12	35	18	4	10
16	3	17	22	0
27	3	24	1	29
13	31	33	25	24
18	35	26	12	1
22	12	29	29	7
31	14	6	5	24
18	19	28	6	18
9	18	26	29	27
25	26	26	11	25
17	24	14	33	16
36	11	26	34	3
17	17	13	12	9
20	3	4	1	12

Fig. 7-49. BASIC program for generating pseudorandom numbers. This program illustrates the use of the RND and INT library functions.

In the previous random number example (Fig. 7-49), we used the INT function without explaining how it worked. Let us examine that function now. The statement

```
20  LET A = INT (146.3)
```

when executed in a program would cause the value 146 to be assigned to the variable A. In other words, the INT function truncates any fractional part of the argument, and the result is a whole number. The following examples should illustrate this point:

Value of x:	23.40	-6.3	0	$-.10$	.0004
Value of INT (X):	23	-6	0	0	0

The general form of the *user-defined* function is

$$\text{DEF FN } a \ (v) = e$$

where a is any letter of the alphabet, v is an unsubscripted variable, and e is an expression that uses the variable v. The expression e may contain library functions, but it cannot reference other user-defined functions. Consider the user-defined function

```
DEF FNA (X) = SQR(X ↑ 4)
```

which is used in the statement

```
20  LET R = FNA(3) + 10
```

This statement would first cause 3 to be assigned to X (the argument of the function), then compute the square root of the fourth power

$$\sqrt{3^4} = \quad \sqrt{81} = 9$$

then add 10 to this value, and finally assign the value 19 to the variable R.

The user-defined function is useful when a particular one-statement computation is required at several different points in the program. As another example, suppose that at several points in a program we need to compute the value of

$$x = 2 \ \sqrt{y^2 + \frac{3y}{2}}$$

Instead of writing explicit statements at each point in the program, we write, just once, a user-defined function:

```
40  DEF FNP (Y) = 2*SQR(Y ↑ 2 + 3*Y/2)
```

Then, at each point where X is to be computed, we could use the statement

    60   LET X = FNP(K)

The function would be evaluated, based on the current value of K, and the result assigned to X; e.g., if K had been 6 at the time of execution of the LET statement, then the evaluation of

$$2\sqrt{6^2 + 9}$$

would be assigned to X.

The program shown in Fig. 7-50 uses the SIN, COS, and TAN functions to print a table of trigonometric values. It also uses a DEF function to specify the computation of the cotangent, using the relationship

$$\text{cotangent } x = \frac{\text{cosine } x}{\text{sine } x}$$

Note that degrees had to be represented in radians before the functions could be used. Radian measurement can be obtained from an angle expressed in degrees by using the conversion factor

$$x \text{ (radians)} = x \text{ (degrees)} \times \frac{\pi}{180}$$

The conversion factor can be represented in BASIC in one of two ways:

    190   LET R = D*3.14159/180

or

    190   LET R = D/57.2958

The program of Fig. 7-50 used the latter form to eliminate a multiplication operation. A flowchart of this program is shown in Fig. 7-51.

SUBROUTINES

A *subroutine* is essentially an independent program, but it is written in such a way that it can be executed only when called by another statement. Subroutines, like functions, are used to perform tasks that are needed on more than one occasion. A subroutine call can be written at any place in a program; that is, at different times and/or in different

```
100 REM TRIGONOMETRIC TABLE PROGRAM
110 REM COTANGENT FUNCTION
120 DEF FNC(H)=COS(H)/SIN(H)
130 LET D=0
140 PRINT "DEGREES","SINE","COSINE","TANGENT","COTANGENT"
150 PRINT
160 PRINT "0","0","1","0","INF"
170 LET D=D+1
180 REM CONVERT DEGREES TO RADIANS
190 LET R=D/57.2958
200 PRINT D,SIN(R),COS(R),TAN(R),FNC(R)
210 IF D<45 THEN 170
220 PRINT
230 PRINT "DEGREES","SINE","COSINE","TANGENT","COTANGENT"
240 END
```

RUN

DEGREES	SINE	COSINE	TANGENT	COTANGENT
0	0	1	0	INF
1	1.74524E-2	.999848	.017455	57.2901
2	3.48994E-2	.999391	3.49207E-2	28.6363
3	5.23359E-2	.998629	5.24077E-2	19.0812
4	6.97563E-2	.997564	6.99267E-2	14.3007
5	8.71556E-2	.996195	8.74886E-2	11.4301
6	.104528	.994522	.105104	9.51438
7	.121869	.992546	.122784	8.14436
8	.139173	.990268	.140541	7.11538
9	.156434	.987688	.158384	6.31376
10	.173648	.984808	.176327	5.67129
11	.190809	.981627	.19438	5.14456
12	.207911	.978148	.212556	4.70464
13	.224951	.97437	.230868	4.33148
14	.241922	.970296	.249328	4.01079
15	.258819	.965926	.267949	3.73206
16	.275637	.961262	.286745	3.48742
17	.292371	.956305	.30573	3.27086
18	.309017	.951057	.324919	3.07769
19	.325568	.945519	.344327	2.90421
20	.34202	.939693	.36397	2.74748
21	.358368	.933581	.383864	2.60509
22	.374606	.927184	.404026	2.47509
23	.390731	.920505	.424474	2.35585
24	.406736	.913546	.445228	2.24604
25	.422618	.906308	.466307	2.14451
26	.438371	.898775	.487732	2.05031
27	.45399	.891007	.509525	1.96261
28	.469472	.882948	.531709	1.88073
29	.48481	.87462	.554309	1.80405
30	.5	.866026	.57735	1.73205
31	.515038	.857168	.60086	1.66428
32	.529919	.848049	.624869	1.60034
33	.544639	.838672	.649407	1.53987
34	.559193	.829039	.674508	1.48256
35	.573577	.819153	.700207	1.42815
36	.587785	.809018	.726542	1.37638
37	.601815	.798637	.753553	1.32705
38	.615662	.788012	.781285	1.27994
39	.629321	.777147	.809783	1.2349
40	.642788	.766046	.839099	1.19176
41	.656059	.754711	.869286	1.15037
42	.669131	.743146	.900403	1.11061
43	.681998	.731355	.932514	1.07237
44	.694658	.719341	.965688	1.03553
45	.707107	.707107	1	1
DEGREES	SINE	COSINE	TANGENT	COTANGENT

Fig. 7-50. BASIC program for printing a table of trigonometric values. This program illustrates the use of the SIN, COS, and TAN library functions, and also the user-defined function, DEF FN.

locations, a main program may call upon a subroutine to perform a certain operation.

In Fig. 7-52, statement 5 of the main program transfers control to

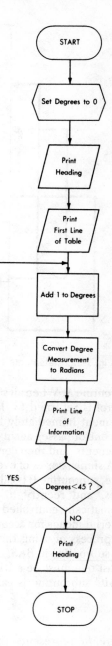

**Fig. 7-51. Flowchart for the program
shown in Fig. 7-50.**

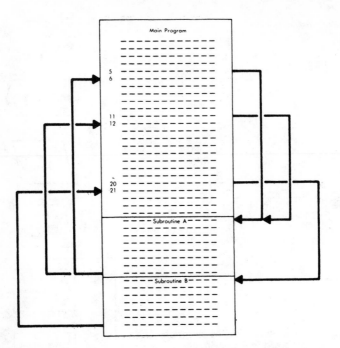

Fig. 7-52. Statements in main program referencing two subroutines.

subroutine A. When all statements in subroutine A have been executed, control is returned to the main program at statement 6; that is, the statement immediately following the calling statement. At statement 11, control passes again to subroutine A for the execution of all of its statements, and then control returns to the main program at statement 12. A similar series of events occurs between statements 20 and 21, but there, subroutine B is called. A subroutine may be called any number of times, and reentry to the main program at the proper point is automatically controlled by the calling statement. Subroutines offer a powerful means for accomplishing a very basic task in programming—the process of using the same set of statements repeatedly.

A subroutine in BASIC may consist of any number of statements, but its last one must be a RETURN statement. The statement by which a BASIC subroutine is called has the general form

$$\text{GOSUB } ln$$

where ln represents the line number of the first statement in a subroutine.

A subroutine can also call another subroutine. Fig. 7-53 illustrates a

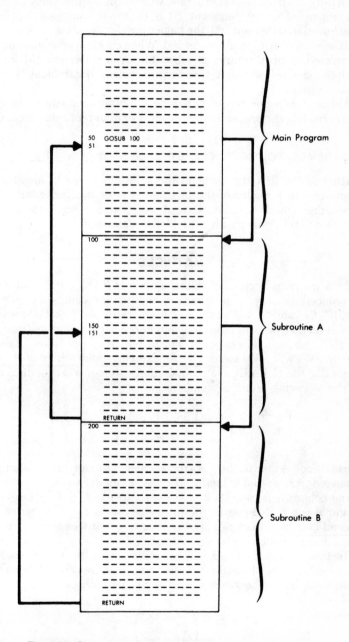

Fig. 7-53. One subroutine referencing another subroutine.

main program that calls a subroutine, which calls another subroutine. In this example, when statement 50 is executed, program control is transferred to statement 100, the beginning of subroutine A. Statement 150 transfers control to statement 200. When exection of subroutine B is completed, control returns to subroutine A at statement 151 for the completion of subroutine A; then control returns to statement 51 in the main program.

Although it is not necessary to give a subroutine a name, doing so makes reading the program much easier. For example, a statement such as

50   REM SUBROUTINE TO COMPUTE CUBE ROOT OF N

written as the first statement in the subroutine, would identify the subroutine to a reader of the program. Under this procedure, each subroutine could be characterized as starting with such a REM statement and ending with a RETURN statement.

MATRICES

In a previous section of this chapter *(ARRAYS)*, the reader was introduced to arrays of numbers; or, as they are commonly called in BASIC, *lists* and *tables*. An *array* of numbers can also be called a *matrix*. In this section, we will refer to two-dimensional arrays as *matrices* and we shall also learn how to perform many important operations of matrix algebra. We will cover some of the fundamental points about matrices in order that the 11 BASIC matrix-operation statements can be discussed.

The following arrays of numbers:

$$\begin{bmatrix} 1 & 6 & 2 \\ 3 & 1 & 9 \end{bmatrix} \qquad \begin{bmatrix} 3 & 1 \\ 4 & 2 \end{bmatrix} \qquad \begin{bmatrix} 1 & 2 & 2 \\ 6 & 4 & 5 \\ 3 & 1 & 6 \end{bmatrix}$$

are matrices. A matrix, then, is a rectangular or square array of numbers, arranged in rows and columns. The first example, with two rows and three columns, is called a 2 × 3 matrix (read "2 by 3"); the second example is a 2 × 2 matrix; the third example is a 3 × 3 matrix. The second and third examples are called *square* matrices since they have the same number of rows as columns.

In this section, matrices will be written with brackets around the rectangular array of numbers. Other notations are acceptable and are used in other publications. For example, parentheses

$$\begin{pmatrix} 12 & 14 \\ 26 & 32 \\ 41 & 16 \end{pmatrix}$$

and double-bar notations

$$\left\| \begin{array}{ccc} 63 & 12 & 37 \\ 41 & 61 & 64 \\ 18 & 19 & 23 \end{array} \right\|$$

are sometimes used.

Two matrices are equal if, and *only* if, they are of the same order, and each entry of one is equal to the corresponding entry of the other. For example,

$$\begin{bmatrix} a_{11} & a_{12} \\ a_{21} & a_{22} \end{bmatrix} = \begin{bmatrix} b_{11} & b_{12} \\ b_{21} & b_{22} \end{bmatrix}$$

if, and only if, $a_{11} = b_{11}$, $a_{21} = b_{21}$, $a_{12} = b_{12}$, and $a_{22} = b_{22}$.

The BASIC language contains 11 statements designed for matrix operations. Each begins with MAT, followed by the specific operation. Table 7-6 lists examples of the 11 statements, along with their identifications. The matrix in each case is named C, and A and B represent values involved in the given operation. All other characters are fixed parts of the statements.

Table 7-6. Matrix Operation Statements Used in BASIC

Statement	Identification
MAT READ C	Read Matrix
MAT PRINT C	Print Matrix
MAT C = TRN (A)	Transpose Matrix
MAT C = ZER	Zero Matrix
MAT C = IDN	Identity Matrix
MAT C = CON	J Matrix
MAT C = A + B	Add Matrix
MAT C = A − B	Subtract Matrix
MAT C = (A) * B	Scalar Multiplication
MAT C = A * B	Multiply Matrix
MAT C = INV (A)	Invert Matrix

Before the BASIC matrix operations can be used, each matrix must be declared in a DIM statement, which reserves computer storage for it. For example, the statement

```
10   DIM A(2,4), B(10,12), C(30,30)
```

reserves storage for a 2 × 4 matrix named A, a 10 × 12 matrix named B, and a 900-element square matrix named C. The first number in parentheses specifies the number of rows in the matrix; the second number specifies the number of columns. Thus, a 4 × 6 matrix could be dimensioned by the statement 10 DIM P(4,6), which specifies that the matrix named P has four rows and six columns. Note that a matrix name must be a single letter, such as D, R, or W.

Before any computations can be made by means of a matrix statement, the size of the matrix must be established and values must be assigned to it. The size of a matrix named C may be established by any of the following statements: DIM C (M,N), MAT READ C (M,N), or MAT C = ZER (M,N), MAT C = IDN (M,N), or MAT C = CON (M,N), where M is the number of rows in the matrix and N is the number of columns.

Values may be assigned to the matrix C by any of the following statements: MAT READ C, MAT C = ZER, MAT C = IDN, or MAT C = CON. The MAT READ statement is used to read values from a DATA statement into a specified matrix. The general form is

$$\text{MAT READ } v$$

where v is the name of a matrix that has been dimensioned by a DIM statement. The MAT READ statement can also specify more than one previously dimensioned matrix. The general form is then

$$\text{MAT READ } v_1, v_2, \ldots, v_n$$

The sequence of statements

```
10   DIM A(4,3)
20   MAT READ A
30   DATA   1, 2, 3, 4, 5, 6, 7, 8, 9, 10, 11, 12
```

would cause the values 1, 2, and 3 to be established as the values for row 1 of the matrix named A; 4, 5, and 6 for row 2; 7, 8, and 9 for row 3; and 10, 11, and 12 for row 4. Note that the MAT READ statement reads the values from the DATA statements in *row* order; i.e., row 1 first, then row 2, then row 3, then row 4, etc.

It is possible to reserve more storage than is actually needed. When in doubt, indicate a larger dimension than you expect to use. This precaution will allow you to expand the size of the matrix at some future date without changing the DIM statement, provided that you do not exceed the size that was originally dimensioned. For example, if you wanted to create a list of 12 numbers, you might write the program segment shown in Fig. 7-54. Statements 200 and 600 could have been eliminated by writing statement 300 FOR J = 1 TO 12, but the form as written allows for the lengthening of list X by changing only statement 600, as long as it does not exceed 100.

```
100 DIM X[100]
200 READ K
300 FOR J=J TO K
400    READ X[J]
500 NEXT J
600 DATA   12
700 DATA   6, 7, 4, 3, 10, 14, 36, 9, 12, 9, 1, 17
```

Fig. 7-54. Segment of BASIC program illustrating the use of the DIM statement.

The general form of the MAT PRINT statement is

$$MAT\ PRINT\ v$$

where v is the name of a matrix that has been dimensioned in a DIM statement. Like the MAT READ statement, the MAT PRINT statement can contain the names of several previously dimensioned matrices.

There are two types of printing formats, (1) *regular* and (2) *packed*. If the matrix name is followed by a semicolon, the matrix is printed in packed format; otherwise, regular format is used. The program shown in Fig. 7-55 establishes values for and prints the matrix W in packed format.

A matrix is transposed when the elements in the rows become the elements in the columns, and vice versa. For example, the 2×4 matrix

$$\begin{bmatrix} 8 & 6 & 7 & 2 \\ 3 & 5 & 6 & 1 \end{bmatrix}$$

```
10 DIM W[2,5]
20 MAT   READ W
30 MAT   PRINT W;
40 DATA   4, 24, 8, 36, 12, 3, 18, 6, 27, 9
50 END

RUN


4      24      8      36      12

3      18      6      27      9
```

Fig. 7-55. BASIC program illustrating the use of the MAT READ and MAT PRINT statements. The semicolon at the end of statement 30 causes the printout to be in packed format.

Computers and Programming Guide for Scientists and Engineers

when transposed becomes the 4×2 matrix

$$\begin{bmatrix} 8 & 3 \\ 6 & 5 \\ 7 & 6 \\ 2 & 1 \end{bmatrix}$$

The general form of the BASIC matrix transposition statement is

$$\text{MAT } v_1 = \text{TRN } (v_2)$$

where v_1 and v_2 are matrices. It would transpose matrix v_1 and assign it in the new form to matrix v_2. For example, the program shown in Fig. 7-56 uses the matrix transposition statement to transpose a 4×5 matrix. The program assigns the original values to matrix S, transposes matrix S, assigns the transposed values to matrix Y, and prints both matrices.

```
100 DIM S[4,5],Y[5,4]
110 MAT   READ S
120 PRINT "MATRIX S"
130 PRINT
140 MAT   PRINT S
150 MAT Y=TRN(S)
160 PRINT "TRANSPOSE OF MATRIX S IS"
170 PRINT
180 MAT   PRINT Y
190 DATA   6, 14, 3, 5, 24, 2, 6, 15, 9, 13, 12, 2, 5, 8, 11, 1, 23, 16, 4, 9
200 END

RUN
MATRIX S
```

6	14	3	5	24
2	6	15	9	13
12	2	5	8	11
1	23	16	4	9

```
TRANSPOSE OF MATRIX S IS
```

6	2	12	1
14	6	2	23
3	15	5	16
5	9	8	4
24	13	11	9

Fig. 7-56. BASIC program illustrating the use of the matrix transposition statement, MAT C = TRN(A).

A matrix whose elements are all zeros is called the *zero* matrix. The BASIC statement

$$\text{MAT } v = \text{ZER}$$

can be used to place zeros in all elements of the matrix represented by v. For example, the statement

```
800  MAT R = ZER
```

will cause all elements of matrix R to be replaced by zeros.

The *identity* (or *unit*) matrix is a square matrix with all elements zeros except those that are on its main diagonal, which are all ones. The BASIC statement

$$\text{MAT } v = \text{IDN}$$

may be used to set up matrix v as an identity matrix. Note that only a square matrix can be set up as an identity matrix.

A matrix whose elements are all ones is called the J matrix. The statement

$$\text{MAT } v = \text{CON}$$

may be used to place ones in all elements of matrix v.

Addition of two matrices of the same order is accomplished by adding the elements of one to the corresponding elements of the other, and placing the sums in a third matrix of the same dimensions. The addition of matrices a and b to produce matrix c can be expressed by the equation

$$c_{ij} = a_{ij} + b_{ij}$$

where c_{ij}, a_{ij}, and b_{ij} are corresponding elements of the three matrices. The general form of the matrix addition statement is

$$\text{MAT } v_1 = v_2 + v_3$$

To illustrate this instruction, let us consider a BASIC program to perform the addition

$$\begin{bmatrix} 2 & 1 & 7 \\ 4 & -6 & 2 \\ 0 & 3 & -3 \end{bmatrix} + \begin{bmatrix} 16 & 8 & -1 \\ 4 & 6 & 9 \\ -3 & 2 & 8 \end{bmatrix} = \begin{bmatrix} \; ? \; \end{bmatrix}$$

and print the result. The program shown in Fig. 7-57 assigns the name X to the first matrix, Y to the second, and Z to the summation matrix.

```
100 DIM X[3,3],Y[3,3],Z[3,3]
110 MAT    READ X,Y
120 PRINT "MATRIX X"
130 PRINT
140 MAT    PRINT X
150 PRINT
160 PRINT "MATRIX Y"
170 PRINT
180 MAT    PRINT Y
190 PRINT
200 REM ADD MATRICES X AND Y
210 MAT  Z=X+Y
220 PRINT "SUM OF MATRICES X AND Y IS LOCATED IN MATRIX Z"
230 PRINT
240 PRINT "MATRIX Z"
250 PRINT
260 MAT    PRINT Z
270 DATA   2, 1, 7, 4,-6, 2, 0, 3,-3, 16, 8,-1, 4, 6, 9,-3, 2, 8
280 END

RUN
MATRIX X


 2              1              7

 4             -6              2

 0              3             -3
MATRIX Y


 16             8             -1

 4              6              9

-3              2              8
SUM OF MATRICES X AND Y IS LOCATED IN MATRIX Z

MATRIX Z


 18             9              6

 8              0             11

-3              5              5
```

Fig. 7-57. BASIC program illustrating the use of the matrix addition statement, MAT C = A + B.

Subtraction of two matrices of the same order is accomplished by the same method that is used for addition, except that corresponding elements are, of course, subtracted. The BASIC statement is

$$\text{MAT } v_1 = v_2 - v_3$$

To illustrate, let us perform the subtraction

$$
\begin{bmatrix} 6 & 1 & 6 \\ 4 & 0 & 7 \\ 2 & 3 & 2 \end{bmatrix} - \begin{bmatrix} 2 & 4 & 6 \\ 6 & 3 & 2 \\ 1 & 7 & 4 \end{bmatrix} = \begin{bmatrix} ? \end{bmatrix}
$$

The program shown in Fig. 7-58 names the minuend matrix A, the subtrahend matrix B, and the difference matrix C.

```
100 DIM C[3,3],A[3,3],B[3,3]
110 MAT    READ A,B
120 MAT    C=A-B
130 PRINT "MATRIX A"
140 MAT    PRINT A
150 PRINT
155 PRINT
160 PRINT "MATRIX B"
170 MAT    PRINT B
180 PRINT
185 PRINT
190 PRINT "MATRIX C"
200 MAT    PRINT C
210 DATA   6, 1, 6, 4, 0, 7, 2, 3, 2, 2, 4, 6, 6, 3, 2, 1, 7, 4
220 END

RUN
MATRIX A

6            1            6

4            0            7

2            3            -2

MATRIX B

2            4            6

6            3            2

1            7            4


MATRIX C

4            -3           0

-2           -3           5

1            -4           -2
```

Fig. 7-58. BASIC program illustrating the use of the matrix subtraction statement, MAT C = A − B.

Scalar multiplication is performed by multiplying each element of a matrix by the same factor, called a *scalar*. In the following example, the scalar is 6:

$$6 \times \begin{bmatrix} 6 & 4 \\ 3 & 2 \\ 1 & 7 \end{bmatrix} = \begin{bmatrix} 36 & 24 \\ 18 & 12 \\ 6 & 42 \end{bmatrix}$$

In BASIC, the scalar may be a constant, a variable, or an expression. The general form of the statement is

$$\text{MAT } v_1 = (s) \times v_2$$

Note that parentheses around the scalar, s, distinguish this form of multiplication from matrix multiplication. The program shown in Fig. 7-59 gives the matrix

$$\begin{bmatrix} 6 & 1 & 2 \\ 2 & 4 & 4 \\ 3 & 7 & 5 \end{bmatrix}$$

the name W and multiplies it first by the constant 6 and then by the expression $N \times 13$, in which N is equal to 8 as indicated in statement 130. The program causes both the original matrix and the two calculated matrices to be printed.

The multiplication of two matrices is an interesting operation. The products of the *row* elements of one, and the corresponding *column* elements of the other, are added together to form the elements of a product matrix having the same number of rows as the first, and the same number of columns as the second. Consequently, if two matrices are to be multiplied, the first must have the same number of elements in each *row* as the second has in each *column*. To illustrate, let us compute the product of the following two matrices:

$$\begin{bmatrix} a_1 & a_2 & a_3 \\ b_1 & b_2 & b_3 \end{bmatrix} \times \begin{bmatrix} x_1 & x_2 \\ y_1 & y_2 \\ z_1 & z_2 \end{bmatrix}$$

The clearest way to explain this operation is to show how the individual products are obtained and combined to form the product matrix:

$$\begin{bmatrix} a_1x_1 + a_2y_1 + a_3z_1 & a_1x_2 + a_2y_2 + a_3z_2 \\ b_1x_1 + b_2y_1 + b_3z_1 & b_1x_2 + b_2y_2 + b_3z_2 \end{bmatrix}$$

```
10    DIM W[3,3],S[3,3]
20    MAT    READ W
30    PRINT "MATRIX W"
40    MAT PRINT W
50    PRINT
60    REM   --- MULTIPLY MATRIX W BY 6
70    MAT S=(6)*W
80    PRINT
90    PRINT "MATRIX W MULTIPLIED BY 6"
100   MAT PRINT S
110   PRINT
120   REM   --- MULTIPLY MATRIX W BY N*13
130   LET N=8
140   MAT S=(N*13)*W
150   PRINT
160   PRINT "MATRIX W MULTIPLIED BY N * 13"
170   MAT PRINT S
180   DATA 6, 1, 2, 2, 4, 4, 3, 7, 5
190   END

RUN
MATRIX W
```

6	1	2
2	4	4
3	7	5

```
MATRIX W MULTIPLIED BY 6
```

36	6	12
12	24	24
18	42	30

```
MATRIX W MULTIPLIED BY N * 13
```

624	104	208
208	416	416
312	728	520

Fig. 7-59. BASIC program illustrating the use of the scalar multiplication
statement, MAT C = (A) * B.

If we now assign arbitrary values to our two original matrices, we can compute their product as follows:

$$\begin{bmatrix} 1 & 3 & 2 \\ 0 & -1 & 2 \end{bmatrix} \times \begin{bmatrix} 3 & 6 \\ -1 & 2 \\ 2 & 1 \end{bmatrix} =$$

$$\begin{bmatrix} 1(3) + 3(-1) + 2(2) & 1(6) + 3(2) + 2(1) \\ 0(3) + (-1)(-1) + 2(2) & 0(6) + (-1)(2) + 2(1) \end{bmatrix}$$

$$= \begin{bmatrix} 4 & 14 \\ 5 & 0 \end{bmatrix}$$

The BASIC statement for multiplying two matrices is

$$\text{MAT } v_1 = v_2 \times v_3$$

The program shown in Fig. 7-60 determines the product of the following two matrices:

$$\begin{bmatrix} 1 & -2 & -3 \\ 2 & 3 & -4 \\ 5 & 0 & 2 \end{bmatrix} \times \begin{bmatrix} 2 & 1 & -1 \\ 4 & 3 & 2 \\ 0 & 1 & -1 \end{bmatrix}$$

The program (Fig. 7-60) also prints all three matrices.

Previously, we encountered the *identity* matrix in which the elements of the main diagonal are ones and the other elements are zeros. Let us now see the reason for that name by multiplying a square matrix by the identity matrix:

$$\begin{bmatrix} a_1 & a_2 & a_3 \\ b_1 & b_2 & b_3 \\ c_1 & c_2 & c_3 \end{bmatrix} \times \begin{bmatrix} 1 & 0 & 0 \\ 0 & 1 & 0 \\ 0 & 0 & 1 \end{bmatrix} = \begin{bmatrix} a_1 & a_2 & a_3 \\ b_1 & b_2 & b_3 \\ c_1 & c_2 & c_3 \end{bmatrix}$$

The principle involved here may, of course, be applied to a square matrix of any size. If we represent the identity matrix by the symbol i, then $a \times i = a$ for any matrix, a.

For every *nonsingular** square matrix there exists an *inverse*; the product of the matrix and its inverse is the identity matrix. Thus,

$$a \times a' = a' \times a = i$$

---

*A matrix is called *nonsingular* when its determinant, written a, is nonzero. If the determinant is zero, the matrix is singular.

```
10   DIM C[3,3],A[3,3],B[3,3]
20   MAT    READ A,B
30   PRINT "MATRIX A"
40   MAT    PRINT A
50   PRINT
60   PRINT "MATRIX B"
70   MAT    PRINT B
80   PRINT
90   REM  --- DETERMINE PRODUCT OF A * B
100  MAT C=A*B
110  PRINT "MATRIX C"
120  MAT    PRINT C
130  DATA  1,-2,-3, 2, 3,-4, 5, 0, 2, 2, 1,-1, 4, 3, 2, 0, 1,-1
140  END

RUN
MATRIX A
```

1	-2	-3
2	3	-4
5	0	2

```
MATRIX B
```

2	1	-1
4	3	2
0	1	-1

```
MATRIX C
```

-6	-8	-2
16	7	8
10	7	-7

Fig. 7-60. BASIC program illustrating the use of the matrix multiplication statement, MAT C = A * B.

where a is a nonsingular square matrix and a' is its inverse. Let us now determine the inverse, a', of a given a by means of the equation $a \times a' + i$:

$$\begin{bmatrix} 9 & 5 \\ 7 & 4 \end{bmatrix} \times \begin{bmatrix} x & u \\ y & v \end{bmatrix} = \begin{bmatrix} 1 & 0 \\ 0 & 1 \end{bmatrix}$$

$$\quad a \qquad\qquad a' \qquad\qquad i$$

By the rules of matrix multiplication, we obtain the following equations:

$$9x + 5y = 1 \qquad 9u + 5v = 0$$
$$7x + 4y = 0 \qquad 7u + 4v = 1$$

Solving these equations, we get $x = 4$, $y = -7$, $u = -5$, and $v = 9$. Therefore,

$$\begin{bmatrix} 4 & -5 \\ -7 & 9 \end{bmatrix}$$

By the same procedure, the inverse of the matrix

$$\begin{bmatrix} 1 & 2 & 0 \\ -1 & 1 & 3 \\ 0 & 1 & -1 \end{bmatrix}$$

is

$$\begin{bmatrix} 4/6 & -2/6 & -1 \\ 1/6 & 1/6 & 3/6 \\ 1/6 & 1/6 & -3/6 \end{bmatrix}$$

The answer can be checked by performing the following matrix multiplication:

$$\begin{bmatrix} 4/6 & -2/6 & -1 \\ 1/6 & 1/6 & 3/6 \\ 1/6 & 1/6 & -3/6 \end{bmatrix} \times \begin{bmatrix} 1 & 2 & 0 \\ -1 & 1 & 3 \\ 0 & 1 & 1 \end{bmatrix} = \begin{bmatrix} 1 & 0 & 0 \\ 0 & 1 & 0 \\ 0 & 0 & 1 \end{bmatrix}$$

Finding the inverse of a large matrix is obviously a complex procedure, but in scientific work it is often necessary to find the inverse of a matrix with several hundred rows. Therefore, several different methods have been developed for performing this computation. In BASIC, the inverse of a matrix may be determined by using the statement

$$\text{MAT } v = \text{INV}(v_2)$$

Let us now consider the program shown in Fig. 7-61, which determines the inverse of matrix R.* This program prints the original matrix R (statement 50), computes its inverse J (statement 80), and prints J (statement 120).

An important application of matrix inversion in BASIC is the solution of simultaneous linear equations such as the following:

$$x + 2y + 3z = 26$$
$$3x + 5y + 2z = 39$$
$$2x + 4y + z = 27$$

---

*Matrix R, as read from the DATA statement in the program, must be nonsingular to produce a valid result, since singular matrices have no inverses.

```
10   DIM R[4,4],J[4,4]
20   MAT  READ R
30   PRINT "MATRIX R"
40   PRINT
50   MAT  PRINT R
60   PRINT
70   REM  -- DETERMINE INVERSE OF MATRIX R
80   MAT J=INV(R)
90   PRINT
100  PRINT "INVERSE OF MATRIX R"
110  PRINT
120  MAT  PRINT J
130  DATA  2, 3, 8, 4, 7, 1, 6, 0, 8, 0, 3, 3, 5, 2, 0, 4
140  END

RUN
MATRIX R
```

2	3	8	4
7	1	6	0
8	0	3	3
5	2	0	4

INVERSE OF MATRIX R

-8.02675E-2	.100334	.013378	7.02342E-2
-3.00999E-2	.287625	-.494982	.401338
9.86621E-2	1.67298E-3	6.68892E-2	-.148829
.115385	-.269231	.23077	-3.84618E-2

Fig. 7-61. BASIC program illustrating the use of the matrix inversion statement, MAT C = INV(A).

It is possible to represent these equations as a simple matrix equation in the following manner:

$$\begin{bmatrix} 1 & 2 & 3 \\ 3 & 5 & 2 \\ 2 & 4 & 1 \end{bmatrix} \times \begin{bmatrix} x \\ y \\ z \end{bmatrix} = \begin{bmatrix} 26 \\ 39 \\ 27 \end{bmatrix}$$

To determine the inverse of the square matrix in our equation, we will name it M, and then write and execute the program shown in Fig. 7-62A. With the inverse printed by this program, we can now determine the values of x, y, and z. We multiply the inverse matrix by

$$\begin{bmatrix} 26 \\ 39 \\ 27 \end{bmatrix}$$

```
100 DIM M[3,3],D[3,3]
200 MAT   READ M
300 MAT D=INV(M)
400 MAT   PRINT D
500 DATA  1, 2, 3, 3, 5, 2, 2, 4, 1
600 END

RUN
```

-.6	2	-2.2
.2	-1	1.4
.4	0	-.2

(A) Program to determine the inverse of the square matrix, M.

```
10 DIM   D(3,3), S(3,1), A(3,1)
20 MAT READ D, S
30 MAT A = D * S
40 MAT PRINT A
50 DATA -.6, 2, -2.2, .2, -1, 1.4, .4, 0, -.2
60 DATA 26, 39, 27
70 END

RUN
   3.

   4.

   5.
```

(B) Program to determine the values of x, y, and z.

Fig. 7-62. Illustration of how matrix inversion is used in BASIC to solve simultaneous linear equations.

since this would give us

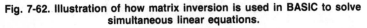

$$\begin{bmatrix} 1 & 0 & 0 \\ 0 & 1 & 0 \\ 0 & 0 & 1 \end{bmatrix} \times \begin{bmatrix} x \\ y \\ z \end{bmatrix} = \begin{bmatrix} -.6 & 2 & -2.2 \\ .2 & -1 & 1.4 \\ .4 & 0 & -.2 \end{bmatrix} \times \begin{bmatrix} 26 \\ 39 \\ 27 \end{bmatrix}$$

A BASIC program to perform this multiplication is given by the program shown in Fig. 7-62B. The matrix printed by this program gives us the unknown values for the original equations: $x = 3$, $y = 4$, and $z = 5$.

SAMPLE PROGRAMS

The programs in the preceding sections were quite simple. The programs that follow in this section are slightly more complex. The purpose is to afford the engineer an opportunity to test his ability to read BASIC programs on engineering and mathematical problems. The discussion is organized around the following framework:

- *Problem*—A brief statement of the problem to be solved.
- *Flowchart*—Figure number of the flowchart.
- *Program Listing*—Figure number of the BASIC program.
- *Program Comments*—Description of how the program solves the problem.
- *Program Results*—Figure number of the printout from the program.

Coordinate Geometry

Problem—The distance between two points (x_1, y_1) and (x_2, y_2) is determined by the formula

$$\sqrt{(x_1 - x_2)^2 + (y_1 - y_2)^2}$$

We can find the coordinates of the midpoint of two points from

$$\left(\frac{x_1 + x_2}{2}, \frac{y_1 + y_2}{2} \right)$$

and the slope of the line segment from

$$\frac{y_1 - y_2}{x_1 - x_2}, \ x_1 \neq x_2$$

For example, let us consider the points (4,6) and (8,9) and determine the previously defined items.

$$\text{Distance} = \sqrt{(4 - 8)^2 + (6 - 9)^2} = \sqrt{4^2 + 3^2}$$

$$= \sqrt{16 + 9} = \sqrt{25} = 5$$

$$\text{Midpoint} = \left(\frac{4 + 8}{2}, \frac{6 + 9}{2}\right) = \left(\frac{12}{2}, \frac{15}{2}\right)$$

$$= \left(6, \frac{15}{2}\right)$$

$$\text{Slope} = \frac{6 - 9}{4 - 8} = \frac{-3}{-4} = \frac{3}{4}$$

Flowchart—See Fig. 7-63.

Program Listing—See Fig. 7-64.

Program Comments—A step-by-step explanation of the program follows:

100	Program name.
110	Supplementary program information.
120	Establishment of coordinates of points (X1, Y1), and (X2, Y2).
130	Supplementary program information.
140–160	Computation and printout of the distance between the two points.
170	Supplementary program information.
180–210	Computation and printout of the coordinates of the midpoint.
220	Supplementary program information.
230	Determination of whether X1 equals X2.
240	Printout of message if X1 = X2.
250	Transfer of control to statement 120.
260–280	Computation and printout of the slope of the line segment.
290	Transfer of control to statement 120.
300–340	Data for five sets of points.
350	Termination of program.

Program Results—See Fig. 7-65.

Satellite Orbit

Problem—Fig. 7-66 shows the path of a satellite and an *x-y* coordinate system fixed to the center of the earth. The points labeled 1, 2, and 3 specify the positions of the satellite at equal time intervals; i.e., the satellite requires the same time to move from position 2 to position 3 as from position 1 to position 2. The coordinates of position 3 can be

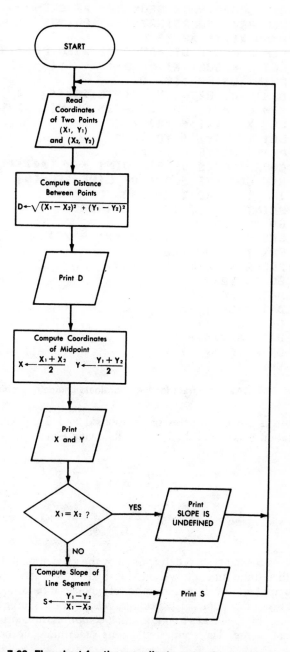

Fig. 7-63. Flowchart for the coordinate geometry program.

```
100 REM COORDINATE GEOMETRY PROBLEM
110 REM READ COORDINATES OF POINTS
120 READ X1,Y1,X2,Y2
130 REM COMPUTE DISTANCE BETWEEN POINTS
140 LET D = SQR((X1 - X2)↑2 + (Y1 - Y2)↑2)
150 PRINT USING 160, D
160:DISTANCE BETWEEN POINTS IS ###.##
170 REM COMPUTE COORDINATES OF MIDPOINT
180 LET X = (X1 + X2) / 2
190 LET Y = (Y1 + Y2) / 2
200 PRINT USING 210, X,Y
210:COORDINATES OF MIDPOINT --- (##.##,##.##)
220 REM COMPUTE SLOPE OF LINE SEGMENT
230 IF X1 <> X2 THEN 260
240 PRINT "SLOPE IS UNDEFINED"
250 GO TO 120
260 LET S = (Y1 - Y2) / (X1 - X2)
270 PRINT USING 280, S
280:SLOPE OF LINE IS ##.##
290 GO TO 120
300 DATA 4,6,8,9
310 DATA -3,6,5,8
320 DATA 3,5,7,8
330 DATA 6,4,6,8
340 DATA 16,5,-8,-10
350 END
```

Fig. 7-64. BASIC program for the coordinate geometry problem.

computed if the coordinates of positions 1 and 2 are known. This computation is accomplished by the following equations:

$$x_3 = 2x_2 + x_1 \left(\frac{c}{(x_1^2 + y_1^2)^{3/2}} - 1 \right)$$

$$y_3 = 2y_2 + y_1 \left(\frac{c}{(x_1^2 + y_1^2)^{3/2}} - 1 \right)$$

where c is a constant that is determined by the gravitational attraction of the earth and the time interval previously discussed. After point 3 has been computed, any desired number of points can be computed from the two preceding points. The program reads in values for n, c, and the coordinates for the first two points, and it computes the coordinates of n additional points. The computed points determine the orbit of the satellite.

```
DISTANCE BETWEEN POINTS IS    5.00
COORDINATES OF MIDPOINT --- ( 6.00, 7.50)
SLOPE OF LINE IS    .75
DISTANCE BETWEEN POINTS IS    8.25
COORDINATES OF MIDPOINT --- ( 1.00, 7.00)
SLOPE OF LINE IS    .25
DISTANCE BETWEEN POINTS IS    5.00
COORDINATES OF MIDPOINT --- ( 5.00, 6.50)
SLOPE OF LINE IS    .75
DISTANCE BETWEEN POINTS IS    4.00
COORDINATES OF MIDPOINT --- ( 6.00, 6.00)
SLOPE IS UNDEFINED
DISTANCE BETWEEN POINTS IS   28.30
COORDINATES OF MIDPOINT --- ( 4.00,-2.50)
SLOPE OF LINE IS    .63

OUT OF DATA IN 120
```

Fig. 7-65. Printout of the results from the coordinate geometry program.

Flowchart—See Fig. 7-67.

Program Listing—See Fig. 7-68.

Program Comments—Statement 120 causes a message to be printed on the teletypewriter. Statement 140 is used to input the coordinates of the first two points (X1, Y1) and (X2, Y2), as well as the number of points (N) to be computed by the program, and a constant (C). The next five statements cause a table heading to be printed on the teletypewriter. Statements 260 and 280 cause the first two lines of table data to be printed.

Statements 300 and 460 set up a loop that is repeated N times. Each time through the loop, the coordinates for a new point are computed and printed by statements 320, 340, and 360. Statements 380 through 440 are used to update the variables X1, X2, Y1, and Y2 for use in computations during the next pass through the program loop. The END statement terminates the program.

Program Results—See Fig. 7-69.

Polynomial Evaluation

Problem—Write a BASIC program to evaluate the 6th-degree polynomial

$$y = x^6 - 3x^5 - 93x^4 + 87x^3 + 1596x^2 - 1380x - 2800$$

for all integer values of x between -12 and $+16$. The program should print the heading

VALUES OF X WHEN THE POLYNOMIAL IS ZERO

and the values of x when y is zero. After examining all values of x, the program is to print the values of x for which the polynomial is the largest and smallest.

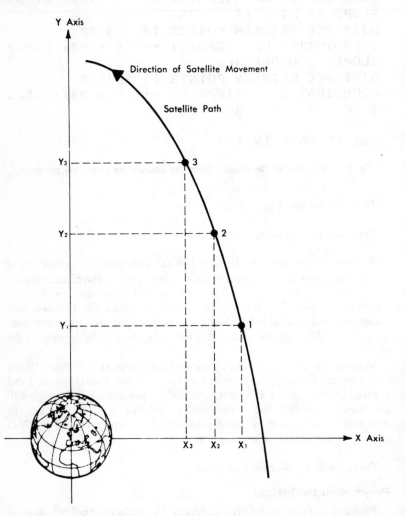

Fig. 7-66. An x-y coordinate system for the path of a satellite.

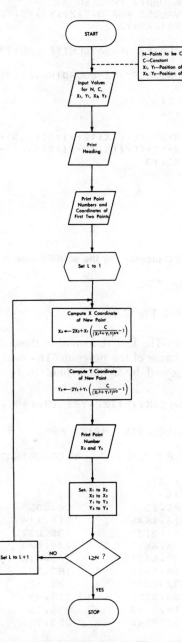

Fig. 7-67. Flowchart for the satellite orbit program.

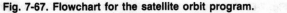

```
100 REM SATELLITE ORBIT PROBLEM
120 PRINT "TYPE VALUES FOR N,C,X1,Y1,X2,Y2";
140 INPUT N,C,X1,Y1,X2,Y2
160 PRINT
180 PRINT "COORDINATES OF SATELLITE ORBIT"
200 PRINT
220 PRINT "POINT NUMBER","X COORDINATE","Y COORDINATE"
240 PRINT
260 PRINT "1",X1,Y1
280 PRINT "2",X2,Y2
300 FOR K=1 TO N
320   LET X3=2*X2+X1*(C/((X1↑2+Y1↑2)↑1.5)-1)
340   LET Y3=2*Y2+Y1*(C/((X1↑2+Y1↑2)↑1.5)-1)
360   PRINT K+2,X3,Y3
380   LET X1=X2
400   LET X2=X3
420   LET Y1=Y2
440   LET Y2=Y3
460 NEXT K
480 END
```

Fig. 7-68. BASIC program for the satellite orbit problem.

Flowchart—See Fig. 7-70.

Program Listing—See Fig. 7-71.

Program Comments—The first statement in the program is a REM statement giving the name of the program. The next two statements cause a heading, followed by a blank line, to be printed on the

```
RUN
TYPE VALUES FOR N,C,X1,Y1,X2,Y2? 10,1000,103,64,94,81

COORDINATES OF SATELLITE ORBIT

POINT NUMBER    X COORDINATE    Y COORDINATE

1               103             64
2               94              81.
3               85.0578         98.0359
4               76.1648         115.114
5               67.3107         132.237
6               58.4856         149.404
7               49.6811         166.612
8               40.8907         183.855
9               32.1098         201.131
10              23.3351         218.433
11              14.5642         235.76
12              5.79542         253.107
```

Fig. 7-69. Printout of the results from the satellite orbit program.

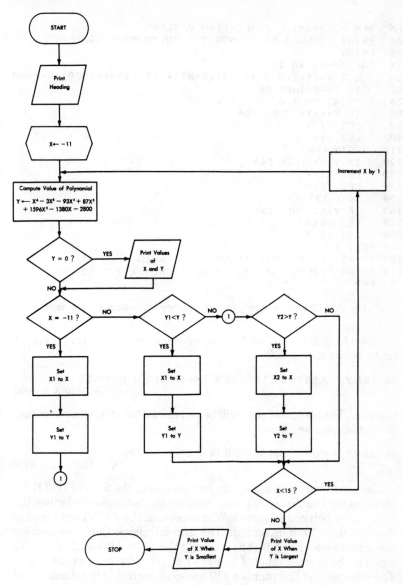

Fig. 7-70. Flowchart for the polynomial evaluation program.

teletypewriter. The group of statements beginning with the FOR statement at line number 40 and through the NEXT statement at line number 190 are repeated for all integer values of X between − 12 and 16 (− 11, − 10, − 9, . . . , + 13, + 15). The first statement in this

```
10    REM POLYNOMIAL EVALUATION PROGRAM
20    PRINT "VALUES OF X WHEN THE POLYNOMIAL IS ZERO"
30    PRINT
40    FOR X=-11 TO 16
50       LET Y=(((((X-3)*X-93)*X+87)*X+1596)*X-1380)*X-2800
60       IF Y<>0 THEN 80
70       PRINT "P = 0 WHEN X = ";X
80       IF X<>-11 THEN 120
90       LET X1=X
100      LET Y1=Y
110      GOTO 170
120      IF Y1<Y THEN 160
130      LET X1=X
140      LET Y1=Y
150      GOTO 190
160      IF Y1>Y THEN 190
170      LET X2=X
180      LET Y2=Y
190   NEXT X
200   PRINT "POLYNOMIAL IS SMALLEST WHEN X = ";X1
210   PRINT "POLYNOMIAL IS LARGEST WHEN X = ";X2
220   END
```

Fig. 7-71. BASIC program for the polynomial evaluation problem.

program loop (line number 50) computes a value for Y. This statement could be written as follows:

50   LET Y = $X \uparrow 6 - 3{\ast}X \uparrow 5 - 93{\ast}X \uparrow 4 + 87{\ast}X \uparrow 3 + 1596{\ast}X \uparrow 2$
$- 1380{\ast}X - 2800$

however, less computer time will be required if the statement is written in *nested* form as follows:

50   LET Y = $(((((X - 3) \ast X - 93) {\ast}X + 87){\ast}X + 1596)$
${\ast}X - 1380) {\ast}X - 2800$

Contained within this loop are four checks in the form of IF-THEN statements. The first check (line number 60) determines whether the value of the polynomial is zero. Whenever it is, the PRINT statement at line number 70 is executed. The second check (line number 80) determines whether X is at its starting value of − 11, and if so, sets X1 equal to the current value of X, and Y1 equal to the current value of Y. The statement at line number 110 transfers control to the statement at line number 170. The third IF-THEN statement determines whether the value of Y1 is less than the value of Y. If so, program control is transferred to the statement at line number 160; if not, the values of X1 and Y1 are set to the current values of X and Y, respectively. The fourth check determines whether the value of Y1 is greater than the value of Y. If not, the values of X2 and Y2 are set to the current values of X and Y.

The statements at line numbers 200 and 210 cause two messages to be printed after all values of X have been determined. In addition, the PRINT statement at line number 200 causes a printout of the value of X for which the polynomial is the smallest, and the statement at line number 210 causes a printout of the value of X for which the polynomial is the largest. The program terminates with the END statement at line number 220.

Program Results—See Fig. 7-72.

```
VALUES OF X WHEN THE POLYNOMIAL IS ZERO

P = 0 WHEN X = -7
P = 0 WHEN X = -5
P = 0 WHEN X = -1
P = 0 WHEN X =  2
P = 0 WHEN X =  4
P = 0 WHEN X = 10
POLYNOMIAL IS SMALLEST WHEN X =  8
POLYNOMIAL IS LARGEST WHEN X =  16
```

Fig. 7-72. Printout of the results from the polynomial evaluation program.

Geometry Calculation

Problem—Given the coordinates of the vertices of a triangle ($x_1, y_1; x_2, y_2; x_3, y_3$), compute (1) the length of the sides a, b, and c; (2) the area of the triangle; (3) the radius of the inscribed circle r_i; (4) the radius of the circumscribed circle r_c; and (5) the angles in radians of the angles α, β, and γ. The program uses the mathematical relationships shown in Fig. 7-73.

Flowchart—See Fig. 7-74.

Program Listing—See Fig. 7-75.

Program Comments—The following step-by-step assessment of the BASIC program in Fig. 7-75 is intended to provide a confirmation of the rules developed in this chapter and to suggest ideas for readers who may be undecided on directions to take.

| 10 | Name of program. |
| 20–30 | Message to teletypewriter operator requesting input. |

40	Input of values of coordinates X1, Y1, X2, Y2, X3, Y3 by teletypewriter operator.
50	Informative message.
60–80	Computation of a, b, and c and storage in A, B, and C, repectively.
90	Informative message.
100–110	Computation of s and A and storage in S and A1.
120	Informative message.
130	Computation of r_i and storage in R1.
140	Informative message.
150	Computation of r_c and storage in R2.
160	Informative message.
170–190	Computation of α, β, and γ and storage in X, Y, and Z, respectively.
200	Informative message.
210	Heading to be printed.
220–230	Messages and values to be printed.
240	Instruction to skip a line.
250	Informative message.
260–320	Messages and values to be printed.
330	Termination of program.

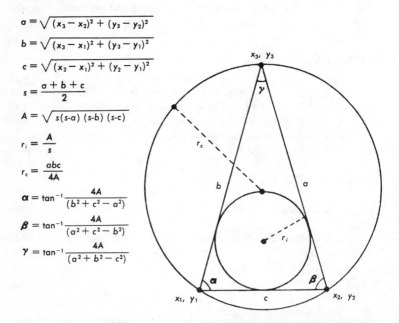

$$a = \sqrt{(x_3 - x_2)^2 + (y_3 - y_2)^2}$$

$$b = \sqrt{(x_3 - x_1)^2 + (y_3 - y_1)^2}$$

$$c = \sqrt{(x_2 - x_1)^2 + (y_2 - y_1)^2}$$

$$s = \frac{a + b + c}{2}$$

$$A = \sqrt{s(s\text{-}a)\,(s\text{-}b)\,(s\text{-}c)}$$

$$r_i = \frac{A}{s}$$

$$r_c = \frac{abc}{4A}$$

$$\alpha = \tan^{-1} \frac{4A}{(b^2 + c^2 - a^2)}$$

$$\beta = \tan^{-1} \frac{4A}{(a^2 + c^2 - b^2)}$$

$$\gamma = \tan^{-1} \frac{4A}{(a^2 + b^2 - c^2)}$$

Fig. 7-73. Formulas for solving a problem in geometry.

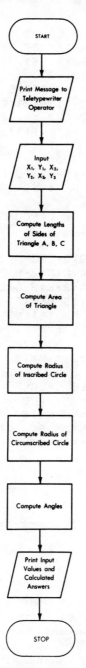

Fig. 7-74. Flowchart for the geometry calculation program.

```
10    REM GEOMETRY PROGRAM
20    PRINT "TYPE COORDINATES OF TRIANGLE IN THE"
30    PRINT "FOLLOWING ORDER: X1,Y1,X2,Y2,X3,Y3";
40    INPUT X1,Y1,X2,Y2,X3,Y3
50    REM COMPUTE LENGTHS OF SIDES
60    LET A=SQR((X3-X2)↑2+(Y3-Y2)↑2)
70    LET B=SQR((X3-X1)↑2+(Y3-Y1)↑2)
80    LET C=SQR((X2-X1)↑2+(Y2-Y1)↑2)
90    REM COMPUTE AREA
100   LET S=(A+B+C)/2
110   LET A1=SQR(S*(S-A)*(S-B)*(S-C))
120   REM COMPUTE RADIUS OF INSCRIBED CIRCLE
130   LET R1=A1/S
140   REM COMPUTE RADIUS OF CIRCUMSCRIBED CIRCLE
150   LET R2=A*B*C/(A1*4)
160   REM COMPUTE ANGLES
170   LET X=ATN((4*A1)/(B↑2+C↑2-A↑2))
180   LET Y=ATN((4*A1)/(A↑2+C↑2-B↑2))
190   LET Z=ATN((4*A1)/(A↑2+B↑2-C↑2))
200   REM PRINT COORDINATES OF TRIANGLE
210   PRINT "COORDINATES OF TRIANGLE ARE"
220   PRINT "X1 = ";X1,"Y1 = ";Y1
225   PRINT "X2 = ";X2,"Y2 = ";Y2
230   PRINT "X3 = ";X3,"Y3 = ";Y3
240   PRINT
250   REM PRINT CALCULATED VALUES
260   PRINT "A = ";A,"B = ";B,"C = ";C
270   PRINT "AREA OF TRIANGLE IS";A1
280   PRINT "RADIUS OF INSCRIBED CIRCLE IS";R1
290   PRINT "RADIUS OF CIRCUMSCRIBED CIRCLE IS";R2
300   PRINT "ALPHA = ";X
310   PRINT "BETA = ";Y
320   PRINT "GAMMA = ";Z
330   END
```

Fig. 7-75. BASIC program for the geometry calculation problem.

Program Results—See Fig. 7-76.

Student Grade Computation

Problem—In a Fluid Mechanics course at "Space Engineering College," five examinations are given. Final grades for the course are to be based exclusively on examination scores, but the individual examinations are to be weighted differently in the computation. Scores received by six students are shown in the following table, which includes the weighting of each examination in parentheses following its number.

Student	Examination and Weight				
	1 (.10)	2 (.15)	3 (.25)	4 (.15)	5 (.35)
1	63	68	72	89	93
2	99	100	76	83	94
3	53	68	63	75	78
4	93	97	100	89	91
5	75	72	81	78	84
6	78	81	69	75	79

The program is to compute the final score for each student in the Fluid Mechanics class.

Flowchart—See Fig. 7-77.

Program Listing—See Fig. 7-78.

Program Comments—REM statements 100, 110, 150, and 210 appear in the program only as supplementary information to the reader. Statements 120 through 140 cause the program to read the weight of each examination into list W. Statements 160 through 200 cause the grades that each student received on the examinations to be read into table M. Statements 220 through 280 determine the final score received by each student and print each final score as it is computed. DATA statements 290 through 350 contain the weight and student score data that is used by READ statements 130 and 180. Statement 360 terminates the program.

Program Results—See Fig. 7-79.

```
TYPE COORDINATES OF TRIANGLE IN THE
FOLLOWING ORDER: X1,Y1,X2,Y2,X3,Y3? 6,6,2,2,7,1 COORDINATES OF TRIANGLE ARE

X1 =  6        Y1 =  6
X2 =  2        Y2 =  2
X3 =  7        Y3 =  1

A =  5.09902    B =  5.09902    C =  5.65685
AREA OF TRIANGLE IS 12
RADIUS OF INSCRIBED CIRCLE IS 1.51373
RADIUS OF CIRCUMSCRIBED CIRCLE IS 3.06413
ALPHA =  .982793
BETA =  .982793
GAMMA =  1.17601
```

Fig. 7-76. Printout of the results from the geometry calculation program.

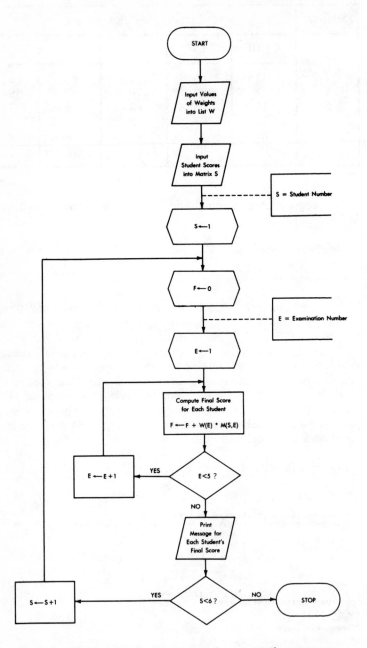

Fig. 7-77. Flowchart for the student grade computation program.

```
100 REM STUDENT GRADE COMPUTATION
110 REM READ WEIGHTS
120 FOR E=1 TO 5
130   READ W[E]
140 NEXT E
150 REM READ STUDENT SCORES ON EXAMINATIONS
160 FOR S=1 TO 6
170   FOR E=1 TO 5
180     READ M[S,E]
190   NEXT E
200 NEXT S
210 REM COMPUTE FINAL SCORE FOR EACH STUDENT USING WEIGHTS
220 FOR S=1 TO 6
230   LET F=0
240   FOR E=1 TO 5
250     LET F=F+W[E]*M[S,E]
260   NEXT E
270   PRINT "STUDENT";S,"HAS A FINAL SCORE OF ";F
280 NEXT S
290 DATA  .1,  .15,  .25,  .15,  .35
300 DATA  63, 68, 72, 89, 93
310 DATA  99, 100, 76, 83, 94
320 DATA  53, 68, 63, 75, 78
330 DATA  93, 97, 100, 89, 91
340 DATA  75, 72, 81, 78, 84
350 DATA  78, 81, 69, 75, 79
360 END
```

Fig. 7-78. BASIC program for the student grade computation problem.

```
STUDENT 1      HAS A FINAL SCORE OF   80.4
STUDENT 2      HAS A FINAL SCORE OF   89.25
STUDENT 3      HAS A FINAL SCORE OF   69.8
STUDENT 4      HAS A FINAL SCORE OF   94.05
STUDENT 5      HAS A FINAL SCORE OF   79.65
STUDENT 6      HAS A FINAL SCORE OF   76.1
```

Fig. 7-79. Printout of the results from the student grade computation program.

Function Evaluation

Problem—Fig. 7-80 is a graph of the function $f(x) = x^2 - 6x + 5$ with domain $-1 \le x \le 7$, and x a real number. The graph of f is a parabola with minimum point at $(-4,3)$ and with x-intercepts at 1 and 5. The program listing will find two successive values of x between which the value of the function changes from positive to negative or from negative to positive when x takes on integral values from -4 to 10 inclusive. The curve crosses the x-axis between 0 and 2 and between 4 and 6. This tells us that the value of the function changes sign between these values of x. As x changes from 0 to 2, the value of the function changes from positive to

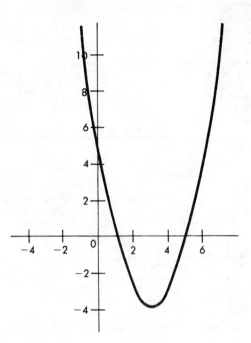

Fig. 7-80. Graph of the function f(x) = x² − 6x + 5.

negative; and as x changes from 4 to 6, the value of the function changes from negative to positive.

Flowchart—See Fig. 7-81.

Program Listing—See Fig. 7-82.

Program Comments—Statement 100 gives the program name. The next statement defines the function, FNA(X), as X ↑ 2 − 6 * X + 5. Statement 120 establishes an initial value for X1, which denotes the first value of x; the variable X2 denotes the second value of x. The initial value of X1 is − 4, and the initial value of X2 is −2, or X1 + 2. Statement 140 computes a value of the function when x = X1 for X1 = − 4: FNA(X1) = $(-4)^2 - 6(-4) + 5$, or 16 + 24 + 5, or 45. It then assigns this value to Y1. Similarly Y2 = FNA(X2) = $(-2)^2 - 5(-2) + 5$, or 4 + 10 + 5, or 19.

Statement 160 uses the SGN function to test for a sign change. If

SGN(Y1)*SGN(Y2)<> − 1

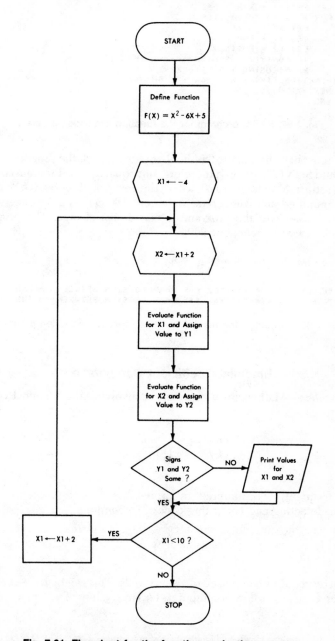

Fig. 7-81. Flowchart for the function evaluation program.

```
100 REM FUNCTION EVALUATION PROGRAM
110 DEF FNA(X) = X↑2 - 6*X + 5
120 FOR X1 = -4 TO 10 STEP 2
130     LET X2 = X1 + 2
140     LET Y1 = FNA(X1)
150     LET Y2 = FNA(X2)
160     IF SGN(Y1) * SGN(Y2) <> -1 THEN 190
170     PRINT USING 180, X1, X2
180:FUNCTION F(X) = X↑2 -6X + 5 CHANGES SIGN BETWEEN ## AND ##
190 NEXT X1
200 END
```

Fig. 7-82. BASIC program for the function evaluation problem.

they must have like signs. On the first pass through the program, SGN (Y1) and SGN (Y2) are + 1; therefore, not equal to − 1. Program control then returns to statement 120, where the next pair of successive Y values are computed and compared. Statement 180 causes a message to be printed whenever the program detects a sign change. The program terminates with statement 200.

Program Results—See Fig. 7-83.

```
FUNCTION F(X) = X↑2 -6X + 5 CHANGES SIGN BETWEEN  0 AND  2
FUNCTION F(X) = X↑2 -6X + 5 CHANGES SIGN BETWEEN  4 AND  6
```

Fig. 7-83. Printout of the results from the function evaluation program.

Binomial Coefficient Computation*

Problem—Mathematical expressions involving the binomial coefficient

$$\binom{n}{k} = \frac{n!}{k! \, (n - k)!}$$

are frequently encountered in probability theory problems or in error-detecting and correcting codes. To compute

$$\binom{n}{k}$$

directly requires computing three factorials. This can be time-consuming and cause overflow in computers for large values of n. A method that

---

*Program designed by Ronald Lambert, Design Engineer, General Electric Company.

prevents overflow, unless the final answer itself causes overflow, is as follows: If $n \geq 2k$, start with

$$\binom{n}{1} = n$$

Recursively compute

$$\binom{n}{j}$$

for $j = 2, 3, 4, \ldots, k$. Then

$$\binom{n}{j} = \binom{n}{j-1}\left(\frac{n+1-j}{j}\right)$$

If $n < 2k$, initialize

$$I = 1$$

Start with

$$\binom{k+I}{k} = \binom{k+1}{k} = k+1$$

Recursively compute

$$\binom{k+I}{k}$$

for $I = 2, 3, 4, \ldots, n - k$. Then

$$\binom{k+I}{k} = \binom{k+I-1}{k}\left(\frac{k+I}{I}\right)$$

Flowchart—See Fig. 7-84.

Program Listing—See Fig. 7-85.

Program Comments—The program performs the computation of $\binom{9}{4}$, $\binom{11}{6}$, and $\binom{100}{70}$, and indicates that $\binom{100}{70}$ has the largest value of these binomial coefficients.

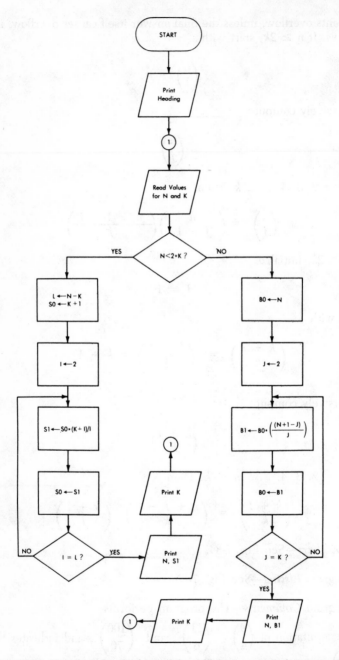

Fig. 7-84. Flowchart for the binomial coefficient computation program.

```
30    REM BINOMIAL COEFFICIENT COMPUTATION
40    PRINT "N","BINOMIAL"
50    PRINT "K","COEFFICIENT"
60    PRINT
70    READ N,K
80    IF N<2*K THEN  180
90    LET B0=N
100   FOR J=2 TO K
110     LET B1=B0*((N+1-J)/J)
120     LET B0=B1
130   NEXT J
140   PRINT N,B1
150   PRINT K
160   PRINT
170   GOTO 70
180   LET L=N-K
190   LET S0=K+1
200   FOR I=2 TO L
210     LET S1=S0*(K+I)/I
220     LET S0=S1
230   NEXT I
240   PRINT N,S1
250   PRINT K
260   PRINT
270   GOTO 70
280   DATA  9, 4, 11, 6, 100, 70
290   END
```

Fig. 7-85. BASIC program for the binomial coefficient computation problem.

Program Results—See Fig. 7-86.

N	BINOMIAL
K	COEFFICIENT
9	126
4	
11	462
6	
100	2.93722E+25
70	

Fig. 7-86. Printout of the results from the binomial coefficient program.

Bias Circuit Design*

Problem—This program solves the circuit equations for a stabilized self-biased transistor operating as a class-A amplifier under small-signal conditions. A typical bias network is illustrated by the engineer making the following entries to the program:

- Germanium transistor.
- Minimum design temperature $= -30°C$.
- Maximum design temperature $= 60°C$.
- Minimum beta $= 50$.
- Maximum beta $= 150$.
- Supply voltage $= 10$ V.
- Emitter resistor $= 2000$ Ω.
- Resistance tolerance $= 5\%$.
- $V_{CE} = 5$ V.
- $I_{CBO} = 0.002$ mA (minimum).
- $I_{CBO} = 0.78$ mA (maximum).
- $I_E = 1.18$ mA.

Program Listing—See Fig. 7-87.

```
 70  PRINT "FOR SILICON TRANSISTOR, ENTER 1, FOR GERMANIUM, ENTER 0";
 80  INPUT S
 90  PRINT "ENTER MIN. & MAX. DESIGN TEMPERATURES, MIN. & MAX. BETA"
100  INPUT T1, T2, H1, H2
110  PRINT "ENTER SUPPLY VOLTAGE, EMITTER RESISTOR, RES. TOLERANCE IN %"
120  INPUT V0, R4, P
130  PRINT "ENTER V(CE), I(CBO) IN MA, MIN. & MAX. I(E) IN MA"
140  INPUT V1, I0, I1, I2
150  LET I1 = I1*(1+.03*P)
160  LET I2 = I2*(1-.03*P)
170  LET H1 = H1*.865*EXP(.00575*T1)
180  LET T3 = T2-25
190  LET H2 = H2*(.865*EXP(.00575*T2)-(S-1)*(.00895-.00565*T3+.00048*T3+2))
200  IF S = 1 THEN 220
210  LET I0 = I0*EXP(.075*T3)
220  LET R3 = 2000*(V0-V1)/(I1+I2)-R4
230  LET R6 = ((I2-I1)*R4+2.5*(T2-T1))/(I0+I1/(H1+1)-I2/(H2+1))
240  IF R6>0 THEN 270
250  PRINT "I(E) RANGE TOO NARROW"
260  STOP
270  LET V6 = I1*.001*(R6/(H1+1)+R4)+.2+.5*S-.0025*(T1-25)
280  PRINT
290  PRINT "BIAS VOLTAGE =";V6;"VOLTS"
300  PRINT "BIAS RESISTOR =";R6;"OHMS"
310  PRINT
320  PRINT "FOR STABILIZED BIAS CIRCUIT:"
330  PRINT "R(B-VCC) =";V0*R6/V6
340  PRINT "R(B-GND) =";V0*R6/(V0-V6)
350  PRINT "R(COLL.) =";R3
360  PRINT "R(EMITTER) =";R4
370  END
```

Fig. 7-87. BASIC program for the bias circuit design problem.

---

*Program designed by Charles H. Popenoe, Physicist, U.S. Dept. of Commerce, National Bureau of Standards.

Program Comments—The program considers the following factors:

- Type of transistor (silicon or germanium).
- The manufacturer's specified spread of current gain (beta or h_{FE}) at the operating point for the transistor used.
- The variation of beta with temperature. For this, a typical measured variation was approximated with an analytic function.
- The variation of collector leakage current (I_{CBO}) with temperature. Again, typical curves were approximated with analytic functions.
- The variation of base-to-emitter voltage drop (V_{BE}) with temperature. Under normal conditions, V_{BE} at 25°C is about 0.2 volt for germanium and 0.7 volt for silicon, with temperature dependence of $-$ 2.5 mV/°C.
- The variation of circuit element values due to tolerances.

The generalized circuit contains three resistors and two batteries. This is later converted by Thevenin's theorem into a more practical circuit using four resistors and a single battery. The method of solution involves writing the circuit equations at both temperature extremes and solving simultaneously for the values of the bias battery and base resistor, with the assumption that I_{CBO} = 0 at the low temperature extreme. Input quantities required are

- Minimum and maximum temperatures (°C).
- Minimum and maximum beta at 25°C.
- Supply (collector) voltage (V_{CC}).
- Emitter resistor in ohms.
- Component tolerance in percent (%).
- Quiescent operating point, specified by V_{CE} and allowable minimum and maximum I_E in milliamperes.
- Collector leakage current (I_{CBO}) in milliamperes at 25°C.

```
FOR SILICON TRANSISTOR, ENTER 1, FOR GERMANIUM, ENTER 0?0
ENTER MIN. & MAX. DESIGN TEMPERATURES, MIN. & MAX. BETA
?-30,60,50,150
ENTER SUPPLY VOLTAGE, EMITTER RESISTOR, RES. TOLERANCE IN %
?10,2000,5
ENTER V(CE), I(CBO) IN MA, MIN. & MAX. I(E) IN MA
?5,.002,.78,1.18

BIAS VOLTAGE = 2.35223    VOLTS
BIAS RESISTOR = 9202.79   OHMS

FOR STABILIZED BIAS CIRCUIT:
R(B-VCC) = 39123.6
R(B-GND) = 12033.3
R(COLL.) = 3263.16
R(EMITTER) = 2000
```

Fig. 7-88. Printout of the results from the bias circuit design program.

The program computes the required values of the base resistor and bias battery for the generalized two-battery circuit, and of all four resistors for the practical circuit.

Program Results—See Fig. 7-88.

Fig. 7-89 illustrates the program output in circuit-diagram form.

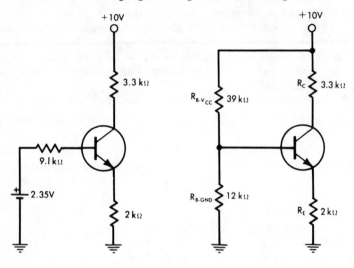

(A) Generalized bias circuit.　　　(B) Practical bias circuit.

Fig. 7-89. Circuit diagrams representing the results from the bias circuit design program.

EXERCISES

1. Determine which of the following are acceptable as variables and constants:

   (a) .63E2
   (b) R6
   (c) 71
   (d) 7S
   (e) 0
   (f) − .0008
   (g) A + 2

2. Write a BASIC expression for each of the following algebraic expressions:

   (a) $(x + y)^2$

   (b) $\dfrac{a + b}{c - d}$

(c) $28 (a + b)$

(d) $a + b^2$

(e) $a + \dfrac{b}{c} - d$

(f) $\sqrt{x^2 + y^2}$

(g) πr^2

3. Write LET statements for each of the following:

   (a) $F = ma$
   (b) $S = \frac{1}{2} (a + b + c)$

   (c) $A = \sqrt{S (S - a) (S - b) (S - c)}$

   (d) $R = \dfrac{1}{R_1} + \dfrac{1}{R_1}$

4. Write a LET statement to increase R by 1.

5. Write a complete BASIC program to do the following 50 times: read a, compute $x = a^2$, print x.

6. Write a program that will read a, b, and n; compute $y = (a + b)^n$, and print y. The data values are $a = 27$, $b = 4$, and $n = 3$.

7. Write a PRINT statement that will cause the following message to be printed: HOW DO YOU SPELL APE?

8. Draw a flowchart and write a BASIC program to compute the sum of the first 200 integers squared.

$$\sum_{i = 1}^{200} i^2$$

9. Write a program to calculate 10 factorial (10!).

10. Find the intermediate values of R in the following BASIC program:

```
10   LET R = 3.0
20   FOR I = 1 to 4
30       LET R = R * 2 + B(I)
40   NEXT I
50   END
```

List B

B(1)	= 2
B(2)	= 0
B(3)	= 3
B(4)	= 4

11. Find the final value of N in the following BASIC program:

```
100   LET N = 1
110   FOR I = 1 TO 2
120       FOR K = 1 TO 2
130           LET N = N + L(I,K)
140       NEXT K
150   NEXT I
160   END
```

Table L

2	2
3	4

12. The length of the hypotenuse of a right triangle may be found from the formula

$$c = \sqrt{a^2 + b^2}$$

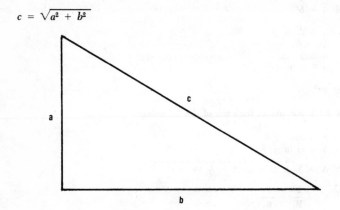

Write a program that will establish values for a and b and then compute and print c.

13. Consider the following table named X:

3	3	3	1	3
3	3	1	3	3
3	1	3	3	1
1	3	3	3	3
1	1	3	3	3

Each 3 represents a true value; each 1 a false value. Write a program that will examine the table and print the location of each false value; i.e., the value of the subscripts I and J when the contents of X(I,J) represent a false value.

14. Write a BASIC program that will establish values for list A, calculate the sum of the values, and print the sum. The values of A are 10, 31, 22, 9, 14, 106, 39, 42, 18, 2.

15. The equation for determining the current flowing through an ac circuit is

$$I = \frac{E}{\sqrt{R^2 + \left(2\pi fL - \dfrac{1}{2\pi fc}\right)^2}}$$

where,
    I is the current in amperes,
    R is the resistance in ohms,
    C is the capacitance in farads,
    π = 3.14159,
    E is the voltage in volts,
    L is the inductance in henrys,
    f is the frequency in hertz.

Write a program to compute the current for a number of equally spaced values of capacitance for voltages of 1.0, 2.0, and 3.0. Use the following data values: R = 100, F = 0.006, L = 50. Use a starting value of capacitance of 0.0003, a terminating value of capacitance of 0.001, and an increment of 0.0001.

16. Draw a flowchart and write a BASIC program to calculate the volume of the hollow cylinder shown in the accompanying sketch. Assume that only the dimensions shown are in the computer's memory. Use the formula

$$V = \frac{\pi L (D^2 - d^2)}{4}$$

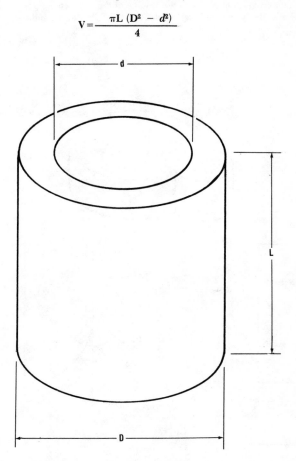

17. Write a program to compute and print the sum of the natural logarithms of the odd integers from 151 to 275, inclusive.

18. Write a BASIC program that will multiply the following matrices:

$$A = \begin{bmatrix} 1 & 2 & 4 \\ 3 & -2 & 5 \\ 4 & 2 & -1 \end{bmatrix} \quad B = \begin{bmatrix} 0 & 1 & -2 \\ 3 & 0 & 1 \\ 4 & 0 & 2 \end{bmatrix}$$

19. Write a BASIC program that will transpose the matrix:

$$\begin{bmatrix} 6 & 3 & 4 \\ 1 & 0 & 7 \\ 8 & 4 & 3 \\ 2 & 2 & 1 \\ 6 & 1 & 4 \end{bmatrix}$$

20. Write a program to compute the volume of the intersecting parallel cylinders shown in the accompanying sketch. Use the following formula:

$$V = L \left([\pi(R_1^2 + R_2^2)] - [R_1^2(\theta_1 - \tfrac{1}{2} \sin 2\theta_1)] - [R_2^2(\theta_2 - \tfrac{1}{2} \sin 2\theta_2)] \right)$$

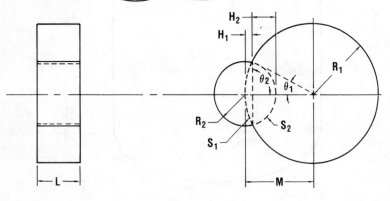

CHAPTER 8
PROBLEM-ORIENTED PROGRAMMING LANGUAGES

Many people view procedure-oriented languages as problem oriented because they tend to be used for certain classes of applications; i.e., FORTRAN is used primarily for scientific or engineering applications, COBOL and RPG are used primarily for business applications, JOVIAL and CS/1 are used primarily for real-time control applications, etc. However, I prefer to use the term *problem oriented* with programming languages that are designed for solving more specialized problems, such as numerical control, investment analysis, civil engineering, simulation, equipment checkout, circuit analysis, etc. These languages adopt specific phrases and key words from the standard vocabulary of the prospective user. For example, COGO is a language for civil engineers and surveyors, and uses phrases containing key words that are indigenous to the vocabulary of those professions. This language enables the user to describe computations by using such key words as ANGLE, AREA, CURVE, DISTANCE, GIRDER/LENGTHS, LO-CATE/AZIMUTH, SEGMENT, and SUBGRADE.

Most problem-oriented languages are interpretively translated and executed, thus allowing them to be used in commercial time-sharing systems as well as in batch-processing systems. This should be important to the operators of small engineering shops who cannot afford and do not need a large computer system. They can, however, have a terminal installed in their offices and have the use of high-level programming facilities to help them solve many of their problems.

One of the main advantages of problem-oriented languages is that they can be learned by the prospective user in a relatively short time. For example, a freshman or sophomore engineering student should be able to write competent programs in COGO after only one hour of instruction. Programming languages that can be learned with such ease could be factored into all beginning courses in civil engineering and surveying. Using languages of this type will allow instructors to assign students more complex problems without overloading them with tedious calculations.

345

This chapter contains brief descriptions of several problem-oriented languages. Because many of these languages contain concepts and terms that are of a specialized nature, only introductory information is provided. What I have attempted to do is present a general description of the language and, where appropriate, list several of the language statements and show an example.

COGO

COGO (*CO*ordinate *GeO*metry) is the most widely implemented problem-oriented language for civil engineering applications. The language has been implemented on several computer systems.

Civil engineers work on surveying, layout, and highway-design problems, and use certain common terms and operations; e.g., *point, area, coordinate, line, azimuth, station,* and *intersect*. COGO assists civil engineers and surveyors in doing plane-geometry computations. With COGO, the engineer writes a simple listing to locate points, find areas, adjust traverses, and do those calculations that occur frequently in his work. Commands such as ANGLE, DISTANCE, and AREA permit him to find the angle formed by three points, the distance between two points, and the area of a polygon—all without writing a single equation.

Each COGO command consists of a name and relevant data; e.g., AREA 1 14 63, which computes the area in square feet and acres of the triangle identified by corner points 1, 14, and 63. When using COGO, the engineer must determine which commands to use, the proper order of the commands, and the data to be included with the commands. Table 8-1 lists the commands available in COGO.

Table 8-1. List of COGO Commands

ADJUST/ANG/LS	DISTANCE/SAVE	POINTS/INTERSECT
ADJUST/AZ/LS	DIVIDE/LINE	REDEFINE
ALIGNMENT	DIVIDE/STATION/LINE	RT/TRI/HYP
ANGLE	DUMP	RT/TRI/LEG
ANGLE/SAVE	EVEN/STATIONS	SEGMENT
ARC/ARC/INTERSECT	EXTERNAL/TANGENT	SEGMENT/MINUS
ARC/LINE/AZ	FINISH	SEGMENT/PLUS
ARC/LINE/POINTS	GIRDER/LENGTHS	SPIRAL/CURVE/INTER
AREA	INVERSE/AZIMUTH	SPIRAL/LINE/INTER
AREA/AZIMUTHS	INVERSE/BEARING	SPIRAL/SPIRAL/INTER
AREA/BEARINGS	LINES	START
AZ/INTERSECT	LOCATE/ANGLE	STATION/EL/POA
BR/INTERSECT	LOCATE/AZIMUTH	STATION/POA
CLEAR	LOCATE/BEARING	STORE
COORD/EL/OFFSET	LOCATE/DEFLECTION	STORE/SUPER
COORD/EL/POA	LOCATE/LINE	SUBGRADE
COORD/OFFSET	OFFSET/ALIGN	SUPER/EVEN
COORD/POA	OFFSET/ELEV	SUPER/SPECIAL
CROSS/TANGENT	OFFSET/EL/ALIGN	SURVEX/STATION
CURVE/SPIRAL	ORIGIN	TERMINUS
DEFINE/CURVE	PARALLEL/LINE	VERTICAL/SEGMENT
DISTANCE	PI	

COGO enables an engineer to solve, *in minutes*, such problems as right-of-way survey, interchange design, highway design, control surveys, land surveying, construction layout, subdivision analysis, and bridge geometry. The heart of the COGO method is the simple concept of a coordinate table. Each point involved in a problem is given an identification number. As each point is "located," the coordinates of the point are stored in the coordinate table and are, henceforth, available for subsequent computations by simply referring to the point number.

The use of the coordinate table and the system may be illustrated by a simple example. In the problem shown in Fig. 8-1, the following data are known:

(a) The coordinates of points 9, 103, and 115.
(b) The clockwise angle at point 9 from point 103 to point 111.
(c) The length of the line from point 8 to point 111.

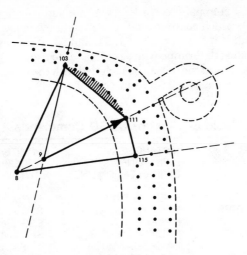

Fig. 8-1. Civil engineering problem solved by the COGO program of Fig. 8-2.

The following are the desired answers:

(a) The coordinates of points 8 and 111.
(b) The area bounded by points 8, 103, 111, and 115, and the lengths and azimuths of the sides.
(c) The bearings of the sides.
(d) The area of the segment defined by points 103 and 111 with the radius determined internally as the distance from point 9 to point 111. Also, the chord length and arc length between points 103 and 111.
(e) The area noted in (b) plus the area of the segment in (d).
(f) The area noted in (e) minus the area of the segment in (d).

Fig. 8-2 illustrates the COGO program used to compute the desired answers. This program uses the following COGO commands:

STR	STORE
LAN	LOCATE/ANGLE
LLN	LOCATE/LINE
ARE	AREA
ARZ	AREA/AZIMUTHS
ABR	AREA/BEARINGS
SGM	SEGMENT
SPL	SEGMENT/PLUS
SMI	SEGMENT/MINUS

The underlined portions of the program are the user responses.

```
?STR 9 134.8695 45.4597 103 314.1014 80.2988
  9       134.869500        45.459700

103       314.101400        80.298800


?LAN 103 9 111 D 9 103 51 0 0.0
111       220.588720        206.674006

?LLN 111 9 8 249.4049
  8       103.500155        -13.537420

?STR 115 151.0889 231.2852
115       151.088900        231.285200

?ARE 8 103 111 115 8
AREA=     26787.9986 SQ.FT.,         .614968 ACRES

?ARZ 8 103 111 115 8
PT.    8 TO PT. 103 DIST=      230.5604   AZ=  24-  0- 57.7

PT. 103 TO PT. 111 DIST=      157.2111   AZ= 126- 30-   .0

PT. 111 TO PT. 115 DIST=       73.7288   AZ= 160- 29- 59.9

PT. 115 TO PT.   8 DIST=      249.4049   AZ= 259-  0-   .0

AREA=     26787.9986 SQ.FT.,         .614968 ACRES

?ABR 8 103 111 115 8
PT.    8 TO PT. 103 DIST=      230.5604   BR=  24-  0- 57.7  QUAD= 1

PT. 103 TO PT. 111 DIST=      157.2111   BR=  53- 30-   .0  QUAD= 2

PT. 111 TO PT. 115 DIST=       73.7288   BR=  19- 30-   .1  QUAD= 2

PT. 115 TO PT.   8 DIST=      249.4049   BR=  79-  0-   .0  QUAD= 3

AREA=     26787.9986 SQ.FT.,         .614968 ACRES

?SGM 103 111 D 9 111
CHORD=      157.2111 ARC=      162.5236 SEG AREA=      1883.1212 SQ.FT
                                                      .043231 ACRES

?SPL 103 111 D 9 111
CHORD=      157.2111 ARC=      162.5236 SEG AREA=      1883.1212 SQ.FT
                                                      .043231 ACRES

AREA=     28671.1198 SQ.FT.,         .658198 ACRES

?SMI 103 111 D 9 111
CHORD=      157.2111 ARC=      162.5236 SEG AREA=      1883.1212 SQ.FT.
                                                      .043231 ACRES

AREA=     26787.9986 SQ.FT.,         .614968 ACRES
```

Fig. 8-2. COGO program for the problem of Fig. 8-1.

STRESS

STRESS (*STRuctural Engineering Systems Solver*) is a problem-oriented language used for solving structural engineering problems. It consists of a language that describes the problem and a translator that accepts the language and produces the requested results.

A problem is described with the STRESS language by writing statements specifying the nature and size of the structure, the loads, a solution procedure, and the results desired. The STRESS language is easily understood and the engineer needs no conventional programming experience in order to solve problems with it.

From the engineer's viewpoint, STRESS has the following principal characteristics:

- Communication with the computer is entirely in the engineer's language.
- A STRESS program consists of commands and data.
- A STRESS program, once written, can easily be modified to allow for updated changes, thus making it a dynamic structural design facility.

STRESS can handle small and medium-size structural problems as well as large ones. It has been implemented to perform the linear analysis of elastic, statically loaded framed structures. Analysis means the computation of member distortions, member end forces, reactions, joint displacements, and support displacements for a structure. The engineer describes the problem in a series of statements that specify the makeup and orientation of all the members, and the type, position, and magnitude of all the applied loads, displacements, and distortions.

The term *framed structure* is used to denote structures composed of slender elements. The structure itself may extend in two or three dimensions. Any structure that can be described by the language can be analyzed. The engineer may have to make supplementary computations if a structure cannot be completely described by the language.

Table 8-2 illustrates the statement types available in the STRESS language. The data in STRESS is more complicated than the data in

Table 8-2. Statement Types in the STRESS Programming Language

Classification	Statement Type	Description
Header	STRUCTURE	Program start.
Size Descriptors	NUMBER OF JOINTS NUMBER OF SUPPORTS NUMBER OF MEMBERS NUMBER OF LOADINGS	Define the size of the problem.
Process Descriptors	TYPE METHOD TABULATE SELECTIVE OUTPUT PRINT	Information about the procedures to be used.
Structural Data Descriptors	JOINT COORDINATES JOINT RELEASES MEMBER INCIDENCES MEMBER PROPERTIES MEMBER RELEASES CONSTANTS	Describe a framed structure.
Loading Data Descriptors	LOADING JOINT LOADS JOINT DISPLACEMENTS MEMBER DISTORTIONS MEMBER LOADS COMBINE	Describe loading.
Modification Descriptors	MODIFICATION ADDITIONS CHANGES DELETIONS	Permit program and data modifications.
Termination Statements	SOLVE SOLVE THIS PART FINISH	Terminate input of problem.

COGO because STRESS requires topological and mechanical properties as well as other information, whereas COGO requires only geometric data.

Let us examine a sample STRESS problem illustrating the use of several statements. The plane frame shown in Fig. 8-3 is to be analyzed for two loading conditions: (1) the uniform load of 1.2 kips*/ft on all horizontal members, and (2) horizontal loads of 20 kips on the two floors. The first step is to identify the joints and members as shown in Fig. 8-3. Next, the coordinate origin is identified as joint 5. The program shown in Fig. 8-4 performs the necessary computations and prints the data shown in Fig. 8-5.

---

*The *kip* is a unit of force (weight) used to express deadweight loads and is an acronym for *kilo*pound (1.0 kip = 1000 pounds). In the SI metric system of units, 1.0 kip = 4448 newtons.

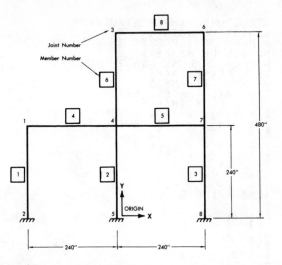

Fig. 8-3. Sample structure showing joint and member numbers.

APT

APT (*A*utomatically *P*rogrammed *T*ools) is a system consisting of a collection of computer programs designed to eliminate some of the tedium and drudgery from producing paper-tape programs to control machine tools. *Numerical control*, as applied to machine tools, is the automatic control of all machine functions through a complete cycle by means of coded instructions. This means that once the work is placed in position on the machine, a coded program controls selection of the tools, feed rate, coolant setting, spindle speed, and the direction and distance of movements until the piece of work is complete. Coded instructions to machine tools are usually in the form of punched paper tapes. Fig. 8-6 illustrates the procedure used in producing these control tapes. The circled numbers on the illustration correspond to the following procedural steps:

1. The part programmer writes a program (*part program manuscript*) in a language such as APT.
2. The program is keypunched on cards. Each card contains a specific machine-tool instruction.
3. The APT program is used to accept the sequence of instructions (part program) and calculate the coordinate points that the machine tool will follow in producing the part.
4. Because one machine tool and control system may differ from another, a program called a *post processor* is used to account for

```
STRUCTURE SAMPLE STRUCTURE
NUMBER OF JOINTS    8
NUMBER OF SUPPORTS  3
NUMBER OF MEMBERS   8
NUMBER OF LOADINGS  2
TYPE PLANE FRAME
METHOD STIFFNESS
TABULATE FORCES, REACTIONS
JOINT COORDINATES
1 X -240. Y 240. FREE
2 X -240. Y   0. SUPPORT
5 X    0. Y   0. S
8 X  240. Y   0. S
4 X    0. Y 240.
7 X  240. Y 240.
3 X    0. Y 480.
6 X  240. Y 480.
MEMBER INCIDENCES
121
254
387
414
547
643
776
836
MEMBER PROPERTIES
8 PRISMATIC AX 10.0 IZ 300.0
4 PRISMATIC AX 10.0 AY 0.0 IZ 300.0
MEMBER PROPERTIES, PRISMATIC
1 AX  20. IZ 200.
2 AX  20. IZ 200.
3 AX  20. IZ 200.
5 AX  10. IZ 300.
6 IZ 100. AX  20.
7 IZ 180. AX  20.
CONSTANTS E, 30000.,ALL
LOADING 1 UNIFORM ALL BEAMS
MEMBER LOADS
8 FORCE Y UNIFORM, -0.1
4 FORCE Y UNIFORM, -0.1
5 FORCE Y UNIFORM, -0.1
LOADING 2 WIND FROM RIGHT
JOINT LOADS
6 FORCE X -20.
7 FORCE X -20.
TABULATE DISPLACEMENTS
SOLVE THIS PART
```

Fig. 8-4. STRESS program to analyze the sample structure of Fig. 8-3 for two loading conditions.

these differences. The post processor uses the computed machine-tool location data to produce control data in the proper format for a specific machine tool.

5. The computer is used to accept the APT program, the part program, and the post processor program. Using these programs, the computer executes the instructions specified by the part program.

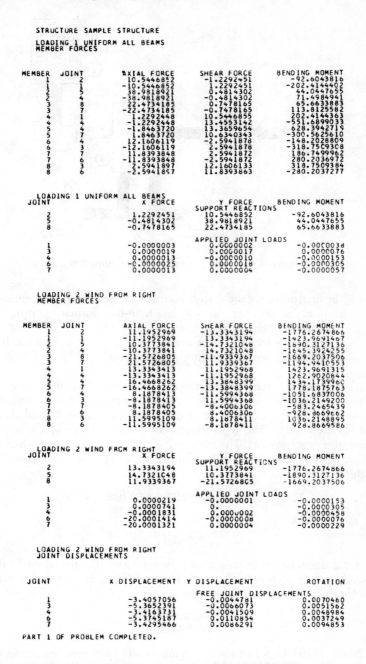

```
STRUCTURE SAMPLE STRUCTURE
LOADING 1 UNIFORM ALL BEAMS
MEMBER FORCES


MEMBER   JOINT      AXIAL FORCE        SHEAR FORCE      BENDING MOMENT
  1        2        10.5446852         -1.2292451        -92.6043816
  1        1       -10.5446852          1.2292451       -202.4144402
  2        5        38.9818921          0.4814302         44.0447655
  2        4       -38.9818921         -0.4814302         71.4984941
  3        8        22.4734185         -0.7478165         65.6633883
  3        7       -22.4734185         -0.7478165        113.8125582
  4        1         1.2292448         10.5446855        202.4144363
  4        4        -1.2292448         13.4553142       -551.6899033
  5        7        -1.8463720         13.3659654        628.3942719
  5        7         1.8463720         10.6340343       -300.5625610
  6        4        12.1606119         -2.5941878       -148.2028809
  6        3       -12.1606119          2.5941878       -318.7509308
  7        7        11.8393848          2.5941872        186.7499962
  7        6       -11.8393848         -2.5941872        280.2036972
  8        3        -2.5941897         12.1606133        318.7509384
  8        6        -2.5941857         11.8393863       -280.2037277


LOADING 1 UNIFORM ALL BEAMS
JOINT                 X FORCE            Y FORCE        BENDING MOMENT
                                   SUPPORT REACTIONS
  2                  1.2292451         10.5446852        -92.6043816
  5                 -0.4814302         38.9818921         44.0447655
  8                 -0.7478165         22.4734185         65.6633883

                                   APPLIED JOINT LOADS
  1                 -0.0000003          0.0000002         -0.0000038
  3                  0.0000019          0.0000017          0.0000076
  4                  0.0000013         -0.0000010         -0.0000153
  6                 -0.0000025          0.0000018         -0.0000305
  7                  0.0000013          0.0000004         -0.0000057


LOADING 2 WIND FROM RIGHT
MEMBER FORCES


MEMBER   JOINT      AXIAL FORCE        SHEAR FORCE      BENDING MOMENT
  1        2        11.1952969        -13.3343194      -1776.2674866
  1        1       -11.1952969         13.3343194      -1423.9691467
  2        5        10.3773841        -14.7321048      -1890.3127136
  2        4       -10.3773841         14.7321048      -1645.3924255
  3        8       -21.5726805        -11.9339367      -1669.2037506
  3        7        21.5726805         11.9339367      -1194.9410553
  4        1        13.3343413         11.1952968       1423.9691315
  4        4       -13.3343413        -11.1952968       1262.9020844
  5        7        16.4668262         13.3848399       1434.1739960
  5        7       -16.4668262        -13.3848399       1778.1875763
  6        4         8.1878413        -11.5994368      -1051.6837006
  6        3        -8.1878413         11.5994368      -1036.2149200
  7        7        -8.1878405         -8.4006306       -583.2465439
  7        6         8.1878405          8.4006306       -928.8669662
  8        3        11.5995109          8.1878411       1036.2148895
  8        6       -11.5995109         -8.1878411        928.8669586


LOADING 2 WIND FROM RIGHT
JOINT                 X FORCE            Y FORCE        BENDING MOMENT
                                   SUPPORT REACTIONS
  2                 13.3343194         11.1952969      -1776.2674866
  5                 14.7321048         10.3773841      -1890.3127136
  8                 11.9339367        -21.5726805      -1669.2037506

                                   APPLIED JOINT LOADS
  1                  0.0000219         -0.0000001         -0.0000153
  3                  0.0000741          0.                -0.0000305
  4                 -0.0001831          0.0000002         -0.0000458
  6                -20.0001414         -0.0000008         -0.0000076
  7                -20.0001321          0.0000004         -0.0000229


LOADING 2 WIND FROM RIGHT
JOINT DISPLACEMENTS


JOINT            X DISPLACEMENT     Y DISPLACEMENT        ROTATION
                                   FREE JOINT DISPLACEMENTS
  1                 -3.4057056         -0.0044781          0.0070460
  3                 -5.3652391         -0.0066073          0.0051562
  4                 -3.4163731         -0.0041509          0.0048984
  6                 -5.3745187          0.0110854          0.0037249
  7                 -3.4295466          0.0086291          0.0094853
PART 1 OF PROBLEM COMPLETED.
```

Fig. 8-5. Output produced by the STRESS program of Fig. 8-4.

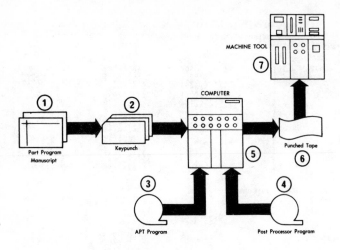

Fig. 8-6. Steps in computer programming for numerical control.

6. The final output of the system contains all the commands required to produce the part in the machine-tool format. Output is 8-channel punched paper tape.
7. The machine tool that uses the control tape can be a contouring lathe, a drill press, a milling machine, etc.

APT allows the part programmer to define points, lines, circles, planes, geometric surfaces, and canonical surfaces. Having defined these locations, there are action (major) words that guide the tool along the defined path. The instructions are written sequentially as in computer programming. The basic unit of APT is the *statement,* which is either a command or a unit of information. It may be a complex statement, such as

TL LFT, GORGT/LIN2, PAST (LINE/1.0, 3.0, S., S.)

or as simple as

HEAD/2

A statement can be broken up into two sections. The major words are usually in one section, and words that modify the major words are in another section:

FEDRAT/30
GO/FWD,L2

Many FORTRAN rules about symbols and functions also apply to APT. In fact, FORTRAN-like statements may be used within an APT

Table 8-3. Partial APT Vocabulary List

Coordinate Transformation Declarations
- REFSYS

Function Designators
- DOTF
- LNTHF
- SQRTF
- SINF
- COSF
- EXPF
- LOGF
- ATANF
- ABSF

Geometric Expressions
- POINT
- LINE
- PLANE
- CIRCLE
- CYLNDR
- ELLIPS
- HYPERB
- CONE
- GCONIC
- LCONIC
- VECTOR
- MATRIX
- SPHERE
- QADRIC
- POLCON
- TABCYL

Array Declarations
- RESERV

Arithmetic Transfer Statements
- IF
- JUMPTO

Geometric Transfer Statements
- TRANTO

Direction Declarations
- INDIRP
- INDIRV

Z-Surface Declarations
- ZSURF

Input/Output Control Statements
- PRINT
- READ
- TITLES
- PUNCH

Remarks
- REMARKS

Explicit Positioning Statements
- FROM
- GODLTA
- GOTO

Initial Continuous Motion Statements
- GO
- OFFSET

Intermediate Continuous Motion Statements
- GOLFT
- GORGT
- GOFWD
- GOBACK
- GOUP
- GODOWN

Termination Statements
- FINI

Statements
- LOOPST
- LOOPND

Procedure Statements
- CALL

Tolerance Specifications
- TOLER
- INTOL
- OUTTOL

Post Processor Control Statements
- SADDLE
- LOADTL
- SELCTL
- CLEARC
- CYCLE
- DRAFT
- RITMIDI
- PLOT
- OVPLOT
- LETTER
- PPRINT
- PARTNO
- INSERT
- CAMERA
- END
- STOP
- OPSTOP
- ISTOP
- RAPID
- SWITCH
- RETRCT
- DRESS
- PICKUP
- UNLOAD
- PENUP
- PENDWN
- ZERO
- CODEL
- RESET
- PLABEL

Table 8-3. Partial APT Vocabulary List (cont)

HEAD	TANCRV
MODE	TLONPS
CLEARP	TLOFPS
TMARK	**Cutter Specifications**
REWIND	CUTTER
CUTCOM	**Calculation Constant Controls**
REVERS	CUT
FEDRAT	DNTCUT
DELAY	2DCALC
AIR	3DCALC
OPSKIP	NDTEST
LEADER	TLAXIS
PPLOT	MULTAX
MACHIN	MAXDP
MCHTOL	NUMPTS
PIVOTZ	THICK
MCHFIN	NOPS
SEQNO	PSIS
INTCOD	**Modifier Words**
DISPLY	MULTRD
AUXFUN	XYVIEW
CHECK	YZVIEW
POSTN	ZXVIEW
TOOLNO	SOLID
ROTABL	DASH
ORIGIN	DOTTED
ARCSLP	CL
COOLNT	DITTO
SPINDL	PEN
TURRET	SCRIBE
THREAD	BLACK
TRANS	XYPLAN
TRACUT	XYROT
INDEX	RPM
COPY	MAXRPM
PREFUN	TURN
COUPLE	FACE
PITCH	BORE
CLAMP	XYZ
ENDMDI	TRFORM
ASLOPE	NORMAL
Procedure Declarations	UP
MACRO	DOWN
TERMAC	LOCK
Vocabulary Equivalence Declarations	SFM
SYN	XCOORD
Tool Position Declarations	YCOORD
TLLFT	ZCOORD
TLRGT	TYPE
TLNDON	NIXIE
TLON	LIGHT
	FOURPT

Table 8-3. Partial APT Vocabulary List (cont)

TWOPT	XAXIS
PTSLOP	YAXIS
PTNORM	ZAXIS
SPLINE	TOOL
RTHETA	AUTO
THETAR	RIGHT
YLARGE	SCALE
YSMALL	SMALL
YZPLAN	TANTO
YZROT	TIMES
ZLARGE	TRANSL
ZSMALL	UNIT
ZXPLAN	XLARGE
ZXROT	XSMALL
3PT2SL	TAPKUL
4PT1SL	STEP
5PT	MAIN
INTERC	SIDE
SLOPE	LINCIR
SUNTRN	MAXIPM
ATANGL	REV
CENTER	RANGE
FUNOFY	PSTAN
INTOF	CSTAN
INVERS	FRONT
LARGE	REAT
FEFT	SADTUR
MINUS	MILL
NEGX	THRU
NEGY	DEEP
NEGZ	TRAV
NOX	NORMPS
NOY	CONCRD
NOZ	GECENT
IN	NOMORE
OUT	MODIFY
ALL	MIRROR
LAST	START
MILWAK	ENDARC
BENDIX	CCLW
DYNPAT	CLW
TRW	MEDIUM
CINCY	HIGH
TRUTRA	LOW
PRATTW	CONST
FOSDIK	DECR
BURG	INCR
PROBOG	ROTREF
DVLIEG	TO
POSY	PAST
POSZ	ON
RADIUS	OFF

Table 8-3. Partial APT Vocabularly List (cont)

RED	CAXIS
GREEN	CIRCUL
BLUE	LINEAR
LITE	PARAB
MED	PARLEL
DARK	PERPTO
CHUCK	PLUS
AAXIS	POSX
BAXIS	FLOOD

statement. Table 8-3 lists the APT vocabulary list. These words have specific meanings and are understood by people working in the numerical-control and machine-tool areas.

Some of the characteristics of the APT language are illustrated in the following examples of usage. Fig. 8-7 shows a two-dimensional cam that is to be produced by the APT program* shown in Fig. 8-8. Each statement in the program is accompanied by an explanation of the instructions contained in the statement.

---

*Program from the following brochure: Hori, S., *Future of Numerical Control in Industry.* Chicago: Armour Research Foundation of Illinois Institute of Technology.

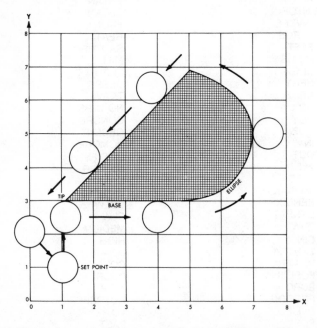

Fig. 8-7. Part to be produced by a numerically controlled machine tool as specified by the APT program shown in Fig. 8-8.

Part Program	Explanation
CUTTER/1	Use a 1-inch diameter cutter.
TOLER/.005	Tolerance of cut is 0.005 inch
FEDRAT/80	Use feed rate of 80 inches per minute.
HEAD/1	Use head number 1.
MODE/1	Operate tool in mode number 1.
SPINDL/2400	Turn on spindle; set at 2400 r/min.
COOLNT/FLOOD	Turn on coolant; use flood setting.
PT1 = POINT/4, 5	Define a reference point (PT1) as the point with coordinates (4, 5).
FROM/(SETPT = POINT/1, 1)	Start the tool from the point called SETPT, which is defined as the point with coordinates (1, 1).
INDIRP/(TIP = POINT/1, 3)	Aim the tool in the direction of the point called TIP, which is defined as the point with coordinates (1, 3).
BASE = LINE/TIP, AT ANGL, 0	Define the line called BASE as the line through the point TIP which makes an angle of 0° with the horizontal.
GO/TO, BASE	Go to the line BASE.
TLRGT, GORGT/BASE	With the tool on the right, go right along the line BASE.
GOFWD/(ELLIPS/CENTER, PT1,3,2,0)	Go forward along the ellipse with center at PT1; semimajor axis = 3, semiminor axis = 2, and major axis making an angle of 0° with the horizontal.
GOLFT/(LINE/2,4,1,3), PAST, BASE	Go left along the line joining the points (2,4) and (1,3) past the line BASE.
GOTO/SETPT	Go to the point SETPT in a straight line.
COOLNT/OFF	Turn off coolant flow.
SPINDL/OFF	Turn off spindle.
END	This is the end of the machine control unit operation.
FINI	This is the finish of the part program.

Fig. 8-8. APT program for machining the part shown in Fig. 8-7.

Another example of an APT program is shown in Fig. 8-9. This program describes the motions of a cutting tool 0.5 inch in diameter, revolving at 2600 revolutions per minute, moving at 30 inches per minute around a simple figure bounded by two lines (L1 and L2) and two circular arcs (C1 and C2) (see Fig. 8-10). Statements are made that specify the part number, the machine that the output will be used on,

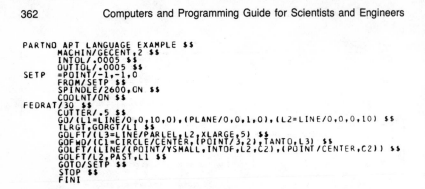

```
PARTNO APT LANGUAGE EXAMPLE $$
        MACHIN/GECENT,2 $$
        INTOL/.0005 $$
        OUTTOL/.0005 $$
SETP    =POINT/-1,-1,0
        FROM/SETP $$
        SPINDLE/2600,ON $$
        COOLNT/ON $$
FEDRAT/30 $$
        CUTTER/.5 $$
        GO/(L1=LINE/0,0,10,0),(PLANE/0,0,1,0),(L2=LINE/0,0,0,10) $$
        TLRGT,GORGT/L1 $$
        GOLFT/(L3=LINE/PARLEL,L2,XLARGE,5) $$
        GOFWD/(C1=CIRCLE/CENTER,(POINT/3,2),TANTO,L3) $$
        GOLFT/(LINE/(POINT/YSMALL,INTOF,L2,C2),(POINT/CENTER,C2)) $$
        GOLFT/L2,PAST,L1 $$
        GOTO/SETP $$
        STOP $$
        FINI
```

Fig. 8-9. APT program for describing the motions of the cutting tool shown in Fig. 8-10.

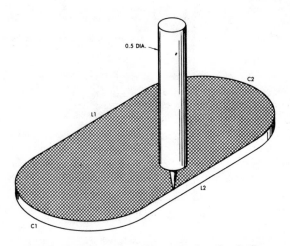

Fig. 8-10. Cutting tool moving around a simple figure.

and the maximum deviation tolerance into and away from the part being machined. Statements are provided to control machine functions, such as turning the spindle on at a selected r/min, turning the coolant on, and specifying the rate of feed of the cutter. The geometry of the part is described in terms similar to those used in plane and solid geometry: *points, lines, circles, planes, cylinders, spheres, cones,* etc. These may be described easily by noncomputer-oriented personnel. The cutter is commanded to move along the part with terms such as GOLFT (go left), GORGT (go right), GOFWD (go forward), and GOTO (go to).

DATAPOINT

DATAPOINT is a two-axis point-to-point programming language developed by Data General Corporation to run on their line of

"WOW! TALK ABOUT FAST WORK—I JUST SENT A NOTE IN
A BOTTLE APPLYING FOR A COMPUTER DATE LAST WEEK!"

minicomputers. The language is easy to learn, consisting of a small number of supervisory and editing commands and a number of geometric statements. The commands are brief and generally self-explanatory. The geometric statements for parts programming are equally simple.

Users can prepare parts programs that define a limited number of machine operations and then incorporate them into larger programs by using the "define pattern" statement. In this way, operations can be checked out easily and large parts programs can be written. Punched paper tapes produced by DATAPOINT may be used to automatically control tools.

Geometric Commands

DATAPOINT uses the following geometric commands:

1. OFFSET Xn Yn—Allows the coordinates Xn, Yn to be used as the reference point for all input following the offset command.
2. AT Xn Yn—Moves the current location to the new position Xn, Yn but does not output a coordinate at Xn, Yn. Used in locating the starting point for other commands. This command may either appear on the same line as other geometric commands, or on a separate line.
3. LINE θ d h—Outputs h coordinates, the distance d apart, and along the line θ degrees from the X axis.

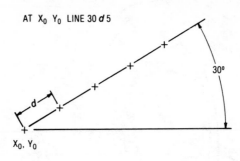

4. BHC θ r h—Outputs h coordinates, equally spaced around the circumference of a circle of radius r with the initial coordinate θ degrees from the X axis.

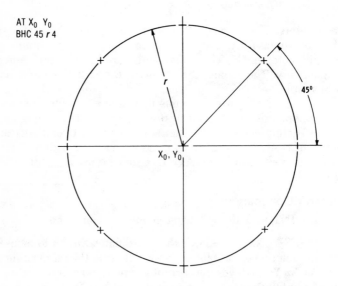

5. ARC θ_i, θ_f r h—Outputs h coordinates, equally spaced along the circumference of an arc of radius r. The first coordinate is θ_i degrees from the X axis, and the last coordinate is θ_f degrees from the X axis.

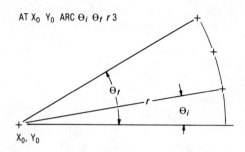

6. GRID $\theta_x d_x h_x \theta_y d_y h_y$—Outputs a series of coordinates in a grid (rectangular or trapezoidal) pattern. The h_x coordinates are produced along a line θ_x degrees from the X axis with d_x distance between them. The h_y coordinates are produced along a line θ_y degrees from the X axis with a distance d_y between them.

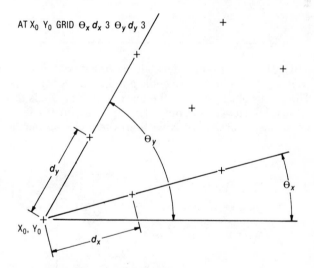

The arguments of the geometric commands may be arithmetic expressions. For example, LINE θ $(2 \times 1.375)/4h$ is evaluated as LINE θ 0.6875 h.

Contour Definition

The geometric commands can be used to profile the following contours:

1. BHC θ r b rt—Produces all coordinates to profile a circular hole of radius r. The maximum allowable burr is given by b. The

radius of the tool used is given by rt. The first coordinate is produced θ degrees from the X axis.

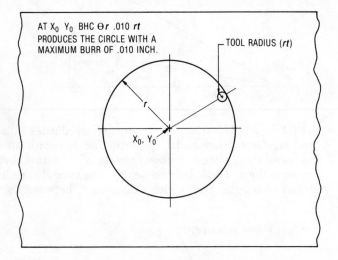

AT X_0 Y_0 BHC Θr .010 rt
PRODUCES THE CIRCLE WITH A
MAXIMUM BURR OF .010 INCH.

TOOL RADIUS (rt)

X_0, Y_0

2. ARC $\theta_i \theta_f$ r b rt—Produces all coordinates to profile an arc starting at θ_i degrees and ending at θ_f degrees from the X axis. The radius of the arc is r, the maximum burr size is b, and the radius of the tool is rt. If only r is written, the arc is understood to be an inside arc. If ro is written, the arc is an outside arc.

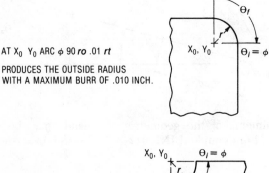

AT X_0 Y_0 ARC ϕ 90 ro .01 rt

PRODUCES THE OUTSIDE RADIUS
WITH A MAXIMUM BURR OF .010 INCH.

AT X_0 Y_0 ARC ϕ D r .01 rt
PRODUCES THE INSIDE ARC.

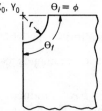

3. HOLE *x y t*—Produces all coordinates to profile a rectangular hole *x* by *y* inches using a square tool of dimension *t*. The entire center is punched away.

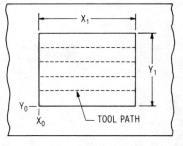

AT X_0 Y_0 HOLE X_1 Y_1 *t*

PRODUCES THE CUTOUT BY PUNCHING AWAY THE CENTER.

4. TRIM *x y t*—Produces the coordinates to profile a rectangular hole *x* by *y* inches using a square tool of dimension *t*. The hole is created by trimming around the perimeter of the rectangle, leaving the center portion in one piece.

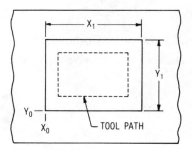

AT X_0 Y_0 TRIM X_1 Y_1 *t*

PRODUCES THE CUTOUT BY PUNCHING AROUND THE PERIMETER, LEAVING THE CENTER INTACT.

Pattern Definition

Coordinates may also be combined with the geometric commands to define a pattern. This allows the parts programmer to make his own patterns. All patterns are terminated by the END statement. The following example illustrates how a pattern (pattern 1) is defined and used within another pattern definition (pattern 2):

```
DEFINE PATTERN 1          (Begin pattern definition.)
AT X1 Y2 BHC 06.08
X6.0 Y7.25
END                       (End pattern definition.)
```

```
DEFINE PATTERN 2
AT X10.0 Y8.0
ARC 30 60 2.03
1X 1.0
PAT 1                        (Pattern 1 is nested
END                              within pattern 2.)
```

Setback Commands

Up to four unique setbacks can be defined. The setbacks can then be used by calling their names. The setback arguments can be arithmetic expressions:

SBAn	[The four setbacks
SBBm	(A,B,C,D) are defined
SBCl	as the numbers
SBDk	n, m, l and k.]
SBA (071*T) + (1.57*R)	(Specifying T and R, the setback A would be equal to the results of the expression.)
X10.5 − SBB	(If setback B were previously defined to be 0.060, the expression would be evaluated.)
X10.44	(Evaluated coordinate.)

Material Thickness Command

The material thickness command is similar to the setback command:

THKn	(The thickness is specified by the dimension n.)
X2.5 + THK	(Would be evaluated as the second expression.)
S2.5 + n	

Offpart Warnings

X and Y limit dimensions may be set. If any coordinate outside of these limits is programmed, an error message will be typed out.

XLMn	(Sets the maximum value of the X coordinate to be less than or equal to n.)
YLMm	(Sets the maximum value of the Y coordinate to be less than or equal to m.)

Error Messages

DATAPOINT performs 60 unique error checks on all input coordinates and geometric commands. These 60 checks are combined into 15 error messages which can appear to the parts programmer. This extensive checking makes it virtually impossible to execute a program containing programming errors. The DATAPOINT error messages are as follows:

0001	Decimal point error.
0002	Illegal character in arithmetic.
0003	Arithmetic format error.
0004	Arithmetic format error.
0005	X-Y format error.
0006	Illegal command name/number combination.
0007	Input error.
0008	Argument count wrong.
0009	Geometric line-length error.
0010	Geometric angle error.
0011	Geometric hole-count error.
0012	Command definition error.
0013	Command recall error.
0014	Memory full.
0015	:T/:M command error.

The part illustrated in Fig. 8-11 is programmed in DATAPOINT as shown in Fig. 8-12.

ECAP

ECAP was designed for the engineer with little programming experience and for the technician without a background in circuit

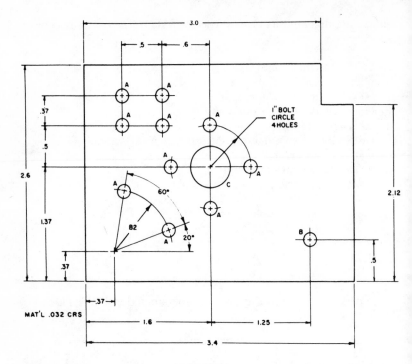

Fig. 8-11. Part produced by the DATAPOINT program shown in Fig. 8-12.

```
X00.953     Y00.582     AT X.37 Y.37 ARC 20 60 .622    :T1
X00.68      Y00.907
X02.6       Y01.37      AT X1.6 Y1.37 BHC 0   1.0 4
X01.6       Y02.37
X00.6       Y01.37
X01.6       Y00.37
X01.        Y01.87      AT X1.6-6 Y1.37+.5 GRID R .5 2 U .37 2
X01.5       Y01.87
X01.5       Y02.24
X01.        Y02.24
X01.6       Y01.37      X1.6 Y1.37                      :T2
X02.85      YC0.5       X1.6+1.25 Y.5                   :T3
X03.5       Y02.62      X3.0+.5 Y2.12+.5                :T4
```

Fig. 8-12. DATAPOINT program for the part shown in Fig. 8-11.

theory. It is a nonlinear dc and transient circuit-analysis language that uses a free format for describing circuit parameters and topology. In terms of the input language, the user may easily describe his circuit, define the types of analysis to be performed, and specify the desired output.

ECAP includes a nested model feature that permits the engineer to store circuit descriptions of devices and subcircuits for subsequent recall and insertion into larger circuits. ECAP also contains a diagnostic feature which indentifies input format errors or inconsistencies in the circuit description. ECAP has been implemented on the IBM System/360 and other computers.

Several circuit-design programs were in use during the 1960s. Today, many engineers find these programs an indispensable aid in designing circuits of many kinds. The syntax of the ECAP language is patterned after some of the early circuit-analysis programs. Alphanumeric names may be assigned to circuit components. Components are described by their values and names, which designate the nodes to which they are connected. For example, a 5300-ohm load resistance from node A to B would be written:

$$\text{RLOAD, A-B} = 5.3\text{K}$$

Sample ECAP statements are as follows:

```
CIRCUIT, 3N4629A:A MODEL
                (Starts the definition
                of the circuit and labels it.)
J2, 4-6 = DIODE(VJ2,28,3.5745E − 12):
DEFINES D2
                (Defines a base-emitter diode.)
STORE, EXT = A-B-C
                (Causes a circuit to be
                stored in the model library
                with external nodes A,B, and C.)
```

The system uses a model library identified by a name, the external nodes, and the basic transistor type described as an equivalent circuit. These notations can then be stored in the model library. Primitive subcircuits (NOR, NAND, INVERTER) may also be named, assigned external nodes, and stored in the library. These individual subcircuits may then be assembled into more complex arrays (such as full adders or latches) by recalling each subcircuit from the library and specifying its terminal connections. In this manner, nested models to a depth of 20 levels can be used to design a very large circuit. A given circuit may be stored away in the library and later recalled for modification and reanalysis. The ECAP program shown in Fig. 8-13 is used to define and analyze the transistor circuit shown in Fig. 8-14.

Exercises

1. List some applications where COGO could be used.

2. Can you describe an engineering problem where STRESS could be used?

3. The world's tallest building (Sears Tower in Chicago) was designed with the aid of a problem-oriented language. Can you identify the areas where the computer might have been used?

```
CIRCUIT,JCNDIODE   STANDARD DIODE MODEL
J1,2-1=DIODE(VJ1,K,PISAT)  DIODE CURRENT,AMPS
K=28   Q/KT FACTOR,PER VOLT
PISAT=1.0E-12   REV SAT CURRENT,AMPS
STORE,EXT=2-1,DES= "STANDARD DIODE MODEL"
CIRCUIT,2N2369A   TRANSISTOR MODEL
RBB,B-4=30   BASE RESISTANCE
R1,5-C=0   DUMMY,TO MEASURE JBC
R2,6-E=0   DUMMY,TO MEASURE JBE
CTE,4-E=3.0PF
CDE,4-E=6.72E-9*IR2
CTC,4-C=2.0PF
CDC,4-C=185E-9*IR1
J2,4-6=DIODE(VJ2,28,3.5745E-12)   DEFINES D2
D1,4-5=JCNDIODE,K=32,PISAT=7.3801E-12
   J1,4-5=DIODE(VJ1,K,PISAT)   DIODE CURRENT,AMPS
   K=32   Q/KT FACTOR,PER VOLT
   PISAT=7.3801E-12   REV SAT CURRENT,AMPS
JREV,E-4=0.474*IR1   REVERSE ALPHA*JBC
JFWD,C-4=0.978*IR2   FORWARD ALPHA*JBE
STORE,EXT=E-B-C,DES="TRANSISTOR MODEL FOR HIGH SPEED SWITCHING APPL"
CIRCUIT
ES1,0-3=6
ES2,5-0=6
EIN,1-0=TAB1(TIME)   TAB1 DEFINES INPUT WAVEFORM
TAB1,0,0,1NS,9,2NS,8,100NS,8,101NS,-1,102NS,0,110NS,0
C1,2-0=3.6PF
C2,4-0=3.9PF
RIN1,1-2=5.6K
RBIAS,2-3=10K
RLOAD,5-4=1K
T1,0-2-4=2N2369A,RBB=30   TRANSISTOR MODEL WITH RBB=30
   RBB,2-4.T1=30   BASE RESISTANCE
   R1,5.T1-4=0   DUMMY,TO MEASURE JBC
   R2,6.T1-0=0   DUMMY,TO MEASURE JBE
   CTE,4.T1-0=3.0PF
   CDE,4.T1-0=6.72E-9*IR2
   CTC,4.T1-4=2.0PF
   CDC,4.T1-4=185E-9*IR1
   J2,4.T1-6.T1=DIODE(VJ2,28,3.5745E-12)   DEFINES D2
   D1,4.T1-5.T1=JCNDIODE,K=32,PISAT=7.3801E-12
      J1,4.T1-5.T1=DIODE(VJ1,K,PISAT)   DIODE CURRENT,AMPS
      K=32   Q/KT FACTOR,PER VOLT
      PISAT=7.3801E-12   REV SAT CURRENT,AMPS
   JREV,0-4.T1=0.474*IR1   REVERSE ALPHA*JBC
   JFWD,4-4.T1=0.978*IR2   FORWARD ALPHA*JBE
SAVE1,VC1("BASE VOLTS"),VC2("OUT VOLTS")
PRINT1,VC1,VC2,CDE.T1,CDC.T1,TIME
PRINTERPLOT1,SAVE1,VS=TIME,TITLE=TITLE1
TITLE1,"DIGITAL LOGIC INVERTER","VC1=BASE VOLTAGE"," VC2=OUTPUT VOLTAGE"
TSTOP=200NS
TRUNC=0.50
ANALYZE,DC,TR
```

Fig. 8-13. ECAP program for analyzing the transistor circuit shown in Fig. 8-14.

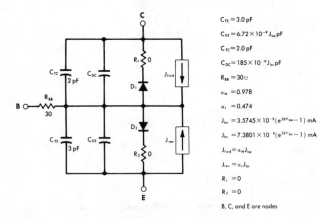

Fig. 8-14. Transistor circuit with component values used in the ECAP program of Fig. 8-13.

4. For what application was APT designed?

5. List two problem-oriented languages designed for numerical-control applications.

6. Discuss a language that was developed for use in designing circuits.

CHAPTER **9**

SIMULATION LANGUAGES

Simulation is a technique that provides an effective means of testing, evaluating, and manipulating a proposed system without any direct action on the real system. Several hours, days, weeks, or even years of operation can be simulated in a matter of minutes on a computer. In most cases, simulation is not a precise analog of the actual system, but rather, a symbolic representation of the system. It can, however, provide measurements that would be impossible to obtain in any other way.

Digital-computer simulation of real systems has become a valuable aid to analysts, engineers, and managers in such diverse fields as transportation, military operations, production facilities, manufacturing, and economics. Computer programs have been developed to simulate the behavior through time of transportation systems, military systems, manufacturing systems, etc.

In modeling a system, the analyst studies the system as it exists (or as it is proposed if the system is not actually in operation) by running the model. If desired, he can then change the logic of the system (its decision rules) to see what effect these changes will have. He then runs the model again over the simulated "run time."

In the simulation of transportation systems, for example, the computer is told how to simulate the movement of motor vehicles or aircraft. Likewise, in a manufacturing system, the computer is told the physical structure of the manufacturing facility. These simulated systems can then be operated with variations in the load to be processed, the configuration of the physical system, or the decision rules to be followed.

Another example of how the simulation process works might be the study of a truck-loading dock where inadequate facilities are causing inordinate delays in loading the trucks. By constructing a model of the system as it exists and running the model over a simulated time period (say a day), the analyst can see where the bottlenecks in the system are; by changing the facilities in subsequent model runs (for example, constructing additional loading docks), the analyst can see how the performance will be improved.

Simulating the dynamics of alternate systems under a variety of conditions often uncovers potential difficulties. If the real system is a large, complex one, the use of a simulated computer system is usually inexpensive compared to the cost of a trial-and-error approach with the real system.

Digital simulation has proven to be an extremely valuable tool; however, developing the computer programs was found to be time consuming and expensive. In fact, it often took longer to develop the computer program than it did to formulate the simulation model. Thus, there was a need for programming systems and languages designed specifically for computer modeling and simulation applications.

Among the various simulation languages there are two major types: (1) *continuous* and (2) *discrete*. Continuous simulation is more closely associated with analog computers than with digital computers. The continuous simulation languages are not covered in this book. The discrete simulation languages use either program statements or blocks to define the system being simulated. Simulation languages are designed for the purpose of eliminating much of the tedium involved and to simplify the procedures in preparing simulations for computer implementation.

There are a variety of simulation languages. Each language has certain characteristics and applications. Several of the most used simulation languages are discussed in this chapter.

GPSS

GPSS (General Purpose Systems Simulator) was originally developed by IBM and has been implemented on several computer systems. In constructing a model using GPSS, the user first draws a block diagram that represents the system he wishes to simulate. The block diagram shows the interaction of the various events that take place within the system. Each block in the diagram represents some basic system action.

GPSS elements are *transactions, system resources,* and *blocks.* Transactions represent physical units flowing through the system. Each transaction interacts with other transactions by competing for the system resources. They represent the units of traffic, such as ships in a ship transportation system, vehicles in a highway traffic flow system, or shop orders in a factory operation system. Transactions are created and destroyed as required during the simulation run and can be thought of as causing actions to occur while moving through the system. Associated with each transaction are a number of "parameters," which can be assigned values by the user to represent characteristics of the transaction. For example, a transaction representing a ship might carry in a parameter the amount of cargo to be unloaded. This number could then be used in the simulator logic to determine how long the unloading operation would take.

System resources represent elements of system equipment—*facilities, storages,* and *logic switches.* A facility can handle only one transaction at a time and could represent a toll booth or a particular machine in a factory. It represents a potential bottleneck. A storage can handle several transactions concurrently and could be used to represent a parking lot or a group of identical machines in a factory. In defining resources, ambiguity sometimes arises. For example, machines in a factory can be modeled as facilities if they are to be considered individually, or as a storage if several machines are identical and it is immaterial which of the machines is actually used by the transaction. The exact nature of the transactions, facilities, and storages depends on the system under study. The analyst assigns meaning to each when he constructs the model.

A logic switch is a two-state indicator that can be set on or off by one transaction to modify the flow of other transactions. It could model a traffic light or the next-window sign of a bank teller. Blocks provide the logic of a system, instructing the transactions where to go and what to do next. Each block, in effect, represents a command to the transaction to perform in a certain manner as it passes through the model. Eventually, each block becomes one punched card in a GPSS program deck. Specific blocks have a name, a characteristic symbol, and a block number. Some of the block formats and the descriptive symbols associated with them are shown in Fig. 9-1.

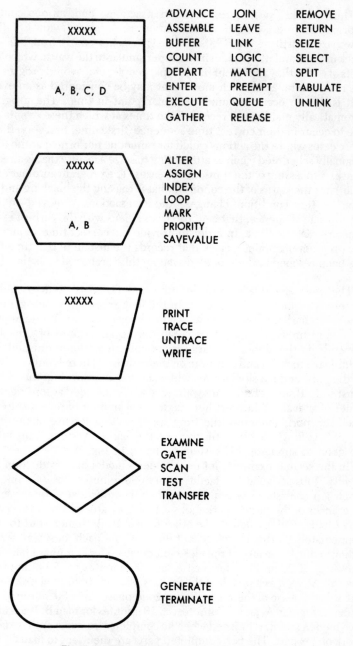

ADVANCE	JOIN	REMOVE
ASSEMBLE	LEAVE	RETURN
BUFFER	LINK	SEIZE
COUNT	LOGIC	SELECT
DEPART	MATCH	SPLIT
ENTER	PREEMPT	TABULATE
EXECUTE	QUEUE	UNLINK
GATHER	RELEASE	

ALTER
ASSIGN
INDEX
LOOP
MARK
PRIORITY
SAVEVALUE

PRINT
TRACE
UNTRACE
WRITE

EXAMINE
GATE
SCAN
TEST
TRANSFER

GENERATE
TERMINATE

Fig. 9-1. GPSS block formats and symbols.

Thus, blocks, system resources, transactions, and various control information (e.g., length of simulation run), along with a GPSS flowchart, constitute the GPSS model. Transactions move from block to block in the simulation model in a manner similar to the way in which the units of traffic they represent (i.e., ships, people, etc.) would progress in the real system. Each such movement may be considered as an event that is due to occur at some particular point in time. The program automatically maintains a record of the times at which these events are due to occur in their correct time sequence (first come, first served). In those cases where the actions called for cannot be performed at the time originally scheduled (such as attempting to seize a facility that is already in use), processing of the transaction ceases. The program automatically maintains the status of the condition that is causing the blocking and, as soon as this condition changes, the transaction is moved in the appropriate sequence; that is, those transactions with the earliest event time are serviced first. In order to provide the correct time sequence, the program maintains a clock that records the instant of real time that has been reached in the modeled system; this is referred to as the *clock time*.

The most effective way to describe how GPSS is used to study a system is by means of examples. In the first example, we are going to examine a harbor where ships arrive in a known pattern. While in port, each ship unloads some of its cargo during an amount of time that depends on the amount of cargo to be unloaded. When finished, the ships leave the port and continue on their voyage. There is only one pier in the port, and if a ship arrives while another is unloading, the second must wait. If several ships are waiting, each is unloaded according to its order of arrival. Of interest here is the total amount of time a ship will spend in port, including the time spent waiting for use of the pier. Fig.9-2 is a GPSS block diagram of the harbor system. The GPSS program to simulate this system is shown in Fig. 9-3.

In the second example, let us consider a model of a production line facility. Jobs arrive at the facility every 300 minutes, ± 100 minutes. Each job consists of two functions that are interrelated by the close tolerances of the parts. As the jobs arrive they are split into two parts; one part is given to man A, the other to man B. Both men start to work immediately on the first phase of their jobs, but each must wait for the other to finish because of the close tolerances. The first phase takes 100 minutes, ± 20 minutes for man A, and 90 minutes, ± 20 minutes for man B. As soon as a match of the parts is assured, both men proceed to the second phase of their jobs. The second phase takes 50 minutes, ± 5 minutes for man A, and 70 minutes, ± 10 minutes for man B. Each of the two men (A and B) is finished when he completes the second phase of the work on his part. The two completed parts are then sent to man C, who assembles the final product. The final assembly (which takes 50 minutes,

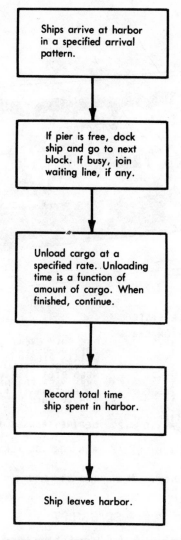

Fig. 9-2. GPSS block diagram of a harbor system.

± 5 minutes) cannot begin, of course, until both of the original parts are completed. A GPSS block diagram for this example is shown in Fig. 9-4. The GPSS program is shown in Fig. 9-5.

GPSS is less flexible than statement-oriented languages, such as SIMSCRIPT; however, it is easier to learn and use. It provides excellent program diagnostics whenever an error is made, either when assembling the program, inputting data, or executing a simulation run.

```
*              HARBOR SYSTEM
*
*  BLOCK DEFINITION CARDS
      GENERATE    32,5       ONE SHIP EVERY 32+-5 HOURS
      QUEUE       1          JOIN QUEUE, WAIT FOR PIER
      SEIZE       1          OBTAIN PIER WHEN FREE
      DEPART      1          LEAVE QUEUE (NO LONGER WAITING)
      ADVANCE     25,20      HOLD PIER 25+-20 HOURS
      RELEASE     1          FREE PIER FOR NEXT SHIP
      TABULATE    10         ENTER TRANSIT TIME IN TABLE 10
      TERMINATE   1          REMOVE SHIP FROM SYSTEM
*
*  TABLE DEFINITION CARD
   10 TABLE       M1,10,5,20 DEFINE TRANSIT TIME TABLE
*
*  CONTROL CARD
      START       100        RUN FOR 100 TERMINATIONS
```

Fig. 9-3. GPSS program to simulate the harbor system of Fig. 9-2.

SIMSCRIPT

SIMSCRIPT was intially developed at the Rand Corporation under the sponsorship of the U.S. Air Force. The Air Force used the language in the simulation of aircraft maintenance procedures. They also used SIMSCRIPT to study the effects of prepositioning critical supplies at various worldwide locations, versus airlifting these same supplies when and where needed. The language has been implemented on several computer systems.

To build a discrete-event simulation model using SIMSCRIPT, the modeler must describe the system in terms of *entities, attributes* of

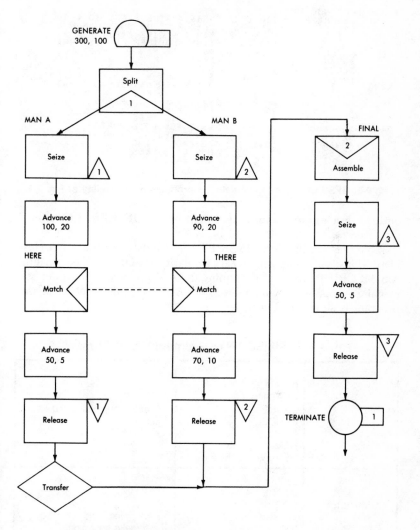

Fig. 9-4. GPSS block diagram of a production line facility.

entities, and *sets* of entities. Entities are basically the physical elements of the system being studied; for example, trucks in a transportation system, or machines in a machine shop. Attributes of entities are properties associated with entities or items that describe entities. For example, in a machine shop, only certain machines can be used; or, in a transportation system, only certain trucks carry regular gasoline. These attributes are specified by the modeler. Sets of entities are groups of

```
* JOB SHOP MODEL
         GENERATE    300,100    JOBS ARRIVE EVERY 300+-100 MIN.
         SPLIT       1,MANB     SEND PART OF JOB TO MAN B
         SEIZE       1          MAN A BEGINS FIRST PHASE
         ADVANCE     100,20     TIME REQUIRED FOR 1ST PHASE
HERE     MATCH       THERE      WAIT FOR MAN B
         ADVANCE     50,5       FINISH PART A
         RELEASE     1          MAN A IS FREE
         TRANSFER    ,FINAL     SEND PART A TO FINAL ASSEMBLY
MANB     SEIZE       2          MAN B BEGINS WORK ON PART B
         ADVANCE     90,20      TIME REQUIRED
THERE    MATCH       HERE       WAIT TO MATCH PARTS
         ADVANCE     70,10      FINISH PART B
         RELEASE     2          MAN B IS FREE
FINAL    ASSEMBLE    2          WAIT FOR BOTH PARTS
         SEIZE       3          MAN C BEGINS FINAL ASSEMBLY
         ADVANCE     50,5       ASSEMBLY TIME
         RELEASE     3          MAN C IS FREE
         TERMINATE   1          JOB ENDS
```

Fig. 9-5. GPSS program to simulate the production line facility of Fig. 9-4.

entities. For example, an entity might be ENGINEER, an attribute might be SEX, and sets might be IEEE.

Table 9-1 is a list of SIMSCRIPT commands and phrases. A close inspection of this table will reveal a similarity to FORTRAN commands. A SIMSCRIPT program, describing the end process for an order at a machine shop, is shown in Fig. 9-6. A detailed description of this program is shown in Fig. 9-7.

Table 9-1. SIMSCRIPT Commands and Phrases

Entity Operations	CREATE DESTROY CAUSE CANCEL FILE REMOVE FIRST REMOVE "SPECIFIC"	Creating and destroying entities.
Arithmetic and Control Commands	LET STORE FOR WITH OR AND DO TO LOOP REPEAT	Performing and controlling arithmetic operations.
Decision Commands	IF Unconditional GO TO Computed GO TO FIND FIRST WHERE	Selecting among alternatives.

Table 9-1. SIMSCRIPT Commands and Phrases (cont)

Input/Output Commands	SAVE READ FORMAT WRITE ON ADVANCE BACKSPACE REWIND ENDFILE LOAD RECORD MEMORY RESTORE STATUS	Tape-handling commands.
Miscellaneous Commands	ACCUMULATE COMPUTE STOP DIMENSION FORTRAN INSERTS STATEMENT CON- TINUATION	

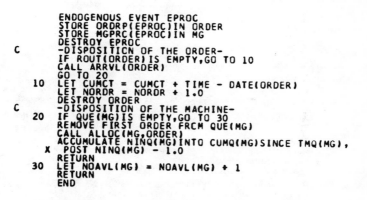

```
         ENDOGENOUS EVENT EPROC
         STORE ORDRP(EPROC)IN ORDER
         STORE MGPRC(EPROC)IN MG
         DESTROY EPROC
   C     -DISPOSITICN OF THE ORDER-
         IF ROUT(ORDER)IS EMPTY,GO TO 10
         CALL ARRVL(ORDER)
         GO TO 20
   10    LET CUMCT = CUMCT + TIME - DATE(ORDER)
         LET NORDR = NORDR + 1.0
         DESTROY ORDER
   C     -DISPOSITION OF THE MACHINE-
   20    IF QUE(MG)IS EMPTY,GO TO 30
         REMOVE FIRST ORDER FRCM QUE(MG)
         CALL ALLOC(MG,ORDER)
         ACCUMULATE NINQ(MG)INTO CUMQ(MG)SINCE TMQ(MG),
   X       POST NINQ(MG) - 1.0
         RETURN
   30    LET NOAVL(MG) = NOAVL(MG) + 1
         RETURN
         END
```

Fig. 9-6. SIMSCRIPT program describing the end process for an order at a machine shop.

DYNAMO

DYNAMO (*DYNA*mic *MO*dels) was developed at the Massachusetts Institute of Technology. DYNAMO is a system of translating and running continuous models (models that are described by a set of different equations). It was developed for simulating dynamic feedback models of business, economic, and social systems; however, there is nothing in its design that precludes its use for any continuous system.

The DYNAMO language includes time subscripts that easily enable

Program	Explanation
ENDOGENOUS EVENT EPROC	Indicates an event routine describing an endogenous event called EPROC.
STORE ORDRP(EPROC) IN ORDER	Sets the local variable ORDER equal to the identification of the order that has finished processing.
STORE MGPRC(EPROC) IN MG	Sets the local variable MG equal to the machine group that has just completed the process.
DESTROY EPROC	Sets the contents of the end-of-process record equal to zero and makes this storage space available to subsequent CREATE statements.
C —DISPOSITION OF THE ORDER—	A comment; does not affect the object program.
IF ROUT(ORDER) IS EMPTY, GO TO 10	Tests to see if any destinations remain in the routing of the order.
CALL ARRVL(ORDER)	Calls the previously described subroutine describing the arrival of an order at a machine group.
GO TO 20	Transfers control to statement number 20.
10 LET CUMCT = CUMCT + TIME − DATE(ORDER)	Adds the elapsed time the order has been in the shop to the cumulative cycle time of all previously completed orders.
LET NORDR = NORDR + 1.0	Increases the number of orders completed by one.
DESTROY ORDER	Sets the record of the order to zero and makes the space available for the use of subsequent CREATE statements.
C —DISPOSITION OF THE MACHINE—	A comment.
20 IF QUE(MG) IS EMPTY, GO TO 30	Tests to see if there is another order in the queue of the machine group that just completed the process.
REMOVE FIRST ORDER FROM QUE(MG)	Removes the order that is first in the queue of the machine group. The local variable ORDER now identifies the order just removed from the queue.
CALL ALLOC(MG,ORDER)	Calls the previously described subroutine that allocates a machine to an order.
ACCUMULATE NINQ(MG) INTO CUMQ(MG) SINCE TMQ(MG), POST NINQ(MG) − 1.0	Updates the cumulative number in queue and decreases the number in queue by one.
RETURN	Returns control to the timing routine.
30 LET NOAVL(MG) = NOAVL(MG) + 1	Increases the number of machines available by one if the queue is empty.
RETURN	Returns control to the timing routine.
END	Indicates the physical end of the subprogram.

Fig. 9-7. Detailed description of the SIMSCRIPT program shown in Fig. 9-6.

anyone to comprehend how the calculations are made. As the user soon gains confidence that DYNAMO is doing no more for him than he asks, he can direct his attention to the model's design rather than to the mastery of some sophisticated tool.

DYNAMO's "load-and-go" feature simplifies running a model; the user does not have to master the vagaries of link-editors and loaders. The output facilities include both tabular and plotted results that can easily be specified, and which include automatic scaling features. An example of plotted output is shown in Fig. 9-8. Program coding for a DYNAMO model is shown in Fig. 9-9.

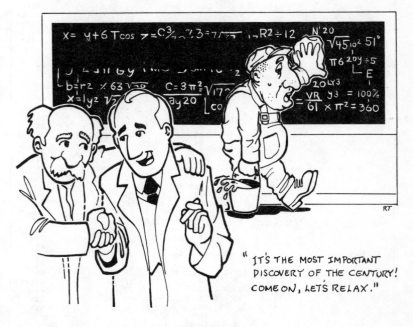

" IT'S THE MOST IMPORTANT DISCOVERY OF THE CENTURY! COME ON, LET'S RELAX."

MILITRAN

MILITRAN is a simulation-oriented general-purpose language developed specifically for the purpose of simulating military systems; however, it is not restricted to just this application area. All of the general processing and computational features familiar to users of FORTRAN and other algorithmic languages are present in MILITRAN, in addition to the special simulation features. Simulations often contain a considerable amount of straightforward computation and data handling; thus, to provide excess special features at the expense of general computational power would be like "robbing Peter to pay Paul."

In defining the elements of a simulation model, the modeler frequently finds that it is convenient to refer to abstract objects (submarines, missiles, passengers, telephone lines, etc.) as well as to purely numerical parameters. These objects may further be grouped into classes associated with other objects, or have numerical characteristics describing them. A conventional programming language would either force the user to specify his model in an unnatural way, or to develop a scheme of artificial numerical codes, flags, and indices.

```
IAR=I,UOR=U,RRR=R,SSR=S,PSR=P,SRR=Q,DFR=•

   7500.          8000.          8500.          9000.          9500. I
    850.           950.          1050.          1150.          1250. U
    900.          1000.          1100.          1200.          1300. RSPQ
     .95             1.           1.05            1.1           1.15 •
    .0- - - - - - - I- - - U - - - - - - - - - - - - - - - - - - IRSPQ•
    .              I       U       .              .              . IRSPQ•
    .              I       U       .              .              . IRSPQ•
    .              I       U       .              .              . IRSPQ•
    .              I       U       .              .              . IRSPQ•
    .              I       U       R              .              . ISPQ•
    .             IQ    •P S       R   U          .              .
    .           I Q        •S P R       U         .              .
    .         I   .Q          S  R      P      U  .              . R•
    .        I     . Q         S  R       •      P  U            .
   10.- - - I - - - - - Q - - - S  R - - - - •- - - -PU - - - - -
    .      I         .          Q  S R          •.       UP
    .      I         .            QSR            •.      U  P
    .     I          .            SR  Q          •.      U  P
    .     I         .             R    Q      • •    U    P  . RS
    .      I        .             R        Q    •.      U  P . RS
    .        I      .             RS          • Q.      U P
    .        I      .             RS          •    Q    UP
    .         .I    .             R S      •      .   PU      . PQ
    .              I              R S      •    .P U Q       . S•
   20.- - - - - - - - - - •R S - - - - - P - -U- - Q - - - -
    .              •  I   R  S         P       U    Q
    .              .    RIS  P          U .     Q
    .           .      RPS   I       U    .    Q
    .         •.    P     R  S       IU      .Q
    .         .     P    RS       U   I   Q.
    .        •.       P     RS       U   Q I  .
    .        .         P     RS     UQ         I
    .        •.    P         R   QU            .I        . RS
    .       •.     P          RQ    U          .I        . RS
   30.- - - - •- - -P- - - -QR - -U- - - - - - -I - - - - . RS
    .       •.      P     Q    R     U          .I        . RS
    .        •.       P Q       R     U          I        . RS
    .         •.    P          R      U        I.         . RS, PQ
    .         .     Q  P       R      U    I    .         . RS
    .          •.    Q   P     R      U    I    .         . RS
    .           .     Q        PR      U I       .        . RS
    .            •     Q      SRP      UI        .
    .             .    Q     SR  P     IU        .
    .              •   Q    SR    P I   U        .
   40.- - - - - - - - - •- - Q -SR - -I- -U- - - - - - - - IP
```

Fig. 9-8. Plotted results of a DYNAMO simulation run.

MILITRAN allows any natural system definition to be programmed directly.

In addition to the usual numerical and logical variables, the MILITRAN user may use *program-object* variables to manipulate abstract objects. The following two statements are analogous:

$$I = 5$$
$$ATTACKER = SEA\ WOLF$$

The first statement assigns the value 5 to the numerical variable I, while the second assigns the value SEA WOLF to the program-object variable ATTACKER. Program-object variables may be used with essentially the same freedom as numerical variables—they may be compared, used in logical conditions, placed in vectors and other arrays, used as subscripts

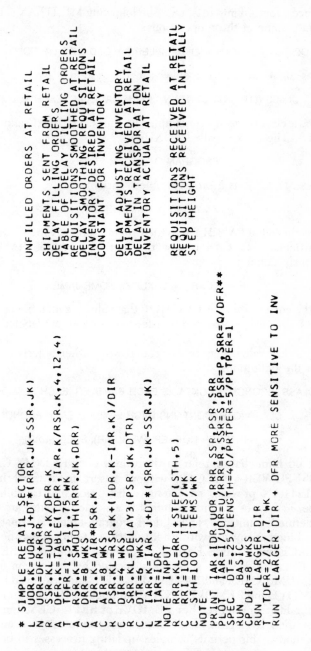

```
* SIMPLE RETAIL SECTOR
L   UOR.K=UOR.J+DT*(RRR.JK-SSR.JK)          UNFILLED ORDERS AT RETAIL
N   UOR=DFR*RRR
R   SSR.KL=UOR.K/DFR.K                       SHIPMENTS SENT FROM RETAIL
A   DFR.K=TABLE(TDFR,IAR.K/RSR.K,4,12,4)      DELAY FILLING ORDERS
T   TDFR=1,5,10,1.75 WK                       TABLE OF DELAY FILLING ORDERS
R   RSR.K=SMOOTH(RRR.JK,DRR)                  REQUISITIONS SMOOTHED AT RETAIL
C   DRR=8 WKS                                 DELAY SMOOTHING REQUISITIONS
A   IDR.K=AIR*RSR.K                           INVENTORY DESIRED AT RETAIL
C   AIR=8 WKS                                 CONSTANT FOR INVENTORY
A   PSR.KL=RSR.K+(IDR.K-IAR.K)/DIR
C   DIR=4 WKS                                 DELAY ADJUSTING INVENTORY
R   SSR.KL=DELAY3(PSR.JK,DTR)                 SHIPMENTS RECEIVED AT RETAIL
C   DTR=6 WKS                                 DELAY IN TRANSPORTATION
L   IAR.K=IAR.J+DT*(SRR.JK-SSR.JK)            INVENTORY ACTUAL AT RETAIL
N   IAR=IDR
NOTE INPUT
R   RRR.KL=RRI+STEP(STH,5)                    REQUISITIONS RECEIVED AT RETAIL
C   RRI=1000 ITEMS/WK                         REQUISITIONS RECEIVED INITIALLY
C   STH=100 ITEMS/WK                          STEP HEIGHT
NOTE
PRINT IAR,IDR,UOR,RRR,SSR,PSR,SRR
PLOT IAR=I/UOR=U/RRR=R,SSR=S,PSR=P,SRR=Q/DFR=**
SPEC DT=.25/LENGTH=40/PRTPER=5/PLTPER=1
RUN BASIC
CP DIR=8 WKS
T TDFR=2/1/.7 WK
RUN LARGER DIR
RUN LARGER DIR + DFR MORE SENSITIVE TO INV
```

Fig. 9-9. Program coding for a DYNAMO model.

or indices, formed into lists, etc. The following MILITRAN statements illustrate some of these operations:

OBJECT PLYMOUTH (2), RAMBLER (3), CADILLAC (1), ROLLS (2)

defines eight cars as basic objects in the system.

CLASS (LUXURY) CONTAINS EACH*CADILLAC, EACH*ROLLS

defines a class or group containing the one CADILLAC and the two ROLLS. The class is called LUXURY.

PROGRAM OBJECT MY CAR

defines MY CAR as a program-object variable.

MY CAR = RAMBLER (1)

assigns the value RAMBLER to the program-object variable MY CAR. In particular, MY CAR is now the first of the three RAMBLERS previously defined.

IF (MY CAR .IN. LUXURY), HOME JAMES

tests the current value of MY CAR. If that value is a member of the class called LUXURY, control will transfer to the statement labeled HOME JAMES.

Numerical values may be associated with either objects or classes. Given the definitions

CLASS (ECONOMY) CONTAINS EACH RAMBLER, EACH PLYMOUTH

CLASS (CAR) CONTAINS EACH LUXURY, EACH ECONOMY

INTEGER HORSEPOWER(CAR), SPEED(CAR)

we could immediately refer to the values of SPEED(MY CAR) and HORSEPOWER (MY CAR) without resort to artificial indexing.

MILITRAN provides an extensive list-processing capability. The number and types of items included in a single list entry are entirely user-defined; numerical, logical, and program-object information may be combined in any way within a list entry. List entries may be created by PLACE and PLACE ENTRY statements, modified by REPLACE and REPLACE ENTRY statements, located by the system functions MINIMUM INDEX and RANDOM INDEX, and destroyed by means of REMOVE and REMOVE ENTRY statements. The entry, or entries, to be modified or removed by a REMOVE or REPLACE statement may be specified by logical conditions of any complexity on any or all components. This permits complex updating processes to be accomplished by a single MILITRAN statement.

The flexibility of MILITRAN list processing is best demonstrated by example:

LIST OPERATING ((VEHICLE, DESTINATION, PASSENGERS), CAR)

PROGRAM OBJECT VEHICLE, DESTINATION

INTEGER PASSENGERS

The preceding statements define a list and indicate the nature of information stored in each component of its entries. The use of CAR as a dimension indicates that the maximum number of entries possible is the number of objects in the class CAR. Operations on the list might include some of the following:

PLACE (MY CAR, CHICAGO, 3) IN OPERATING

records the status of a car carrying three passengers to Chicago.

REPLACE (MY CAR) BY (*, NEW YORK, *— 1) IN OPERATING

updates the status of that car after dropping one passenger.

REPLACE (,,* .L. 6) BY (*,*,* + 1) IN OPERATING

adds one passenger to every car in the list that is now carrying less than six passengers.

REMOVE (,LOS ANGELES) FROM OPERATING

causes every entry whose DESTINATION is LOS ANGELES to be removed from the list.

REPLACE ( ) BY (*,WASHINGTON,*) IN OPERATING

resets the DESTINATION component of every entry to the value WASHINGTON.

The central dynamic feature of most simulation programs is the processing of simulated events occurring either at regular intervals or at critical points in time. MILITRAN provides a convenient and flexible means of implementing both "time-step" and "critical-point" algorithms. Full control of event structure is retained by the user, and automatic features may be overridden without system alterations.

The iterative processes in a simulation program often involve incrementation and termination criteria. The MILITRAN DO-loop form allows modification of termination criteria, increment values, and even the index itself within the iteration. Furthermore, exit from the loop may be made at any point without loss of current values, and indices are defined even after normal exits. A second form of the DO statement permits iteration over all members of a class to be specified in a convenient and concise manner. Both forms of DO loop may be nested to any depth.

A list of MILITRAN statements is provided in Table 9-2. A sample MILITRAN simulation program is shown in Fig. 9-10.

Table 9-2. MILITRAN Statements

Environment Declarations
REAL $n_1(i_1,i_2, \ldots ,i_k), \ldots ,n_m(i_1,i_2, \ldots , i_j)$
INTEGER $n_1(i_1,i_2, \ldots ,i_k), \ldots ,n_m(i_1,i_2, \ldots ,i_j)$
LOGICAL $n_1(i_1,i_2, \ldots i_k), \ldots ,n_m(i_1,i_2, \ldots ,i_j)$
OBJECT $n_1(i_1),n_2(i_2), \ldots ,n_m(i_m)$
PROGRAM OBJECT $n_1(i_1,i_2, \ldots ,i_k), \ldots$
   $,n_m(i_1,i_2, \ldots ,i_j)$
CLASS (c) CONTAINS $a_1,a_2, \ldots ,a_m$
NORMAL MODE $m_1(a_1,a_2, \ldots ,a_k),m_2(b_1,b_2,$
   $\ldots ,b_l)$
VECTOR N $(a_1,a_2, \ldots ,a_l),d_1,d_2, \ldots ,d_l)$
COMMON $n_1,n_2, \ldots ,n_i$

Substitution Statement
$a = b$

Control Statements
GO TO s
PAUSE j
STOP
IF (b), s_t,s_f
UNLESS (b), s_f,s_t
DO (s) UNTIL $b,n = e_1,e_2$
DO (s) FOR a . IN . b
CONTINUE

List Processing Statements
LIST n $((c_1,c_2, \ldots ,c_i),d)$
LENGTH (n)
RESET LENGTH (n) to p
PLACE $(e_1,e_2, \ldots ,e_i)$ IN n
REMOVE ENTRY n (k)
PLACE ENTRY m (j) IN n
REPLACE ENTRY n (k) BY $(e_1,e_2, \ldots ,e_i)$
REPLACE ENTRY n (k) BY ENTRY m (j)
REMOVE $(b_1, b_2, \ldots ,b_i)$FROM n
REPLACE $(b_1,b_2, \ldots ,b_i)$ BY $(e_1,e_2, \ldots ,e_i)$IN
   n

REPLACE $(b_1,b_2, \ldots ,b_i)$ BY ENTRY $m(j)$ IN n
MINIMUM INDEX $(n(b_1,b_2, \ldots ,b_i,b_x),s)$
RANDOM INDEX $(n(b_1,b_2, \ldots ,b_i,b_x),s)$

Event Statements
PERMANENT EVENT $n((a_1,a_2, \ldots ,a_i),d)$
CONTINGENT EVENT $n((a_1,a_2, \ldots ,a_i),d)$
NEXT EVENT
NEXT EVENT $(n_1,n_2, \ldots ,n_i)$
NEXT EVENT EXCEPT $(n_1,n_2, \ldots ,n_i)$
END
END CONTINGENT EVENTS (s)

Procedure Statements
PROCEDURE n
PROCEDURE n $(a_1,a_2, \ldots ,a_n)$
EXECUTE n
EXECUTE $n(a_1,a_2, \ldots ,a_n)$
RETURN
RETURN a

Input/Output Statements
FORMAT (Format Specification)
READ (t,s) List
WRITE (t,s) List
READWRITE (t_1, s_1, t_2, s_2) List
BINARY READ (t) List
BINARY WRITE (t) List
END FILE RETURN (s)
END RECORD RETURN (s)
BACKSPACE (t)
BACKSPACE FILE (t)
END FILE (t)
REWIND (t)
UNLOAD (t)

EXERCISES

1. Define computer simulation.

2. What is a model?

3. Name the two major types of simulation languages.

4. List several simulation languages.

5. Obtain a manual for a simulation language such as GPSS or SIMSCRIPT. Study the manual carefully. Learn the contents and decide upon application of the language. Prepare a critique of the simulation language.

6. What are the advantages of simulation languages?

STATEMENT LABEL	MILITRAN STATEMENT
	READ (5, INPUT) ARRIVAL RATE, SERVICE RATE, DAYS PER RUN,
	PROFIT PER TRUCK, COST PER SPACE PER DAY
INPUT	FORMAT (5F10.3)
	PLACE (DAYS PER RUN) IN END OF RUN
	PLACE (-LOG(RANDOM)/ARRIVAL RATE) IN ARRIVAL
	NEXT EVENT ... SIMULATION BEGINS
	CONTINGENT EVENT ARRIVAL ((ARRIVAL TIME), 1)
	IF (LENGTH (SERVICE QUEUE).GE. SPACES), NEXT TRUCK
	SERVE TIME = MAX (TIME, SERVE TIME) -, LOG(RANDOM)/SERVICE RATE
	PLACE (SERVE TIME) IN SERVICE QUEUE
NEXT TRUCK	REPLACE ENTRY ARRIVAL (1) BY (TIME-LOG(RANDOM)/ARRIVAL RATE)
	END .... THIS STATEMENT IS, ALSO, INTERPRETED AS 'NEXT EVENT'
	CONTINGENT EVENT SERVICE QUEUE ((SERVICE TIME), SPACES)
	PROFIT = PROFIT + PROFIT PER TRUCK
	REMOVE ENTRY SERVICE QUEUE (INDEX)
	END
	CONTINGENT EVENT END OF RUN ((END TIME), 1)
	WRITE (6, OUTPUT) PROFIT -, SPACES*TIME* COST PER SPACE PER DAY
OUTPUT	FORMAT (9H, PROFIT = F7.2)
	STOP
	END

Fig. 9-10. Sample MILITRAN simulation program.

"MARK MY WORDS, BESSIE, SOME DAY THERE'LL BE COMPUTERS THAT'LL BE ABLE TO DETERMINE A BETTER TRAIL TO THE COAST!"

CHAPTER **10**
COMPUTER PROCESSING CONCEPTS

The majority of present computer applications fall into the category of *information systems*. In these applications (Table 10-1 lists a few of them), the computer is used as a massive filing system. The files are updated and analyzed by the computer, information is retrieved rapidly, and individual documents or reports are prepared automatically from information in the files. Since the 1950s, computers have been the central controlling element of such systems. Today, computers handle information processing in a variety of different ways: by allowing time sharing between several users, by providing data processing in real-time, etc. A few methods for processing information will be discussed in this chapter.

Table 10-1. Information Systems Applications

Credit Card Processing	Newspaper Printing
Record Keeping	Menu Planning
Book Publishing	Law Date Bank
Movie Production	Stock Market Analysis
School Administration	Test Grading
Production Control	Report Preparation
Scheduling	Market Research
Accounting	Election Returns
Inventory Control	Income Tax Returns
Reservation Control	Language Translation
Sales Analysis	Hospital Administration
Billing & Invoicing	Economic Analysis
Actuarial Research	Census Data Analysis
Library Search & Retrieval	Medical Data Bank
Personnel Files	Patent Search

TIME SHARING

Time sharing is the simultaneous shared use of a computer system by independent users. A time-sharing computer system enables several users to share space in the computer memory and to share computation time. Among the many advantages offered by this type of system are:

1. Users can prepare their own programs in an easy-to-learn conversational language. This eliminates having the problem solved by a professional programmer.
2. Since time-sharing users receive their answers immediately, there is no time delay as found in batch-processing systems. What is the time delay in an average batch-processing computer system? First, users must define their problems and provide data to a programmer who, after a short period of time, produces a computer program. The program is written (or coded) in a programming language for the specific computer being used. The program is then punched on either cards or paper tape and sent to the computer center for processing. After a few hours, the program will be run on the computer. If the program is incorrect (it almost always is on the first attempt), the programmer must debug the program and correct the problem. After several days, the program will be working properly and the problem answers will be satisfactory.
3. Time sharing places a powerful computer at the hands of many users who would not normally be able to afford the use of a computer system.
4. The manufacturers and suppliers of time-sharing systems often furnish many "application" programs for use by the user.

The time-sharing concept is based on the principle that there is enough capacity in a computer system for multiple users, provided that each user console is active only a small fraction of the time. The components of a time-sharing system are the operating system (time-sharing executive, language compilers, application programs, etc.), hardware (computer, data communications equipment, auxiliary storage, etc.), and remote-user terminals (teletypewriters, typewriters, crt display devices, etc.). It is the responsibility of the operating system to determine what each user is attempting to do and to schedule all communications between the computer system and the user. In a simple system, the user programs are stored in an auxiliary storage and transferred in and out of the computer main memory as needed. The operating system would determine what programs needed swapping and when this swapping must occur.

Users of a time-sharing system have the illusion that each is the only one using the system. This illusion is false, however, as each user has the use of the computer for only a specified amount of time. The computer picks up orders from one user, works on this problem for a short period of time, such as 1/200 of a second, and stores the partial answer. The computer then moves to the next user, receives the orders, works on the second problem for 1/200 of a second, and moves on to the third user, etc. When a specific user's problem is completed, the results are transmitted to the user's console. The computer accomplishes the orders of several users so fast that they all receive the impression the system is working for them full time.

In a typical time-sharing system, the users communicate with the computer by means of remote consoles. The computer may only be a few yards from the console or it may be several thousand miles away (Fig. 10-1). Communications between these remote consoles and the computer system is via the normal telephone service. A remote terminal is connected with the computer by using a dataphone set which may be leased from the local telephone company. The dataphone is a modulator/demodulator unit used for converting the keyboard signals of the terminal into two-level tones for transmission over the voice-grade telephone lines. As a demodulator, it converts the received signals to activate the display or print mechanism of the terminal.

Fig. 10-2 shows an engineering designer using a terminal that is connected to a time-sharing computer system. A user can use this unit to prepare programs, check out programs, or run previously written programs.

The time-sharing computer uses the same basic equipment as a computer used for batch processing. However, not all machines suitable for batch-processing work are for use in time-sharing systems. This may be because certain hardware features are not available or that time-sharing software is not available.

Hardware items that are peculiar to time-sharing computer systems are data communications control units (for gathering and routing all input/output communications between the computer and remote units), memory protection features, remote terminal units, and large auxiliary storage units. In addition, the computer equipment must be reliable. When equipment failure occurs in a normal batch-processing computer system, only a few users voice their complaints. In a time-sharing system it is possible to expect complaints from several hundred irate users whenever the time-sharing system is not functioning properly.

A typical time-sharing hardware system is diagrammed in Fig. 10-3. This system contains the equipment normally found in a computer system (central processing unit, auxiliary storage devices, and input/output equipment) plus the data communications equipment and remote terminal units. The data communications equipment performs similar to a telephone exchange in routing incoming calls to the computer and outgoing information to the correct remote unit.

The largest users of time-sharing systems are schools, universities, large industrial companies, small engineering companies, small research firms, and small businesses.

Fig. 10-1. In a time-sharing system, the computer user communicates with the computer through normal telephone service. The computer can be a few blocks or many miles from the user.

Courtesy Xerox Corp.

Fig. 10-2. An engineer using a time-sharing computer system to help him solve a problem.

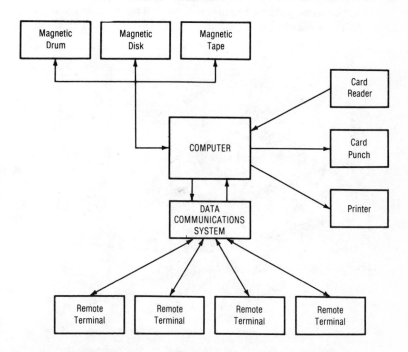

Fig. 10-3. Hardware configuration of a typical time-sharing system.

To engineers, scientists, businessmen, or any other user, the time-sharing system is just a useful tool. It allows them to solve their problems more rapidly. The users want to simply use an application program that has been written by someone else or they want to write programs easily. With a language such as BASIC, the user communicates with the computer in a conversational mode. In this mode, the user communicates or converses directly with the computer in tems of requests and acknowledgment dialogues. The user can prepare a program, one instruction at a time or several at a time, and can change any instruction in the computer at any time.

In the field of education, time sharing makes computers available to many students. This allows students to become familiar with the use of a computer and to use this capability in the solution of problems in their prime area of interest. As the use of computers in industry, government, and business increases, the need for training becomes more acute. Time sharing is certainly not limited to university students only, as students in secondary and elementary schools are easily able to learn how to use these systems.

The use of time-sharing systems varies with the manufacturer; however, they all follow a similar pattern. First, the user dials the computer by using either a telephone mounted on the teletypewriter or a telephone connected to a dataphone set. This call goes through the

"HE SAYS HE DOESN'T LIKE BEING DIAGNOSED BY A REMOTE COMPUTER..."

normal telephone exchange network and establishes contact with the
computer system. When contact is made, the user will be asked for
identification and to select the programming system to be used. If a
program that is already written and stored in the time-sharing system
library is to be used, the user simply requests to execute the program. If,
however, a new program is being prepared, the user will type the
program in some conversational programming language and, when
complete, inform the computer that the program is to be executed. The
computer will then run the program and transmit the program results to
the remote unit. The user also has the option of storing this newly
created program in the system library for use on some future occasion.

MULTIPROCESSING

A *multiprocessing* computer system is one that contains two or more
interconnected central processng units, each with its own arithmetic
and logic units, and each capable of independent operation (see Fig.
10-4A).

A computer system operating in a multiprocessing configuration must
be able to interpret and execute its own programmed instructions. In

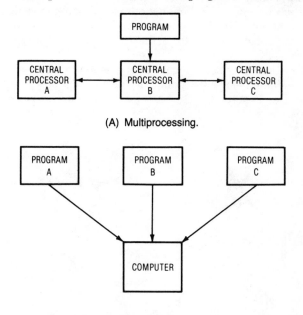

(A) Multiprocessing.

(B) Multiprogramming.

Fig. 10-4. Comparison of multiprocessing and multiprogramming configurations.

addition, facilities must be available to transfer data from one CPU to another, to transfer data and instructions to and from internal storage, and to transfer data and instructions to and from a common auxiliary storage device.

The requirements for multiprocessing in terms of both equipment and programs are extensive. One of the first multiprocessors consisted of 10 small computers, each capable of performing input, output, and processing, while connected to a main central processing unit. The main CPU included many multiply, add, shift, and test units which could operate at the same time to improve processing speed.

Multiprocessing offers data-processing capabilities that are not available when only one central processing unit is used. With a multiprocessing system, many complex operations can be performed at the same time.

MULTIPROGRAMMING

There is an extreme difference in the speeds at which a computer is able to perform calculations and the speeds at which even the fastest input/output devices can operate. In the time taken to print one line on a line printer working at 1200 lines per minute, a computer could perform 10,000 additions. *Multiprogramming* is a technique developed to relieve this imbalance and to further increase the utilization of the computer.

Multiprogramming is the concurrent execution of two or more programs simultaneously residing in the internal storage unit of a computer (see Fig. 10-4B). The basic principle of multiprogramming is

that the programs in internal storage share the available time of the central processing unit and the input/output units. Each program is written as a completely independent program. While input/output operations of one program are being handled, the CPU is essentially idle and can handle some non-input/output processing of another program at the same time. For example, a program to read data from punched cards and transcribe it to magnetic tape will only require the use of the computer for a small fraction of the program running time. The remainder of the time represents input/output transfer time during which other programs can use the central processing unit.

Benefits to be gained from multiprogramming include the elimination of *off-line* equipment normally used to transcribe data onto a faster medium for input. While this activity is proceeding, using limited numbers of input/output devices and little processing time, other more productive programs can use the remaining input/output devices and CPU time.

REAL-TIME PROCESSING

Real-Time is a term used to describe a system that controls an ongoing process and delivers its outputs not later than the time when these are needed for effective control. An example of a real-time system is an airline reservations system in which each reservation must be processed by the system immediately after it is made so that a complete, up-to-date picture of available seating is maintained by the computer at all times. With a real-time airline reservations system, a customer can request space for a specific date between cities. A reservations agent then inserts a flight card in the computer, querying it on seat availability. Instantaneously, the computer searches for the appropriate flight record and transmits the latest availability information back to the agent. This information is then displayed for the agent on a crt viewing screen. When a seat is sold, the agent presses a button and the computer center then updates the seat inventory for that flight. Fig. 10-5 illustrates the computer-controlled terminals used by an airline reservations center.

A real-time system network is also being used in the railroad industry where, in a matter of seconds, recording of and access to freight car location and movement information can be accomplished. The system enables a railroad to supply shippers with freight car location, as well as approximate time of freight car arrival within seconds after an inquiry is received. The system also makes it possible to eliminate many handwritten daily reports that have been a burden on operating personnel since the inception of railroads.

Many department stores, insurance companies, and banks use real-time systems. Banks and other financial establishments use these systems to send transactions from branches to a central computer

Fig. 10-5. Remote crt terminals at an airline reservations center.

installation. Real-time terminals are being used on bank counters to check customer balances and sometimes to produce statements or to process the customer transactions on-line.

Boston's State Street Bank, the country's largest custodian/transfer agent for mutual funds, uses a real-time computer system to maintain up-to-the-minute records for its customers. Using display terminals, personnel can enter information directly into the computer and receive instantaneous answers to questions.

Real-time data-processing equipment also controls dissemination of the New York Stock Exchange trading data, runs stock tickers, and even "speaks" to member subscribers over the Exchange's telephone quotation service. Trading information, which was previously transmitted by pneumatic tubes and voice, is now sped to a computer center in the Exchange via direct electronic signals from *data readers* on the trading floor. The system prints sales on exchange tickers across the United States in as little time as a half-second after a special reporting card is "read" on the floor.

Common elements of all these applications of real-time systems include a file to store information, a computer to process it, and communications lines and terminals to provide access to or for someone remotely located.

The impetus for acquiring a real-time operation is the need for immediate information. With a real-time system, information managers have the capability of making human judgments based on the most recent data.

Real-time systems normally require the use of data communications equipment to feed data into the system from remote terminals, direct-access storage devices to store incoming data in large volumes, and computers capable of executing the programs needed to validate data and control the input data at the same time as this data is being used for the particular application.

Real-time systems have definite advantages over more conventional methods of processing data. These systems provide immediate interaction between people and machine, or between machine and machine (computer to computer, terminal to computer, etc.).

REAL-TIME COMPUTER

A *real-time computer* is one that has an interrupt capability that will permit input/output components, such as interrogating keyboards and random-access devices, to signal the processor when they are ready to enter a message. The computer can then interrupt its current program and issue appropriate instructions to receive the incoming message before the message is destroyed in the line buffers by the arrival of subsequent messages.

For example, using a real-time system in an airline reservations system, the computer would interrupt its current operation to input and store a reservation request message whenever one occurred. This capability would eliminate the possibility of the message being lost in a waiting position.

Here, the important distinction is the ability to respond to the stimuli in a time period that will permit servicing of the stimuli before the reason for the stimuli is no longer valid. The computer must be capable of servicing multiple interrupts so that an interrupt signal is not lost because of servicing of prior interrupt signals.

The computer must have an expandable internal memory. Accurate memory requirements for real-time programs are often very difficult to estimate when a system is originally designed. Thus, the ability to add additional memory to the computer (if required) can prevent the possible reprogramming of parts of the system.

The real-time computer must have an asynchronous input/output capability. The computer must be able to perform input/output operations and processing functions simultaneously. Other features, such as a built-in clock, methods to protect information in storage, and methods to automatically relocate computer programs in storage, are desirable on many real-time computers.

DESIGNING A REAL-TIME SYSTEM

In designing a real-time system, it is possible to break down the process into various steps and examine each in detail: system design, hardware selection, program design, testing, and integration.

System Design

It is generally agreed that problems in real-time systems to date have not been those of hardware or even of generalized software, but rather, problems of systems design and programming—notably, problems of communication between the people involved. Because of the inherent complexity of real-time programs, the systems design work—the foundation for the programming itself—is exceedingly important. The makeup of the design team, the documentation and communications standards adopted, and the feedback system are all critical.

The use of an interdisciplinary team for system design is strongly recommended. The team should include programmers who have intimate knowledge of the hardware being considered and its accompanying software, the customer who will be serviced by the system, and representatives of the advanced planning section. The team should be supervised by an individual who is familiar with management's plans and objectives, both immediate and future.

This team must be responsible for problem definition and the operational specifications of the system. They must also be responsible for the broad system, which includes a functional breakdown, a diagram of the main information flow, the initial sequencing of functions and transaction types, and the general allocation of computer capacity among the many tasks set for the system by the various parties involved.

Because programming for large systems costs more per instruction than does programming of less complex jobs, and because real-time programming is normally accomplished (because of its size and complexity) by concurrently writing separate segments of the program, great emphasis must be placed on systems design. The key is to ensure adequate design controls while the system is still in the formative stages.

The design team must also consider costing. At this juncture, the programming manager must be consulted. Estimates must be made as to memory and file requirements and educated guesses ventured as to computer running times. The cost of a particular program feature must be compared to the operational value of its result, or to its effect on the available computer capacity. Features must then be deleted or added in an attempt to balance the system to acceptable requirements.

Another part of the initial systems design is to identify how all programs will work together as a system. Too often, this is left to develop during the coding process, and experience has shown that this leads to extensive and costly reprogramming at late stages in development of a system.

"In accordance with the divorce settlement, a fifty-fifty split, Frank, you get the microcomputer and Lenna gets the disk file and line printer."

The systems design team should not be disbanded after preliminary development of the system, but should continue to operate even into the implementation phase. The later work of this team will include the design of operational procedures, the investigation of message format options, the evaluation of alternative computational methods, and the design and specification of testing procedures. The team operates as a control and coordination group. Their work and its documentation is of the utmost importance to the success of any real-time system.

Hardware Selection

After systems requirements have been determined, the selection of hardware must be made. Basically, there are three criteria for the choice: (1) size, (2) operating speed, and (3) reliability.

The *size* of the computer must be considered, with special attention given to the potential modularity of the hardware. Because real-time subsystems (e.g., shop order location and inventory control) cross functional lines, real-time systems have a marked tendency to grow. Therefore, it is very important that the computer system selected have the capacity to expand in terms of the number of communications channels, the size of the internal memory, and the capacity of auxiliary storage.

The *operating speed* of the computer must be taken into account. The internal and input/output speeds of the hardware must be such that the complex programs typical of a real-time system can operate at the necessary speeds, with a safety factor allotted for scanning or switchover. The requirements of the system under development must be considered. Usually, system response time on the order of several seconds, or even minutes, is sufficient to fulfill requirements.

There is no more important criteria for hardware selection than that of *reliabilty*. The reliability of not only the central computer, but also of the communications channels and of the auxiliary storage devices must be carefully evaluated. Usually, the question of reliability centers around cost versus system requirements.

Programming

Real-time programs are usually composed of many separate segments written concurrently by many different programmers. All of these segments are linked through both independent overlays and access to the executive routine. The programs are large and very complex, and yet must be very fast. They must provide for a validity check of all input data and proper disposition of errors, and the programming system must recognize hardware failure and provide for alternative handling at microsecond speed. It must be stressed that program segments must "fit" each other exactly under all circumstances.

There are many constraints imposed on programs by the real-time system. The real-time program must sample data from input devices at prescribed intervals, thereby placing a constraint on the time spent in performing computations and other processing functions. This time limitation and the complexity of program interfaces mean that real-time computer programs cannot be organized in as simple and logical a manner as in batch processing; i.e., they must be time conscious. A system may consist of scores of tables, 50 to 100 program segments, and hundreds of data items all interacting in real-time, with the sequence of execution dependent upon the contents of the incoming data. Yet, no matter how these factors may vary, the system must continue to operate within the time constraint imposed by input volume. In addition, real-time programs must deal successfully with a great variety of input/output devices of disparate speeds. The problem of equipment malfunction and programming or data errors in a real-time system places additional burdens on the people developing the system. Data errors must be dealt with in such a way that the system is protected against the broadening ripples of false information that are the effect of erroneous data being admitted to the system. Yet, the program must keep pace with the ever-present time requirements.

The *executive program* is the keystone of any real-time program. It functions as a scheduler and housekeeper accomplishing the handling of all inputs and outputs, including the construction of queues and the determination of individual transaction priorities. It is responsible for supplying all necessary subroutines and data to the operational programs. In addition to these duties, the executive routine provides the accounting for the system in terms of message volumes, controls program allocation in the internal memory of the computer, and performs the necessary recovery procedures in case of equipment malfunction.

With all of these functions to perform, the executive program has a tendency to become very large and complex. A better procedure is to design separate subroutines for each major function and have the executive program simply reference these subroutines whenever it is time for them to be executed. In this way, the executive program can be fully debugged and ready for use when the first program segments are to be tested. Furthermore, changes can be made in any of the individual functions performed by the executive program without having to change the executive itself.

Programming Standards

The need for complete programming standards is obvious. As part of these standards, a formal system of documentation plays a large part in determining the relative success of the effort. These standards must include strict rules for the use of the selected programming language, a functional description of the executive program (including entrance and exit locations), detailed data formats, locations of logical program interfaces, design of major subroutines (input/output, standard computations, etc.), and explicit rules for programming procedures.

Program Testing and Integration

Program testing involves a verification that all of the permissible inputs to the system are received properly, processed properly, and the results returned correctly to the proper destination. This is usually an obvious and simple task for non–real-time programs, and it is often performed only after the programmer is fairly confident that the program works. In a real-time system, however, the magnitude of the testing effort precludes such an approach. Test programs should be used whenever possible, to avoid making the user a human *"guinea pig."* The danger of this is that the user tends to lose confidence in the system very quickly, and regains that confidence at an agonizingly slow rate. In many cases, a shaky system tends to aggravate a user's basic distrust of computers.

From the programmer's point of view, the most annoying characteristic of *"guinea-pig"* testing is that it may take months or years to uncover some problems, and often it is nearly impossible to recreate the conditions that caused the problem. A good test program, on the other hand, can check all of the features of the system in an organized manner. If an error should occur in the system, the programmer usually has a good idea of the cause of the error, simply because he knows what the test program was doing at the time of the error. A test program also has the advantage that it can be repeated indefinitely, thus giving the programmer the opportunity to retry the test several times while searching for the error, and also to retry it at periodic intervals in the future to guarantee that new errors have not crept into the system.

The process of testing a real-time system must be very well organized and very carefully controlled if it is to be effective. The manner in which components of the system are to be tested, the order in which they are to be tested, and the manner in which the results of test runs are to be saved and compared with other runs of the same test are all important for a good testing environment.

Probably the most agonizing task a programmer faces is the elimination of "bugs" from his program. The simple bugs may be found by extensive desk-checking, but the more obscure bugs have traditionally required the use of selective dumps, test programs, and other procedures that attempt to catch a program in the act of performing some incorrect action.

Program testing is an area that deserves the closest scrutiny. This function is much more important in real-time than in batch-processing systems. Each program segment must be individually tested for logic and clerical errors, run in conjunction with the executive routine to check linkage, and then incorporated into the system and tested once again. Experience has shown that the errors that are the most difficult to detect show up when the program segment is incorporated into the system.

This phase of testing, called *system integration*, should be carried out over as long a period of time as possible. The entire system should be retested with the addition of each program segment or subroutine. Throughout the testing procedure, extensive test tools must be used. Test data generators are invaluable. Simulators must be sophisticated enough to manipulate all of the variables present in the real environment. Because errors often refuse to repeat themselves during debugging, sampling programs that monitor the running system and print out the contents of certain storage areas should be used throughout the testing of a program segment. Equipment failure must be introduced in order to test switchover and recovery procedures.

The programming package for a real-time system generally consists of an executive program and a package of *operational programs*. In most cases, a different group of programmers is assigned to each project, and their testing needs are quite different.

While the executive program is being tested, another group of programmers is often working on a package of operational programs. In a real-time system, this involves many different subroutines. The operational programs tend to be more *logic oriented* and less *input/output oriented* than the executive system. Thus, a large part of an operational program might be tested with the standard procedures of dumps and test programs.

Operational programs can be partially tested in a *stand-alone environment*; however, there comes a time when all further work must be done under the executive system. It would be convenient at this point to have a program-testing tool under the control of the executive system. This tool would allow the programmer to maintain control over the running of the program from a terminal.

It must be stressed that program-testing aids and test programs can never act as a substitute for careful design procedures. The most sophisticated testing program in the world cannot correct design errors; it can only help the programmer find them.

Real-Time Software

Real-time software requirements differ from those associated with general-purpose data processing in several aspects. These differences have made many standard vendor-supplied software packages partly or wholly unusable for real-time work.

One of the basic and most important requirements of real-time software is that it must operate in a real-time environment. For example, signals and control lines between input/output interface equipment and the computer must be serviced on demand. Furthermore, accurate time synchronization to initiate data conversions and other events must also be handled on an interrupt basis. Thus, the executive program must be capable of processing both synchronous and asynchronous priority interrupt requests initiated by an arbitrary number of external sources.

The real-time user requires general software control over interrupt hardware. In some cases, it is important to disable interrupts during program execution to assure immediate completion of the associated function. In such a case, it is important that the interrupt signals not be lost during the period of disablement.

An implicit software requirement for real-time systems is the generation of efficient object programs. The user can frequently trade accuracy for execution speed in certain areas, since there are many programming techniques for accomplishing this tradeoff. Thus, computer programs designed for maximum accuracy and capable of full-word precision are not always needed or desirable. Most standard software, however, is so characterized.

On-line problem debugging and optimization are commonplace in real-time systems. Moreover, the ability to monitor problem solutions on benchboards and consoles, and then adjust the program structure on-line, is typical of the human/machine relationship that exists in real-time systems. Although it is not a strict software requirement, this direct communication between human and machine should be emphasized in the software design.

The previous paragraphs indicate some of the more important considerations in the development of real-time software. These factors, however, are in no way intended to minimize the necessity for software features usually associated with general-purpose computation. For example, the capability for batch assemblies and compilations is also a requirement in a well-organized real-time computing system. This feature is important, not only for multiple assemblies and compilations of computer programs, but also for off-line debugging. More simply stated, the automatic processing features that are commonplace in the

"IT'S COMFORTING TO KNOW THAT 200 HUMANS WOULD HAVE TO WORK 100 YEARS TO MAKE SO MANY MISTAKES AS WE DO IN ONE SECOND."

digital computation system should be equally available to the real-time system user.

BATCH PROCESSING

Batch processing is a method of processing data in which transactions are accumulated for a predetermined period of time and prepared for input to the computer for processing as a single unit. Input is collected in batches and sorted in the same sequence as it is to be processed. For example, all memos of transactions (invoices, sales slips, etc.) are collected. The batch of memos is then sorted numerically or alphabetically for posting to accounts. The indicated time period may be any length—an hour, a day, a week, or a month. In batch processing, however, there is often some delay between the occurrence of original events and the eventual processing of the transactions. This type of processing is contrasted with real-time processing in which transactions are dealt with as they arise and are automatically applied to files held in a direct-access storage device.

Batch processing has several important advantages. It makes mechanization of processing operations more feasible by assuring that a large number of items will be processed at one time. Preparation time for processing data is reduced since a few large processing runs are made instead of numerous smaller processing runs.

STRUCTURED PROGRAMMING

Structured programming is concerned with improving the programming process through better organization of programs and better programming notation to facilitate correct and clear descriptions of data and control structures.

Improved programming languages and organized programming techniques should help one produce programs that are (1) more understandable and, therefore, more easily modified and documented, (2) more economical to run because good organization and notation make it easier for a compiler to "understand" the logic of the program, and (3) more correct and, therefore, more easily debugged.

The physical structure of a well-organized program corresponds to the sequence of steps in the algorithm being implemented. At a lower level, all parts of the implementation of one idea are grouped in a structure that clearly indicates how the various parts are selected and sequenced, and the relation of this idea to neighboring ideas.

The program should be expressed in the most natural and appropriate representation. The program should not contain a GOTO statement when a better representation is available. A program designer should, however, use a GOTO statement when the alternatives are worse.

Whenever a GOTO statement is used in a program, it should be accompanied by enough comments to make its purpose perfectly clear.

Some program designers limit their conception of structured programs to programs with structured control, and ignore the equally important factor of structured data. When the data has to be manipulated to fit the available data-structure representations, the program becomes less readable. The program designer should inform the reader and the computer how to represent his data-structure representations into computer representations, and then go about using his representations in his program.

A good language for structured programming has a carefully thought-out assortment of control structures and data-structure definition facilities. If a language provides one kind of iterative control statement for counter-controlled loops, and others for loops controlled by a decision value of an expression, then the former should be used when the loop is expected to terminate as a result of the counter reaching its terminal value. The others should be used when some other condition is expected to terminate the loop. This makes it easier for a reader to distinguish between the "nature" of the control being exercised by the loop.

When a line of code is a continuation of a previous line or a subsidiary idea, it should be indented from the left margin established by the

"ACTUALLY, YOU WERE MADE POSSIBLE
BY A GRANT FROM GENERAL MOTORS!"

principal statement. When an indented code might be so complex or long as to obscure the principal level of control, then one should consider making this code into a procedure. A good "rule of thumb" is to try to get each principal idea to fit on a single page.

Structured programming is often associated with "top-down programming." Although this technique is a useful tool for explaining a program and illustrates how much easier it is to explain a structured program than a haphazardly written one, it is unlikely that the art of programming can be restricted to the use of a single technique.

TELEPROCESSING

Teleprocessing is a term formed by a combination of the words *telecommunications* and *data processing*. It is a form of information handling in which a data-processing system utilizes communications facilities to permit processing of data at a point remote from its origin. Fig. 10-6 illustrates a system that has five remote locations. Data communications between the central processing facility and the remote locations is accomplished by such communications facilities as telephone lines, electric cables, or microwave systems. The source or destination points of data are called *terminals*.

A terminal can have one or a combination of input/output devices. A large variety of such devices are available for use at remote terminals.

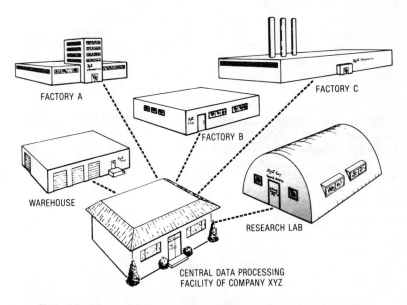

Fig. 10-6. A teleprocessing network that has five remote locations.

These include special keyboards, crt graphic display devices, printers, card read/punch units, and telephones. In addition, a remote terminal may have a remote processing system, in which case the application is not only a teleprocessing one, but a *multiprocessing* one as well.

Teleprocessing applications range from those in which data is received by a central processing system and merely stored for later processing, to large complex systems in which the hardware and information resources of the central system are shared among many users at remote locations. Teleprocessing capabilities are particularly useful in situations where a central computer can coordinate several facilities remote from each other.

The three major types of teleprocessing are (1) *data collection*, (2) *data communications*, and (3) *data transmissions*. A single teleprocessing system may include any combination of these three.

Data Collection

Data collection implies that data is received by a central processing system from one or more remote terminals and is stored for later processing. Depending on the specific application, the transfer of data may be initiated either at the terminal or by the central processing system.

An example of a data collection application would be one in which data is received intermittently during the day (as it is generated) and is processed, when convenient, during the second or third shift, taking advantage of lower data-processing rates for those shifts. This could be an application in which production workers, upon completion of their jobs, transmit by means of special input devices such data as their ID numbers, the number of work units they completed, and other pertinent data. The central system, after all the data for the day has been collected and stored, could then process it for accounting and production control purposes.

In other applications, data may be accumulated during the day and then placed on an input device such as a punched-card reader. The data could be collected by the central computing system during off-peak hours in order to take advantage of lower communication-line rates for those hours.

Data Communications

Data communications is the movement of data by means of electrical transmission systems. The terms *data* and *information* are often considered synonymous, although there is a subtle difference between the two. Data may be regarded as one or more facts not necessarily meaningful. Information, however, is always meaningful. For example, the apparently meaningless series of digits 326432521125 could be called data. To a payroll clerk, however, to whom the figures could mean

that employee number 3264 worked 32.5 hours and should be paid
$211.25, the series of digits would be information.

Thus, the language of machines is called data—a word that represents
various kinds of information. For example, data can be represented by
typed letters and numbers or by punched holes or magnetized material.
Machines pass the data back and forth with electrical signals.

Data can be sorted out, compiled in many ways, and subjected to
arithmetic operations. That is why the machine for handling these
operations—the computer—is frequently called a *data-processing*
machine. Similarly, that is why the conveyance of machine information
from one place to another is called *data communications*.

Today, machines communicate with each other by means of *lines*.
These lines may be wires, cables, or microwave circuits (see Fig. 10-7).
A wide range of transmission services is available from such firms as
American Telephone and Telegraph (AT&T), General Telephone and
Electronics (GTE), and Western Union (WU).

Data Transmission

Data transmission is the sending of data. Magnetic-tape-to-computer
communications are examples of data transmission. It is important
wherever large amounts of data must be conveyed at high speeds from
one location to another. In Fig. 10-6, a design modification to some
electrical apparatus might be sent from engineers in the research lab to
the central data-processing facility. Likewise, new circuit diagrams
resulting from the modification might be sent to factory A.

Data Communications Terminals

Terminals range from a simple send-only teleprinter, to a complicated
terminal computer with considerable data manipulation power. The
basic common denominators of these terminals are the capability to
transmit and/or receive data over communications lines, and an input
and/or output medium.

In terms of function, terminals can be divided into transmitters,
receivers, and transceivers. They communicate with computers and
other terminals equipped with appropriate interface devices. The type
of communications circuit required is most often a voice-grade line,
either via the direct-dial network or a private line. Some terminals may
achieve higher throughput by using a broadband or microwave link.
Telegraph lines are also used.

The transmitters accept as input media the keyboard, punched card,
voice message, magnetic tape, magnetic disk, plastic card, punched
paper tape, pencil-marked card, edge-punched card, etc. Receivers
output data in the form of printed hard copy, punched-card voice
message, magnetic tape, magnetic disk, punched paper tape,
cathode-ray tube, or in direct signals to the computer memory.

Modems and Acoustic Couplers

Modems and acoustic couplers are essential in data communications, because common-carrier telephone lines cannot carry signals as they are emitted from computers or other digital machines, nor can they input signals directly into the machines. Either a modem or an acoustic coupler is required to convert the signals to telephone-line language for data transmission.

A modem is used between the communications line and the digital machine. It converts digital output signals from the machine into analog signals for transmission, and vice versa on the receiving end, as shown in Fig. 10-8. Modems are made by the telephone companies and computer equipment manufacturers. They are often called *data sets*.

Many computer centers now have a large number of dial-up lines connected into them. Fig. 10-9 shows a rack of many data sets connecting telephone lines to the computer system.

The acoustic coupler is an alternate way of connecting digital terminals to a computer system. It accepts a conventional telephone handset and does not require special wiring. To use the coupler, one merely uses an ordinary telephone, dials the telephone number, and places the telephone handset into a cradle on the acoustic coupler.

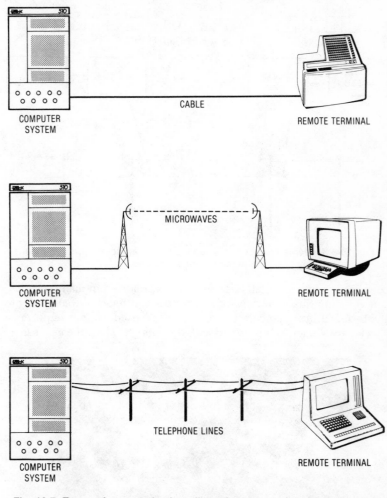

Fig. 10-7. Types of communications lines that are used to connect remote terminals to computer systems.

There are differences in the performance capabilities of the two devices. One of the major differences is the speed of data transmission. Most couplers have a maximum transmission rate of 300 bits per second, although a few can handle rates as high as 1800 bits per second. Some modem transmission rates are as high as a million bits per second. The data transmission speed, of course, is largely dependent on the type of communications line used.

Although both devices operate with equal efficiency, the acoustic

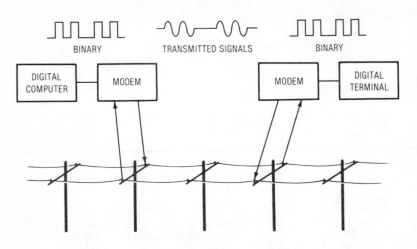

Fig. 10-8. Modems are used to interface digital equipment with standard communications facilities.

coupler provides a portable feature and is preferred in many systems. The coupler utilizes the data tone that is transmitted by the computer to the terminal. Any standard telephone can be used without requiring a special installation as is required with the data set. Thus, the user can go

Courtesy Bolt Beranek and Newman, Inc.

Fig. 10-9. Rack of data sets connecting many dial-up telephone lines to a large computer system.

wherever a telephone is available, dial the computer, and start processing data.

Most modems and acoustic couplers employ serial transmission, which can be synchronous (in which the sending and receiving terminals are synchronized bit for bit) or asynchronous (in which the start and end of each character is indicated by signal elements).

Another characteristic to be considered is the directionality of the unit. Simplex units operate in one direction only, half duplex indicates two-way alternate transmission, and full duplex indicates two-way simultaneous transmisson. A modem or acoustic coupler may have numerous interchange circuits.

Teleprocessing Applications

Message switching is a type of teleprocessing application in which a message received by the central computing system from one remote terminal is sent to one or more other remote terminals. Message switching can be used in a nationwide or worldwide telegraph system, or it can be used by a geographically dispersed business or scientific enterprise to provide instantaneous communication within the enterprise.

Remote job processing is a type of application in which data-processing jobs, like those that are entered into the system locally, are received from one or more remote terminals and processed by the operating system.

On-line problem solving is a teleprocessing application in which a number of users at remote terminals can concurrently use a central computing system in solving problems. In this type of application, each user at a terminal has the impression that he is the sole user of the computing system. In reality, however, the resources of the system are shared among several users. Accordingly, such applications are often referred to broadly as *time sharing*. When the use of the computing system is momentarily not required by one user, it is available to satisfy the needs of others. Because of its speed, the computing system can respond to the needs of all the users within a few seconds.

Often, in this type of application, a dialogue or conversation is carried on between the user at a remote terminal and a program within the central computing system. The program may be designed to interrogate the user and immediately respond to his replies or requests, or even his mistakes.

On-line problem solving has a great many potential applications in the fields of education, engineering, and research. Because the system can respond immediately to the needs of the user, it can directly participate in, and speed up, the problem-solving process as well as other similar processes, such as program design and learning. Thus, if a user makes a mistake in the course of designing a program, he may be immediately alerted to take corrective action by a program in the central computing system. Therefore, he need not wait until the complete program is compiled and tested before the mistake is detected. Similarly, in a *computer assisted instruction* (CAI) system—an important variation of on-line problem solving—a student is immediately informed of, and learns from, mistakes as they are made.

EXERCISES

1. Indicate which of the following complete(s) the statement correctly: Time sharing

    (a) is the simultaneous use of a computer system by a number of different persons.
    (b) is the use of a computer at different times by different people.
    (c) consists of stacking jobs in order to enable the computer to process them at one time.
    (d) always involves the use of two or more digital computers.

2. List three devices commonly maintained as user terminals in a time-sharing system.

3. How is a communications processor used in a time-sharing system?

4. Why is it necessary to have a large direct-access storage device in a time-sharing system?

5. What is meant by multiprocessing?

6. Define multiprogramming and give an example.

7. Define the following terms:

    (a) Real-time.
    (b) Real-time computer.

8. List four applications where real-time systems are used.

9. Describe the system design process used in developing real-time systems.

10. Is computing equipment selected before or after the system is designed? Why?

11. Why is developing real-time programs more difficult than developing programs for a batch-processing environment?

12. What is an executive program?

13. What is the difference between program testing and system integration?

14. What is meant by on-line program debugging?

15. Explain how a bank might use a real-time computer system. A department store. An airline company.

16. Compare batch processing with real-time processing.

17. What is meant by structured programming?

18. Define teleprocessing.

19. What is a terminal?

20. What are the three major types of teleprocessing?

21. How is it possible for a computer system located in New York to communicate with a machine in Southern California?

22. What is a modem? An acoustic coupler?

23. List some common communications services that are available for data communication.

24. Describe a teleprocessing activity that you are familiar with.

CHAPTER 11
SYSTEMS
DEVELOPMENT

A *systems study* is the investigation made in an organization to determine and develop needed informational improvements in specified areas. In some cases, the needed improvements will involve using a computer to achieve objectives. There are at least three reasons for making a systems study. First, substantial investment may be involved in using a computer, and a proper study reduces the risk of loss. Second, many of the common pitfalls associated with inadequate planning may be avoided. Finally, the study may point the way to substantial benefits.

In this chapter, we will examine an approach for a business to follow in conducting a systems study.

SYSTEMS ANALYSIS AND DESIGN

Systems analysis and design is the evaluation and creation of computer-based information systems. Its relationship with computer programming is shown in Fig. 11-1. The process begins with the *recognition* of a *problem* or an opportunity (step 1). The problem may be specific, such as payroll for 120 employees, or the general idea that control could be enhanced by a more effective computer-based information system. In either case, the next step is *systems analysis* (step 2), which is to learn enough about the present system to design a better one. This step involves collecting, organizing, and evaluating facts about a system and the environment in which it operates. The systems analysis step is intended to evaluate the necessity and the economic and technological feasibility of a solution to the problem. The written report produced in the systems analysis step is the *feasibility study*.

The third step is *systems design*. Once it is determined that the project is feasible, a general outline of the proposed solution (feasibility study) is used to produce a detailed design. This detailed design is literally the specifications that are supplied to programming (step 5).

The fourth step is *equipment selection and acquisition*. The object of

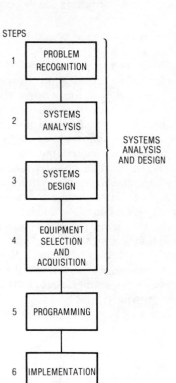

STEPS

1 — PROBLEM RECOGNITION

2 — SYSTEMS ANALYSIS

3 — SYSTEMS DESIGN

4 — EQUIPMENT SELECTION AND ACQUISITION

SYSTEMS ANALYSIS AND DESIGN

5 — PROGRAMMING

6 — IMPLEMENTATION

7 — EVALUATION

Fig. 11-1. Steps in the process of developing a computer-based system.

this step is to select and acquire the computer system that will do the job effectively at the lowest possible cost. This step is accomplished by converting the feasibility study to a nonhardware-oriented specification. To obtain the lowest price, computer vendors are invited to submit bids based on the specifications. The user evaluates the bids and selects the vendor from which to buy or lease the equipment.

The first four steps—problem recognition, systems analysis, systems design, and equipment selection and acquisition—constitute systems analysis and design. The remaining three steps are *programming, implementation,* and *evaluation.* The objectives of the programming and implementation steps (steps 5 and 6) are to write, test, and check out (debug) the programs for the new system. More personnel resources are expended for the programming and implementing steps than for any of the other steps in the development cycle. The evaluation step (step 7) involves reviewing and checking the effectiveness of the process and the finished product.

The role of the *systems analyst* in the last three steps varies from organization to organization. In some businesses, the systems analyst has no control or authority over the programming, implementing, or evaluating. However, in other instances, the systems analyst has total responsibility for and control of these functions. In this chapter, we will consider the systems analyst in the latter role.

Systems analysts accumulate a great deal of data as they work. Initially, the data are objective and appear as grid charts, flowcharts, or on data sheets. However, systems analysts also obtain much subjective information. They draw conclusions about the present system. First, they acquire a complete understanding of the data flow of the system. Second, they know the actions taken by each work center in the system. Third, they know the total activity of the system from data organization to product delivery. Fourth, they identify the possible areas for integration of functional areas. This step is important when the work progresses to systems design. Fifth, they produce a written report—the feasibility study.

"THERE GOES SOMEBODY'S BRILLIANT
SYSTEMS ANALYSIS."

FEASIBILITY STUDY

The *feasibility study* analyzes the practicality and economics of installing a new system in one or more application areas within an organization. It is a familiar technique used for years by systems personnel. Its name describes its function—a study to determine the feasibility of a request for a change from one method to another in accomplishing certain processing functions. The request normally involves a major system change. Performing a study has the effect of averting certain problems because:

1. It forces the requestor to examine in detail the system under consideration and to reduce the proposal to writing.
2. It induces a broader look at the system under study. Many related functions must be examined, such as data conversion and input, audit and control, and the interrelationship with other departments and system functions.
3. It includes the participation and contribution of members of the user department. Too often, the request for a new system technique comes from a source outside of the department most directly affected.
4. It prohibits a one-sided proposition from being adopted. Public acknowledgment that a study is in progress alerts other interested parties and gives them a chance to participate.
5. It enables the study to be reviewed in terms of other studies being performed and allows corporate management to properly forecast potential future expenditures.

A feasibility study should be as factual as possible and all-inclusive in examining the many factors that affect system selection. The study results in a document of a few pages, or a substantial report of many pages, depending on the magnitude of the system investigated. The study should outline the scope of the system, the objectives that such implementation would, hopefully, accomplish, and the desired results as far as its contribution to overall corporate processing is concerned. In addition, it should be a vehicle to obtain approval from the user department manager and any other responsible individuals. Included with the goals must be an estimate of systems personnel-hours required, a general assignment of personnel, and a plan for integration of this request with other current and future projects.

Frequently, the study can deteriorate into a one-sided attempt to place an application on the computer, so it is important to outline both advantages. Such seemingly incidental factors as user training, user-department documentation, program maintenance, and forms design and cost should be included. The finished study should allow management to make an unbiased decision.

As the systems analyst or the systems team approaches a feasibility study, there are four basic solutions to the request for a computer system implementation:

1. *Develop a computer system as a solution.* In these days of microcomputers, minicomputers, large disk-storage units, virtual storage, multiprogramming, time sharing, and improved programming techniques, a computer may be the most obvious (although not necessarily the best) solution. Generally, the request for a system is proposed on the assumption that a computer system would be designed and implemented.

2. *Develop a manual system as a solution.* If a new system must be designed, then it is often less expensive and simpler to develop a manual system and operate it at least until it is error free. In addition, performing the job manually allows the user to develop a better understanding of what the system entails. Historical information can be accumulated, and the initial data base can be developed under the manual system. Later, automation of the system as experience and volume grow may offer the most efficient solution. Systems people should not be blinded by the computer. Sometimes, modifications to a manual system can accomplish corporate purposes.

3. *Develop an integrated manual and computer system as a solution.* With any computer system, there is some manual effort in its initial processes, but it may be determined that other intermediate steps or validation techniques could be performed more economically.

   Occasionally, when computerizing a system, one small part may require an inordinate amount of time for programming and testing, or it may require a large amount of hardware resources. To do this manually would be the best solution.

4. *Do not change the current method.* Frequently, a manual system or a manual/computer system cannot be improved enough to justify the expense involved in the change. Do not change something for the sake of change. It is important that the information processing manager select or recommend the method that is most beneficial to the company, whether it be computer, manual, or a combination. This selection cannot be done by viewing only cost savings as the determiner, but by evaluating all factors.

User-department participation in feasibility studies is important to success. This participation not only provides a better and more comprehensive study and system, but also makes the user department feel that the system is its own.

Participation should be by a designated individual or individuals to provide continuity. On major projects it is important, if not imperative, that a member of the user department be assigned to work full time on the study. This lets the user staff member identify with the system from the beginning, understand why certain things are done or are not done, and have a say about how and what should be done. It also dispels any feelings among user-department personnel that a system is being imposed upon them. In addition, the participation promotes cooperation during the design, training, conversion, and implementation phases of the project.

A system must be designed for the user, not for the convenience of the computer. The best computer system can fail without user-department cooperation.

Several important steps need to be taken before actually starting a feasibility study. First, the systems analyst together with the requestor and appropriate systems and user-department personnel should:

1. Define, review, and confirm the study scope, objectives, and desired results in a preliminary form that includes the purpose, extent, and limitation of the study. This phase should point out the possible effects of the proposed system on other systems, sections, and departments. It may also result in dropping the project or significantly widening its scope.
2. Develop a preliminary study approach, timetable, and personnel requirements. This step will document a proposed study approach and estimate the following requirements of the study: total personnel-months, total elapsed time, number of systems personnel, number of user-department personnel, and number of other personnel.
3. Review the previous steps with management. The scope, objectives, desired results, study approach, timetable, and estimated personnel requirements should be reviewed with the user department head and head of the systems department. The objective of this review is to obtain approval for making the study, the scope and desired results of the study, and commitment of personnel and projected start date.

When time and personnel requirements are significant, a cost estimate for the feasibility study may be required. In many companies, for any significant project, it is necessary to obtain high-management approval and an assignment of project priority from the total company view.

All full-time team members of a feasibility study should be selected and be given any necessary education or orientation. It is helpful to give nonsystems team members a course in information processing systems or at least a short course covering flowcharts, vocabulary, and methods of documentation. It is also a good idea to have a member of the user department spend some time outlining the department work that the study will affect.

"NO, THIS IS LOVER'S LEAP. PROGRAMMERS
LEAP IS FARTHER UP THE HILL."

Once the team has been formed, the study plan can be reviewed, modified if necessary, and made formal. From this an outline of the various steps to be followed can be produced, including the company areas and/or departments to be contacted and external visits or contacts to be made to avoid duplication of work already done.

A timetable should be set up. It will either reinforce the original estimates or allow them to be modified prior to the actual start of the study.

One of the most important steps to include in the outline and timetable is periodic review and reporting. This should not be just a frequency, it should be specific dates and times; for instance, the first and third Monday of each month at 10:00 a.m. in the conference room. A set time will ensure that meetings occur, whereas a vague "once a month" may never come. Without reporting and review by the whole team and the respective section or department heads, a study may go off on an unwanted tangent or the timetable may become so warped that it cannot be fulfilled.

After establishing goals and objectives, the feasibility study team begins to collect information about the current system and its environment. All information gathered, including minutes of meetings, should be documented, categorized, indexed, and copied so that each member of the team has a complete set. Included in this documentation should be any suggestions or comments on the design of the system that have been made during the fact-finding phase. In most cases, some of the information will need expansion. This additional information should be documented and indexed and, if appropriate, cross-keyed to previous documentation. As in all systems work, "documentation" is the byword.

Using the facts and documentation developed in earlier steps and any additional information needed, begin to develop possible solutions. Identify the areas of difficulty and examine their implications. This step helps determine the requirements of the system. A good system does not have to be automatic from beginning to end. Manual intervention may easily overcome some of the problem areas at certain points in the system.

Develop as many alternative solutions and approaches as possible. Weed out those that are obviously unworkable. Then evaluate the remaining solutions from the standpoint of technical, economic, administrative, and implementation feasibility. Be sure to project the volumes for the current system and for the proposed systems three to five years in advance. A system that is marginal now may be a real money-saver at the increased volumes. In addition, it may show the total inability of the current system to cope with future volumes. After this preliminary evaluation, select the preferred solutions for further evaluation. For the chosen solutions, you must next design approaches to the overall design, a systems-approach programming implementation, and evaluation.

First, develop the personnel requirement for analysts, programmers, training and followup, and user-department personnel. Second, using the estimated personnel requirement, develop a detailed schedule for the completion of the system. Actually, both the first and second points are handled together, as one depends on the other. Do not forget vacations and allowances for sick time, meetings, and any other factor that may require time of the project personnel. If omitted, these items can quickly wreck the best schedule.

Develop an economic evaluation. Develop all costs for the system, both recurring and nonrecurring. Costs deriving from the implementation of the system include:

- Cost of the computer hardware system.
- Cost of the software system.
- Additions to the programming and systems staff.
- Site preparation.
- Staff training.
- Systems analysis and design.
- Software development and checkout.
- User training.
- Security.
- Physical facilities (floor space, lighting, heating, and air conditioning).
- Conversion.
- Printed forms.

The final report on the feasibility of a system should be produced professionally. A hastily typed, slapped-together document with sloppy handwritten material makes poor backup and starts readers off with a negative attitude. A good feasibility report contains at least the following:

1. A *summary* that states the recommended solution to the request or problem. This summary should be the first page of the report.
2. A list of any *new equipment* necessary, with details of why the particular equipment was chosen.

3. An estimated *cost* of the system, including a future projection of the costs and savings for the next three to five years.
4. A list of *intangible benefits*.
5. If the new jobs have been created, then new *job descriptions* should be written. Identify old jobs that are no longer necessary.
6. A recommended *schedule* for design, programming, system checkout, training, conversion, implementation, and documentation.
7. An estimate of the *useful life* of the system.
8. Indicate the future growth pattern and the *ease of system expansion*.
9. A list of the *advantages* and *disadvantages* of the system.
10. A *conclusion* which provides some detail.
11. An *index* if the report is large enough to warrant it.

During the preparation phases of a system feasibility study, the systems analyst's greatest assets are an *open mind* and a *willingness to be convinced*. One should avoid tunnel vision by looking at all solutions.

"I TOLD YOU I DIDN'T WANT TO WATCH ANY X-RATED PROGRAMS!"

EXERCISES

1. What is a system study?

2. List the steps required in the process of developing a computer-based information system.

3. Distinguish between systems analysis and systems design. Discuss the importance of each function.

4. What is the feasibility study?

5. List several qualifications of the systems analyst.

6. What is the difference between a manual system and a computer system?

7. Why should we spend time studying the current system when we are planning another system to replace it?

8. Discuss some of the information that must be collected in a systems study.

9. Why are costs important when one is designing a new system?

10. List several of the items that should be contained in the feasibility report.

11. When conducting a systems study, why is it important that the systems analysts or systems team keep an "open mind"?

12. Develop a plan for the redesign of a system with which you are familiar.

CHAPTER 12
COMPUTER CENTERS

An information processing center is significant in the overall organization of a company not only because of the expense of the equipment, software, and personnel, but also because of its role as a service department which accepts input data, performs processing and storage, and provides information. If the function is not well managed, it can seriously impair the activities of the entire organization.

All of the principles of good organization and management that apply to any business or organization apply to the management of information processing facilities. While information processing may be unique in the type of service that it renders, and possibly in its location in the overall organizational structure, it is nevertheless composed of people, machines, responsibilities, and production deadlines.

In this chapter, we will discuss the placement of the information processing function within the structure of a company, and the organization of an information processing center. The following job descriptions are included in this chapter: manager of information processing, systems analyst, programmer, computer operator, and clerical jobs.

ORGANIZATIONAL CONCEPTS

There is no universal or standard pattern for the location of the information processing center within the organizational structure of a company. Individual company differences influence the nature and location of the information processing function.

Traditionally, the information processing functions were placed under the financial managers, primarily because most of the original information processing applications were related to accounting functions (e.g., payroll, accounts receivable, and general accounting). It was, therefore, somewhat natural that financial managers (usually the controller) should play a large role in the administration of information processing activities.

Today, there is a trend in the more advanced information processing functions to have a vice-president devote full time to the responsibility (see Fig. 12-1.) The designation of a vice-president of information processing can have a positive effect because it reflects a progressive attitude toward information processing activities. It recognizes the need to be flexible and to cope with changes, new technologies, and the state of the economy. The emergence and importance of information processing activites in many organizations warrants suitable organizational status for these functions.

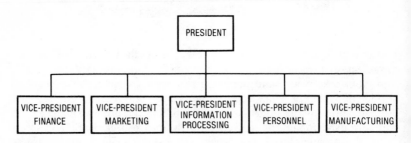

Fig. 12-1. Organizational structure of a typical company.

A major requirement is to develop information processing awareness in all managers and in the rank and file, so that they can appreciate the role of the computer. The managers of a company should be able to identify and articulate problems with the systems analysts and programmers.

Unless information processing has top management backing, the organization will be ineffective in its total systems and management information efforts and in its capability to cope with newer technologies. A lesser reporting relationship will not have the authority, influence, and knowledge of management's requirements to obtain full benefit from the new technology and to get the support of the departments of the company affected by proposed changes. In many small businesses, the function of the vice-president of information may be combined with one or more additional responsibilities (e.g., vice-president of marketing, personnel, and information).

A company or organization may either centralize or decentralize management and staff activites. When centralized, management is concentrated at one location to obtain the benefits of greater specialization and ease of coordination, communication, and top-level decision making. Generally, if management is centralized, information processing is also centralized so that it can support the staff. In fully centralized computer operations, all data to be processed are submitted or transmitted to one central location—the principal offices of the company. Information is provided to the staff agencies at the central location, and certain reports may be forwarded to field locations. Communications and data transmission costs are usually high. Centralized computer facilities ordinarily have larger-scale computer systems than do comparable decentralized locations. Specialized applications dealing with simulation, modeling, operations research, or other management science techniques may be in use.

On the other hand, in a decentralized operation, the authority and responsibility for results may be as far down the line as efficient management permits. Decentralization may imply that the size and volume of the organization's information processing needs are too unwieldly to control from a central point. It may take too long to send facts up the line and wait for the decision to come back down. The basic concept of decentralization is that facts are gathered and decisions are made on the scene of action.

Motivation is often enhanced when personnel are allowed to participate in management decisions at the local level. Information processing is decentralized when it is placed with branch offices to support those components of the company. Generally, these facilities have smaller-scale equipment than do centralized facilities. Products are provided to local agencies, and a modest amount of data is submitted to higher echelons. Transmission and communications costs are moderate.

Some people have envisioned the role of the computer as encouraging a swing to the centralized concept because unlimited amounts of data are readily available at the home office. The lower cost and higher processing output of newer computers (especially minicomputers and microcomputers), however, encourage the decentralized concept. Communications costs are beginning to approach hardware costs for highly centralized operations. Data transmission costs are lower when decentralized units support widely separated branches or divisions.

INFORMATION PROCESSING ORGANIZATION

The internal organization of the information processing function may vary, depending on the size and nature of the business it services. Since these and other factors may influence the exact organizational structure of the information processing function, only a general type of organization is shown (see Fig. 12-2).

COMPUTER CENTER PERSONNEL

Most companies and organizations have job descriptions which identify job titles and clearly describe all job functions required of an employee. Although titles vary between computer installations, the

following general job descriptions cover the most common information processing positions.

Manager of Information Processing

At the head of most computer installations or departments is someone who coordinates and directs the overall efforts of systems analysts, programmers, computer operators, and others involved with the use of the computer. Such department heads may have titles like *manager of information processing*, *manager of computer services*, etc. They generally report to a top executive of the organization.

Management of information processing requires considerable experience, good management skills, and, in most companies, a college

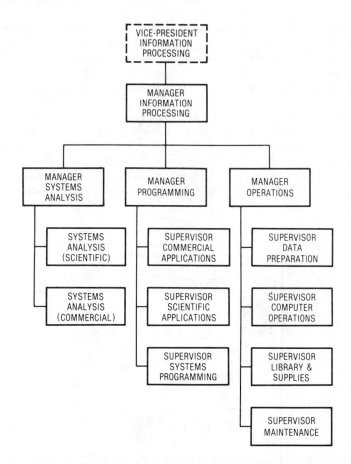

Fig. 12-2. Organizational structure of a typical information processing function.

degree. Salaries vary widely depending on the size of the staff and the organizational level within the company.

Systems Analyst

The work of the *systems analyst* involves both the collection of facts regarding the information requirements of the computer user and the analysis of those facts. Systems analysts formulate efficient patterns of information flow from its sources to the computer, define the computer process necessary to turn the raw data into useful information, and plan the distribution and use of the resulting information.

In smaller computer installations, the functions of systems analysis and programming are frequently combined, while in the larger installations, they are usually separate. No matter what the title, persons performing the analysis have to understand the problem and interpret it correctly and, at the same time, know how to use the computer effectively. They must bring to every problem a deep insight that will enable them to reduce it to its fundamental information-flow terms.

An engineering/scientific analyst may work on such problems as tracking a satellite or controlling a nuclear process. The analyst must consult with and understand top-level scientists and mathematicians and develop mathematical equations that describe the problem and its solution. Such an analyst, of course, must have at least one degree in mathematics, physics, or an appropriate engineering science.

On the other hand, while a formal educational background in business administration is helpful for systems analysts who specialize in business data processing, it is not always required. Business experience and the ability to reason logically are important, however. Typical of the projects that a business systems analyst may work on are the development of an integrated production, inventory control, and cost analysis system.

An area of increasing importance, as businesses grow bigger and more diversified, is operations research. This field is an especially challenging specialty, involving the analyst in the high echelons of decision making in any business or organization. The analyst must formulate a mathematical model of a management problem and use it to provide a quantitative basis for making decisions. Many organizations require that systems analysts have two or more years of programming experience in addition to a college degree.

Programmer

After the analysts have laid out the solution for a problem or the design of an information processing system, it goes to a *programmer*. It is the programmer's job to devise a detailed plan for solving the problem on the computer. This plan is called the *program*, and in final form it consists of a series of coded step-by-step instructions that make the computer perform the desired operations. In most instances, the analysts or the programmer will have prepared a flowchart which graphically illustrates the flow of data through the system and what actions are to be taken when a given condition is met or not met. The programmer generally employs one of several computer languages to communicate with the machine. The programmer checks the program by preparing sample data and testing it on the computer. The programmer also "debugs" the program by making several trial runs with the actual data from the project (see Fig. 12-3). To complete the entire programming process for a large project may take several months or longer, and the program may take up several volumes of flowcharts and listings of program steps.

Programmers often work as part of a team, with different levels of responsibility (see Fig. 12-4). Depending on the size of the project, there may be a programming manager or a senior programmer leading the team, with a staff of programmers, junior programmers, coders, and trainees. The term *coder* is sometimes used instead of junior programmer. The name derives from the fact that machine instructions are often called machine *codes*. A coder takes detailed flowcharts and produces coded instructions.

In some organizations, coders and programmer trainees translate the programmers' instructions into the codes understood by the particular computer being used. The junior programmers write instructions from the detailed flowcharts developed by the programmers, and sometimes receive the opportunity to write specific parts of a broad program. In this way, they develop the skills and experience needed to develop programs on their own. Those who take a full range of computer courses leading to a computer science degree at a college or university can

Courtesy IBM Corp.

Fig. 12-3. A programmer "debugging" (finding and correcting errors) a computer program.

generally skip the initial training-level positions in their first job and go right into full-fledged programming assignments.

The varieties of problems programmers deal with, the different computers they may work with, and the various information processing languages they must know demand a high degree of ingenuity, experience, imagination, and, above all, the ability to think logically. Well-trained and experienced programmers can write programs for many different types of problems.

"I'VE HAD IT WITH HUNTING AND GATHERING! I THINK I'LL BECOME A COMPUTER PROGRAMMER!"

Computer Operator

Look into any busy information processing center and you will see several men and women pushing buttons, changing magnetic tapes, flicking through punched cards, and in other ways supervising the operations of the computer. Computer operators, those who push the buttons and watch the lights, actually do much more than that. They review computer programs and instruction sheets to determine the necessary equipment setup for the job. When the control panel lights indicate that the machine has stopped for some reason, the console operator must investigate and correct the stoppage, or call in a maintenance engineer if the cause is equipment malfunction. The console operator keeps a log of the work done by the computer and writes reports on its use. In large installations, the console operator is assisted by tape librarians and handlers and the operators of peripheral equipment (sorters, collators, high-speed printers, tape-drive units, etc.).

Computer operators usually serve an apprenticeship, during which their main duties are inserting punched cards in card readers and punches, inserting forms in printers, mounting reels of magnetic tape on tape drives, and generally readying peripheral devices for operation. More-experienced operators are usually responsible for actually manipulating the controls that actuate the computer system. The console operator holds a position of much responsibility, since mistakes

Courtesy IBM Corp.

Fig. 12-4. Programmers often work as part of a team.

can be time consuming and costly. Employers require a high-school education, and many of them prefer some college. A college degree is very helpful for those who aspire to progress into programming or systems analysis. Many computer operators have successfully advanced to positions as supervisors of operations, programmers, and managers of information processing centers.

Clerical

Clerical jobs vary, but usually include manual coding of data, verification of totals used for accounting controls, maintaining libraries of magnetic-tape files, and maintaining operating schedules and logs of operations. These tasks provide good on-the-job training for high-school graduates who wish to learn something about computing. These tasks are sometimes "apprenticeship" jobs for computer operators.

Keypunching

Keypunching of data into punched cards or paper tape and operating other key-driven data-recording devices require an ability to type reasonably well (30 to 40 words per minute) and an ability to work in a fairly noisy environment. After two or three weeks of intensive training, a high-school graduate may start as a keypunch operator.

GLOSSARY

Access Time—The time required to read data to/from an imput/output device.

Accumulator—A register in which the result of an arithmetic or logic operation is formed.

Acronym—A word formed from the first letter or letters of the words describing some item; e.g., FORTRAN from *FOR*mula *TRAN*slation.

Address—A name, label, or number that identifies a location in storage.

Algorithm—A computational procedure for solving a problem.

Analog-to-Digital—A device that converts external signals to a form the computer can recognize.

Analysis—The investigation of a problem by some consistent, systematic procedure.

Analyst—A person skilled in the definition and development of techniques for the solving of a problem, especially those techniques for solutions on a computer.

ANSI—*A*merican *N*ational *S*tandards *I*nstitute. An organization that acts as a national clearinghouse and coordinator for voluntary standards in the United States.

APL—*A* *P*rogramming *L*anguage. A higher-level terminal-oriented programming language.

Application—The system or problem to which a computer is applied.

Applications Program—A program that solves a specific problem, such as inventory control or machine control.

Arithmetic Unit—The portion of the central processing unit where arithmetic and logic operations are performed.

Array—A list or table (matrix) of data.

ASCII Code—*A*merican *S*tandard *C*ode for *I*nformation *I*nterchange. A seven-bit code used on many present-day computers.

Assembler—A computer program used to translate a program written in a symbolic programming language into a machine-language program.

Assembly Language—A programming language that allows a computer user to write a program using mnemonics instead of numeric instructions. It is a low-level symbolic programming language that closely resembles machine-code language.

Auxiliary Storage—A storage that supplements the internal storage of the central processing unit. Also called *secondary storage*.

Background Processing—Processing of a low-priority program that takes place only when no higher-priority or real-time processing function is present.

Backup Copy—A spare copy of a program or data for use in the event of accidental erasure or damage of the original copy.

Base—The radix of a number system. See *Radix*.

BASIC—*B*eginners *A*ll-purpose *S*ymbolic *I*nstruction *C*ode. An easy-to-learn and easy-to-use programming language designed for use in scientific work and in business applications. The language is widely used with microcomputers.

Batch Processing—A technique by which items to be processed must be coded and collected into groups prior to processing.

Binary—(1) A condition or situation having only two possibilities. (2) A number representation system with a radix of 2.

Binary Digit—In binary notation, either of the digits, 0 or 1.

Bit—An abbreviation of *binary* digi*t*.

Bit Rate—The rate at which binary digits, or pulse representations, appear on communications lines or channels.

Block—A set of things, such as digits, characters, or words, handled as a unit.

Branch—A technique used to transfer control from one sequence of a program to another.

Buffer—A storage device used to compensate for a difference in the rate or sequence of data flow when transmitting data from one device to another.

Bug—A term used to denote a mistake in a computer program or a malfunction in a computer hardware component.

Bus—A channel or path for transferring data and electrical signals.

Byte—A grouping of adjacent binary digits operated on as a unit by the computer. The most common size of byte contains eight binary digits.

Card—A storage medium in which data is represented by means of holes punched in vertical columns in a paper card.

Card Punch—An output device used to punch cards.

Card Reader—An input device used to transmit punched-card data to the central processing unit of a computer.

Carriage—A control mechanism for a typewriter or printer that automatically feeds, skips, spaces, or ejects paper forms.

Cassette Unit—A magnetic-tape recorder that uses cassette tapes for storage. Widely used with microcomputers.

Central Processing Unit—That portion of the hardware of a computing system containing the control unit, arithmetic unit, and internal storage unit. Abbreviated CPU.

Character—A symbol, mark, or event which a data-processing machine can read, write, or store. It is used to represent data to a machine.

Chassis—A metal structure that supports the component parts of a computer system.

Circuit—A system of conductors and related electrical elements through which electrical currents flow.

Closed Shop—The operation of a computer facility where actual program running service is the responsibility of a group of specialists, thereby effectively separating the phase of task formulation from that of computer implementation. The programmers are not allowed in the computer room to run or oversee the running of their programs. Contrasted with *open shop*.

COBOL—*CO*mmon *B*usiness-*O*riented *L*anguage. A higher-level programming language developed for programming business problems.

Coder—A person who prepares instruction sequences from detailed flowcharts and other algorithmic procedures prepared by others, as contrasted with a programmer who prepares the procedures and flowcharts.

Coding—The process of translating problem logic represented by a flowchart into computer instructions and data.

Coding Form—A form on which the instructions for programming a computer are written. Also called a *coding sheet*.

COM—*C*omputer *O*utput *M*icrofilm. Refers to a method of converting computer output to microfilm form.

Compatible—A term applied to a computer system which implies that it is capable of handling both data and programs devised for some other type of computer system.

Compiler—A computer program used to translate high-level source-language programs into machine-language programs suitable for execution on a particular computing system.

Compiler Language—See *Higher-Level Language*.

Computer—A calculating device which processes data represented by a combination of discrete data (in digital computers) or continuous data (in analog computers).

Computer Operator—A person who manipulates the controls of a computer and performs all operational functions that are required in the computing system, such as loading a tape transport, placing cards in the input hopper, removing printouts from the printer rack, etc.

Computer Program—See *Program*.

Computer Programmer—A person who designs, writes, debugs, and documents computer programs.

Computer Resource—The total devices, storage, and features of a computer system available to the system user.

Computer Science—The field of knowledge that involves the design and use of computer equipment, including software development.

Computer System—A central processing unit together with one or more peripheral devices.

Console—That part of a computer used for communications between the computer operator or maintenance engineer and the computer.

Control Panel—A panel with input switches and output indicators that allows control of a computer system.

Control Unit—The portion of the central processing unit that directs the step-by-step operation of the entire computing system.

Conversational Mode—A mode of operation where a user is in direct contact with a computer, and interaction is possible between human and machine without the user being conscious of any language or communications barrier.

Counter—A device such as a storage location or a register used to represent the number of occurrences of an event.

CPU—*C*entral *P*rocessing *U*nit. The main controlling unit in a computer.

CRT—*C*athode *R*ay *T*ube. An electronic vacuum tube with a screen for visual display of output information in graphical or alphanumeric form. Display is produced by means of proportionally deflected electron beams.

Cycle—An interval of time in which an operation or set of events is completed.

Data—A representation of facts or concepts in a formalized manner suitable for communication, interpretation, or processing by people or by automatic means.

Data Base—A comprehensive data file containing information in a format applicable to a user's needs and available when needed.

Data Collection—The gathering of source data to be entered into a computer system.

Data Processing—A term used in reference to operations performed by data-processing equipment.

Data-Processing Center—An installation of computer equipment which provides computing services for users.

Data Structures—Arrangement of data; i.e., arrays, files, etc.

Debug—To detect, locate, and remove all mistakes in a computer program and any malfunctions in the computing system hardware itself.

Desk Checking—To debug a program by examining the code at a table or desk.

Diagnostics—Statements printed by an assembler or compiler indicating mistakes detected in a source program.

Digit—One of the symbols of a number system used to designate a quantity.

Digital—Pertaining to the utilization of discrete integral numbers in a given base to represent all the quantities that occur in a problem or a calculation.

Digital Computer—A computer that operates on discrete data by performing arithmetic and logic processes on the data.

Digital Plotter—An output unit which graphs data by an automatically controlled pen. Data is normally plotted as a series of incremental steps.

Digital-to-Analog—A device that converts computer digital data into analog signals.

Direct-Access Storage—Pertaining to the process of obtaining data from or placing data into storage where the time required for such access is independent of the location of the data most recently obtained or placed in storage. Also called *random-access storage.*

Disk—See *Magnetic Disk.*

Diskette—See *Floppy Disk.*

Disk Operating System—Software used to manage disk files and programs, and to develop application software. Abbreviated DOS.

Disk Pack—The vertical stacking of a series of magnetic disks in a removable self-contained unit.

Display Unit—A device that provides a visual representation of data. See *CRT.*

Down Time—The total elasped time that a computer system is unusable because of a malfunction.

Dump—Printing all or part of the contents of a storage device.

EBCDIC—*Extended Binary Coded Decimal Interchange Code.* An eight-bit code used for data representation in several computers including the IBM System/360 and System/370.

Emulate—To imitate one system with another, such that the imitating system accepts the same data, executes the same programs, and achieves the same results as the imitated system.

EPROM—*Erasable Programmable Read-Only Memory.* A read-only storage device that can be erased to change its contents.

Erase—To remove data from storage without replacing it.

Execute—To perform the operations specified by computer instructions (programs).

Feasibility Study—A specialized study of data-processing equipment designed to determine what equipment, and in what configurations, would best accomplish the job.

Feedback—The part of a closed-loop system that automatically brings back information about the condition under control.

File—An organized collection of related data. For example, the entire set of inventory master data records makes up the inventory master file.

Fixed-Word Length—The condition in which a machine word always contains a fixed number of bits, characters, bytes, or digits.

Floppy-Disk—A flexible disk (diskette) of oxide-coated mylar that is stored in paper or plastic envelopes. The entire envelope is inserted in the disk unit. Floppy disks are low-cost storage units that are widely used with microcomputers and minicomputers.

Flowchart—A graphical representation for the solution of a problem. It is used primarily to help in the development of a computer program by illustrating how a computer program logic is laid out, and to provide documentation for the program.

Flowchart Symbol—A symbol used to represent operations, data, equipment, or flow on a flowchart.

Flowchart Template—A plastic guide containing cutouts of the flowchart symbols. It is used in the preparation of a flowchart.

Foreground Processing—The automatic execution of the computer programs that have been designed to preempt the use of the computing facilities.

FORTRAN—*FORmula TRANslation.* A higher-level programming language designed for programming scientific-type problems.

Garbage—A term often used to describe incorrect answers from a computer program, usually resulting from equipment malfunction or a mistake in a computer program.

General-Purpose Computer—A computer that is designed to solve a wide class of problems. The majority of digital computers are of this type.

Gigo—*Garbage In-Garbage Out.* A term used to describe the data into and out of a computer system; i.e., if the input data is bad (garbage in) then the output data will also be bad (garbage out).

Hard Copy—A printed copy of computer output; e.g., printed reports, listings, or documents.

Hardware—The physical equipment in a computer system; e.g., mechanical, electrical, or magnetic devices. Contrasted with *software.*

Hexadecimal—A numbering system in which the radix (base) is 16. A shorthand method of representing binary data.

Higher-Level Language—A computer programming language that is intended to be independent of a particular computer. See *Procedure-Oriented Language*.

Hollerith Code—A punched-card code developed by Dr. Herman Hollerith for tabulating census data for the U.S. Census Bureau.

Idle Time—The time a computer is available for use but is not in actual operation.

IFIPS—*I*nternational *F*ederation of *I*nformation *P*rocessing Societies.

Information—Data that has been organized into a meaningful sequence.

Information Retrieval—A technique of classifying and indexing useful data in mass storage devices, in a format amenable to interaction with the user(s).

Input—The introduction of data from an external source into the internal storage unit of a computer.

Input/Output—A general term for the peripheral devices used to communicate with a digital computer, and the data involved in the communication.

Input Unit—A device used to transmit data into a central processing unit; e.g., a card reader, a teletypewriter, a paper-tape reader, an MICR reader, or an optical scanning reader.

Instruction—A set of characters used to define a basic operation and to tell the computer where to find the data needed to carry out the operation.

Instruction Repertoire—The complete set of machine instructions of a computer.

Integer—A whole number which may be positive, negative, or zero. It does not have a fractional part. Examples of integers are 687, -39426, and 0.

Integrated Circuit—A microminiature electronic circuit produced on a single chip of silicon.

Intelligent Terminal—An input/output device in which a number of computer processing characteristics are physically built into, or attached to, the terminal unit.

Interactive—Highly communicative between the user and the computer system.

Interface—A common boundary between two pieces of hardware or between two systems.

Internal Storage—Addressable storage directly controlled by the central processing unit of a digital computer. It is an integral part of the central processing unit. The CPU uses internal storage to store programs while they are being executed. Also called *primary storage, immediate-access storage,* and *main storage.*

Interpreter—A computer program or ROM that translates and executes each source-language expression before translating and executing the next one.

Interrupt—To temporarily disrupt the normal execution of a program by a special signal from the computer.

Iterative Process—A process in which the same procedure is repeated many times until the desired answer is produced.

Job—A specified group of tasks prescribed as a unit of work for a computer.

K—When referring to storage capacity, 2^{10}; in decimal notation, 1024. For example, a storage capacity of 32K is 32,768.

Keyboard—An input device that allows data to be input to a computer. Keyboards are used widely with microcomputers.

Keypunch—A keyboard-operated device that is used to punch holes in punched cards to represent data.

Light Pen—A stylus used with crt display devices to add, modify, and delete information on the face of the crt screen.

Line Printer—An output unit used to record computer output in the form of printed characters.

Loop—A sequence of program instructions that are repeated until a predetermined terminal condition is achieved.

LSI—*L*arge-*S*cale *I*ntegration. Logic used in microprocessors, microcomputers, and other computers.

Machine Address—An address that is permanently assigned by the machine designer to a storage location. Also called *absolute address.*

Machine Independent—A term used to indicate that a program is developed in terms of the problem rather than in terms of the characteristics of the computer system.

Machine Language—Basic language of a computer. Programs written in machine language require no further interpretation by a computer.

Macroinstruction—An instruction, in a source language, that is equivalent to a specified sequence of machine-language instructions.

Magnetic Core—A tiny doughnut-shaped piece of magnetizable material capable of storing one binary digit.

Magnetic-Disk Unit—A device used to read and write data on thin magnetic disks, the surfaces of which have been coated with a magnetizable material.

Magnetic-Drum Unit—A device used to read and write data on a cylinder, the surface of which is covered with a magnetizable material.

Magnetic Ink—An ink that can be magnetized. It is used for printing magnetic characters on forms such as checks, utility bills, invoices, etc. These magnetic characters are subsequently read by magnetic-ink character-reading equipment.

Magnetic-Tape Unit—A device used to read and write data in the form of magnetic spots on reels of tape coated with a magnetizable material. See *Cassette Unit.*

Main Frame—The part of the computer that contains the arithmetic unit, internal storage unit, and control functions. See *Central Processing Unit.*

Main Storage—See *Internal Storage.*

Mark-Sense Card—A card designed to permit data to be entered on it with an electrographic pencil.

Matrix Printing—A method of printing character and other data by combinations of small dots.

Medium—The physical substance upon which data is recorded; e.g., diskette, magnetic tape, etc.

Megahertz—Millions of times per second.

Memory—A term often used to refer to the storage facility of a computer. See *Storage.*

Menu—A display of selections that may be chosen, typically on a visual display screen.

MICR—*Magnetic Ink Character Recognition.* A system of coding in which numeric and special characters are printed with magnetizable ink.

Microcomputer—A computer consisting of a central processing unit, storage, and input/output circuitry. A microcomputer contains at least one microprocessor. It functions much the same way as a minicomputer.

Microelectronics—The field that deals with techniques for producing miniature circuits; e.g., integrated circuits, thin-film techniques, and solid-logic modules.

Microprocessor—The control and processing portion of a minicomputer or microcomputer, which is usually built with LSI circuitry on one chip.

Microsecond—One millionth of a second. Abbreviated µs.

Millisecond—One thousandth of a second. Abbreviated ms.

Minicomputer—A small and relatively inexpensive digital computer.

Mistake—A human failing; e.g., faulty arithmetic, incorrect keypunching, incorrect formula, or incorrect computer instructions.

Modem—A contraction of *MOdulator/DEModulator.* Its function is to interface with data-processing devices and convert data to a form compatible for sending and receiving on transmission facilities.

Monitor—A television receiver without the circuitry to detect transmissions. Used widely with microcomputers.

Monolithic Integrated Circuit—A class of integrated circuits wherein the substrate is an active material, such as the semiconductor, silicon.

Multiprocessing—Independent and simultaneous processing accomplished by a computer configuration consisting of more than one arithmetic and logic unit, each being capable of accessing a common memory.

Multiprogramming—Pertaining to the concurrent execution of two or more programs by a computer. The programs operate in an interleaved manner within one computer system.

Nanosecond—One billionth of a second. Abbreviated ns.

Network—The interconnection of a number of points by data communications facilities.

Nonvolatile Storage—A storage medium that retains its data in the absence of power.

Number Base—See *Radix*.

Number Crunching—The use of computers for processing complex mathematical problems.

Numeric Pad—A special cluster of keys allowing input of the numeric digits 0 through 9.

Object Program—The result of an assembly or compilation, usually close to machine-language form. Contrasted with *source program*.

Octal—A numbering system based on a radix of 8.

Off-Line—Peripheral units which operate independently of the central processing unit. Devices not under the control of the central processing unit.

On-Line—Peripheral devices operating under the direct control of the central processing unit.

Open Shop—A computer installation at which computer operation can be performed by a qualified person. Contrasted with *closed shop*.

Operand—A unit of data that is to be operated upon.

Operating System—Software that controls the execution of computer programs and which may provide scheduling, input/output control, compilation, data management, debugging, storage assignment, accounting, and other similar functions.

Operation Code—The portion of an instruction which designates the operation to be performed by a computer; e.g., add, subtract, or move. Also called a *command*.

Optical Scanning—The translation of printed or handwritten characters into machine language.

Optimize—To rearrange instructions and/or data in storage to minimize time requirements.

Origination—Determining the type, nature, and origin of some documents.

Output—Data transferred from the internal storage unit of a computer to some storage or peripheral device.

Output Unit—A device capable of recording data coming from the internal storage unit of a computer; e.g., card punch, line printer, crt display, magnetic disk, or teletypewriter.

Paper Tape—A continuous strip of paper into which data is recorded as a series of holes along its length. Data is read by a paper-tape reader sensing the pattern of holes, which represent coded data.

Paper-Tape Punch—An output unit used to encode data in paper tape.

Paper-Tape Reader—An input unit used to sense information coded in paper tape.

Pascal—A programming language that is of particular interest to computer scientists and is being used increasingly for many applications.

Patch—To temporarily modify the software or hardware of a computer system.

Peripheral Devices—Input/output and storage devices attached to a computer.

Picosecond—One trillionth of a second. Abbreviated ps.

PL/1—Programming *Language/1*. A general-purpose programming language.

Point-of-Sale (POS) Terminal—An intelligent input/output device that is used to capture data in retail stores; i.e., supermarkets or department stores. POS is a term used to indicate that data regarding a sale is entered directly into the computerized system without having to be converted to another form first.

Precision—The degree of exactness with which a quantity is stated. The result of a calculation may have more precision than it has accuracy. For example, the true value of pi to six significant digits is 3.14159; the value 3.14162 is precise to six digits, given to six digits, but is accurate to only about five.

Preventive Maintenance—The process that attempts to keep computer equipment in continuous operating condition by detecting, isolating, and correcting failures before occurrence. It involves cleaning and adjusting the equipment as well as testing the equipment under both normal and marginal conditions.

Printer—See *Line Printer*.

Problem Definition—The formulation of the logic used to define a problem. A description of a task to be performed.

Problem-Oriented Language—A programming language designed for the convenient expression of a given class of problems; e.g., GPSS and COGO.

Procedure—A precise step-by-step method for effecting a solution to a problem.

Procedure-Oriented Language—A programming language designed for the convenient expression of procedures used in the solution of a wide class of problems; e.g., FORTRAN, APL, PL/1, BASIC, and Pascal.

Program—All of the instructions required to solve a specific problem on a computer.

Programmer—A person who writes computer programs.

Programming—The process of translating a problem from its physical environment to a language that a computer can understand and obey. The process of planning the procedure for solving a problem. This may involve, among other things, an analysis of the problem, preparation of a flowchart, coding of the problem, establishing input/output formats, establishing testing and checkout procedures, allocation of storage, preparation of documentation, and supervision of the running of the program on a computer.

Programming Analyst—See *Analyst*.

Programming Language—A language used to prepare computer programs.

PROM—*Programmable Read-Only Memory*. A read-only memory, programmable by the purchaser, that cannot be erased.

Prompt—A character(s) printed by the program to signal the user that input is required.

Radix—The quantity of characters or digits required by a number system. Same as *base*.

RAM—*Random Access Memory*. A memory that can both be written into and read from.

Random-Access Storage—See *Direct-Access Storage*.

Raw Data—Data that has not been processed.

Read—To sense data from an input medium, such as punched cards, magnetic tape, punched paper tape, or MICR form.

Reader—Any device capable of transcribing data from an input medium.

Real-Time System—A system where transactions are processed as they occur.

Record—A group of related items of data treated as a unit; e.g., the inventory master record. A complete set of such records forms a file.

Register—A temporary storage device used by the computer to store a specified amount of data, such as one word.

Reliability—A measure of the ability to function without failure.

Relocate—To move a routine from one portion of storage to another, and to adjust the necessary address references so that the routine, in its new location, can be executed.

Remote Processing—The processing of computer programs through an input/output device that is remotely connected to a computer system.

Remote Terminal—An input/output device that is remotely located from a computer system. It is used to input programs and data to a computer and to accept computer answers from a computer. Also called *remote station*.

Repertoire—A complete set of instructions that belongs to a specific computer or family of computers.

Report—Any formalized display or printout of data grouped in meaningful form.

Resolution—The "fineness" of a visual display.

Response Time—The time it takes the program or input/output device to respond to a user input or command.

ROM—*Read Only Memory*. A type of memory permanently programmed by the manufacturer.

RPG—*Report Program Generator*. A language designed with built-in logic to produce report-writing programs, given input and output descriptions.

Run—A single, continuous performance of a computer program.

Scan—To retrieve or store data from beginning to end of a list or table.

Screen—The picture tube of a visual display terminal.

Scroll—To display various sections of a long list of lines, similar to viewing a portion of a scroll as it is unwound.

Secondary Storage—Devices that are used to store large quantities of data and programs. To be processed, these data and programs must first be loaded into primary storage. Also called *auxiliary storage.*

Semiconductor Memory—A computer memory that uses silicon integrated-circuit chips.

Service Contract—A contract for maintenance of computer system hardware or software.

Simulate—To represent the functioning of one system by another; i.e., to represent a physical system by the execution of a computer program or to represent a biological system by a mathematical model.

Software—The computer programs, procedures, and documentation concerned with the operation of a computer system; e.g., assemblers, compilers, operating systems, diagnostic routines, program loaders, manuals, library routines, and circuit diagrams. Software is the name given to the programs that cause a computer to carry out particular operations. Contrasted with *hardware.*

Solid State—The electronic components that convey or control electrons within solid materials; e.g., transistors, germanium diodes, and integrated circuits.

Sort—To arrange numeric or alphabetic data in a given sequence.

Source Computer—A computer used to translate a source program into an object program.

Source Deck—A card deck comprising a computer program, in symbolic language.

Source Document—An original document from which basic data is extracted; e.g., invoice, parts list, inventory tag, etc.

Source Language—The original form in which a program is prepared prior to processing by the computer; e.g., FORTRAN or assembly language.

Source Program—A computer program written in a symbolic programming language; e.g., assembly-language program, FORTRAN program, BASIC program. A translator is used to convert the source program into an object program that can be executed on a computer. Contrasted with *object program.*

Special Character—A graphic character that is neither a letter nor a digit; e.g., the plus sign and the period.

Special-Purpose Computer—A computer designed to solve a specific class or narrow range of problems.

Standard—An accepted and approved criterion used for writing computer programs, drawing flowcharts, building computers, etc.

Standardize—To establish standards or to cause conformity with established standards.

Statement—The most elemental instruction to the computer in a higher-level programming language, such as BASIC or FORTRAN.

Storage—The retention of data so that the data can be obtained at a later time.

Storage Allocation—The process of reserving storage areas for instructions or data.

Storage Capacity—The number of items of data that a storage device is capable of containing. Frequently defined in terms of computer words, or by a specific number of bytes or characters.

Storage Device—A device used for storing data within a computer system; e.g., core storage, magnetic-disk unit, magnetic-tape unit, magnetic-drum unit, etc.

Storage Location—A position in storage where a character, byte, or word may be stored.

Storage Map—An aid used by the computer user for estimating the proportion of storage capacity to be allocated to data and instructions.

Storage Protection—A device that prevents a computer program from destroying or writing in computer storage beyond certain boundary limits.

Storage Unit—The portion of the central processing unit that is used to store instructions and data.

Structured Programming—Techniques concerned with improving the programming process through better organization of programs and better programming notation to facilitate correct and clear description of data and control structures.

Subroutine—A set of instructions that directs the computer to carry out a well-defined mathematical, logical, or special operation. It may be used over and over in the same program and in different programs.

Subsystem—A system that is subordinate to the main system.

Summarize—To condense a mass of data into a concise and meaningful form.

Symbolic Address—An address expressed in symbols.

Symbolic Coding—Coding in which the instructions are written in nonmachine language; e.g., a FORTRAN program.

System—An organized collection of machines, methods, and personnel required to accomplish a specific objective.

Systems Analysis—The examination of an activity, procedure, method, technique, or a business to determine what must be accomplished and how the necessary operations may best be accomplished by using electronic data-processing equipment.

Systems Analyst—A person skilled in solving problems with a digital computer. He/she analyzes and develops information systems.

Systems Programs—Computer programs provided by a computer manufacturer. Examples are operating systems, assemblers, compilers, debugging aids, input/output programs, etc.

Systems Study—The detailed process of determining a set of procedures for using a computer for definite operations, and establishing specifications to be used as a basis for the selection of equipment suitable to the specific needs.

Tape—A strip of material that may be punched or coated with a magnetically sensitive substance and which is used for data input, storage, or output. The data is usually stored serially in several channels across the tape transversely to the reading or writing motion.

Telecommunications—Pertaining to the transmission of data over long distances through telephone and telegraph facilities.

Teletypewriter—A keyboard printing unit that is often used to enter information into a computer and to accept output from a computer.

Terminal—A point in a system or communications network at which data can either enter or leave. Any input/output device that allows data entry and display.

Text Editing—The capability to modify text automatically.

Thin Film—A high-speed storage device consisting of a molecular deposit of materials on a substrate.

Throughput—The amount of time required to process a specific application on a computer system.

Time Sharing—A method of operation whereby a computer system automatically distributes processing time among many users simultaneously.

Track—The path along which data is recorded, as in magnetic disks and magnetic drums.

Transistor—A solid-state electronic device developed at Bell Telephone Laboratories in 1948. Used in second-generation computers.

Translate—To change data from one form of representation to another without significantly affecting the meaning.

Translation—Conversion of a higher-level language, or assembly language, to machine-understandable form. See *Assembler, Compiler,* and *Interpreter.*

Turnkey System—A computer system that includes all hardware and software to perform a specified application without the need of professional computer personnel.

Typewriter—An input/output device that is capable of being connected to a digital computer and used for communications purposes.

Variable—A quantity that can assume any of a given set of values.

Verifier—A machine that is used to check the correctness of manually recorded data.

Video—Signals that generate display of data on a visual display terminal.

Virtual Memory—A technique for managing a limited amount of high-speed memory and a (generally) much larger amount of lower-speed memory in such a way that the distinction is largely transparent to a computer user.

Volatile Storage—A storage medium in which data cannot be retained without continuous power dissipation.

Word—An ordered set of characters which occupies one storage location and is treated by the computer circuits as a unit. Ordinarily, a word is treated by the control unit as a quantity. Word lengths may be fixed or variable depending on the particular computer.

Word Length—The number of bits, bytes, or characters in a word.

Word Processing—A text-editing system. A system that is used to prepare text, such as letters, forms, and pages of text.

Write—To transfer information, usually from internal storage to an output device.

Index